The Popes of Egypt

I

The Early Coptic Papacy

The Popes of Egypt

A History of the Coptic Church and Its Patriarchs
from Saint Mark to Pope Shenouda III

Edited by Stephen J. Davis and Gawdat Gabra

Volume One

The Early Coptic Papacy

The Egyptian Church and
Its Leadership in Late Antiquity

Stephen J. Davis

———

The American University in Cairo Press

Cairo   New York

Dar el Kutub No. 16139/03
ISBN 977 424 830 9

Designed by the AUC Press Design Center/ Joanne Cunningham
Printed in Egypt

Contents

Illustrations
(following page 46)

1. Ivory relief depicting Saint Mark with thirty-five successors as Patriarch of Alexandria, early seventh century A.D.; Musée du Louvre, Paris.

2. Five ivory reliefs with scenes from the life of Saint Mark, eighth century A.D.; Museo del Castello Sforzesco, Milan.

3. Wall painting of Saint Athanasius of Alexandria, thirteenth century A.D.; Monastery of Saint Antony, Red Sea.

4. Wall painting of Saint Athanasius of Alexandria, tenth century A.D.; Tebtunis, Fayûm.

5. Manuscript illuminations depicting Theophilus of Alexandria, early fifth century A.D.; W. Goleniscev Collection, Petersburg.

6. Wall painting of Dioscorus of Alexandria, thirteenth century A.D.; Monastery of the Syrians, Wadi al-Natrun.

7. Wall painting of Dioscorus of Alexandria, thirteenth century A.D.; Monastery of Saint Antony, Red Sea.

8. Wall painting of Pope Damian (?), eighth century A.D.; Church of the Holy Virgin, Monastery of the Syrians, Wadi al-Natrun.

9. Coptic inscription of Pope Damian's *Synodical Letter* (A.D. 578), late sixth or early seventh century A.D.; Monastery of Epiphanius at Thebes.

10. Wall painting of Peter I of Alexandria, A.D. 1025–1030; Monastery of the Archangel Gabriel, Fayûm.

Editors' Introduction

The Copts, adherents of the Egyptian Orthodox Church, today represent the largest Christian community in the Middle East. Over the course of its long history, the Coptic Church in Egypt has celebrated the lineage and leadership of Alexandrian bishops who have been accorded the title of Patriarch, or Pope. The term Pope itself originally derived from the Greek word *papas*, meaning "father." By the middle of the third century A.D., however, the term "Pope" *(papas)* had become a formal honorific title of the Alexandrian archbishop, fifty years before the earliest solid evidence for the use of the term as a designation for the Roman archbishop. Over the course of the last two millennia—through the vicissitudes of Roman, Byzantine, Persian, Arab, Ottoman, French, British, and finally Egyptian rule—the Popes of Egypt have often been collectively represented as an emblem of historical continuity for the Coptic Orthodox Church. Such representations raise vital questions about the way that Coptic religious and cultural identity has been shaped in relation to church leadership. How has the history of the Popes of Egypt functioned, in effect, as a monument and marker of Christian identity in Egypt?

In recent decades, there has been an upsurge of interest in the Coptic cultural heritage. Indeed, the second half of the twentieth century witnessed remarkable progress in the study of Egyptian Christianity. The discovery of the Nag Hammadi gnostic library, with its codices written in Coptic, encouraged many scholars to study the Coptic language and literature. The exhibitions of Coptic art in great cities such as Vienna, Paris, Munich, Geneva, and Zurich enhanced the interest of the general public in the material culture of Coptic Egypt. Furthermore, archaeological remains were discovered and carefully

documented at important sites related to Egyptian monasticism and
pilgrimage, including Abu Mina, Kellia, Athribis, Naqlun, Antinoe,
and Esna. The application of modern methods of restoration and
conservation in a number of monasteries led to new discoveries of
beautiful Coptic wall paintings—most recently, murals in the
monastery of Saint Antony at the Red Sea and in the Monastery of the
Syrians (Deir al-Suryan) at Wadi al-Natrun. The foundation of the
International Association for Coptic Studies and the appearance of the
Coptic Encyclopedia have greatly advanced the knowledge of Coptic
culture among scholars in the field.

Surprisingly, however, despite these significant factors, studies on
the history of the Copts in general, and on the Alexandrian patriarchate
in particular have remained relatively rare. The most recent comprehensive historical treatment of Egyptian ecclesiastical leadership from
the early centuries to the modern period is J.M. Neale's *The
Patriarchate of Alexandria*, published in 1847. In the century and a half
since the publication of Neale's two-volume work, much has changed
in the application of historiographical methods, and valuable new
sources have come to light.

The classic primary source for the study of the Coptic papacy is the
Arabic chronicle, *The History of the Patriarchs*, a multi-generational,
serial compilation of biographies (including historical sources and
traditions) for each of the Alexandrian popes. Edited in the eleventh
century, the Arabic *History of the Patriarchs* also includes later recensions designed to update the catalogue, a process of literary expansion
that has extended even into the twentieth century. While this Coptic
chronicle will be a valuable—albeit occasionally problematic—historical
source for the three volumes in this series, the goal here is not simply
to regurgitate its contents or to replicate its structure. To do so would
be to miss a golden opportunity to produce a truly new, critically-
informed reading of this history. The time is ripe for a fresh treatment,
one that draws on recent insights from an array of disciplines, including
theology, social history, papyrology, archaeology, the visual arts, literary
studies, and ideological and cultural criticism.

*The Popes of Egypt: A History of the Coptic Church and Its
Patriarchs from Saint Mark to Pope Shenouda III* represents such an
effort. The three volumes in this series draw on the expertise of
scholars who have dedicated their careers to the study of Egyptian
Christianity, and who are intimately familiar with the material culture
and institutional life of the Coptic Church from years of living and

working in Egypt. Volume One, on the history of Coptic papacy from its origins to the rise of Islam in the seventh century, is authored by Stephen Davis, who currently teaches Christianity in late antiquity in the Religious Studies Department at Yale University. Volume Two of the series, on the period from the rise of Islam to the Ottoman Conquest, will be authored by Mark Swanson, an expert in the Arabic Christian theological heritage who directs the Islamic studies program and teaches early and medieval church history at Luther Seminary in Minneapolis. Volume Three, on the modern Coptic papacy from the Ottoman era to the present, will be co-authored by three scholars: Magdi Girgis (Ph.D., Cairo University), a specialist in Coptic documentary sources during the Ottoman era; Michael Shelley, formerly director of graduate studies at the Evangelical Theological Seminary in Cairo and a specialist in the history of Christian-Muslim relations; and Nelly van Doorn-Harder, associate professor of religion at Valparaiso University and a specialist in both Islamic studies and the modern history of the Coptic Church. The collaborative nature of this series is designed to draw on each scholar's period of expertise, but also to initiate cross-fertilizing, interdisciplinary conversations in the study of Egyptian Christianity. It is our hope that these three volumes— written by academic experts but in an accessible and engaging style— will be of benefit to a wide range of readers, including scholars, teachers, students, as well as persons simply interested in learning more about the Coptic community in Egypt.

Finally, as editors of the series, we want to express our thanks to the American University in Cairo Press, and especially to Mark Linz and Neil Hewison for their vision and abiding faith in this project. The publication of this series is in large part a testament to their professionalism and fine dedication to their craft.

Stephen J. Davis and Gawdat Gabra, co-editors
November 6, 2003

Author's Preface

This book, *The Early Coptic Papacy*, represents the first in a three-volume series on the Popes of Egypt, which will cover the history of the Alexandrian patriarchate (i.e., the Egyptian papacy) from its origins to the present-day leadership of Pope Shenouda III. As mentioned in the Editors' Introduction, such a study is long overdue. The most recent comprehensive treatment of the topic in English is J.M. Neale's *The Patriarchate of Alexandria*, published over a century and a half ago in 1847.[1]

With regard to the period under consideration in this first volume, we face a similar gap in the history of scholarship. Edward R. Hardy, in his book *Christian Egypt, Church and People: Christianity and Nationalism in the Patriarchate of Alexandria* (1952), provided a detailed account of the early Egyptian church and its patriarchs, focusing especially on the period A.D. 325–641. However, his study is now over fifty years old and is considerably dated in the methods and sources used.[2] Other scholars working in the field have either chosen to narrow their focus to a particular century of patriarchal history,[3] or have taken on the much broader task of narrating the history of early Egyptian Christianity (writ large) without concentrating primarily on the leadership role of the Coptic popes.[4] In this book, I will attempt to fill this gap by specifically analyzing the development of the Egyptian papacy from its origins to the rise of Islam. How did the papal office in Egypt evolve as a social and religious institution during the first six and a half centuries A.D.? How do the developments in the Alexandrian patriarchate reflect larger developments in the Egyptian church as a whole—in its authority structures and lines of communication, as well as in its social and religious identity?

My goal here, however, is not simply to produce a critical historiography of important dates, events, and figures. Such an approach would, I fear, cause eyes to glaze over and heads to nod (including my own). Instead, I am interested in writing what I would call a discursive history of the Egyptian papacy—one that takes into account how the Alexandrian patriarchate was rhetorically and socially "constructed" at different points and times in its history. Recently, scholars who work in the field of late ancient Christianity have come to a greater appreciation for how discourses (the ways that people speak) play a performative role in shaping their own sense of social and religious identity.[5] Within social groups, discourses can function in a variety of ways—to negotiate power relationships and authority structures, to endorse shared values and practices, and to define community boundaries.

Thus, in the case of the early Alexandrian patriarchs, I will examine the sources not only for what the patriarchs *did* as leaders, but also for how their leadership and actions were *represented*—or, in the case of their own writings, how they represented themselves. Such representational strategies are laden with cultural value: in this context, how did literary (and artistic) depictions of the patriarchs reflect emerging social and theological concerns within the Coptic church? Or to put it in more dynamic terms, how did such discourses actually *shape* the church's understanding of itself and its leaders? In this book, I will argue that the ways in which the patriarchs portrayed themselves, and the ways their leadership was portrayed by their own and subsequent generations, has something vital to say about the formation of Egyptian Christian identity (or identities) in late antiquity.

Acknowledgments

This book has been a pilgrimage of sorts. Begun in Cairo, completed in New Haven, Connecticut, it has been enriched by colleagues—fellow pilgrims—in both places. The idea of writing a book (and later a three-volume series) on the Popes of Egypt grew out of conversations with Neil Hewison and Mark Linz at AUC Press in the spring of 2001. I first want to thank them (along with the other editors at AUC), and to express my gratitude for their vision, flexibility, and expert guidance throughout the process of making this book a reality.

I am also indebted to others who have been valuable conversation partners during my research and writing. In particular, I must mention my co-editor, Gawdat Gabra, and the other collaborators on this series: Mark Swanson, Magdi Girgis, Mike Shelley, and Nelly van Doorn-Harder. Our conversations—by phone, over a cup of tea, or over a shared meal—have done much to sustain and encourage me, and I look forward to more fruitful work together in the future. In the later stages of writing and revision, Mark Swanson, Dale Martin, Bentley Layton, Paul Dilley, and Gawdat Gabra all read the entire manuscript and offered detailed comments and suggestions. The published form of this book has greatly benefited from their critical eye and scholarship. Finally, my students and colleagues at the Evangelical Theological Seminary in Cairo and at Yale University also deserve my special appreciation: they often provided fresh insights (or welcome distractions!) that kept my approach to this material from getting too stale.

Of all these friends and colleagues, I want to single out my wife, Jenny, who continues to be my most cherished conversation partner in matters both personal and professional. Time and again, her skill as a

proofreader and her patience as a "prooflistener" helped her husband
through rocky patches in his pilgrimage with the Popes. This book is
lovingly dedicated to her.

Stephen J. Davis
New Haven, Connecticut
November 6, 2003

Abbreviations

ACO   Acta conciliorum oecumenicorum, ed. E. Schwartz. Berlin: Walter de Gruyter, 1924–1940.

ACO²   Acta conciliorum oecumenicorum. Second series. Berlin: Walter de Gruyter, 1984– .

ANF   Ante-Nicene Fathers, ed. A. Roberts and J. Donaldson. Buffalo: Christian Literature, 1885–1896. Repr. Grand Rapids, MI: Eerdmans, 1951–1956.

CSCO   Corpus scriptorum christianorum orientalium, ed. J.-B. Chabot et al. Paris: Reipublicae; Leipzig: Harrassowitz, 1903– .

CSEL   Corpus scriptorum ecclesiasticorum latinorum. Vienna: Geroldi, 1866– .

FC   Fathers of the Church. Washington, D.C.: Catholic University of America Press, 1947– .

GCS   Die griechischen christlichen Schriftsteller. Berlin: Akademie, 1897– .

HE   *Historia ecclesiastica* (= *Ecclesiastical History*)

NPNF   Nicene and Post-Nicene Fathers, ed. P. Schaff et al. 2 series. New York: Christian Literature, 1887–1894. Repr. Grand Rapids, MI: Eerdmans, 1952–1956.

PG   Patrologia Graeca, ed. J.-P. Migne. 162 volumes. Paris, 1857–1886.

PL   Patrologia Latina, ed. J.-P. Migne. 217 volumes. Paris, 1844–1864.

PO   Patrologia Orientalis, ed. R. Graffin and F. Nau. Paris: Firmin-Didot, 1907–1922.

SC   Sources chrétiennes, ed. H. de Lubac, J. Daniélou, et al. Paris: Cerf, 1942– .

TU   Texte und Untersuchungen. Berlin: Akademie, 1883– .

One

The Succession of St. Mark

Apostolic Traditions and the Origins
of the Egyptian Church
(Saint Mark to Demetrius)

On an early seventh-century ivory relief from Alexandria, now preserved in the Musée du Louvre in Paris (Fig. 1),[1] the figure of Saint Mark the Evangelist appears in the foreground, seated on a throne and surrounded by a group of bishops who are gathered together beneath the gate of a city. In the background, tiny human figures lean out of the windows and balconies of a miniature cityscape—the residential skyline of late antique Alexandria—in order to catch a glimpse of the holy gathering below.

This Alexandrian relief, carved virtually on the eve of Arab rule in Egypt, conveys to the viewer a vivid, visual sense of the emerging self-identity of the Coptic church and its patriarchate during the first six and a half centuries of its existence. The haloed figure of Mark—enlarged in relation to the other figures, seated in honor on an episcopal throne, holding his Gospel in his left hand and raising his right in a gesture of blessing—was viewed in church tradition as the founder of the Egyptian church and the first in a long line of bishops (also known as Alexandrian patriarchs or popes) who would succeed him in leadership of the church. Early Christian traditions recording Saint Mark's reputation as the founder of the church in Alexandria will be a primary focus of this first chapter.

In the Louvre relief, the thirty-five bishops who stand in a semi-circular choir around Mark are meant to represent his immediate successors as patriarchs—or popes[2]—of Alexandria. The number of bishops depicted here has helped scholars to date the relief: it was probably carved during the reign of the thirty-sixth patriarch of Alexandria, Pope Anastasius (A.D. 607–619), or perhaps on the occasion

1

of his death and the consecration of his successor Andronicus in the year 619. It is noteworthy that the seventh-century artist of the ivory relief has portrayed the successors to the throne of Saint Mark in mute imitation of the evangelist: those on his left (the viewer's right) hold copies of Mark's Gospel in their left hands; those on his right (the viewer's left) raise their right hands, mirroring his silent gesture of holy blessing. Throughout the history of the Coptic church, the authority of the Egyptian patriarchs has been understood to derive from the imitation of Mark's virtues and from a direct lineage of apostolic succession.

This book begins by mining the ecclesiastical ideologies behind this artifact from the early history of the Egyptian papacy. The stories about Saint Mark's founding of the church in Alexandria, and the discourses about apostolic succession and papal authority, not only reflected the self-perception of the Egyptian church in late antiquity but also helped shape that identity in a determinative way. How and when did these stories and discourses develop, and what do they say about how the church in Alexandria (and the rest of Egypt) viewed its leadership? As has been noted already in the preface, this book is not just about the Alexandrian patriarchs themselves, but about the developing relationship between the patriarchs and their church—more specifically, about what the discourses surrounding the patriarchs (in historical, hagiographical, and liturgical sources) tell us about the evolving identity of the Egyptian church leadership and its relation to its local setting.

In this context, it is important not to ignore the tiny figures peopling the cityscape background of our ivory relief from the Louvre. Indeed, our task in this first chapter and throughout this book is to place ourselves as historians in the texture of this Alexandrian scene, to climb up onto their balconies and to peer down with them, straining to hear the whispers of the gathering below. Those whispered discourses— found in private (and public) letters, lives of martyrs and saints, and manuscript illuminations, as well as "official" church histories—will tell us much about the emergence of the Coptic papacy in late antique Egypt, and even more about how the identity of the Coptic church was shaped in relation to its leadership.

Traditions about Saint Mark and the Founding of the Church in Egypt

Traditionally, Mark the evangelist has been viewed by Copts as the founder of their church and as the first in the line of Alexandrian patriarchs. What do we know about Mark as an historical figure?

What early Christian sources witness to the tradition of associating Mark with the earliest Alexandrian church? Finally, what does the development of this tradition tell us about the emerging identity of the Alexandrian patriarchs as successors to Saint Mark?

The Search for the Historical Mark

While the New Testament writings give us some information about Mark, they do not connect him directly with the early Christian mission to Alexandria. In fact, there is no mention of the Alexandrian mission in the New Testament itself. Mark (also known in the book of Acts as John Mark)[3] was a companion of the early Christian missionaries, Paul and Barnabas. Mark's close relationship to Barnabas apparently even involved family ties: he is identified as Barnabas' cousin (Gr. *anepsios*) in Colossians 4:10.

In the version of events recorded in Acts, Mark first accompanied Paul and Barnabas on their first journey to Seleucia and Cyprus as a "helper" (*hupêretês*; Acts 13:5). Then, he traveled with them to Pamphylia in Asia Minor (modern day Turkey), where he left the party and returned to Jerusalem (13:13). Mark's departure was later a source of tension within the group. The author of Acts reports that when Paul suggested to Barnabas that they make a second missionary journey to revisit churches, Barnabas wanted to take Mark along again. However, Paul adamantly refused to take with them "one who had deserted them in Pamphylia and had not accompanied them in the work" (Acts 15:36–41, esp. verse 38). As a result of their disagreement, Paul and Barnabas parted ways, with Barnabas taking Mark with him again to Cyprus, and Paul himself traveling back to Syria and Cilicia (15:39–40). The Acts narrative provides no more information about Mark's role in the early Christian mission.[4]

Mark is also linked with the apostle Peter in the New Testament and other early Christian sources. In the closing salutation of 1 Peter (5:13), the writer conveys greetings to his readers from Mark.[5] Early Christian traditions surrounding the writing of the canonical Gospel of Mark have also connected Mark with the figure of Peter. Even though its writer is never identified in the work itself, Mark was credited as the author of the Second Gospel at least by the early second century.[6] This tradition of authorship first appears in the writings of Papias, bishop of Hieropolis (A.D. 120–130).[7] Papias describes how Mark, while not an eyewitness to the life of Christ, acted as Peter's "translator" or "interpreter" *(hermêneutês)* in the writing of the Gospel.[8]

According to Papias, Mark "wrote accurately, although not in order, the things that had been said and done by the Lord," and in doing so followed Peter, "who used to compose his teachings for practical use and not as a systematic arrangement of the Lord's sayings." It is debatable whether Papias provides us with reliable evidence concerning the process by which the Second Gospel took shape;[9] indeed, one scholar has suggested that Papias' primary concern was to defend the trustworthiness of Mark's account by linking his role as interpreter as closely as possible to Peter as an apostolic source.[10]

Nonetheless, this tradition about Mark's role as the associate and interpreter of Peter also appears in other second-century Christian writings, where Mark's writing of the Gospel is further connected with Peter's mission at Rome. Irenaeus of Lyons, in his work *Against Heresies* (ca. 180–200), describes how, after Peter's death in Rome, "Mark, the disciple and interpreter of Peter, also handed down to us in written form the things that had been preached by Peter."[11] Clement of Alexandria (ca. 160–215) preserved a variant tradition in which Mark is said to have written his gospel in Rome while Peter was still alive, as a record of Peter's preaching.[12] The accounts recorded in these two sources were probably based on the earlier tradition found in Papias and represent later developments upon that tradition that link Mark's Gospel more closely to the prestige of Peter's church in Rome."[13]

The reference to Mark in 1 Peter 5:13 would only seem to reinforce this early link between Mark, Peter, and the church at Rome. In that text, the writer sends final greetings to his readers in Asia Minor:

> She who is in Babylon *(hê en Babulôni)*, chosen together with you, sends you greetings; and so does my son Mark.

This short passage, with its cryptic reference to "she who is in Babylon," has been the subject of considerable debate. Most scholars accept that the Mark mentioned here is the evangelist (referred to in this verse as Peter's spiritual son), and that the female pronoun "she" refers not to an actual person, but to the church (which is a feminine noun in Greek, *hê ekklêsia*). Thus, the passage should read: "The church who is in Babylon . . . sends you greetings."

However, we are left with questions concerning the reference to Babylon. Does this suggest that the writer (whether Peter or a later follower) was sending this letter from the city of Babylon in

Mesopotamia? This is quite doubtful, as there are no early Christian traditions from this period connecting Peter (or Mark for that matter) with Babylon of Mesopotamia.

Some scholars have tried to argue that this reference in 1 Peter actually gives us our first evidence for Mark's association with the church in Egypt.[14] In antiquity, Babylon was also the name of a Roman garrison town on the Nile just south of modern day Cairo.[15] In light of later traditions about Mark's founding of the Alexandrian church (discussed below), it would be tempting to read 1 Peter 5:13 as corroborating evidence; however, two problems make such an interpretation unlikely. First, despite Mark's reputation as the founder of the church in Alexandria, the stories told about him in the early church make no mention of his traveling to the fort at Babylon or other parts of Egypt. Second, there is no evidence from early Christian sources that that military post became a Christian center in the first few centuries A.D.[16] As one scholar has noted, a small military camp at the branch of the Nile does not seem like the likeliest place to locate the writing of this letter addressed to congregations in Asia Minor.[17] Third and finally, recent archaeological investigation has demonstrated that the fortress at the site of Babylon in Old Cairo was not built until the last decade of the third century, during the reign of the Roman emperor Diocletian (A.D. 284–305).[18]

In light of these problems, it is wise to look elsewhere for a solution. Most now opt to interpret "Babylon" metaphorically as a reference to the city of Rome. By the end of the first century, ancient Jewish and Christian apocalyptic writers both began using "Babylon" as a symbolic name for the imperial city.[19] In the early church, this symbolic usage is typified by the writer of Revelation (14:8; 16:19; 17:5; 18:2, 10, 21), who envisions the fall of Babylon (Rome) as the result of God's judgment. In ancient Jewish and Christian interpretation, Babylon was often remembered as a place of exile; thus, in the context of 1 Peter, the writer may be evoking Babylon at the conclusion of his letter to convey to his readers his sense of solidarity with them as "exiles of the Dispersion" (cf. his opening greeting in 1:1).[20] In any case, both the contemporary use of "Babylon" as a coded reference to Rome and the context of 1 Peter itself would seem to support a Roman setting for the letter and for Mark's association with the apostle Peter in that setting. To find the earliest evidence for Mark's association with the Egyptian church, one must look elsewhere.

The Earliest Sources and Traditions
about Saint Mark as the Founder of the Egyptian Church

The earliest undisputed witness to Saint Mark's role as founder of the church in Egypt is the fourth-century church historian, Eusebius of Caesarea. In his landmark *History of the Church* (completed in the year 325), Eusebius writes: "Now, they say that this Mark was the first to have set out to Egypt to preach the gospel, which he had already written down for himself, and the first to have organized churches in Alexandria itself."[21] Several points are worth noting about Eusebius' account.

First, Eusebius connects the tradition about Mark's founding of the Alexandrian church with the earlier traditions about Mark's writing of his gospel in Rome, and attempts to establish a basic chronology of Mark's ministry. In the paragraph preceding his account of Mark's mission in Alexandria, Eusebius relates how Mark wrote his gospel in Rome in response to personal appeals among the Christians in that city for him to write down the apostle Peter's teachings.[22] In fact, Eusebius cites Clement of Alexandria, and then refers to the writings of Papias of Hieropolis to confirm the tradition that Rome was the setting for the composition of Mark's gospel. (In the case of the latter, Eusebius notes how Papias understood the reference to Mark and the church in Babylon in 1 Peter in light of this Roman provenance.) Immediately after this, Eusebius enters into his account of how, while in Egypt, Mark preached from the gospel he had written. Here we see an example of how apostolic traditions were collected and "collated" in the early church. Thus, in his account, Eusebius brings together two separate regional traditions about Mark and sets them in order within an abbreviated chronological narrative.

As an aside, Eusebius' concern with establishing an apostolic chronology is also evident in his work entitled the *Chronicle*, in which he places Mark's arrival in Alexandria in the third year of Claudius' reign, or A.D. 43.[23] The dating of Mark's arrival would become a contested issue in the history of the Egyptian church: different sources from the early and medieval church present dates that range from A.D. 39 to the year 49 or 50.[24] The "official" medieval church history of the Copts, the *History of the Patriarchs*, eventually dated his arrival "in the fifteenth year after the Ascension of Christ" (ca. A.D. 48).[25] These divergent datings reflect the difficulty of the historical task in the early church: beginning with Eusebius, church writers tried to pinpoint the date of Mark's mission in Alexandria despite a preponderant lack of available information.

Second, what do we in fact know about Eusebius' sources of information regarding this tradition? While he attempts to establish a chronology of Mark's work in Rome and Egypt, Eusebius does not specify where he learned about the story of Mark's founding of the Alexandrian church. In contrast to other places in his *History* where he credits previous writers as sources of information (as in the case of Mark's mission to Rome), Eusebius does not explicitly mention any written sources regarding Mark's activity in Alexandria. The language he uses (the Greek verb, *phasin*—"they say," or "it is said") may suggest that he is relying on hearsay or some form of orally-transmitted tradition, or alternatively it may refer to some unspecified written source.[26] In any case, given the context of the passage, it is likely that Eusebius is alluding to a by-then well-known tradition in the Egyptian church.

Third and finally, Eusebius actually gives us very little information about Mark's mission to Alexandria. Indeed, we learn only that Mark preached "the gospel, which he had already written down," a detail that may derive simply from Eusebius' attempt to combine the Roman and Alexandrian traditions about Mark into a coherent and unified historical narrative. Other than this, his account reads like a stereotypical summary, reporting Mark's establishment of churches, and extolling the numerical success of his mission: "Such a great assembly of those who had come to believe in that place—both men and women— came together from his first effort . . . that Philo deemed their pastimes, gatherings, meals, and every other aspect of their life worthy of being recorded in writing."[27] Even in adding this last detail about the nature and size of the community Mark founded, Eusebius betrays the limitations of his knowledge, as he mistakenly identifies the earliest Alexandrian church with a community of Jewish ascetics that the writer Philo of Alexandria documented in the first century A.D.[28] The relatively late date of Eusebius' recording of this tradition about Mark, the sparseness of the information he provides, and his susceptibility to historical error in reporting this tradition have led many Western scholars to doubt the historicity of Mark's reputation as the father of the Egyptian church.[29] For such scholars, the story of Mark's establishment of churches in Alexandria is more easily explainable as a later attempt by the church to ground its history in the life of a revered, apostolic figure. Was this tradition about Saint Mark, then, simply a product of the historical consciousness of the fourth-century Alexandrian church?

While this judgment prevails among many Western scholars, in the last half century the situation has grown even more complicated with the discovery of a previously unknown letter attributed to the second-century writer Clement of Alexandria that refers to Mark's mission in Alexandria.[30] The contents of the letter are controversial. The writer tells his recipient (a man named Theodore) about a secret gospel written by Mark while the evangelist was in Alexandria, and includes a fragment from that gospel, in which Jesus raises a youth from the dead and then receives him in a mysterious, nightlong ritual of initiation. This account of a secret gospel written by Mark in Alexandria is intriguing for our purposes, especially in light of the testimony of the late fourth-century theologian John Chrysostom that the evangelist wrote his gospel in Egypt.[31]

Unfortunately, however, the authenticity of this discovery remains the subject of heated debate. While some scholars have supported the claim that Clement was the original author of the letter, the issue of its authorship has also sparked strenuous opposition.[32] In fact, on the basis of the available textual evidence some critics have even raised the possibility that the work might be a modern forgery.[33]

That being said, if this letter proved to be authentic, it would provide us with our earliest evidence to date for the tradition locating Mark's ministry in Alexandria. Like Eusebius, the writer of the letter links this Alexandrian tradition with the tradition surrounding Mark's writing of his (canonical) gospel in Rome:

> [As for] Mark, then, during Peter's stay in Rome he wrote [an account of] the Lord's doings, not, however, declaring all [of them], nor yet hinting at the secret [ones], but selecting those he thought most useful for increasing the faith of those who were being instructed. But when Peter died as a martyr, Mark came over to Alexandria, bringing both his notes and those of Peter, from which he transferred to his former book the things suitable to whatever makes for progress toward knowledge [*gnosis*]. [Thus] he composed a more spiritual Gospel for the use of those who were being perfected. Nevertheless, he yet did not divulge the things not to be uttered, nor did he write down the hierophantic teaching of the Lord, but to the stories already written he added yet others and, moreover, brought in certain sayings of which he knew the interpretation would, as a mystagogue, lead the hearers into the innermost sanctuary of that truth hidden

by seven [veils]. Thus, in sum, he prearranged matters, neither grudgingly nor incautiously, in my opinion, and, dying, he left his composition to the church in Alexandria, where it even yet is most carefully guarded, being read only to those who are being initiated into the great mysteries.[34]

Interestingly, in this text, there is no mention of Mark's *founding* of the church in Egypt. Indeed, the author's words imply that there were already Christians in Alexandria when he arrived ("those who were being perfected"). The focus of the passage is upon Mark's role as editor of the gospel he wrote in Rome, and his composition of "a more spiritual Gospel" in which he supplemented some of Peter's secret teachings about Christ. It was this secret gospel that Mark is supposed to have left in the care of the Alexandrian church at his death.

Even if authentic, this letter attributed to Clement ultimately gives us precious little information about Mark's mission in Egypt. Moreover, when compared with the account of Eusebius, the text presents an inconsistent witness concerning his activity there. For example, according to Eusebius, Mark founded the church in Alexandria, while the letter attributed to Clement seems to imply the presence of Christians before Mark's arrival. Furthermore, the letter reports that Mark *wrote* a "secret gospel" in Egypt, while Eusebius only mentions that he *preached* the gospel there.

These apparent discrepancies and the questions surrounding the authenticity of the letter only leave church historians with further questions. Was Mark, in fact, the founder of the Egyptian church? If so, what exactly did he do while he was there? Unfortunately, the earliest historical sources do not allow us to answer these questions with any certainty. In the end, perhaps the best we can do is to heed the words of a recent Coptic scholar who, when faced with the difficulties in assessing this evidence, remarked that the historicity of Mark's association with Alexandria, "though unprovable, should not be ruled out."[35]

The Later Development of Traditions about Saint Mark in the Late Ancient and Early Medieval Egyptian Church

The lack of information in the earliest written sources concerning Mark's activities in Alexandria soon led to the rise of oral traditions that tried to fill in the historical gaps—that is, traditions that tried to answer the question of what Mark might have done and where he might have gone while he was in the city. Eventually, these oral traditions were written down and recorded for posterity in the church. This process was an ongoing one throughout late antiquity and the early medieval period, as the Egyptian church continued to collect new stories that enhanced Mark's reputation and expanded his legend.

The *Acts of Mark* is one example of a source that has collected these early oral traditions and has set them within a larger narrative describing the details of Mark's mission and martyrdom in Alexandria.[36] The *Acts* actually incorporates two streams of tradition within a single narrative. The first stream of tradition concerns Mark's founding of the church in Alexandria and his encounter with a sandal-maker named Anianus (or Ananias, depending on the version), who would become his successor as leader of the Alexandrian church. The second stream of tradition concerns Mark's martyrdom itself, and provides an explanation for the establishment of his martyr church on the outskirts of Alexandria. While the exact date of composition for the *Acts of Mark* is uncertain, these traditions are traceable at least to the late fourth or early fifth century.[37]

The first half of the *Acts of Mark* (chapters 1–5) describes in detail how Mark came to Egypt and founded the church there.[38] According to the account, among the apostles Mark was appointed by lot to evangelize Egypt and the surrounding areas (1.1). He first went to Cyrene in Pentapolis where he preached the gospel, performed miracles of healing and exorcism, and baptized many converts (2.1). However, while he was there, he received a vision that he should go to Alexandria (2.2). The next day, Mark sailed there by ship and arrived at a place in the city called Mendion (3.1). However, while he was entering the city, the strap of his sandal broke, and Mark was forced to seek out a local cobbler to mend it (3.1–4). As the cobbler was trying fix the sandal, he accidentally struck his hand and cried out in pain, "God is one *(heis theos)*" (3.5). This exclamation caught Mark's attention (he saw it as a sign that he had come to the right place) and he promptly healed the cobbler's hand (3.8). In thanks, the cobbler invited Mark back to his home for a meal (3.9–4.2). There, the cobbler asked him about the source of his healing power, and Mark began to preach to him about Jesus Christ, whom he calls "Son of God, Son of Abraham," and about the prophets who spoke of him (4.3–7). As a result, the cobbler, whose name was Anianus (Ananias), believed in Christ and was converted, along with his entire household and many others living in his neighborhood (4.10–11). The news of these conversions angered some of the pagan "men of the city," who began to plot a way to kill Mark (5.1). However, Mark heard that his life was in danger and made plans to return to Pentapolis; before he did so, he ordained Anianus (Ananius) as bishop, along with three presbyters named Milaius, Sabinus, and Cerdo, seven deacons, and eleven others for "ecclesiastical service" in the Alexandrian church (5.2).

The second half of the *Acts of Mark* (chapters 6–10) describes the series of events that led up to Mark's martyrdom. After spending two years in Pentapolis (where he was busy ordaining bishops and clerics for that region), Mark returned to Alexandria and found that the people in the community there "had flourished in the grace and the faith of God, and had built a church for themselves"[39] in a place called Boukolou located near the sea (5.3–4). However, this state of affairs (and the news of Mark's return) continued to anger the pagan populace of the city (6.1–2). That year a festival of the cult of the Egyptian god Serapis happened to fall on the same day as the church's Easter celebration (7.1). Incited to take action, a crowd of pagans entered the church, seized Mark in the midst of the service, and dragged him through the streets of Alexandria until "all his flesh was falling on the ground and the rocks were stained by his blood" (7.2–4). When evening came, the crowd finally threw Mark—still alive and thanking God—into prison (8.1). That night, while Mark was praying, there was a great earthquake, and an angel appeared to him, addressing him with the words, "O Mark, servant of God, the foremost of the saints in Egypt, behold your name has been written in the book of eternal life and you have been counted among the holy apostles. Your memory will not be forsaken forever . . ." (8.3). After the angel, Christ himself appeared to Mark, identifying him as "my evangelist" (8.6). In the morning, the pagan mob came and dragged Mark's body through the city once again until he died (9.1–3). However, when the crowd tried to burn Mark's body on a pyre (in a place called Angeloi), Christ, having foreseen their action, sent a violent storm that caused the crowd to disperse in terror (9.4–6). Finally, a group of the faithful came and took Mark's body back to the church, prepared it for burial, and placed it in a stone tomb on the eastern outskirts of the city (10.1). According to this account, Mark's death occurred on the thirtieth of the Egyptian month of Pharmouthi (April 25), the traditional feast day of Saint Mark in the Coptic church (10.2).

I have summarized the *Acts of Mark* in detail in order to make several observations about the traditions it preserves. First of all, it has been recognized that, despite its relatively late date, the *Acts* may contain elements that are, in fact, reminiscent of the very earliest social context of Christianity in Egypt. The monotheistic exclamation ("God is one!"), the name of the first convert Anianus, Mark's references to Old Testament prophecy in his preaching about Christ, and the place names mentioned in the work all may recall vestiges of the social identity of the earliest church in Alexandria—a community composed largely of converts from Hellenistic Judaism.[40]

Second (and perhaps more importantly), the traditions preserved in the *Acts of Mark* reveal to the reader something about the emerging self-identity of the Egyptian church in late antiquity (i.e., the fourth and fifth centuries). The *Acts* itself functions as an etiology for the existence of the Alexandrian church—specifically, an attempt to explain the origins of the patriarchate itself and the church's identity as a community founded on the blood of the martyrs. The Egyptian church's identity as a "church of the martyrs" will be the subject of the next chapter: there, I will discuss the account of Mark's martyrdom in more detail. Here, however, I want to concentrate on Mark's encounter with Anianus. What does this story tell us about Egyptian perceptions of the patriarchal (papal) office in late antiquity?

As early as the fourth century, in Eusebius' *History of the Church*, Anianus was identified as "the first after Mark the evangelist" to assume responsibility for serving "the districts in Alexandria."[41] However, Eusebius provides no other information about Anianus or about how he was named as Mark's successor. In the *Acts of Mark*, then, the story of Mark's ordination of Anianus as bishop (and his ordination of the three presbyters) is an attempt to demonstrate and reaffirm the direct link between Saint Mark and his successors as bishops of Alexandria. Indeed, one of the three presbyters ordained by Mark in the story—Cerdo—is also recognized by Eusebius as the third successor to Mark as bishop of Alexandria. In this way, Mark's meeting with Anianus in the *Acts of Mark* served as a "foundation legend" that helped the late antique Egyptian church make sense of its own (apostolic) history and leadership.

This "foundation legend" exerted a strong influence over the literature and art of the Egyptian church during the early medieval period. The *History of the Patriarchs* attributed to Sawirus ibn al-Muqaffa is one text that directly reflects this influence.[42] The work is actually a multi-generational compendium of Egyptian church history that relies on several early Coptic sources but was redacted and translated into

Arabic in the eleventh century,[43] and it preserves the stories of Mark's encounter with Anianus and of Mark's martyrdom in the *Acts* almost verbatim. Yet, it also expands Mark's legend even further by appending material from another (anonymous) source about Mark's life as a young man before his mission to Egypt, in particular by placing emphasis upon Mark's early association with the apostle Peter and his ability to perform miracles in the face of "pagan" resistance. Once again, in this later text as in the *Acts*, Mark's association with the apostles and his spiritual power are understood to be fundamental for the identity of the Egyptian church he founded.

Another interesting example of the influence of this legend about Mark is found in a series of eighth-century ivory reliefs preserved in Milan.[44] The ivories, probably commissioned in Egypt but produced by Syrian-trained artists,[45] depict scenes from Mark's encounter with Anianus in the *Acts*. The first of the ivories seems to present a scene of Mark's missionary work in Alexandria: in the relief, Mark holds his gospel in his hand and preaches to a small crowd, who stand before an architectural façade with a cityscape in the background (Fig. 2a).[46] In the second of the series, Mark heals the hand of Anianus, who sits on a cobbler's stool with the buildings of Alexandria behind him (Fig. 2b).[47] In the third ivory, Mark baptizes Anianus and two other unidentified, smaller figures, who stand in a river with the walls of Alexandria as a backdrop (Fig. 2c).[48] The fourth ivory shows Mark laying his hands on Anianus in front of a shell arcade, with four other figures looking on—a scene of Anianus' ordination as bishop (Fig. 2d).[49] The fifth ivory belonging to this same series is only partially preserved: Mark is depicted striding forward with a book under his arm—behind him, part of a man's head appears at the left; to the right, there is a door visible (Fig. 2e).[50] Unfortunately, not enough details are present for a certain identification of the scene.

The fragmentary nature of this fifth scene reminds us of the fact that this set of five ivories probably originally belonged to a larger series that included other scenes from Mark's life and martyrdom. The size and shape of the ivories suggest that they may have originally been set in the panels of a wooden door to a church. A similar example of a carved door relief—in this case, all in wood and from the sixth century—survives from the Church of St. Barbara in Old Cairo.[51] Set within the panels of a door leading into an Egyptian church, the Milan ivories depicting Mark's missionary work in Alexandria and his ordination of Anianos would have had an important social function. They would not only have reminded everyday Christians of the stories about their church's origins, but also of the continuing identity of the church and its leadership as successors to Saint Mark.

The Earliest Successors of Saint Mark: Apostolic Lineage and Orthodox Self-Definition

"A Mere Echo and a Puff of Smoke": Saint Mark's Earliest Successors and the Silence of History

During the first part of this chapter, I have traced the development of some of the most important traditions surrounding Saint Mark in the ancient and early medieval Egyptian church. Now, I want to return again to the first two centuries and to Mark's immediate successors in the see of Alexandria. As I mentioned earlier, no sources earlier than Clement of Alexandria (late second or early third century A.D.) even mention Mark's connection with the church in Egypt, and the authenticity of Clement's testimony continues to be disputed. In the case of Mark's successors, our sources are even later and less forthcoming. Of Anianus, nothing is known prior to Eusebius' fourth-century account—and there, Eusebius merely records Anianus' name as Mark's first successor and provides no other information. If Eusebius knew anything about the story of Mark's encounter with Anianus as it appears in the later *Acts of Mark*, he strangely had nothing to say about it in his *History*. Unfortunately, the same is the case for each of Mark's first ten successors as bishop of Alexandria: Eusebius simply lists them in order without providing any substantive comments about their lives or accomplishments. A comparison of Eusebius' comments about each reveals scarcely any variation, only a stark repetition of their order of succession and their years of rule:

> (2.24) When Nero was celebrating the eighth year of his reign, **Anianus**, as the first after Mark the evangelist, received the responsibility for serving the districts in Alexandria.

> (3.14) In the fourth year of Domitian, the first bishop of Alexandria, Anianus, died after having fulfilled twenty-two years (of service), and the second, **Abilius**, succeeded him.

> (3.21) Trajan succeeded Nerva after the latter had reigned a little more than a year. It was during Trajan's first year that **Cerdo**

succeeded Abilius, who had presided over the districts of Alexandrian for thirteen years. Cerdo presided as the third bishop of that area after Anianus, the first.

(4.1) About the twelfth year of Trajan's reign the bishop of the districts in Alexandria mentioned to us a little earlier passed away, and **Primus** was chosen to serve there as the fourth from (the time of) the apostles.

(4.4) Around the same time (the third year of Hadrian's reign) **Justus** succeeded Primus, who had passed away in the twelfth year of his leadership.

(4.5) After a year and some months had passed, **Eumenes** took up the leadership of the districts belonging to the Alexandrians in the sixth election, the bishop before him having remained in office for eleven years.

(4.11) At Alexandria **Mark** (**Marcianus**) was publicly declared pastor after Eumenes had fulfilled, in all, thirteen years (of service).

(4.11) And when Mark took his rest from ten years of service, **Celadion** received the responsibility for serving the church of the Alexandrians.

(4.19) But when Celadion had headed the districts of Alexandria for fourteen years, **Agrippinus** took up the succession.

(5.9) In (the Emperor Commodus') first year, **Julian** was entrusted with the archbishopric of the Alexandrian churches, with Agrippinus having fulfilled his service in twelve years.

(5.22) At the same time (in the twelfth year of Commodus' reign), after Julian had fulfilled his tenth year (of service), **Demetrius** was entrusted with the responsibility for serving the districts at Alexandria.

It is only with Demetrius, the eleventh bishop after Mark, that we finally begin to get something other than the most stereotypical report.

Later, in Book 6 of his *History of the Church*, Eusebius goes on to provide more detailed information about Demetrius' term of leadership,
including his correspondence and his further efforts in the area of
church organization (see chapter two).[52]

However, for much of the first two centuries we know almost
nothing about those who served as bishops of Alexandria. Given the
importance of Egypt as an ecclesiastical center in the early church and
as a reservoir for the discovery of early Christian documents, the lack
of information about the first two centuries of Egyptian church
leadership has caused historians much consternation. In this context,
Walter Bauer has written his famous words that the first ten
Alexandrian bishops "are and remain for us a mere echo and a puff of
smoke."[53] C.H. Roberts, another scholar specializing in early Egyptian
Christianity, has also lamented the "obscurity that veils the early history
of the Church in Egypt."[54] What, then, is the reason for the deafening
silence of our sources during this period? And how are we to understand the succession list that Eusebius provides in light of this silence?

In his landmark and controversial study, *Orthodoxy and Heresy in
Earliest Christianity*, Walter Bauer argued that the reason for the
silence in the early sources about Egyptian church leadership in the first
two centuries stems from the fact that this leadership was not yet well
defined during this period, and that the dominant form of earliest
Christianity in Egypt was of a Gnostic type that would later be considered heretical by the larger church. As evidence for the presence of
this unorthodox kind of Christianity, Bauer points to the existence of
ancient Gnostic gospels from Egypt—especially the *Gospel of the
Egyptians* and the *Gospel of the Hebrews*—which, in his opinion,
represent a version of Christianity that predated the rise of orthodox,
ecclesiastical forms. In Bauer's view, orthodox faith and practice was
only successfully imposed upon the Egyptian church toward the end of
the second century during the reign of Demetrius (bishop of Alexandria
from 189 to 231).[55] At that time, earlier Gnostic literature would have
begun to be suppressed, and along with it the earliest historical records
of Egyptian Christianity. Thus, the reason that Eusebius gives us so little
information about the first ten orthodox bishops is simply that he never
had much reliable, surviving information to work with: for Bauer, the
bishops in his list are "a mere echo and a puff of smoke; and they
scarcely could ever have been anything but that."[56]

Bauer's study has provided valuable insights into the processes by
which "orthodoxy" was defined (or constructed) in the late second

century, and by which the emerging orthodox leadership suppressed alternative forms of belief in the late second century. However, his argument that heresy preceded orthodoxy in the early Egyptian church has caused (as one might imagine) a considerable amount of controversy in ecclesiastical circles. In addition, it has also prompted criticism from certain scholars who believe that he went too far in his "argument from silence." One of the most cogent critiques has been offered by C.H. Roberts, who has argued that Bauer failed to provide an accurate account of the diverse array of sources actually available to us from the first two centuries in Egypt. In his book entitled *Manuscript, Society and Belief in Early Christian Egypt*, Roberts reexamined the papyrological evidence for second-century Christianity in Egypt, and concluded that this evidence did not support Bauer's thesis of a "heretical" or "Gnostic" hegemony. Of fourteen extant Christian Greek papyri that perhaps may be assigned a date before the year A.D. 200, only one (a fragment of the *Gospel of Thomas*) is debatably Gnostic. Of the remaining papyri, ten are biblical texts, while the others include an *Unknown Gospel* (not Gnostic in character), the *Shepherd of Hermas*, and Irenaeus' anti-Gnostic treatise *Against Heresies*.[57] Most certainly, the *Gospel of Thomas* fragment and the papyrus with Irenaeus' anti-Gnostic treatise give witness to the early presence of "heterodox" forms of Christianity in Egypt (albeit from very different perspectives). However, it is clear that "Gnosticism" (itself a phenomenological category that has recently been called into question by historical scholars)[58] is by no means the only Christian world view represented in the papyri. From this and other evidence from the period (including early Coptic writings), Roberts concludes that the situation of earliest Christianity in Egypt is better characterized as a "fluid" one, in which various types of Christians coexisted in a community not yet differentiated sharply along theological lines.[59] Such a situation—in which church leadership roles were still in the process of being defined and negotiated—prevailed throughout the first two centuries of Egyptian church history.

Defining Orthodoxy in the Late Second Century: Succession Lists and the Discourse of Apostolicity

The late second century was a crucial time for the Egyptian church and its process of theological and ecclesiastical self-definition. The presence of a late second- or early third-century fragment of Irenaeus' treatise *Against Heresies* in the Egyptian papyrological records testifies loudly to this fact.[60] Written around the year 180 in Lugdunum (modern Lyons, France), the treatise was one of the earliest attempts in the Christian church to define the boundaries of "orthodox" faith and to label beliefs outside those boundaries as "heresies." The Roman church utilized Irenaeus' work in its nascent war against heresy, and—judging by the papyrological evidence—the treatise circulated quickly in the eastern Mediterranean world to Egypt, where it would have been used to similar purpose.[61]

Key strategies in this process of orthodox self-definition were discourses of apostolicity and the publication of succession lists. In antiquity, the concept of succession, or pedigree, was typically employed as a means to establish legitimacy and power in the face of competing claims to authority. The use of succession as an ideological and polemical concept predated the rise of Christianity and took two main forms: 1) intellectual pedigrees (e.g., pedagogical genealogies) and 2) institutional pedigrees (e.g., royal dynasty lists).[62] Both types of succession rhetoric are attested in ancient Christianity. In the second century, various Christian teachers appealed to apostolic pedigrees to defend the authority of their theological instruction, while bishops (somewhat belatedly) began invoking the principle of succession to bolster their right to govern the church.

In the churches at Alexandria and Rome, independent Christian teachers had been claiming apostolic authority for their own teaching since the early decades of the second century. The earliest evidence for such practice is connected with a Christian philosopher named Basilides who was active in Alexandria during the final years of the Emperor Hadrian's rule (ca. A.D. 132–135). Specifically, Basilides identified himself as the student of a man named Glaucas, who had been an "interpreter" *(hermêneus)* of the apostle Peter.[63] Around the same time, a Christian Gnostic named Valentinus was making similar apostolic claims. A younger contemporary of Basilides, Valentinus likewise lived and taught in Alexandria during the early decades of the second century (sometime between the years 117 and 138). By 140, he had migrated to Rome, where he became a prominent instructor in the faith and attracted numerous students. In his case, Valentinus traced his apostolic connections through his teacher Theudas back to the apostle Paul.[64] Valentinus' disciple Ptolemy, who was active in Rome around the year A.D. 150, alludes to this intellectual pedigree in his *Letter to Flora* when he talks about "the apostolic tradition, which even we have received by succession."[65]

For the earliest evidence of an apostolic genealogy conceived on *institutional* lines, we must turn once again to Irenaeus, who supplies us with our first succession list for Roman bishops almost fifty years after Basilides and Valentinus began their public teaching careers in Alexandria. In his treatise *Against Heresies* (ca. 180), Ireneaus lists the first twelve bishops of Rome between Peter and Eleutherius, and grounds that list on an apostolic claim: "It is available to all who truly desire to see in every church to observe the tradition of the apostles manifest in all the world, and we are able to enumerate those who were appointed bishops in the churches by the apostles, as well as their successors, down to our time."[66] By defining an exclusive apostolic lineage of Roman bishops, Irenaeus sought to exclude from the church any leaders or teachers who claimed a different heritage.

In Egypt, a similar impetus toward self-definition and the establishment of more rigid standards of institutional succession seems to have gripped the church in the final decade of the second century, a process undoubtedly spurred on by the circulation of Irenaeus' anti-Gnostic treatise and by the leadership of Demetrius, the first Alexandrian bishop for whom we have specific biographical information.[67] The succession list of early Egyptian bishops that was eventually handed down to Eusebius (see discussion above) was probably originally compiled and published during this period, perhaps even by bishop Demetrius himself. As such, it reflects a self-conscious attempt by the late second-century Egyptian church leadership to define its apostolic pedigree in terms of a succession of bishops, and to counter and combat independent teachers like Basilides and Valentinus who claimed a different kind of apostolic authority for their own instruction.

Thus, the late second century witnessed a sharp conflict between two models of authority in the Alexandrian church. In this period, Christian bishops like Demetrius began to claim apostolic sanction for their administrative leadership of the church. Through the publication of episcopal succession lists, the ecclesiastical leadership increasingly moved to suppress alternative, academic (i.e., intellectual) sources of authority in the church. Most prominent among these were the apostolic claims of certain circles of Christian philosophers and Valentinian Gnostics who had previously (in the absence of strong bishops) wielded considerable social influence in the Alexandrian church.

Interestingly enough, while the emerging episcopal hierarchy in Alexandria proved successful in ostracizing the intellectual heirs of

Basilides and Valentinus and relegating them to sectarian status, other non-clerical academic models survived within the bounds of the church. In particular, two well-known Christian academicians, Clement (ca. A.D. 160–215) and Origen (ca. 185–253), were tolerated (at least for a time) by bishop Demetrius and achieved public recognition as representatives of an Alexandrian theological school. Significantly, both of these men employed the rhetoric of apostolic succession as a stamp or guarantee of their own theological orthodoxy. Clement of Alexandria describes his apostolic teaching lineage in almost biological terms. Speaking of his own teacher Pantaenus (regarded in tradition as the first head of the Alexandrian catechetical school) and Pantaenus' other students, Clement remarks: "Now these men, preserving the true tradition of the blessed teaching straight from the holy apostles Peter and James, John and Paul, receiving as a son from a father . . . came with God, depositing those ancestral, apostolic seeds even up to our time."[68] A generation later, Origen would emphasize the same point: "The teaching of the church is preserved unaltered handed down in unbroken succession from the apostles and existing to this day in the churches."[69]

In the end, however, such rhetoric could not prevent the scholastic tradition of Clement and Origen from coming into conflict with the emerging power of the Alexandrian episcopate. In the next chapter, I shall discuss Origen's increasingly rocky relationship with bishop Demetrius, and the concerted steps Demetrius and his successors took to regulate and control the teaching office of the Alexandrian church in an era of persecution.

Two

_____

Bishops, Teachers, and Martyrs

The Shaping of Episcopal Authority in
an Age of Persecution (Demetrius to Peter I)

With the election of Demetrius as bishop of Alexandria in
189, the history of the Egyptian church entered a new era.
During this era, Demetrius and his successors began to
make concerted efforts to consolidate their authority in the Egyptian
church. This consolidation of authority was nowhere more evident
than with regard to the teaching office of the church. The first part of
chapter two will focus especially on the relationship between the episcopal leadership and the church's theological school in Alexandria.
Little concrete historical information survives concerning the activity
of the earliest Alexandrian bishops prior to 189. However, in the last
decade of the second century, beginning with Demetrius' rule, the
sources suddenly become more forthcoming, providing us with evidence from which we can begin to reconstruct more precisely the
social role of the church leadership in Alexandria.

These early attempts by the Alexandrian bishops to consolidate
their authority and to begin to stake out the boundaries of theological
orthodoxy were made more urgent by a new, external threat—the
threat of persecution. While Christians during the first two centuries
were occasionally subject to outbreaks of local hostility, it was only in
the third century that churches in Egypt began to experience more
widespread, systematic forms of persecution. Indeed, from the beginning
of the third century to the first decade of the fourth century, the
Egyptian church was wracked by three periods of intense persecution,
separated by longer stretches of sometimes-uneasy calm: the Severan
persecution (202–206), the Decian persecution (249–251), and the
Diocletianic (or "Great") persecution (303–311). The second part of
this chapter will concern the issues raised by the latter two persecutions

for the leadership of the Egyptian church. How did the Alexandrian bishops continue to consolidate their authority in the face of such a threat? And finally, how was the identity of the Egyptian church and its leadership shaped by the experience of persecution and martyrdom?

The Bishop of Alexandria and the Alexandrian Catechetical School

In antiquity, Alexandria earned an international reputation as a center of learning.[1] The Alexandrian Museum ("Shrine of the Muses"), established early in the Ptolemaic period (323–30 B.C.), became an academic think tank, research center, and social club for the intellectual elite. There, even Roman emperors like Claudius and Hadrian came to give lectures and participate in debates. Founded at around the same time and situated nearby, the Great Library of Alexandria served the clientele of the Museum. By ancient standards, the size of the Library collection was staggering—in its heyday, the Library is reported by some ancient writers to have contained as many as four (or even seven) hundred thousand rolls of papyri. Modern statistical calculations have shown such figures to be considerably inflated—an estimate in the tens of thousands is probably more accurate—but that is not to diminish the fact that the Alexandrian collection was "comprehensive for its time."[2] In any case, the size of the Library eventually led to the creation of a separate branch elsewhere in the city at the Serapeum, the temple complex dedicated to the Egyptian god Serapis—today, visitors to the remains of the Serapeum can still see ancient wall niches that may have originally been used to hold those books.[3]

While Alexandria had long enjoyed its reputation as a center of literary scholarship and scientific enquiry—boasting such lights as Callimachus and Apollonius of Rhodes in the field of poetry and Euclid, Archimedes, Eratosthenes, and Herophilus in the fields of mathematics, physical mechanics, geography, and medicine—by the end of the Ptolemaic period the most publicized scholarly work at the Museum was taking place in the area of philosophy. During the period from the first century B.C. to the second century A.D., Middle Platonic philosophy—an eclectic form of Platonism that borrowed extensively from Stoicism and other schools of thought—became very popular in both intellectual and popular circles. This philosophical ethos would come to have a profound influence on early Christian theologians who lived and worked in Alexandria.[4]

It should not be surprising then that Alexandrian Christians, raised in the shadow of the Alexandrian Library and philosophical academy, soon developed their own institutions of learning. Indeed, in late antiquity, the Alexandria church became renowned throughout the Mediterranean world for its theological academy (often referred to as the Alexandrian "catechetical school"), and for the biblical and philosophical scholarship of its teachers.

The roots of the Alexandrian catechetical school are difficult to trace with certainty. As with his succession list of Alexandrian bishops, the historian Eusebius attempts to trace a lineage of academic leadership for the school, identifying three men—Pantaenus, Clement, and Origen— as early heads of the institution. Pantaenus is the first person to be associated with the leadership of the catechetical school, even though Eusebius seems to imply that the school was in existence even before Pantaenus became its head. Concerning the school, he writes, "From ancient times, there was an established custom among them of having an academy for sacred learning."[5] Of Pantaenus himself, we actually know quite little. Eusebius describes him as a philosophical theologian who was influenced by Stoic thought and whose legacy as principal of the catechetical school apparently included a corpus of writings.[6] Among Pantaenus' disciples was Clement of Alexandria, who recognizes his indebtedness to him in his writings and who, according to Eusebius, became the next head of the catechetical school after Pantaenus' death.[7] Finally, in A.D. 202, Origen, who is identified by Eusebius as one of Clement's students, became the third in this line of academic principals when Clement left Alexandria during the Severan persecutions.[8]

Unfortunately, the historical relationship between Pantaenus, Clement, and Origen is not as easy to characterize as Eusebius would want to suggest. It is especially curious that Origen himself never mentions Clement by name in any of his extant writings.[9] Different explanations have been offered for Origen's reticence concerning Clement—perhaps a doctrinal disagreement over Clement's use of the term "gnostic,"[10] perhaps a reluctance on the part of Origen to associate himself with views of Clement not in favor with Demetrius, the bishop of Alexandria,[11] or perhaps even a strong difference of opinion concerning the proper response to persecution.[12] In any case, the silence in Origen's writings concerning his supposed predecessor has led some to raise questions about Eusebius' account of an orderly succession of leadership at the catechetical school.[13]

It has been argued quite persuasively that prior to Origen there was actually no formal theological "academy" in Alexandria (only a common "school of thought"), and that it was only after bishop Demetrius entrusted Origen with responsibility for "elementary instruction" *(hê tôn grammatikôn logon didaskalia)* in the church that such an institution was officially established.[14] Prior to that, theological instruction in the church may have been conducted on a more independent basis, with teachers like Pantaenus and Clement (like Basilides and Valentinus before them) attracting small groups of philosophically-inclined Christians as disciples. In this context, Eusebius' inclusion of Pantaenus and Clement in his "succession list" may reflect more his general concern with establishing the antiquity of church teaching traditions than with any formally organized, institutional reality already existing in the late second century.[15]

In any case, regardless of when the catechetical school was founded— either at the time of Origen or at some earlier stage—it is clear that Demetrius' appointment of Origen as head of the school marked an important juncture in the Alexandrian bishop's attempts to organize and regulate the teaching office of the church. Eusebius notes that, prior to Origen, "no one was dedicated to the elementary instruction of Alexandria Christian teaching, as everyone had left under threat of persecution."[16] Apparently, Origen had recognized this need even before his official appointment by Demetrius: Eusebius tells us that Origen had been approached by "some from the pagans who had heard the Word of God," and that Origen subsequently began instructing them in private.[17] In this context, Demetrius' appointment of Origen— whether it represented the founding of a formal school or the reform of previous practice—takes on new significance. Undoubtedly, Demetrius' action was designed to meet the needs of a church that lacked adequate resources for educating new converts in the face of persecution, but it was also an attempt to bring Alexandrian catechetical teaching more directly under the control of the bishop.

Demetrius' efforts to exert his authority over the teaching office of the church eventually became a source of tension between him and his appointee Origen.[18] Before becoming head of the catechetical school, Origen had been trained as a teacher of Greek literature *(grammateus)* and had also sat at the feet of Ammonius Saccas, one of the masters at the Alexandrian philosophical academy.[19] In his time as head of the catechetical school in Alexandria, from 202 to 234, Origen put this philological and philosophical training to good use, producing an impressive corpus of writings, including a work of textual criticism comparing different manuscripts of the Old Testament (the *Hexapla*), a number of biblical commentaries (on Psalms 1–25, Lamentations, Genesis, and the Gospel of John), and his masterwork of speculative and systematic theology entitled *On First Principles*. Given his intellectual interest in exploring deeper matters of theology, Origen soon found the limitations of offering only "elementary instruction" to be too restrictive. A brief trip to visit the church in Rome may have exacerbated such feelings in him: Eusebius reports that, although Origen was ostensibly enthusiastic to resume his teaching upon his return, Demetrius "still urged and all but begged him to continue to give assistance to the brethren without hesitation."[20]

Demetrius' efforts to channel (and perhaps restrain) Origen's intellectual energies would prove to be in vain. Shortly after his return from Rome, Origen—seeing that "he would not be able to breathe if he could not engage in deeper, scholarly discussion of theology, or the examination and interpretation of sacred writings, over and above the basic catechetical instruction *(katêxêsis)* of those who were coming and meeting with him"—decided to institute a reform to the organization of the catechetical school. He divided the school into two divisions: one for "elementary instruction" *(eisagogê)* and one for "those who have attained a state of intellectual maturity."[21] He assigned the former to one of his students, Heraclas. The latter—the division of advanced studies—he assigned to himself. Eusebius' language gives no indication that Demetrius was involved in this reorganization, and perhaps this was a factor that contributed to the rising tensions between the two. In any case, the reforms that Origen instituted—designed to bring his teaching and research closer together and to give his students an opportunity for advanced work—may have been viewed by Demetrius as a subtle betrayal of the original vision of the school, namely, to provide basic catechetical instruction for those inquiring about conversion to the Christian faith.

The tension between Demetrius and Origen eventually led to Origen's departure from Alexandria. In his *History of the Church*, Eusebius writes that Origen left Alexandria secretly when "no small warfare was rekindled in the city," and settled for a time in Caesarea of Palestine, where he was invited to give public lectures on biblical interpretation.[22] For a long time, scholars thought that the phrase, "no small warfare," referred to a massacre of Alexandrian citizens instigated by the Emperor Caracalla in the year 215. Yet, there is no indication that Caracalla's action targeted Christians, or that Origen would have felt especially threatened by what has become known as "Caracalla's fury." More recently, the French scholar Pierre Nautin has argued that Eusebius, in referring to this local "warfare," was, in fact, alluding to the ecclesiastical conflict that had erupted between Demetrius and Origen, a conflict that may have induced Origen to take temporary leave of his position in Alexandria.[23]

As mentioned before, Demetrius's primary concern throughout his episcopacy seems to have been to reassert the institutional authority of the bishop and to standardize church organization. This is illustrated by his response to Origen's leave-taking. The Alexandrian bishop wrote a letter to his counterparts in Jerusalem and Caesarea criticizing them for allowing Origen, a layperson, to preach in the presence of bishops, contending that this was something that "had never been heard of and had never taken place" in the church before. (The Palestinian bishops responded by enumerating examples in other locales where laypersons were called upon to assist the clergy in preaching.) Eventually, Demetrius, by writing a more conciliatory letter and sending a delegation of deacons to Palestine, managed to persuade Origen to return to Alexandria.[24] However, the *détente* between the two would not be permanent. By the year 231, Origen had decided to leave Alexandria for the final time, traveling again to the church in Caesarea, where he was persuaded to be ordained as a priest and to set up his own school.[25]

Demetrius' reaction to Origen's final departure and his ordination sheds further light on the social construction of episcopal authority in early Christian Egypt. Angered by what he considered an intrusion upon his jurisdiction as a bishop, Demetrius wrote a series of letters to the bishops of the other dioceses in the Mediterranean world, protesting the irregularity of Origen's ordination.[26] The significance of Demetrius' correspondence, along with his earlier letter to the bishops of Jerusalem and Caesarea, should not be underestimated, as they represent the earliest documented attempts by an Alexandrian bishop to coordinate canonical policy and to raise ecumenical support for his local episcopal authority. In this case, Demetrius' letter-writing campaign had an observable effect: his excommunication of Origen was supported by a Roman church synod and a number of other church centers (with only the bishoprics of Palestine, Arabia, Phoenicia, and Achaia voicing dissent).[27] Demetrius' eventual successor, Heraclas would also uphold this sentence of excommunication of Origen (despite the fact that he had been a pupil and colleague of Origen at the Alexandrian catechetical school).

Another important consequence of Origen's departure from Alexandria was a change in the organization and leadership of the catechetical school. When Origen relocated to Palestine, he effectively took with him the division for advanced study he had established as head of the catechetical school (along with his sizeable personal library).[28] In Caesarea, he resumed his teaching, attracting a new cadre of students and establishing an extensive library collection for theological research—one that Eusebius of Caesarea would make use of seventy-five years later in the writing of his *History of the Church*. In Alexandria, only the division for "elementary instruction" remained, with Origen's former pupil Heraclas as its head. At the time of Origen's departure, there seems to have been no attempt to reestablish an institute for higher theological education in the city.[29]

With Origen out of the picture, the catechetical school in Alexandria became more intimately linked with the authority of the bishop. This is illustrated by the fact that, after Demetrius' death in 233 (only two years after Origen's departure), it was Heraclas, the recently installed head of the catechetical school, who succeeded him as bishop of Alexandria. The succession of Heraclas (231–247) set an important, new precedent for the selection and promotion of episcopal candidates. For the rest of the third century, the Alexandrian bishopric would be filled exclusively by candidates who had previously served as heads of the catechetical school. Heraclas' immediate successors, Dionysius (247–264), Maximus (264–282), and Theonas (282–300), all served in that capacity before their elevation to the office of bishop.[30] This method of promotion reflects another way that the catechetical school was increasingly brought under auspices and authority of the Alexandrian episcopacy. As a consequence, Heraclas and those who came after him were ultimately able to exert more direct control over the teaching office of the church.

Heraclas' role in trying to define and defend orthodox teaching is personally attested by his successor Dionysius in one of his letters. Dionysius writes, "I inherited this rule and example from our blessed pope Heraclas," and then goes on to describe how Heraclas disciplined students "who associated with one of the heterodox teachers."[31] Here, for the first time in our sources, the bishop of Alexandria is accorded the title of "Pope" (in Greek, *papas*) fifty years before that same title was applied to the bishop of Rome.[32] Originally, the Greek term *papas* simply meant "father," but it increasingly came to be applied as a formal title of respect for the archbishops of Alexandria and of Rome.[33] It is

significant that Dionysius first uses this title in describing Heraclas'
efforts to provide a "rule and example" guiding the regulation of
church teaching. As such, the use of the title "Pope," from its inception, evoked the process by which Alexandrian episcopal authority
was consolidated and expanded during the first half of the third
century.

The "Church of the Martyrs"
Episcopal Leadership in an Age of Persecution

Dionysius of Alexandria and the Decian Persecution

Just a year after Dionysius' election as bishop in 247, the world of the
Alexandrian church was thrown into turmoil when an unruly mob
rose up against the Christians in that city. In a letter written later to
bishop Fabius of Antioch, Dionysius describes how the ringleader of
the mob, a pagan prophet, incited them to attack local Christians by
"rekindling their local superstition."[34]

> First, they carried off an old man named Metras, and commanded
> him to say impious words. When he did not obey, they struck his
> body with wooden clubs, stabbed his face and his eyes with sharp
> reeds, led him to the suburbs, and stoned him to death.

Others suffered a similar fate: a female convert named Quinta was
dragged through the city, beaten and stoned to death; an old woman
named Apollonia had her teeth knocked out and was burned to death;
and finally, a man named Serapeum was tortured, had his limbs broken, and was then thrown off the upper story of a building.[35]

This outburst of local violence against the Christians in Alexandria
flamed out quickly—Dionysius reports that the uprising soon
devolved into factional fighting and civil war and that the focus of the
violence shifted away from the Christians ("we enjoyed a brief
respite").[36] However, this reprieve would not last. After a new emper-
or, Decius, took office in 249, another, much larger, wave of persecution would strike. In contrast to earlier outbreaks of violence against
the Christians (which, like the events in the summer of 248, were largely sparked by local unrest),[37] the persecutions initiated by Decius were
systematic, widespread (although varying in intensity), and govern-
ment-sponsored, affecting Christians not only in Egypt, but all
throughout the Mediterranean world.

In his letter to Fabius of Antioch, Dionysius describes the beginning of the Decian persecution as the arrival of "the edict." Early in the year 250, Decius published an edict requiring citizens in the empire to sacrifice to the Roman gods. Originally, this edict probably represented an attempt by Decius to restore traditional Roman discipline in the army and traditional Roman *mores* in the larger society.[38] Government officials supervised the administration of the sacrifices, and official certificates (called *libelli*) were issued to verify that individuals had sacrificed. These *libelli* followed a standardized formula, and more than forty examples have been preserved on Egyptian papyri, all dating from mid-June to mid-July 250.[39]

Christians in Egypt responded to the edict and the call to sacrifice in a variety of ways. Dionysius describes how many capitulated and renounced their faith:

> Everyone has been cowering out of fear. This has also been the case for many of the most prominent citizens: some immediately began presenting themselves (to the magistrate) because they were afraid; others who were working for the state were led (to sacrifice) by career concerns; still others were dragged forward by their neighbors. . . . Some came forward pale and trembling . . . but some others ran more readily toward the altars, insisting overboldly that they had never before been Christians.[40]

Dionysius goes on to describe the fate of other Christians who submitted to imprisonment and torture only to relent and sacrifice in the end. Still others seem to have gotten their slaves to sacrifice for them or bribed officials to issue them counterfeit *libelli*.[41]

Not all Christians capitulated, however. Some remained faithful, even in the face of imprisonment, torture, and death. Dionysius himself names fifteen more Egyptian Christians who perished during this wave of persecutions and describes the atrocities they suffered: four had their flesh dissolved by quicklime, one was beheaded, one was burned alive, four (all women) died by the sword, four were torn in pieces and then burned, and one was disemboweled with a sharp stick.[42] Those who were imprisoned because they confessed their faith publicly were called "confessors" *(homologêtês)*. The courage of the Egyptian confessors as they awaited their deaths quickly became a rallying point for the Christian community: among the rank and file, the confessors were thought to possess a special *charisma*, or spiritual authority, that made them qualified to forgive sins in a church whose institutional leadership had been largely decimated or dispersed.[43]

Indeed, the first stage of the Decian persecution seems to have especially targeted the church leadership (bishops and clergy).[44] During January of 250, Fabian, the bishop of Rome, was arrested, bishop Alexander of Jerusalem (along with Origen) was imprisoned and tortured in Palestine (both would later die as a result of their wounds), and Babylas of Antioch was martyred. Dionysius of Alexandria and Cyprian of Carthage managed to escape persecution by fleeing their capital cities: from their places of hiding both tried to direct church affairs and offer pastoral guidance by means of letters. However, almost two years later, when the persecutions suddenly came to an end after the Emperor Decius' death, their decision to go into hiding would raise problems for their leadership of the church. Both Dionysius and Cyprian were forced to defend themselves against accusations that their flight was a sign of cowardice and that they had abandoned the church in its hour of need. Why should the church honor a leader who had hidden himself away while faithful Christians were going to their deaths?

In Cyprian's case, he would argue in his own defense that his decision to hide was "for the safety of the brethren" (i.e., so that the church would not be such a visible target) and that his numerous pastoral letters allowed him, while absent in body, to be still present "in spirit."[45] As for Dionysius, he presented himself as one who had been fully expecting to be martyred (and who faced that expectation bravely), but whose plans were ultimately thwarted by divine providence. In a later letter, he writes:

> I speak even as in the presence of God, and he knows whether I am lying. I did not give any thought to myself, nor did I conceive of my flight apart from God. But earlier, when the persecution had been instituted by Decius, Sabinus in that very hour sent a police agent (*frumentarius*) to search for me, and I remained at home for four days awaiting his arrival. But even though he went around searching everywhere . . . he was smitten with blindness and did not find the house. For he did not believe that I, being an object of persecution, would remain at home. It was only after four days, after God commanded me to change location and miraculously paved the way, that I went out, along with the young men and many of the brethren. The

events that happened next—during which perhaps I became useful to some—demonstrated that this was a work of God's providence.[46]

While Dionysius alludes here to the usefulness of his continued pastoral role during his self-imposed exile, he grounds his defense of his flight in language his critics would have understood well—a discourse of divine guidance and miraculous intervention, perhaps mixed with a tinge of pious victimization (in the letter, he casts himself as "an object of persecution").

This discourse becomes more pronounced when Dionysius describes how he was later captured and imprisoned by soldiers, but then miraculously rescued by a group of local, pagan villagers who had learned of his plight. Here, Dionysius portrays himself as a most reluctant participant in his own rescue:

> Then, having understood why they had come, I cried out, begging and beseeching them to go away and leave me alone. If they wanted to do something good, they ought to waylay the ones who abducted me and cut off my head themselves. While I was shouting such things, as those who are my companions and partners in all things know, they lifted me up by force. I began to stretch myself back on the floor, but they, having grabbed hold of my hands and dragging my feet, carried me out, and the witnesses (martyres) of all of these events—Gaius, Faustus, Peter, and Paul—followed. These witnesses, having picked me up in a rushing motion, took me out of the village. And, having put me upon a bareback donkey, they led me away.[47]

The scene Dionysius describes seems almost comedic, but his carefully crafted self-presentation in this letter actually had quite serious implications for his role and authority as bishop. By showing himself to be a bishop who had been dragged away from the martyr's altar kicking and screaming (and who had witnesses to prove it), Dionysius was seeking legitimacy in the eyes of those in the church who had suffered, and who would not abide a leader who had not actually suffered in solidarity with them. His need to defend his actions in the aftermath of the persecution sheds further light on his letter to Fabius of Antioch (introduced earlier), where he extols "the divine martyrs among us," enumerating their tortures and describing "how many and how great were the terrors that befell us."[48] Like his description of his own brief imprisonment, Dionysius' chronicling of the martyrs' stories would have had a similar rhetorical function of underscoring his solidarity with those who had suffered and died for the faith. Thus, in the correspondence of Dionysius of Alexandria, one sees for the first time how an Alexandrian bishop began to utilize the early Christian discourse of holy suffering to shape the identity of the Egyptian church as a church of heroic martyrs, and to shape perceptions of his own episcopal leadership in the midst of persecution.[49]

In the aftermath of the persecution, Dionysius would face an even thornier challenge to his authority as bishop, and this challenge appeared on two separate but related fronts. First, the Egyptian church (like Cyprian's church in North Africa) was confronted with the dilemma of what to do with those who had apostatized—that is, those who had denied their faith during the persecution. With the cessation of the persecution in 251, many of these lapsed Christians made petitions to be readmitted into the church. Second, the church was also faced with the challenge of what to do with confessors who had been released from the prisons. As mentioned above, while in prison, these confessors had been credited with the spiritual authority to forgive sins, an authority previously reserved for the bishops alone. What status should the confessors have in the church now that the persecution was over?

To complicate matters, some of the confessors, independent of the bishop, began welcoming those who had "lapsed" back into the church. Thus, in his letter to the bishop of Rome, Dionysius was not simply interested in describing Alexandrian suffering; he was also seeking advice about how he should handle the situation of those who had been pardoned by the confessors:

> Shall we stand with them (i.e., the confessors), as ones who share the same opinion? Shall we defend their judgment and their favor? Shall we be merciful to those who have been shown mercy by them? Or shall we deem their judgment wrong, set ourselves up as the examiners of their conscience, cause grief to their kindness, and undercut their position?[50]

One can see how bishops like Dionysius of Alexandria and Cyprian of Carthage found themselves stuck between a rock and a hard place. On the one hand, if they simply upheld the confessors' pardons, they would effectively validate their claim to having an authority in the church independent of the bishop. On the other hand, if the bishops condemned their actions, they would run the risk of losing the confessors' crucial grassroots support and attracting further criticism regarding their own actions during the persecution.

In the case of Cyprian, he astutely negotiated a compromise solution to this vexing problem: he decided to appoint two young confessors as readers *(lectores)* for the church community in Carthage, and, while he did not immediately ordain them as presbyters, he offered them a salary commensurate with the rank of clergy. Cyprian's brilliant solution was grounded in the social conventions of ancient patron-client relationships. His appointment of these confessors as paid *lectores* was meant "to enhance the status of his new clients" and, at the same time, to win for himself (as high patron of the church) the loyalty of the people who had been granted pardon by the confessors.[51]

We know much less about how Dionysius responded to this same dilemma. Like Cyprian, he seems to have tried to carve out a middle ground between the lenience of the confessors and the intransigence of the more hard-line members of the church, who saw sacrifice during the persecution as tantamount to the unforgivable sin. In Dionysius' letter to the bishop of Antioch, for example, one gets a sense of how he tried to impose more specific penitential standards for the readmission of the lapsed—often postponing their readmission until right before the time of death—while at the same time presenting himself (along with the confessors) as an advocate for their ultimate absolution. In this letter, Dionysius relates the story of a man named Serapion, an old Christian who had sacrificed during the persecution. He describes how Serapion finally received the Eucharist on his deathbed after numerous unsuccessful appeals for readmission to the church. The administration of the sacrament was irregular—his young grandson had to bring him the elements from the local priest, who was also sick in bed. However, Dionysius reaffirms the validity of the rite, saying that he had ordered that "those who were departing from this life, if they wanted it, and especially if they happened to have made petition previously, should be forgiven."[52]

When Eusebius reports on the many letters Dionysius wrote on the subject of repentance, he may be giving us a further clue of how the bishop exercised his skill in correspondence as a way to address the concerns of different constituencies within the church. Judging by Eusebius' account, Dionysius seems to have written a total of at least seven letters on repentance, including correspondence with the churches in Antioch, Laodicea, Armenia, and Rome, as well as three more letters directed to the churches in Alexandria and Upper Egypt.[53] Thus, at the same time that he was negotiating a solution to the problem of the confessors at home, Dionysius was also working to strengthen the bonds between Alexandria and other episcopal sees throughout the Mediterranean.

Before his death in 264, Dionysius would experience a renewal of persecution in 257 under the emperor Valerian. In some of his later correspondence, he presents detailed accounts of his imprisonment, trial, and exile to Libya—accounts he hoped would further demonstrate his solidarity with the confessors. Writing from exile, he describes how he had been "forcibly dragged away" and "confined in a desolate and dry place in Libya." There, a small group of presbyters went underground and secretly made pastoral visits to the beleaguered Christian inhabitants of the city. Among these presbyters was the man who would eventually succeed him as bishop of Alexandria—Maximus.[54]

Dionysius' episcopacy was forged in the fire of persecution, and yet the final years of his reign would witness his return from exile and the inauguration of an extended period of peace for the church. After the emperor Valerian was captured by the Persians in 260, his imperial successor Gallienus issued two edicts (in 260 and 262) reaffirming the church's rights and restoring its property. For the next forty years—a period spanning the bishoprics of Maximus (264–282) and his successor Theonas (282–300)—the church in Egypt was not threatened by governmental persecution.[55] In the year 303, however, this period of relative calm gave way to a new storm—the onset of the last, "Great Persecution" of the church.

Peter of Alexandria:
Persecution, Penance, and the Making of a "Martyr Pope"

It was the nineteenth year of Diocletian's reign . . . (when) imperial rescripts were promulgated everywhere, commanding that the churches be brought to the ground and that the Scriptures be destroyed by fire, and proclaiming publicly that those who had attained honor would become dishonored, and that those in household servitude, if they continued in their Christian persuasion, would be deprived of their freedom. Such was the first edict against us.[56]

With these words, Eusebius of Caesarea describes the beginning of the Great Persecution that began in the year 303 under the emperor Diocletian. Three years earlier, at Peter of Alexandria's election as bishop, such a dire turn of events might have seemed unimaginable to many Egyptians. During the early period of Diocletian's reign, Christians in Egypt had enjoyed a period of economic prosperity largely free from government intervention.[57] As emperor, Diocletian had devoted most of his attention to the administrative, military, economic (monetary), and legal reform of the Roman Empire.[58] Among his most famous accomplishments was the reorganization of the empire into four administrative regions, each ruled by its own emperor, with Diocletian himself standing at the head of this imperial Tetrarchy. Through such reforms, Diocletian had hoped to solidify the boundaries of the Roman territories and to restore the empire to its former glory.

However, as Peter took office as the bishop of Alexandria in 300, there were ominous signs that this environment was about to change. In 297, a revolt in Alexandria over Diocletian's new taxation policies had caused the emperor and his army to intervene and spend a year and a half in Egypt suppressing the revolt and restoring peace to the countryside. Then, in 299, suspecting that his attempts at divination were being thwarted by the presence of Christians making the sign of the cross, the emperor issued a local order while in Syria threatening to purge the army of any soldiers who refused to offer sacrifice to the pagan gods.[59] Finally, two years into Peter's reign as bishop, Diocletian, again in Alexandria, issued an edict condemning members of the Manichaean religious sect with the death penalty.[60] The language of the edict—which accuses the Manichaeans of perpetrating crimes against the gods and against "what has been decided and fixed by the ancients"—shows how Diocletian's goal of restoring the glory of ancient Rome intersected with an agenda of promoting religious allegiance and uniformity in the empire. The very next year, this agenda brought Diocletian into direct conflict with the Christian church.

On February 23, 303, Diocletian (at the instigation of his deputy emperor in the East, Galerius) issued the aforementioned edict that mandated the burning of scriptures, the demolition of churches, and the stripping of Christians' social rank. In the next twelve months, a series of other edicts would be promulgated, escalating the terms of the government persecution. Torture was authorized as a form of punishment, Christian clergy were arrested and compelled to sacrifice, and finally (in an act reminiscent of Decius' regime fifty years before) the emperor issued a general order requiring all to sacrifice.[61] For the next ten years—under Diocletian, and then later under his imperial successors Galerius and Maximin—the Egyptian church would be rocked by successive waves of persecution. Once again, in the face of persecution, the Alexandrian church leadership would use the social capital at its disposal—including personal correspondence, ecclesiastical legislation, and the production of hagiography—to promulgate the identity of the Egyptian church as a "Church of the Martyrs."

The renewal of persecution under Diocletian and Galerius brought both old and new challenges to the authority of Peter as bishop of Alexandria. The second edict against the Christians, issued in the spring or summer of 303, especially targeted ecclesiastical leaders, and Peter (like Dionysius before him) was forced to flee. Other Egyptian clergy, including four bishops named Hesychius, Pachomius, Theodorus, and Phileas, were forcibly removed from their dioceses and thrown in jail. From his exile (reportedly in Mesopotamia, Syria, and Palestine), Peter attempted to offer continued guidance and encouragement to the Egyptian church,[62] offering as a defense for his flight Christ's instruction to his disciples in Matthew 10:23—"When they persecute you from this town, flee to the next." In offering this biblical apology for his own actions, Peter was undoubtedly responding to the same kinds of criticism Dionysius had faced several generations before during the Decian persecution. However, while Dionysius had appealed to divine providence and the miraculous intervention of others in explaining his escape from imprisonment, Peter's defense ultimately rested on a biblical discourse in which he portrayed himself in solidarity with the apostles and in obedience to Christ's teaching.[63]

Not everyone was satisfied with Peter's defense of his flight. Despite his efforts at regular correspondence and a brief return to Alexandria in 305–306, some felt that Peter's extended absence (along with the imprisonment of other Egyptian bishops) had left a serious leadership void in the Egyptian church. In 304, the bishop of Lycopolis in Upper Egypt, a man named Melitius, tried to do something to fill that void. Perhaps motivated by a concern for maintaining the liturgical and sacramental life of the church,[64] he ordained new bishops to take the place of the four whose imprisonment prevented them from occupying their sees (Hesychius, Pachomius, Theodorus, and Phileas). However, Melitius' intervention in other dioceses ran directly counter to traditional canonical practice in the church, and the four imprisoned bishops, having gotten wind of his actions, raised a storm of protest. In a letter written from their Alexandrian jail and addressed to Melitius,[65] the four bishops condemned his ordination of bishops in other dioceses as "alien to divine order and the church's rule," and in particular as an affront to the principle of apostolic succession and "the honor of our great bishop and father, Peter."

The bishops' letter is an invaluable source for reconstructing the motivation of Melitius: they specifically contest his claim that "the flocks were in need and forsaken," arguing that adequate provision had, in fact, been made for the visitation of church members during the persecution. The letter also gives witness to the allegiance Peter continued to garner during his time in exile. Indeed, in chastening Melitius, the bishops reconfirm the authority of the Alexandrian patriarch in matters of church jurisdiction: "You (Melitius) ought to have waited for the judgment of the superior father, and for his permission to do this."

Melitius was not to be swayed by the bishops' letter. Within a year, the four bishops had been martyred, and Melitius had come down the Nile from Lycopolis, entered Alexandria, and ordained two more bishops to fill the vacant parishes of the capital city.[66] This latest action by Melitius brought a response from Peter himself. From his place of exile, Peter wrote a letter to his flock in Alexandria, formally excommunicating Melitius from the church, and warning them against associating with him. The letter has been preserved, and it reveals a struggle for authority in a church thrown into turmoil by government persecution:

> Peter, to his beloved brethren, established in the faith of God, greeting. Since I have found out that Melitius acts in no way for the common good—for neither is he contented with the letter of the most holy bishops and martyrs—but invading my parish has assumed so much to himself as to endeavor to separate from my authority the presbyters and those who had been entrusted with visiting the needy; and, giving proof of his desire for preeminence, has ordained in the prison several for himself; now take heed to this and hold no communion with him until I meet him in company with some wise and discreet men, and see what his designs have been. Farewell.[67]

In Melitius' action of persuading some of Peter's presbyters to shift allegiance to him and in his ordination of several imprisoned *confessors* to the priesthood, one sees the roots of a full-fledged schism in the Egyptian church.

Thus, the beginnings of the "Melitian schism" may be traced to a disagreement over the character and shape of church leadership during the persecution. However, this disagreement soon expanded to involve another dispute—specifically, over the familiar question of how the church should provide for the readmission of those who had lapsed in their faith by sacrificing. The crux of the question was not so much *whether* those who had sacrificed should be readmitted, but rather "the interval to be allowed before readmission and the status to be accorded after it."[68] Over against Peter's perceived leniency on this matter, Melitius and his followers took a more hard-line stance, advocating longer periods of penance before the readmission of the lapsed. Melitius' position on this issue may very well have been forged early on during his episcopal career in Upper Egypt: there is intriguing evidence (found in two Coptic fragments) that Melitius' predecessor as bishop of Lycopolis had been found guilty of apostasy (*paradosis*, "treason") during the persecution. His crime (in the eyes of his fellow Christians) may very well have been the act of handing over sacred writings to be burned, as was ordered by the Roman government at an early stage of the persecution. In this context, Melitius' election may, in fact, have reflected a rigorist reaction against any compromise with the Roman authorities.[69]

The disagreement between Peter and Melitius is colorfully illustrated in a story told by the fourth-century church writer Epiphanius.[70] In the story, which is most likely apocryphal, Peter and Melitius find themselves imprisoned in the same jail cell and begin to argue about the readmission of the lapsed. According to Epiphanius, the argument eventually grew so heated between the two that Peter finally hung his cloak across the middle of the cell as a physical barrier to separate himself from his rival. A number of scholars have taken this story at face value, identifying this event as the root cause of the conflict between Peter and Melitius.[71] However, there is no corroborating evidence for such a prison encounter between these two figures (nor is there evidence that either was imprisoned in the early stages of the persecution). The early letters written by the four bishops and by Peter (mentioned above) focus not on the issue of the lapsed, but rather on Melitius' "illegal" action of ordaining bishops outside the boundaries of his episcopal see. Thus, it is more likely that Epiphanius' account is of a legendary character, and that he "is reading back into the early days of the schism . . . divisions articulated later" once the schism had become full-blown.[72]

In any case, Melitius' establishment of a rival episcopal hierarchy and his hard-line stance regarding the readmission of the lapsed ultimately prompted Peter to return to Alexandria from his place of exile (ca. 305–306). His stay there would only be temporary (perhaps only a little over a year later he would be forced to flee again) but during his time back in the capital city, Peter wrote one of his most influential works—his *Canonical Letter* on the issue of the lapsed.[73] In that letter, he attempted to defuse the Melitian challenge to his authority by formulating a systematic set of policies regarding the practice of penance in the church.

While there is evidence for "the rough outlines of a recognized penitential discipline" in Egypt by the middle of the third century,[74] one sees for the first time in Peter's *Canonical Letter* a detailed attempt by an Egyptian bishop to regulate the length of penance connected with different forms of apostasy.[75] Over against Melitius' austere insistence that no penance should be available to the lapsed until the persecution had come to an end,[76] Peter formulated a system of penance designed to respond more immediately to the petitions of those seeking readmission to the church. For example, those who had sacrificed but then later repented, confessed their faith, and subjected themselves to imprisonment or torture were received immediately into communion (*Canon* 8); the same applied even to those who paid money, or gave up property and fled, in order to avoid sacrificing (*Canons* 12–13). In addition, Peter took a moderate stance in relation to those who had sacrificed under the duress of torture or imprisonment and then repented: at the time of the *Canonical Letter*, the persecution had been going on for three years, and Peter was willing to credit them with "time already served," adding only forty days or one year (respectively) to the term of their penance (*Canons* 1–2).

However, at the same time that Peter's canons reflect his pastoral sensitivity to the needs of those who had stumbled during the persecution, they also reveal his concern to demonstrate his solidarity with the *confessors* and to cultivate the support of rigorous elements in the church by taking a firm stand against more egregious transgressions. Thus, he lavishes praise upon the confessors for their bravery and voices his approval for their intercessory prayers on behalf of the lapsed (*Canon* 11).[77] Peter also grants the status of confessor to those who, under torture, were "forced against their will" to sacrifice (and who can produce witnesses to verify their sufferings) (*Canon* 14). When Peter assigns longer terms of penance for certain forms of apostasy, he may be seeking to find some common ground with his critics, especially those in the church attracted by Melitius' penitential rigorism. Thus, to those who had lapsed without any imprisonment or torture, and to those who forced their Christian slaves to sacrifice for them, Peter assigned at least three more years of penance (*Canons* 3 and 7). Of course, those who remained unrepentant after their act of sacrifice were cursed and denied readmission to the church altogether (*Canon* 4). Finally, Peter ruled that lapsed clergy who later repented and suffered for the faith may be readmitted to communion but are barred from future church office. This stance suggests another way that he was trying to appeal to those in the church who, along with Melitius, had become sorely disillusioned with the inconstancy of their clerical leadership.

Thus, Peter's *Canonical Letter* reflected not only his pastoral concern for healing the wounds inflicted by the persecution, but also a larger ecclesiastical competition over the legacy of the martyrs. In assuming their more rigorous posture, Melitius and his followers specifically identified themselves as the true "Martyrs' Church" *(ekklêsia marturôn)*[78] For his part, Peter, while following the moderate course laid out by his predecessor Dionysius, subtly tried to stake a similar claim for the church he represented by lauding the confessors and remaining resolute in the face of those who had committed apostasy by sacrificing to the Roman gods.

The *Canonical Letter* later became foundational for canon law in the eastern churches (hence its title),[79] but at the time of its writing it would do nothing to impede the growth of the Melitian church. With Peter forced to go in exile again in 306, Melitian communities became more entrenched, especially in the towns and countryside of Upper Egypt.[80] Later in the fourth century, the followers of Melitius would get embroiled in the complex theological politics of the Arian Controversy, and would increasingly become associated with the Egyptian monastic tradition (see chapter three).[81] Indeed, there is evidence that the Melitian community survived as a monastic movement into the eighth century A.D.[82]

As for the ecclesiastical competition between Peter and Melitius, it would take Peter's own death in the waning days of the persecution to wrest the legacy of the martyrs away from his rival and reclaim it for the Alexandrian church. On April 30, 311, the emperor Galerius issued his famous *Palinode* (or "Recantation"), revoking the order to sacrifice and granting amnesty to Christians. Peter was free to return to Alexandria. However, only six months later, persecution of Christians would flare up again in the East under the emperor Maximin, and Peter would be arrested. His death at the hands of his Roman persecutors, reported by Eusebius and retold in hagiographical legend, determinatively and finally shaped the identity of the Alexandrian patriarch as head of an Egyptian "Church of the Martyrs."[83]

While Eusebius gives a very spare report of Peter's death by beheading, the later *Martyrdom of Saint Peter* expands the story with a host of pious details not found in Eusebius' account. The *Martyrdom* actually survives in three different recensions.[84] The shortest version (S)[85] ends with an account of Peter's death in jail: it describes how, with the Alexandrian Christians threatening to riot over their bishop's imprisonment, Peter allowed his captors to enter his cell secretly through a hole in the back wall to avoid the attention of the mob, and then offered himself up to his executioner voluntarily in order to protect the populace from further reprisals. In the two longer versions (L and LL),[86] the story is modified considerably. Peter is led out of the hole in the back wall of the jail and then taken (at his request) to the church of Saint Mark at Baucalis (Boukolou) on the eastern outskirts of Alexandria; there, after being allowed to pray at Mark's shrine, Peter meets a martyr's death. The longest recension of the *Martyrdom* (LL) adds several additional details about events that took place after his martyrdom: 1) a local struggle over where to bury Peter's body, 2) the ceremonial enthronement of his corpse and the passing of his clerical garment (Greek, *himation*; Latin, *pallium*) to his successor Achillas, and 3) his burial in a cemetery west of the city.

Most of the details of these expanded narratives do not have an historical basis,[87] but they do tell us quite a lot about how Peter was represented as the ideal martyr in subsequent centuries, and how the Alexandrian patriarchate was shaped by this discourse of martyrdom. In particular, the longer versions of the *Martyrdom of Saint Peter* consciously reinforced the connection between the martyr Peter and his apostolic predecessor, Saint Mark. The narrative relocation of Peter's death to the site of Saint Mark's burial shrine in Baucalis linked Peter's martyrdom spatially to the social practices of pilgrimage and saint veneration connected with Mark's cult. In the *Martyrdom*, Peter's act of kissing Mark's tomb and his prayer before the shrine makes this discursive link even more explicit. In the prayer, he addresses Saint Mark as "the first martyr and patriarch of this see."[88] Later in the same scene, a virgin standing nearby experiences a vision, in which she hears a heavenly voice say, "Peter was the first of the apostles; and now Peter is the last of the martyrs."[89] Here, we see how Peter, the patriarch of

Alexandria, was represented as the ideal martyr bishop—as the
fulfillment and worthy heir of Saint Mark's suffering and Saint Peter's
apostolic authority.

This representation of Peter as the ideal martyr bishop ultimately
helped construct the social identity of both the Alexandrian patriarchate and the Egyptian church in late antiquity. Peter's prayer at the
shrine of Saint Mark not only links his identity with the evangelist
himself, but also with the patriarchal lineage after Mark. In a prayer
invoking Christ, Peter says, "You chose the blessed Anianus because
he was worthy; and after him (you chose) Abilius, and those who
succeeded those two; then Demetrius and Heraclas and Dionysius and
Maximus; and the blessed Theonas, my father, who brought me up
until I came to the ministry of this see after him."[90] In the longest
recensions of the *Martyrdom*, Peter's death also links him with those
who would come after him in the Alexandrian see: at the end of the
story, prior to his burial, the bishops and elders of the city (along with
a crowd of people) take Peter's body, place it on the episcopal throne,
and then consecrate Peter's successor, Achillas, in a rite involving the
physical transfer of the dead bishop's *pallium*. Throughout this section
of the *Martyrdom* account, Peter is referred to as "the most holy and
famous bishop" and "the holy martyr of God."[91] In the narration of
these events, Peter's reputation as the ideal martyr bishop is effectively
transferred onto the papal office itself.

Thus, in history and in later legend, one sees how the Great
Persecution had a profound influence on the social construction of
the Alexandrian patriarchate in late antiquity, as well as on the self-
perception of the Egyptian church. In the medieval period, this
influence would be most strikingly demonstrated in the dating system
employed by Copts. Starting in the fourth century, Egyptians began to
mark Diocletian's imperial inauguration (A.D. 284) as the beginning of
a new era in their history—the "era of Diocletian." Among Christian
communities in Egypt, this way of reckoning dates soon came to be
embraced as a self-conscious marker of their historical identity as a
people who had suffered persecution. Later, this chronological
marking of communal identity would become even more explicit, as the
"era of Diocletian" began to be labeled the "era of the Martyrs." Indeed,
by the twelfth century the latter phrase had largely superceded the
former among the Copts as the preferred way of dating historical
events,[92] and even today, Egyptian Christians continue to count their
years according to the "era of the Martyrs."[93]

Three

Theological Controversy and the Cultivation of Monastic Support
The Alexandrian Patriarchate from 312 to 451
(Achillas to Dioscorus I)

With the end of the Great Persecution, and with the rise to power of the Emperor Constantine (312–337), the fortunes of the Christian church in Egypt and in the rest of the Roman Empire quickly began to change. At Constantine's decisive victory over his imperial rival Maxentius at the Milvian Bridge outside Rome in the fall of 312, he is supposed to have had a vision of Christ and to have subsequently ordered his army to place the sign of Christ (the labarum) on their shields.[1] After his victory and recognition as supreme Augustus by the Roman Senate, the church suddenly became the unexpected beneficiary of imperial patronage (despite the fact that Constantine himself also continued to make public obeisance to Sol, the Roman god of the sun).[2]

Constantine's patronage of the church was wide-ranging. He supported the restoration of Christian-owned property that had been confiscated during the persecution and authorized donations from the imperial treasury for the building, restoration, and decoration of churches, as well as the publication of biblical codices. In addition, he granted Christian clergy special rights and privileges: in particular, they received exemptions from public government service and from taxation. Christian bishops were included in Constantine's circle of confidants in the imperial court and were given the authority to preside over legal disputes involving Christian claimants. Finally, Constantine also instituted legal reforms that reflected his patronage of Christian causes: crucifixions were abolished as a form of punishment, and Sunday ("sun-day") was universally recognized as a holy day, with soldiers in the imperial army being given official leave on that day for the purpose of worship.[3]

No longer under threat of persecution, many Christians began to celebrate the reign of Constantine as an eschatological golden age, as the coming of God's kingdom on earth. The Christian historian Eusebius writes, "Our emperor, friend of God and bearing the image of divine kingship, rules in imitation of the one who is above all things on earth, as he directs the helm of government."[4] For his part, Constantine calls himself "a bishop who has been appointed by God over all things external to the church."[5] For authors like Eusebius, and for Constantine as well, the unity of the church and the unity of the empire went hand-in-hand, sure signs of God's favor and of the renewed glory of Rome.

In some places, however, this utopian vision of a unified church and empire was already starting to show worrying fault-lines. In the North African church, news of the Donatist schism reached Constantine's ears in 313: this ecclesiastical civil war would rage on despite the emperor's repeated attempts to impose his will upon the dissenting Donatist church. Half a decade later, Constantine would be forced to intervene in a theological dispute that originated in Alexandria over the teachings of a priest named Arius. The sixty-year controversy that ensued—most often referred to as the Arian Controversy—would extend beyond the borders of Egypt and would last well beyond the end of Constantine's reign.

The Arian Controversy was only the first in a series of theological disputes that plagued the churches of Egypt and the Mediterranean basin during the rest of the fourth century and the first half of the fifth. No longer faced with the external threat of persecution, the larger church increasingly found itself distracted and divided by internal disagreements over doctrinal matters. As we shall see, the Egyptian ecclesiastical leadership consistently found itself at the center of this theological and political maelstrom.

In this chapter, I focus on three particular "storms" of theological conflict during this period: 1) the Arian Controversy (ca. 318–381); 2) the Origenist Controversy (ca. 390–410); and 3) the so-called Nestorian or Christological Controversy (ca. 428–451). In each of these controversies, the Alexandrian patriarchs positioned themselves as staunch defenders of theological "orthodoxy," often becoming lightning rods for criticism by their opponents. Much of the literature produced by the patriarchs during this period was polemical—writings that document a war of words that was being waged between opposing theological factions. Thus, during the Arian Controversy, the patriarch

Alexander (312–328) circulated a series of letters against the teachings of Arius. Later, his successor Athanasius (328–373) would produce an *Apology*, a *History*, and three formal *Discourses* against Arius' followers (not to mention numerous other letters and treatises). Even Athanasius' famous ascetic biography, *The Life of Saint Antony*, contains an underlying anti-Arian agenda. During the controversy over Origen's theology at the end of the fourth century, the archbishop Theophilus of Alexandria (385–412) likewise used encyclical letters, as well as sermons, to counter those who held Origenist views. Finally, during the Christological Controversy of the fifth century, similar tactics were employed by Cyril of Alexandria (412–444) and his successor Dioscorus (444–454). Amidst Cyril's vast literary output, for example, one finds several full-scale treatises written against Nestorius, including a list of "Twelve Anathemas" condemning specific points of his Christological doctrine.

The importance of the Alexandrian patriarchs during this period, however, was not limited simply to their literary output, or to the role they played in defining and defending the faith of the Egyptian church; they also had an important social and political role to play, one that was inextricably intertwined with their advocacy of specific theological doctrines. On an international level, the patriarchs of the fourth and fifth centuries were key players in the first ecumenical councils that sought to resolve (but, in fact, often exacerbated) the thorny theological debates that lay at the root of these controversies. Indeed, it was during this period that the Egyptian patriarchs began to assume a truly international profile, wielding considerable influence at ecumenical councils and pursuing heated rivalries with the bishops of Rome and Constantinople for preeminence and authority within the larger church.

On the home front, where the theological controversies often played out on a smaller scale between rival factions of the Egyptian church, the Alexandrian patriarchs faced the complex task of cultivating grassroots support for the theological positions they espoused. This process took place on several levels—among the different urban social classes represented in the city of Alexandria, as well as across economic, geographical, and linguistic boundaries in the towns and villages of Upper Egypt.[6] The methods the patriarchs used in cultivating this theological support were intimately tied to the social customs of ancient Roman patronage in which the patron was expected to provide financial support or protection in exchange for loyalty and services rendered by the client.[7] In the case of an Alexandrian patriarch, the support he offered to his clients could take the form of economic and civic benefits (e.g., giving people freer access to the grain dole, or funding the building of newer and larger churches), as well as more traditional ecclesiastical and spiritual ones (e.g., ordaining new priests, and guaranteeing regular access to the Eucharist). In exchange for such forms of patronage, the clients of the bishop offered their continued loyalty, sometimes in the form of public rallies or demonstrations against their bishop's theological opponents.

Among the most important settings for the exercise of such patriarchal patronage were the monastic communities that had just begun to burst like wildflowers onto the Egyptian social landscape in the early fourth century. Monasticism emerged (at least in part) as a reaction or protest against the social conformity of the church in the era of peace initiated by Constantine. On the outskirts of society (and sometimes in urban centers), Egyptian monks established an alternative way of life, with an independent administrative hierarchy that posed an implicit challenge to the general life of the church and to the rule of the bishop.[8] The ecclesiastical leadership, and the monks themselves, both struggled to define how the monasteries should properly relate to society on the one hand, and to the clerical hierarchy on the other. For their part, the patriarchs and local bishops often tried to exert pressure upon monks to become ordained as priests in order to bring them more directly under episcopal authority. Many monks adamantly resisted this ecclesiastical pressure to become ordained against their will. The situation was complicated by the presence of ordained clergy among the monks who found themselves beholden both to their monastic leaders and to their bishops.[9] Thus, in the midst of the theological disputes of the fourth and fifth centuries, the Alexandrian patriarchs were consistently faced with an extremely delicate task—the task of trying to bring the largely autonomous monastic movement into closer conformity with their theological (and political) policies.

This chapter will explore how the patriarchs of this period, in the midst of theological controversy, began to forge vital links with communities of Egyptian monks, links that endure even to the present day. As we shall see, the patriarchs' cultivation of monastic support during the fourth and fifth centuries indelibly shaped the historical identity of the Egyptian patriarchate, and played a crucial role in the establishment of a Coptic doctrinal orthodoxy.[10]

1. Ivory relief depicting Saint Mark with thirty-five successors as Patriarch of Alexandria, early seventh century A.D.; Musée du Louvre, Paris.

a.   b.

c.   d.   e.

2. Five ivory reliefs with scenes from the life of Saint Mark, eighth
century A.D.; Museo del Castello Sforzesco, Milan: a) Mark preaching in Alexandria;
b) Mark healing Anianus; c) Mark baptizing Anianus (and others);
d) Mark laying hands on Anianus (ordination of Anianus as his successor);
e) Fragmentary scene of Mark walking while carrying a book.

3. Wall painting of Saint Athanasius of Alexandria, thirteenth century A.D.; Monastery of Saint Antony, Red Sea.

4. Wall painting of Saint Athanasius of Alexandria, tenth century A.D. (A.D. 953); Tebtunis, Fayûm.

a.

b.

5. Manuscript illuminations depicting Theophilus of Alexandria, early fifth century A.D.; W. Goleniscev Collection, Petersburg; a) Theophilus, holding a Bible and standing below the mummy of his predecessor Timothy; b) Theophilus, holding a Bible and standing on top of a pedestal decorated with a bust of the Egyptian god Serapis.

6. Wall painting
of Dioscorus of
Alexandria (depicted
wearing a monastic
hood), thirteenth century
A.D.; Monastery of
the Syrians, Wadi
al-Natrun.

7. Wall painting of Dioscorus of Alexandria (on right, with the anti-Chalcedonian patriarch Severus of Antioch on left), thirteenth century A.D.; Monastery of St. Antony, Red Sea.

8. Wall painting of Pope Damian (?); eighth century A.D.; Church of the Holy Virgin in the Monastery of the Syrians, Wadi al-Natrun.

9. Coptic inscription of Pope Damian's
Synodical Letter (A.D. 578); late sixth
or early seventh century A.D.;
Monastery of Epiphanius at Thebes.

10. Wall painting of Peter I of Alexandria (on right, with Saint Andrew the Apostle on
left), in which the image of the archbishop Peter is assimilated to that of Saint Peter the
Apostle; A.D. 1025–1030; Monastery of the Archangel Gabriel, Fayûm.

Alexander, Athanasius, and the Arian Controversy in Egypt

From Alexandria to Nicaea:
The Early Conflict Between Alexander and Arius

Sometime around the year 318,[11] the teachings of a presbyter named Arius began to attract public attention in the Alexandrian church. Originally from Libya,[12] Arius had been appointed parish priest in the eastern Alexandrian suburb of Boukolou either during the short six-month tenure of Peter's successor, Pope Achillas (312), or during the very early years of Pope Alexander's reign (312–326).[13] Arius was an eloquent preacher and his sermons attracted a cadre of devotees,[14] but his distinctive teachings also eventually provoked a censuring response from Alexander and the church hierarchy. If Alexander had at one time held Arius in high regard, the growing theological rift between them quickly soured their relationship and threatened to cast the Alexandrian church into schism.

The point at issue in this emerging theological dispute was Christ's identity as divine Word—or, to put it in other terms, the identity of Christ the Son in relationship to God the Father. Unfortunately, most of Arius' original writings have been lost or destroyed: as a result, his teachings on this subject must be carefully reconstructed from fragments of his writings—scattered excerpts and paraphrases that survive in treatises written against him by his opponents. In one of his extant letters, a defense addressed to his accuser, the "blessed Pope" Alexander, he sets forth his view on the nature of the Son:

> Our faith, from our ancestors, which we have learned also from you, is this. We know one God—alone unbegotten, alone everlasting, alone without beginning, alone true, alone possessing immortality, alone wise, alone good, alone master . . . who begot an only-begotten Son before eternal times, through whom he made the ages and everything . . . (The Son) was created by the will of God before times and ages, and he received life, being, and glories from the Father as the Father has shared them with him . . . God being the cause of all is without beginning, most alone; but the Son, begotten by the Father, created and founded before the ages, did not exist before he was begotten . . . But God is thus before all as a

monad and cause. Therefore, he is also before the Son, as we
have learned from you when you preached throughout the
midst of the church.[15]

Arius' assertion that the Son was "created" before time and subordinate to the Father was grounded in his exegesis of specific biblical
texts,[16] and motivated by specific theological and soteriological concerns.

On the one hand, in describing God the Father as "supremely sole"
and "without beginning," Arius seems to have been concerned to safe-
guard the singular perfection and incomparability of the most high God
(here identified with the Father). This was a theological concern that had
long been present in Egypt among early Christian theologians of the
Platonic tradition who shared the assumption that there could only be
one supreme, perfect Being.[17] According to Arius' application of this
logic, if the Father was identified as this High God, all other beings (the
Son included) necessarily had to be of a subordinate status.

On the other hand, Arius' doctrine also seems to have been
grounded in a particular soteriological concern—that is, a concern
about the nature of human salvation. For Arius and his early followers,
the divinity of the Son was granted to him by the Father—as a kind of
advance promotion or divine adoption—in anticipation of his progress
in virtue and attainment of perfection. This notion that the Son could
change (albeit for the good) was a bone of contention for Alexander and
later opponents of the Arians for whom the immutability of the Son
played a crucial role in the drama of human salvation. For Arius and his
early followers, however, the Son's successful advance toward perfection
in this life (and his possession of divine Sonship by virtue of adoption)
provided a model for the Arian understanding of human redemption
through the imitation of Christ's virtues.[18]

Alexander's response to Arius' teaching set the terms for later
stages of the theological controversy. In a letter written to his namesake, Alexander of Thessalonica,[19] the Egyptian bishop rejected both
the theological and soteriological aspects of Arius' position. For
Alexander, the Father and Son were coeternal, both full and equal
participants in the Godhead. Indeed, he asked, how could God as
Father ever have existed without the Son?

It is necessary that the Father is always the Father. But he is
Father of the always present Son, on account of whom he is
called Father.[20]

Alexander's formulation of this idea clearly draws on the Alexandrian theological tradition, especially Origen, who had proposed the idea of the Son's "eternal generation" a century before.[21]

In addition to rejecting Arius' subordination of the Son to the Father, Alexander also opposed Arius' understanding of human salvation as our shared adoption (with Christ) as sons of God. Instead, Alexander insisted that Christ's Sonship was of a completely different character from our own. While we are still sons (and daughters) of God by adoption, Christ is God's Son *according to his unchanging nature*.

> Therefore our Lord, being Son of the Father by nature, is worshiped. And those who have put off the spirit of slavery, from acts of virtue and progress, and who received the spirit of adoption as sons, become sons by adoption being shown a kindness by the Son, who is Son by nature.[22]

The distinction Alexander was making had enormous implications for his understanding of human salvation: it was only through the grace ("kindness") of one who was "Son of the Father by nature" that humans could become "sons by adoption" and receive salvation. This line of defense became the watchword of Athanasius and others who would follow Alexander in opposing Arius' teachings.

The heady theological debate outlined above became the catalyst for a series of events that threatened the unity of the Egyptian church (and eventually the unity of the empire itself). Shortly after recognizing the implications of Arius' teachings, Alexander convened a local council of bishops in Alexandria to deal with the matter (ca. 318).[23] When Arius refused to sign a "confession of orthodoxy" drafted by Alexander at the council, the patriarch proceeded to excommunicate him and a number of his followers. From that point, the conflict between the two sides escalated onto the international stage.

For their part, Arius and his adherents began writing letters and traveling to different bishoprics throughout the eastern Empire, hoping to drum up support for their theological views. Their efforts seem to have met with some success. Arius, in an early letter written to Eusebius of Nicomedia,[24] claimed a number of other eastern bishops among his supporters, including the bishops of Laodicea, Tyre, Anazarbus, Lydda, and the famous historian Eusebius of Caesarea (Palestine). The addressee, Eusebius of Nicomedia—himself regarded as Arius' foremost advocate—was a bishop who wielded considerable influence in the imperial court and who seems to have hosted Arius for a time during his travels. The decisions of two separate councils during this period—one at Bithynia (Asia Minor, ca. 320–321), and one in Caesarea (Palestine, ca. 321–322)—provide evidence for the strong support garnered for Arius' views in some quarters. Both councils reaffirmed the orthodoxy of Arius' theology and called for his reinstatement by the Egyptian patriarch.[25] Encouraged by these conciliar decisions, Arius would eventually return to Alexandria, intent on establishing his own church there.

At the same time, Alexander himself was seeking support from other church leaders through a letter-writing campaign of his own. In opposition to Arius (and Eusebius of Nicomedia), he wrote a circular letter (ca. 319) addressed to various bishops throughout the Mediterranean region, especially those in Syria and Palestine where Arius and his followers had become active.[26] He also sent copies of this encyclical to the clergy of Alexandria and its environs, accompanied by an introductory letter warning them about the new Arian threat and urging them to add their signatures as a sign of their support for him in his campaign against Arius.[27] The writing of such circular letters was a traditional means by which Egyptian patriarchs both strengthened their ties with other church centers and reasserted their pastoral leadership over their constituency in Egypt.

Eventually, the ongoing controversy between Alexander and Arius brought a response from the emperor Constantine, who wrote a formal *Letter to Alexander and Arius* (ca. 324) urging both of them to seek reconciliation.[28] When it became clear that this letter was not having its intended effect, Constantine called for a general council at Nicaea to resolve the disagreement once and for all. In the end, this gathering of bishops at the Council of Nicaea (325) roundly condemned Arius and supported Alexander's theological position by affirming that the Son was "of the same substance" or "of the same essence" *(homoousios)* as the Father. Under the weight of imperial pressure, only a few dissented. However, the word *homoousios*, supposedly proposed by Constantine himself, was a somewhat novel term that was open to multiple interpretations and whose implications for christological doctrine were not yet fully clear to the participants.[29] Many of those who signed their names to the creed came away from the meeting unclear as to its meaning, or dissatisfied with it as a philosophical term with no direct biblical precedent.[30]

Thus, rather than marking an end to the Arian Controversy, the Council of Nicaea in fact ushered in a second, extended phase of debate, during which different theological factions argued over the viability of this key word, *homoousios*. The First Nicene Council would later come to be recognized as the first ecumenical council of the early church, and its creed as the foundation for "orthodox" theological tradition in Egypt and elsewhere, but it would take over fifty-five years before both the eastern and western churches would reach any sort of solid consensus in support of the decision reached there.

The escalation of the Arian Controversy to an international level in the years leading up to the Council of Nicaea in 325 should not obscure the fact that the controversy continued to rage on a local level in Alexandria over the same period. Having noted the theological crux of the dispute and the course of events that brought it onto the world stage, I now want to return to its Alexandrian point of origin and raise questions about the social factors that drove the controversy there. How did the dispute over Arius' teachings play out in the urban landscape of the Egyptian capital—namely, in the public arena of Alexandrian social life? And what old and new challenges did the controversy raise for the authority of the Egyptian patriarch?

On a local level, the Arian crisis in Alexandria was a crucible for long-brewing social tensions related to the life of the Alexandrian church and the leadership of its patriarch. Like his distant predecessor Demetrius who sparred with Origen for control over the teaching office of the church, Alexander found his own "episcopal" model of teaching authority increasingly in conflict with the longstanding Alexandrian "academic" model held by Arius.[31] In the late third century, the Alexandrian catechetical school had effectively become annexed to the office of the patriarch; nonetheless, a number of Christian "study circles" continued to operate, following a longstanding academic tradition in which individual instructors attracted groups of intellectually curious disciples. By Alexander's time, many of these study circles had effectively been assimilated into "the nascent system of parish churches in urban Alexandria," often organized around the authority of popular local priests who offered church members specialized biblical instruction.[32]

As priest of the parish church at Baucalis, Arius seems to have understood himself as a teacher in this academic tradition. Indeed, in his *Thalia*, a theological work written in verse, he self-consciously situates himself in a long lineage of wise sages:

According to the faith of the chosen ones of God, the knowledgeable children of God, the holy orthodox ones who have received the Spirit of the holy God, I have learnt these things from those who share wisdom, smart people, taught of God and wise in every way; in the steps of these I have come, I going along with them, I, the well-known, who have suffered much for the glory of God, who have learnt wisdom from God, and I know (inside) knowledge.[33]

Such claims to privileged divine knowledge inevitably brought Arius into conflict not only with the institutional authority of Alexander, but also with other local priests making similar claims. Indeed, the church writer Epiphanius gives evidence of a "rivalry" that developed during this period between different Alexandrian priests in their role as teachers, and indicates that such inter-ecclesial competition became a source of social and theological discord in the church:

There are many churches in Alexandria. . . . A presbyter named Colluthus served in one of these, Carpones in another, Sarmatas in another, and Arius, who was in charge of one. Each of these plainly caused some discord among the laity by his expositions, when he taught the people entrusted to his care at the regular services. Some were inclined to Arius, but others to Colluthus, others to Carpones, others to Sarmatas. Since each of them expounded the scripture differently in his own church, from their preference and high regard for their own presbyter some people called themselves Colluthians, and others called themselves Arians.[34]

Faced with such a situation, Alexander was eager to reassert his institutional authority as .patriarch over against the competing academic claims of semi-autonomous local presbyters.[35] In opposing Arius' theology, the patriarch was also seeking to suppress a deep-rooted academic ethos in Alexandria that posed an implicit threat to the episcopal "orthodoxy" he was espousing.[36]

This conflict over "academic" models of teaching was an old one in the Alexandrian church, but the Arian crisis also raised new social challenges for patriarchal leadership in the Egyptian church. The theological controversy did not simply play out in church lecture halls or in the private chambers of the episcopal residence; it also played out on the public streets and alleyways of Alexandria. The letters written by Arius and Alexander hint at the popular dimension of the conflict—in particular, they hint at the ways in which both sides tried to gain support for their views among different urban social factions through the use of pithy theological slogans. In their writings, Arius and Alexander each complain about how the other was using such slogans to appeal to the masses. Arius writes about how Alexander was trying to stir up the city against him,

> because we do not agree with him when he states in public, 'Always God always Son,' 'At the same time Father, at the same time Son,' 'The Son ingenerably coexists with God,' . . . 'Always God always Son,' 'The Son is from God himself.'"[37]

For his part, Alexander lodged a similar complaint about how Arius tried to turn people in the church against his episcopal leadership through "sermons that are too persuasive and of low quality" (perhaps a less-than-subtle complaint about their popular appeal). Alexander goes on to quote a number of theological slogans used by Arius and his followers in their public teaching:

> For this reason, with no delay, I aroused myself, beloved, to make clear to you the unbelief of those who say, 'There was once when the Son of God was not' and 'He who before was not, later came into existence . . .' They say, 'God made all things from nothing,' . . . (And) the wretches state, 'Then we too are able to become Sons of God, just as he.'[38]

In the case of Arius, he also is reported to have composed theological poetry that he set to the tune of popular songs sung at work by "sailors and mill-workers."[39] Along with theological slogans, such songs would have functioned as an effective form of propaganda for Arius' views among the working classes in Alexandria.[40] Arius may have been just as adept at communicating his message among the urban proletariat as among the intellectual elite, and Alexander, as patriarch, would have been forced to compete for the theological allegiance of these same groups.

Amidst the social and religious factionalism of Alexandria during the Arian crisis, one group stands out for the critical role it played in this competition for grassroots support. I am referring here to ascetic (or monastic) Christians. Members of the ascetic movement were counted among both Arius' and Alexander's followers. Arius' attraction for those who opted for a lifestyle of ascetic renunciation may originally have been—at least in part—a function of urban geography. His parish church at Boukolou was located in an area to the east of the city not far from a network of tombs where a number of early Christian ascetics had taken up residence. The proximity of Arius' parish to the *martyrium* of Saint Mark—a popular pilgrimage site—may also have been a factor in his recruitment of ascetics visiting the shrine.[41] Ascetic women apparently made up a sizable portion of Arius' following: the writer Epiphanius claimed that Arius had won the allegiance of not less than seventy virgins.[42] While this number cannot be confirmed, the public visibility of this community of virgins was highlighted by Alexander himself when he complained in one of his letters about the allegedly disruptive activity of "young women" in Arius' camp who run around "on every street."[43] Some of these women may have been attracted by the possibility of participating in one of Arius' study circles and engaging other ascetically-minded members in open philosophical debate.[44]

The importance of ascetic backing was not lost on Alexander, who also attracted his own cadre of consecrated virgins as supporters and students. In fact, his immediate successor, Athanasius, recounts an occasion in which some of these virgins came to Alexander seeking instruction. According to Athanasius' report, Alexander responded to their query with an extended "exhortation to christological orthodoxy" in which he warned the virgins specifically against Arian theological propaganda—propaganda that threatened to lead them away from their bridegroom Christ and, by extension, away from the good graces of their bishop.[45]

Thus, during the last decade of his patriarchate, Alexander was engaged in a struggle with Arius over the recruitment of ascetic Christians as supporters of his theological position. Indeed, it was this struggle that Athanasius inherited when he became patriarch after Alexander's death in 328, only three years after the Council of Nicaea. Like his predecessor, Athanasius would actively court communities of urban ascetics in Alexandria, competing with the followers of Arius for their theological allegiance and political backing.[46] Ultimately, Athanasius' success in cultivating monastic support would definitively stamp his legacy and reshape the social contours of Egyptian papal authority.

From Alexandria to the Desert:
Athanasius and the Cultivation of Monastic Support

In the sanctuary of the Old Church of the Monastery of Saint Antony at the Red Sea, a thirteenth-century wall painting depicts the bearded figure of "Father Athanasius, the apostolic Patriarch of Alexandria" (Fig. 3).[47] Seated on a throne and wearing a robe—both signs of his patriarchal status—Athanasius smiles gently at the viewer and cradles a Bible in his arms. Around him, the walls and niches of the sanctuary are lined with portraits of other Egyptian patriarchs (including Saint Mark).[48] Hundreds of kilometers away in another part of Egypt, a tenth-century painting from Tebtunis in the Fayûm offers us another glimpse of how Athanasius was remembered and revered by later Copts (Fig. 4). In this second painting (dated by inscription to 953), Athanasius is located immediately beneath the central apse depiction of Christ in Majesty (a prominent place usually occupied by the Virgin Mary in Coptic iconography).[49] Just as in the wall painting at Saint Antony's, the figure of Athanasius is enrobed and enthroned, gazing on the viewer with a tranquil aspect. However, unlike in the Red Sea painting, at Tebtunis he is flanked not by other patriarchs, but by the two famous monastic pioneers from Egyptian history—Saint Antony and Saint Pachomius.

These two paintings—one from the Red Sea coast, and the other from the inland oasis of the Fayûm—visually attest the privileged status accorded "Athanasius the Great" in later Coptic tradition as both patriarch and as patron of the monastic life.[50] In both paintings, Athanasius is portrayed as a founding father of the Coptic church, and his peaceful visage is meant to inspire the viewer to divine contemplation. However, the historian of late antiquity cannot help but view these paintings with different eyes, for these serene images of Athanasius in fact mask a history of turbulent conflicts and controversies that beset him during his forty-five year reign as patriarch of Alexandria (328–373).

Indeed, Athanasius' reign was beset by conflict from its very inception. Starting in the first few years of his tenure, Athanasius' opponents—first the Melitians and then the Arians—began challenging his authority as patriarch. Such challenges were directed against Athanasius on two fronts. First, some of his opponents contested the validity of his election as the rightful successor to Alexander.[51] Several of the ancient sources (including Athanasius' own Second *Apology*) attest to the fact that Melitian bishops lodged accusations against what they perceived as the irregularity of Athanasius' election: in particular, they accused him of having been elected in secret by a renegade faction of bishops.[52] According to one ancient source, the Melitians in their dissatisfaction actually took the step of electing a rival bishop for the see of Alexandria (a man named Theonas).[53] This course of action (along with their accusations against Athanasius) may have stemmed from the fact that Athanasius and his supporters had tried to exclude Melitian bishops from voting in the election. In any case, the Index to Athanasius' corpus of *Festal Letters* reveals that there was almost a two-month delay between Alexander's death (April 17, 328) and Athanasius' election (June 8, 328).[54] While one account attributes this delay to the fact that Athanasius was away on church business at the time of Alexander's death,[55] it would not be surprising if a disagreement over election procedure also played a role in delaying the outcome.

Second, in addition to their unrest over Athanasius' election, the Melitians, soon joined by the Arians, also accused the new bishop of coercive leadership tactics in his dealings with minority factions within the church. In the early years of Athanasius' episcopate (probably in the summer of A.D. 330), the Meletian and Arian parties rallied around their opposition to Athanasius as a common cause and formed an alliance led by Eusebius of Nicomedia.[56] Together, they brought a series of charges against the Egyptian bishop to Constantine the emperor. Eventually, their insistence in pressing these charges led to Athanasius' ecclesiastical trial at the Council of Tyre in A.D. 335.

According to the fifth-century historian Sozomen, Athanasius' accusers claimed that he had punished Melitians with beatings, imprisoned their leaders, and burned their churches.[57] While a number of the specific accusations proved to be spurious (including a later trumped-up charge of murder), the discovery of new documentary evidence in the last century has lent credence to the fact that Athanasius was not averse to strong-arm tactics in his efforts to suppress ecclesiastical dissent. The new evidence, discovered in 1922, consists of a private letter on papyrus written in Greek by a Melitian Christian named Callistus.[58] In the letter, Callistus relates to his friends that Athanasius had imprisoned or exiled at least eleven Melitian leaders, and that one of them (a man named Heraiscus) had been scourged while imprisoned.[59]

A number of scholars have taken the discovery of this letter as an occasion to reevaluate the personal character of Athanasius as a church leader, in the process often portraying him in starkly negative terms.[60]

Others have attempted to rehabilitate Athanasius' image by offering alternative (more congenial) readings of available sources, by refocusing attention on his masterful theological and pastoral output, or by recognizing how his methods mirrored that of his opponents and simply reflected the polemical spirit of the times.[61] This is not the place to enter into such a debate: suffice it to say that Athanasius' personality is not quantifiable in simplistic terms.

More important for our study of larger trends in the development of the Coptic papacy is the fact that Athanasius' methods in this conflict (as well as his opponents') reflect fundamental changes in the way church leaders (in Egypt and elsewhere) viewed the relation between ecclesiastical and secular authority. By deploying the instruments of Roman civil law (especially imprisonment and sentences of exile) in an effort to disrupt local church leadership and organization among the dissenting Melitians, Athanasius was publicly extending the boundaries of patriarchal authority into the civil sphere. In doing so, he set a precedent that his successors in office would follow, often with considerable zeal.

For their part, the allied Arian and Meletian parties increasingly tried to link their own cause to the mechanisms of *imperial* law and authority, casting Athanasius' actions as treasonous and appealing to the emperor Constantine to intervene on their behalf. In the short term, their accusations and appeals met with success. At the Arian-controlled Council of Tyre in 335, Athanasius was condemned and subsequently sent into exile by the emperor. He would spend 23 of the next 32 years in exile or hiding while the Arian cause gained strength and benefited from imperial support. In all, Athanasius served five separate periods of banishment: the first in Gaul (335–337), the second in Rome and the Italian peninsula (339–346), and the final three in Upper Egypt (356–362, 362–364, 365–366).

It would be difficult to overestimate the extent to which Athanasius' experience of exile stamped the social role and identity of the Coptic papacy. In the figure of the exiled Athanasius, the Coptic papacy was reshaped as an icon of resistance. This reshaping of papal identity was accomplished, in large part, through Athanasius' own representation of himself in relation to imperial authority. In his writings, he portrays himself as a model for such resistance, sometimes casting himself in the role of biblical figures who stood up to the unjust rule of temporal authorities. One example of this appears in Athanasius' *History of the Arians*, a scathing attack against the Arian emperor

Constantius II (337–361 C.E.), the son and successor to Constantine. Writing during his third exile (ca. 357), the exiled bishop depicts Constantius as a latter-day Pharaoh who has abandoned his promises to Athanasius' allies (the "people").[62] Implicit in his intertextual allusion to the Exodus is Athanasius' presentation of himself as a new Moses, the faithful leader of an exiled people. Athanasius' strategy of self-representation would exert a profound influence over later generations of patriarchs: the Egyptian popes of the late-fifth, sixth, and early-seventh centuries would regularly justify their principled resistance to the emperor's will on the basis of similar biblical models and on the basis of Athanasius' own precedent (see chapter 4).

Just as important, Athanasius' experience of exile also provided him with the opportunity to deepen and consolidate his ties with local monastic communities in the Nile Valley and in the Eastern and Western Deserts. Already during the early years of his episcopate Athanasius had begun positioning himself as a patron of Egyptian monasticism: in A.D. 329–330 he conducted a tour of churches and monasteries in Upper Egypt,[63] and in the decades following he addressed several letters and treatises to ascetic communities of women living in Alexandria and its environs,[64] as well as to prominent (male) monastic leaders in Upper Egypt.[65] From early on, Athanasius' patronage of monastic concerns was intimately tied to his larger anti-Arian agenda. In his correspondence with ascetic women, for example, he endeavors to show how the Christological doctrine of Nicaea uniquely satisfied monastic concerns about the human potential to live a virginal life, and (at the same time) how the rival Arian teaching ultimately thwarted these same concerns. This is vividly demonstrated in his First *Letter to Virgins* (written ca. 337–339), where he quotes extensively from his predecessor Pope Alexander's teachings and casts himself as Alexander's rightful successor in both the defense of Christological "orthodoxy" and the patronage of women's monasticism.[66]

Athanasius' third exile in A.D. 356–362 inaugurated a new, intensive stage in his attempts to secure more widespread monastic allegiance to the Nicene cause. Condemned by the Arian-dominated Council of Milan in 355 and forced to go into hiding after his church in Alexandria was raided by a Roman military search party, Athanasius spent most of the next ten years (his final three periods of exile: A.D. 356–362, 362–364, 365–366) living in secret among communities of monks in Upper Egypt.[67] The protection these monks offered Athanasius (including their success at facilitating his initial escape) gives witness to the success of his earlier attempts to cultivate grass-roots loyalty among them. While Athanasius' exact whereabouts and activities during this period remain unknown, it is clear that he used his time in exile as an opportunity to reinforce monastic allegiance to the Alexandrian patriarchate and to Nicene theology. The evidence comes from Athanasius' own writings: a number of his works during this period—including several letters, historical treatises, and an ascetic biography—were either addressed to monks or dedicated to monastic causes. Through these varied literary forms, Athanasius waged an intensive anti-Arian propaganda campaign among his monastic hosts.

In one of his letters addressed to Egyptian monks during this period, Athanasius reveals one of the reasons for his heightened concerns about Arian influence in the monasteries. He warns his readers of "certain persons who hold with Arius and go about the monasteries with no other object save that under color of visiting you," and laments the fact that there are monks who have no qualms about worshiping with their Arian counterparts.[68] Athanasius responds to this perceived threat by urging his followers to withhold hospitality from their Arian visitors, as well as from monks among their own ranks who allowed themselves to mingle with the Arians in worship. The social impact of Athanasius' instruction would have been strongly felt: here, the Alexandrian bishop was asking the monks to forsake a fundamental monastic virtue—the reception of guests—in order to mark the inviolability of certain theological boundaries.[69]

Athanasius also tried to steel his monastic adherents against Arian sympathizers through other rhetorical means. One way was by cataloguing and highlighting the atrocities allegedly committed by the Arians against faithful Athanasian monks. In his *History of the Arians*, for example, Athanasius describes in lurid detail how the Arian persecutors overran monasteries, bound and tortured monks, and subjected virgins to humiliation, vulgar curses, stonings, scourgings, and beatings with palm-tree rods that left thorns in their limbs.[70] Elsewhere in that same work, Athanasius relates how an Arian official had even spit on a letter sent to him by the famous anchorite, Saint Antony. The exiled bishop does not hesitate to note that the man suffered God's judgment shortly thereafter when he died after being bitten and thrown by a horse.[71] These sensationalist accounts of Arian barbarism seem to have been intended for "monks sympathetic to the author,"[72] and as such, they were designed to raise monastic ire against the Arian leadership in Alexandria who had temporarily ousted Athanasius from power.

In the story about Saint Antony mentioned above, Athanasius uses a legendary detail from the life of the famous solitary to promote his "anti-Arian campaign" among Egyptian monks. Athanasius' *Life of Saint Antony*, also written during his third exile, represents this same agenda but on a much larger scale. This ascetic biography became a veritable bestseller in late antiquity. Written shortly after Antony's death in 356, within fifty years his story was known by both monastic and lay readers throughout the Mediterranean world. Indeed, a number of prominent church leaders of the fourth and fifth centuries give accounts of their dependence upon the *Life* in both their writing and their ascetic practice, including Gregory of Nazianzus (Asia Minor), Jerome (Rome/ Palestine), and Augustine (Italy/ North Africa).[73]

The work is not a conventional biography in the modern sense: Athanasius' concern was not so much to chronicle the details of Antony's life as to yoke Antony's monastic calling to Nicene "orthodoxy."[74] He did so, most explicitly, by portraying the monk Antony as an activist for the Nicene cause. In chapter 68, for example, when so-called "Ariomaniacs" come to visit him at his desert cell, the holy man is said to have "chased them away from the mountain, saying that their words were worse than the poison of serpents."[75] For ancient Egyptian readers, the spatial movement of this story would have conveyed a vivid social and theological message. In Egypt, the "mountain" was understood as the high desert terrain that was elevated in relation to the Nile Valley and oases. It was a place that increasingly became associated with scattered settlements of monks who had withdrawn from village life in order to pursue a life of solitude. Thus, Athanasius, in highlighting Antony's act of chasing his Arian visitors off the "mountain," was effectively denying competing Arian claims over monastic patronage and monastic space. As such, the story would have reinforced Athanasius' admonitions in his *Letters to Monks* regarding hospitality offered to Arian visitors.

The very next chapter of the *Life* (ch. 69) once again uses geographical space to press home Antony's opposition to Arian doctrine. It details the story of how Antony "came down off the mountain" and entered Alexandria in order to refute Arian claims that he shared their theological views. Athanasius' account of these events shows how the monk Antony was a hotly contested figure in Arian-Athanasian debates even during his own lifetime. On the one hand, the story gives evidence (in fact, it takes it on assumption) that the Arians were claiming Antony as one of their own. On the other hand, it shows how

Athanasius himself utilized Antony as a mouthpiece for Nicene theology: Antony is depicted as specifically denouncing Arian theological slogans and advocating the distinctively Athanasian-Nicene belief in the uncreated, eternal character of the Son as the Word of God.[76] Elsewhere in the *Life*, Athanasius' characterization of Antony counters Arian claims in more subtle ways. In addition to portraying the monk as a vocal, public proponent of Nicene theology, Athanasius also interprets Antony's actions (especially his encounters with demons) in ways that were meant to show how monastic piety was ultimately compatible with Athanasian (and not Arian) beliefs about human salvation. Over against Arian understandings of salvation as a process in which the believer (in imitation of Christ) advanced in grace and achieved "sonship" by obedience to God's will, Athanasius portrayed Antony's victories over the demons as signs of the grace that Christ alone always possessed by nature, a grace that only Christ himself could bestow upon the faithful.[77] Thus, when the devil first assails Antony with foul thoughts to distract him from his ascetic discipline, Athanasius comments that "it was the Lord who was working with Antony—the Lord who bore flesh for our sake, and gave the body victory over the devil—so that each one of those who truly struggle might say, 'Not I, but the grace of God that is in me (1 Cor 15:10)."[78] As the author of the *Life*, Athanasius seems to have been especially concerned to combat Arian notions that Antony's spiritual successes were attributed to his own progress in virtue (as opposed to Christ's inherent grace). Thus, in remarking that this experience of temptation was "Antony's first trophy (in his fight) against the devil," Athanasius checks himself in order avoid misunderstanding and adds, "rather, this was the success of the Savior in Antony."[79] In this way, Athanasius' biography of Antony stands in contradistinction to other ancient views of the famous monk that saw him primarily as a spiritual patron with healing powers, as a teacher of wisdom, or as the founder of the solitary monastic life. For Athanasius, the events in Antony's life instead are ultimately recast in terms of a larger theological narrative: specifically, the "story of the incarnate Word" that formed the basis for Athanasius' interpretation of Nicene theology.[80]

The extended period of time Athanasius spent with Egyptian monks during his third exile, his correspondence with them regarding the perceived Arian threat, his composition of the *Life of Antony* as a monastic manifesto and narrative apologetic for Nicene beliefs, and even his later attempts to define more carefully the parameters of the biblical canon and promote a uniformity of practice among the monks regarding the use of scripture[81]—all these were key factors in his efforts to link monastic patronage with the theological position of the Alexandrian patriarchate. To a large extent, Athanasius' efforts in this area were successful. Despite the fact that some monastic communities in Egypt continued to maintain a somewhat independent posture toward episcopal leadership, Athanasius' visits and correspondence brought many monasteries (including the influential Pachomian federation) in line with Alexandrian patriarchal authority.[82] Buoyed by such local monastic support, Athanasius would return to Alexandria in 366 from his fifth and final exile as "an elder statesman renowned for his heroic defense of Nicene orthodoxy."[83] He would not witness the end of the Arian conflict, nor would he immerse himself again in international theological debates, and yet during the final seven years of his life (up until his death in 373) the formidable Athanasius remained largely unchallenged in his Egyptian see. His periods of exile behind him, he was free to spend his last years editing his own works, commissioning an official history of the Alexandrian church (one that upheld his version of events), and sponsoring the construction of a basilica that would bear his name.[84] Such literary and architectural acts of patronage were designed to ensure that his stormy tenure of leadership would not be forgotten.

Athanasius' immediate papal successors, Peter II and Timothy, reaped both the blessings and the curses of his controversial legacy. Upon succeeding Athanasius, Peter II (373–380) faced renewed aggression from the Arian faction, who put forward a counterclaimant to the Alexandrian episcopal throne (a man named Lucius of Antioch) and recruited local military assistance for attacks against Peter's churches. Like his predecessor, Peter was forced to go into exile to Rome, remaining there from 373 to 378. Along with him, scores of monks were also sent into exile—some to the mines, some to the Galilee in northern Palestine, and some to remote islands.[85] The common fate shared by these loyalist monks shows that the bonds created by Athanasius' "monastic campaign" continued to endure during Peter's reign as patriarch.

It was not until early in the reign of Peter's brother Timothy (A.D. 380–385) that the Arian controversy itself would finally be resolved. In 381, the Council of Constantinople reaffirmed the theological tenets that were framed at Nicaea and defended for decades by Athanasius.[86] However, at the same time, other decisions of the council planted seeds of conflict for the Alexandrian patriarchate in the near future.

In particular, the Council granted the see of Constantinople "the privileged rights of honor after the bishop of Rome," a decision that quickly became the source of tension between Constantinople and the more
ancient bishopric of Alexandria.[87] This inter-ecclesial rivalry would
erupt into open conflict during the extended reign of Timothy's successor, Theophilus (A.D. 385–412).

Theophilus' Anti-Pagan Campaign and the Battle over Origen's Legacy

The seventh-century Chronicle by the Coptic bishop John of Nikiu
records a legend of how Theophilus and his sister were orphaned as
children, but soon after were brought under the patronage and protection
of Athanasius. Early in the story, Theophilus and his sister, in the
care of an Ethiopian slave who had belonged to their parents, are
brought to a temple dedicated to the gods Artemis and Apollo.
However, "when the children entered, the gods fell to the earth and
were broken." God reveals this miracle to the patriarch Athanasius,
who baptizes the children (along with the now-repentant slave),
places the sister in a convent until ready for marriage, and establishes
Theophilus as a reader in the church. Later, the story tells how
Theophilus would rise to "the throne of Mark the Evangelist in the
city of Alexandria," and how his sister would give birth to Cyril,
Theophilus' eventual successor as patriarch.[88] This legend, probably
not historical in its details, nonetheless had a particular rhetorical
aim: namely, to reinforce the ties of Alexandrian patriarchal succession
and, even more specifically, to link Theophilus and Cyril to their
famous predecessor (and to each other) by means of divine revelations
and familial connections.

Whether or not Theophilus enjoyed Athanasius' patronage as a
young man, it is clear that he inherited his predecessor's mantle as a
controversialist. Early in his career (during the early 390's) he waged
an often violent campaign against paganism in Egypt, a campaign
portended in his childhood legend by the dramatic fall of the idols in
his presence. Later, he waged war against the so-called "Origenists"
who rejected anthropomorphic conceptions of God. As I will show
below, these two social campaigns were in many ways at cross-purposes
theologically, but both had profound implications for the developing,
yet sometimes contentious, relationship between the Alexandrian
patriarchate and Egyptian monks. Theophilus' penchant for controversy
and his policy toward the regulation of monastic beliefs within Egypt

had international ramifications as well—it ultimately brought him into open conflict with the church at Constantinople and its bishop John Chrysostom. The tensions that developed between the two sees in this period in many ways anticipated the eventual schism between the rival sees during the fifth century.

Theophilus' reputation as patriarch and controversialist is vividly documented in a pair of images found in the margins of an illuminated papyrus from the early fifth century.[89] In the first image, a figure identified as "Saint Theophilus" stands below an oblong bodily form wrapped in strips of cloth—the mummified body of his predecessor Timothy (Fig. 5a). As in the legend recorded by John of Nikiu, the apostolic succession of Saint Mark is emphasized—graphically depicted in this case as the transfer of authority between the deceased Timothy and his living successor Theophilus, who is enrobed in the episcopal *pallium*.[90] In the second image (Fig. 5b), Theophilus stands on a pedestal decorated with the bust of the Egyptian god Serapis: as part of his campaign against paganism, Theophilus destroyed the famous Serapeum in Alexandria and built a Christian church on the site. Here, the artist visually celebrates Theophilus' nascent triumph over the Serapis cult and the other indigeneous religions of Egypt.[91] In this context, it is interesting that Theophilus' posture in both images—in each, he stands dressed in an episcopal robe and holds a Bible inscribed with a cross—closely resembles the formulaic way of depicting biblical prophets in the same manuscript.[92] This artistic detail subtly echoes Theophilus' own way of representing himself in many of his writings. In taking the part of the controversialist in combat against both paganism and Origenist thought, Theophilus cast himself in the role of the Old Testament prophets, who stood fast in the face of idols.[93]

According to Rufinus' *History of the Church* (ca. A.D. 402–403), the origins of Theophilus' conflict with the pagan cults of Alexandria lay in the chance discovery of an underground pagan sanctuary during renovations to a Christian church in the city. In an act intended to humiliate the adherents of the cult, Theophilus had their sacred objects of worship paraded through the streets.[94] Enraged by Theophilus' provocative act, local pagans rioted with attacks against Christians. The result was the outbreak of intercommunal violence and the eventual retreat of the pagan militant faction to the Serapeum. The emperor Theodosius responded to the situation by issuing an edict granting the besieged pagans amnesty, but at the same time authorizing the suppression of pagan cults and celebrating the Christians who died in the violence as martyrs. Led by Theophilus, the Christians subsequently dismantled the Serapeum stone-by-stone: they hacked the main statue of Serapis with axes and then burned what was left in different parts of the city.[95]

Ancient sources reveal that Egyptian monks played a leading role in this anti-pagan pogrom. According to one of the *Sayings of the Desert Fathers*, Theophilus actively recruited the support of monks by calling them to the city to help in the destruction of the temples.[96] This evidence is corroborated by the pagan author Libanius, who identifies the monks ("these men clad in black") as those most to blame for destroying one of the most sacred precincts of Alexandrian paganism.[97]

In the case of the Serapeum, Theophilus even went so far as to encourage monks to take up residence at the ruined site after its destruction.[98] He also funded and expedited the construction of a new church at the site.[99] His dedication of the church to John the Baptist and Elijah and acquisition of their relics were acts of patronage that would have subtly underscored his claims to be a worthy heir of the prophets in his fight against pagan belief. At the same time, especially in the context of his support for monastic residence in the ruins of the Serapeum, his dedication of the new church also may have been designed to reinforce his image as a patron of Egyptian monks, many of whom viewed John the Baptist and Elijah as privileged prophetic models for the ascetic life.[100] Theophilus employed a similar policy at Canopus, a location east of Alexandria known as a destination for pagan pilgrimage: he built one of his churches there and persuaded monks from Jerusalem, and later, Egyptian monks from the Pachomian tradition, to establish communities in the vicinity.[101] One pagan author of the period complained about how Theophilus and the Christians "settled these monks at Canopus also, . . . collected the bones and skulls of criminals who had been put to death for numerous crimes (i.e., the martyrs), . . . and haunted their sepulchers (i.e., made pilgrimage to their shrines)."[102] In the case of both the Alexandrian Serapeum and Canopus, one can see how Theophilus' patronage of monastic settlements at formerly pagan sites was linked with a larger political and religious aim of "Christianizing" the Egyptian landscape through extensive building projects and the consecration of sacred relics.[103]

Theophilus' relationship with Egyptian monks was not always so cooperative and congenial; complications soon arose that brought the patriarch into conflict not only with Egyptian monastic leaders, but also with the church at Constantinople. The late fourth and early fifth centuries witnessed the rapid expansion of monastic influence in Egypt: the monasteries at Nitria and Scetis were flourishing, and new communities were established at the fifth, ninth, and eighteenth mileposts along the road west of Alexandria.[104] In Upper Egypt, the abbot Shenoute was directing the White Monastery federation at Atripe (near modern Sohag) through a period of unprecedented growth.[105] The network of Pachomian monasteries also thrived: archaeological evidence from the late fourth or early fifth century confirms the wealth and popularity of the Pachomian monastery at Pbow, where a new basilica was constructed. Measuring 56 meters in length and 30 meters in width, it would have been one of the largest churches in Egypt at the time.[106]

The increasing numbers of Egyptian monks and their sometimes diverse theological perspectives posed new challenges to Theophilus in his attempts to maintain his authority and provide pastoral direction for these burgeoning communities. Indeed, the roots of these complications in Theophilus' relationship with the monks may be traced to one of his annual *Paschal Letters*. Every year, the bishop of Alexandria would write an official letter to inform the country of the Alexandrian calculation regarding the date of Easter and the beginning of the seasonal Lenten observance. In his *Paschal Letter* of 399, which circulated as usual among the monasteries, Theophilus strenuously defended the incorporeality of God over against monks (and others in the church) who held to anthropomorphic conceptions of the divinity. The theme of this letter reflected his indebtedness to the theology of Origen.[107] It also cohered with Theophilus' larger anti-pagan agenda: in it he urged his readers to avoid human images or analogies in thinking about God lest they fall into the trap of pagan "idolatry."[108]

A monk from Scythia (modern day Romania) was visiting the monks at Scetis when Theophilus' letter arrived. This monk, a man named John Cassian, subsequently reported on the uproar that ensued among monks who did not hold Theophilus' viewpoint.

> Now . . . there came, according to custom, the official letters of the bishop Theophilus. In these he made the announcement about Easter and he included a long discussion of the absurd heresy of the Anthropomorphites, a heresy which he leveled with great eloquence. This was received very bitterly by almost every sort of monk throughout all Egypt, monks who, in their

simplicity, had been ensnared by the error. Indeed, the majority of the older men among the brethren asserted that in fact the bishop was to be condemned as someone corrupted by the most serious heresy, someone opposing the ideas of holy Scripture, someone who denied that almighty God was of human shape— and this despite the clear scriptural evidence that Adam was created in His image. Those living in the desert of Scete and who were far ahead of all the Egyptian monks in perfection and knowledge denounced the bishop's letter. Among all the priests only our own Paphnutius was an exception. Those in charge of the three other churches in the desert refused to allow the letter to be read or publicly presented at their assemblies.[109]

Cassian went on to relate the story of one monk in Paphnutius' monastery who, having been "persuaded" to abandon his anthropo- morphic views, "broke down in tears" when the community gathered for worship, "for he sensed that the human image of God which he used to draw before him as he prayed was now gone from his heart." Throwing himself on the ground, the monk cried out, "They've taken my God away from me. I have no one to hold on to, and I don't know whom to adore or address."[110] This monk's heart-tugging lament vividly demon- strates how such anthropomorphite conceptions of God were intimately intertwined with the daily activities of monastic prayer and worship.[111]

Other monks in the Nitrian desert were not content simply to acquiesce and allow their mental images of God to be stripped from them. Indeed, a number of the monks took immediate action: they left their monasteries and traveled to Alexandria, where they raised a riot against the archbishop. Some reportedly even had designs on Theophilus' life. Faced with this threat, Theophilus underwent a sudden change of heart. First, he sought to mollify the enraged monks by greeting them with language that implicitly (but pointedly) endorsed their belief that God had human characteristics: "I see you as *the face of God*" (my emphasis). Then, when the monks pressed him further, he agreed to denounce the theology of Origen, which he had so recently embraced as the rationale for his festal letter.[112]

Theophilus' about turn had dire implications for Nitrian monks who held Origenist beliefs and had previously supported him in his teachings on the incorporeality of God. Among these monks was a man named Isidore, who had served previously as the "guest-master of the church of Alexandria," and four monks called the "Tall Brothers"

(Dioscorus, Ammonius, Eusebius, and Euthymius), former confidants of Theophilus whom he had recruited for clerical service in Alexandria and in Hermopolis (a city in Upper Egypt).[113] Even before Theophilus' decision to transfer his support to the "Anthropomorphites," these monks had grown disillusioned with the patriarch's economic policies—especially his extravagant investments in church building projects—and had withdrawn once again to the desert.[114] Now, the growing tensions in their relationship with Theophilus were exacerbated by theological factors. Once allies in support of Origen's theology, the patriarch and his former friends now found themselves on opposite sides of a theological divide.

Theophilus' actions from this point on seem to have been driven by a volatile mix of theological and political motivations: his subsequent attempts to impose theological conformity among the monks of Nitria reflected his larger concern to consolidate monastic allegiance behind the stated policies of the patriarchate.[115] The implementation of Theophilus' new anti-Origenist policy was both swift and brutal: he excommunicated Isidore and sent letters to local bishops ordering the expulsion of the Origenist leaders in the monasteries under their jurisdiction.[116] When the Tall Brothers came to Alexandria to appeal for clemency, Theophilus turned them away roughly and then convened a synod to condemn the monks formally. In their place, he installed five loyalists from the Nitrian monasteries. Finally, he sent military troops to Nitria to expel the monks by force and to quell resistance.[117]

Writing to Jerome later that same year, Theophilus once again portrays his actions in continuity with those of the Old Testament prophets: "Certain worthless, raving mad men who desired to sow and to scatter the heresy of Origen in the monasteries of Nitria have been cut down with my prophet's sickle."[118] Here one sees how Theophilus tried to turn his earlier anti-pagan rhetoric on its head by radically reorienting his application of biblical models. As mentioned before, Theophilus' original opposition to theological anthropomorphitism had cohered closely with the agenda of his anti-pagan campaign: by portraying himself in solidarity with the biblical prophets, he had underscored his opposition to the (idolatrous) use of human images in worshiping God. However, with his mind now changed, Theophilus readily employed the same biblical rhetoric to argue from the other side. Thus, by characterizing his actions against the Origenist monks in prophetic terms, he was suggesting that adherence to Origen's theology was tantamount to idolatry, even though it eschewed the use of all human images in contemplating the divine. His ally Jerome dips into the same rhetorical well when he calls the Origenist monks "demonic spirits" who have been "crushed by the authority and eloquence" of Theophilus.[119] In the case of both writers, the logical consistency of the analogy employed was less important than its rhetorical force in the public debates over Origen's legacy.[120]

Theophilus' actions against the Origenist monks quickly brought the conflict onto an international stage.[121] Because of the military raid on the monasteries at Nitria, the four Tall Brothers were forced to flee the country—first to Palestine, and then to Constantinople. In the meantime, Theophilus engaged himself in an intensive letter-writing campaign in which he sought to drum up support for the anti-Origenist cause and instructed other bishops in the East (Palestine, Cyprus, and Asia Minor) not to receive the fugitive ascetics. The Egyptian patriarch chose some of his new monastic appointments at Nitria as couriers for this correspondence.[122] This was a further means by which Theophilus consolidated his authority among the monastic leadership and (at the same time) publicly advertised his role as the patron *par excellence* of Egyptian monks. Indeed, his growing antipathy for Isidore may have been grounded in a rivalry for monastic patronage: in one of Theophilus' letters he excoriates Isidore for using his substantial wealth to win support among the monks and to help facilitate the Tall Brothers' escape.[123]

As soon as they reached the imperial capital, the Tall Brothers appealed to the bishop of the city, John Chrysostom, to provide them with protection and to serve as an advocate for their cause against Theophilus' attacks. In response to their petition, Chrysostom wrote to Theophilus, informing him that the exiled monks were thinking about bringing charges against him and urging him instead to welcome the monks peaceably back to their home country. The intervention of the bishop of Constantinople in what Theophilus viewed as an internal Egyptian church matter only enraged the Alexandrian patriarch further. The ill will between the two patriarchs probably originated a few years earlier in 397 when Theophilus had opposed Chrysostom's election and (ironically) proposed his then-friend Isidore as a rival candidate.[124] Now, summoned to Constantinople to defend himself against the monks' grievances, Theophilus decided to lodge his own charges against Chrysostom, accusing him (a double irony) of violating the Canons of Nicaea by interfering in affairs outside the bounds of his own diocese. Theophilus' countersuit, along with his own shrewd political maneuverings while in the capital, eventually contributed to the condemnation of Chrysostom at the Synod of the Oak (A.D. 403, at Chalcedon) and his exile to Bithynia in Asia Minor.[125] By this time, the dispute between Theophilus and the monks had faded into the background. In fact, after the death of two of the Tall Brothers, the other dissenting monks reconciled with Theophilus at the Synod of the Oak.[126] At least for the time being, the Alexandrian patriarch had been able—through the sheer force of his sizable will—to reexert a tenuous control over his Egyptian monastic clientele. There were no more monastic uproars during the remaining ten years of his patriarchate. However, even after the exile and death of Chrysostom, the tensions between the Alexandrian and Constantinopolitan sees would continue to simmer, as both cities continued to vie for preeminent status in the church alongside Rome. With the outbreak of the Christological Controversy in the fifth century during the reigns of Theophilus' successors, Cyril (412–444) and Dioscorus (444–454), these inter-ecclesial tensions would once again come to a raging boil.

Cyril, Dioscorus, and the Controversy over Christ

After his election as bishop of Alexandria in 412, Cyril began to implement policies that bore a strong resemblance to those of his predecessor Theophilus. Such continuity in policy should not be surprising since the two shared a familial tie: Cyril was Theophilus' nephew (his mother was Theophilus' younger sister).[127] As a close relation of the Alexandrian bishop, Cyril would have enjoyed a privileged educational upbringing. Later in his life, at the Council of Ephesus (431), he would celebrate the fact that he had been "nurtured *(etraphên)* at the hands of holy and orthodox fathers."[128] While this was in part a defense of his orthodox theological pedigree, it also probably reflected his awareness of how he had benefited in concrete ways from the watchful guardianship of Theophilus, and early on perhaps even Theophilus' mentor Athanasius.[129] The ramifications of Cyril's family connection with Theophilus were not lost on his contemporaries. The well-known monk Isidore of Pelusium, for one, recognized how Cyril was "his uncle's nephew" not only by blood, but also in his combative public persona.[130]

Cyril followed Theophilus most notably in two areas: first, his continued activism against paganism and heterodox forms of Christianity in Egypt, and second, his theological and political opposition to the bishops of Constantinopole—both their christological doctrine and their aspirations to expand the episcopal authority of their see.[131] In each of these two cases, Cyril's presentation of himself in continuity with Theophilus was coordinated with his monastic policy. His efforts to exert his authority more fully over Egyptian monks and to retain their allegiance would prove especially valuable during the last years of his patriarchate (and during the patriarchate of his successor Dioscorus) when the Alexandrian and Constantinopolitan sees became embroiled in what has come to be called the "Christological Controversy."

Against Pagans, Against Heretics: Religious Intolerance and the Construction of Community Identity under Cyril of Alexandria

In 415 c.e., only the third full year of Cyril's episcopacy, a mob of Alexandrian Christians, led by a lector named Peter, waylaid the carriage of the famous Alexandrian Platonist philosopher Hypatia, dragged her to the church next to Cyril's residence (the *Caesareum*), stripped off her clothing, and murdered her with shards of pottery *(ostraka)*. The historian Socrates continues the account: "After they had torn her apart limb from limb, and had gathered up her body parts at a place called Cinaron, they burned them up in a fire."[132] This brutal assassination of Hypatia is often taken by historians as an emblem of the inter-religious tensions and the atmosphere of intolerance that existed in the church under Cyril. During his first two years in office, Cyril had already acted to seize several synagogues after inter-communal violence had broken out between Jews and Christians;[133] now, a prominent pagan philosopher lay dead—dismembered and burned—at the hands of Christians.

Ancient and modern writers have long argued over the root social causes of Hypatia's death and to what extent this tragic event was attributable to Cyril and the anti-pagan policies of the Alexandrian patriarchate.[134] A pagan writer of the sixth century goes so far as to blame Cyril directly for Hypatia's murder, and this accusation was later picked up by the eighteenth-century historian Edward Gibbon.[135] However, our earliest historical source, the above-mentioned Socrates, does not attribute any specific role to Cyril in the events leading up to Hypatia's murder. He only observes that the violent act subsequently brought "opprobrium" upon both Cyril and his church. While Cyril may have been culpable for cultivating an atmosphere of unrest and religious intolerance among the Alexandrian Christian populace, there is no direct or reliable evidence that he ordered a mafia-style "hit" on Hypatia.

Instead, Hypatia's murder appears to have been the result, at least in part, of a complex ecclesiastical-juridical power struggle between Cyril and Orestes, the prefect of Alexandria. From the time of Cyril's election in 412, the bishop had found himself in sharp conflict with the civil arm of the Alexandrian government. He had been elected despite the vigorous opposition of the local military leadership.[136] Cyril's conflict with the government, and particularly with Orestes, rapidly escalated during the rioting that broke out between Christians and Jews in the city. On the eve of the rioting, Orestes had subjected one of Cyril's most avid supporters to public torture on suspicion of spying. Then, after Cyril's expulsion of the Jews from certain parts of the city, Orestes sent a letter to the emperor complaining about Cyril's activities. When Orestes subsequently rebuffed the bishop's attempts at reconciliation, a large group of Cyril's monastic supporters—reportedly five hundred monks from Nitria who had been part of Theophilus' brigade a decade earlier—accosted the prefect in the streets of Alexandria while he was riding in his chariot. A number of them screamed insults at him, calling him an "idolater" (despite his professed identity as a baptized Christian). One overexcited monk, a man named Ammonius, threw a stone at Orestes and wounded him in the head. Once again, Orestes' official response was to have the offending party arrested and tortured. When Ammonius died as a result of his severe treatment, Cyril immediately had the monk enrolled in the catalogue of Alexandrian Christian martyrs. In late antiquity, the martyrs—their relics and shrines—were thought to be conduits of social and spiritual power. By registering official lists of martyrs and keeping those lists under their own auspices, early Christian bishops like Cyril sought to control, redirect, and channel the power of the martyrs in the service of episcopal policy.

In this case, Cyril's action of recording Ammonius' name in the catalogue of martyrs did not meet with universal support among the Christians living in the capital; some thought it an unnecessarily provocative gesture.[137] Nonetheless, his attempt to canonize Ammonius and the Nitrian monks' accusations of idolatry against Orestes were gestures laden with social significance. They both demonstrate how, in the midst of this crisis, the patriarch and his monastic supporters sought to shape the self-identity of the Alexandrian church: they did so specifically by appealing to the legacy of the Egyptian martyrs—those who had famously stood firm against government oppression and idolatry.

Therefore, Hypatia's death ultimately may be traced to the confluence of two social factors: the increasingly exclusive lines of communal self-identity in the Alexandrian church and the specific circumstances of Cyril's conflict with Orestes. Hypatia was a confidante of Orestes: she enjoyed a "freedom of speech" *(parrhêsia)* with the prefect and the concomitant benefits of patronage enjoyed by only a select few. Even more importantly, her access to the prefect, especially in her role as a philosopher at the Academy, had become public knowledge among the Christians of Alexandria.[138] In her public position, she was viewed as a rival of Cyril for governmental favor: Cyril himself, shut out from such privileges with Orestes, may have contributed to this perception by privately portraying her as a threat to the hegemony of the church in Alexandria, as a vestige of the old pagan order. The eventual murder of Hypatia was the product of this volatile social environment. Here, the details of her assassination are particularly telling. The dismemberment and burning of Hypatia's body was, in effect, a public, ritual act—a dramatic reenactment of the destruction of the Serapeum under Theophilus. By performing violence upon Hypatia's body, the Christian mob was giving stark expression to their own increasingly exclusive sense of civic and religious identity.[139]

While many scholars have been preoccupied with the question of whether the death of Hypatia was the direct *result* of a systematic anti-pagan policy on the part of Cyril (a question now generally answered in the negative given the complexity of his conflict with Orestes), few if any have noted how this event so early in his reign may have equally acted as a *catalyst* that helped crystallize his later policy toward pagan belief and practice. If Hypatia's murder was in fact perceived as a dramatic reenactment of the Serapeum's destruction—a savage, ritual gesture of popular support for the policies of Theophilus—it may have actually served as a public inducement for Cyril to follow his predecessor's lead all the more closely, and thereby to tap into the groundswell of anti-pagan opinion among certain Alexandrian Christians and the monks of the Egyptian desert.[140] This upsurge in anti-pagan sentiment is vividly captured by the seventh-century chronicler John of Nikiu. Describing the people's reaction to the news of Hypatia's death, he writes: "All the people surrounded the patriarch Cyril and named him 'the new Theophilus'; for he had destroyed the last remains of idolatry in the city."[141]

That Cyril was indebted to Theophilus' example in crafting his subsequent policy may be seen most clearly in his response to the presence of the Isis cult at nearby Menouthis. Despite the efforts of church leaders to suppress indigenous forms of Egyptian religion, local cultic practice continued to thrive during the fifth century (and into the sixth and seventh as well).[142] One such still-vibrant cult was the cult of Isis, which maintained an active pilgrimage center at Menouthis, along the Mediterranean coast just east of Alexandria.[143] There, her temple functioned as a center for healing and oracular divination. Pilgrims would come to Menouthis seeking remedies for their ailments, often sleeping overnight at the shrine in the hope of experiencing dreams in which the goddess would come to them and heal them. The shrine of Isis continued to be a popular pilgrimage destination during Cyril's tenure as bishop: for pagan devotees, it seems to have filled a social niche left vacant by Theophilus' destruction of the Serapeum.

Sometime before the year 429 C.E., the popularity of the Isis cult at Menouthis began to raise concerns for Cyril, who observed that Christians were among those making pilgrimage to that shrine.[144] In response, Cyril did not lead a band of enthusiasts to raze the temple of Isis after the fashion of Theophilus; the widespread popularity of the Isis cult and the charged atmosphere after the death of Hypatia would undoubtedly have precluded it. Instead, he took a more subtle, indirect approach in trying to "Christianize" the local topography: he established a Christian martyr shrine in the vicinity that would compete with the Isis cult as a place of healing and a destination for pilgrims—the shrine of Saints Cyrus and John at Menouthis.[145]

The story behind the founding of this pilgrimage center suggests both how Cyril countered the pagan practice of divination with his own claims to divine inspiration, and how his subsequent policy was shaped in light of Theophilus' example. According to the writer Sophronius,[146] Cyril announced a vision in which an angel instructed him to transfer the relics from Alexandria to Menouthis. When the relics of the two saints—identified by the church as Diocletianic martyrs—were finally brought to Menouthis, Cyril left them in the care of the Pachomian monks whom two decades earlier Theophilus himself had established nearby at Canopus. Cyril's founding of a pilgrimage shrine at Menouthis to house those relics may have even involved the architectural adaptation of a church structure Theophilus had originally built there.[147] In any case, like his predecessor, Cyril strategically used sacred artifacts and architecture, coordinated with the local presence of monastic communities, to contest pagan cultic space and to reclaim the Egyptian landscape as Christian territory.

In his promotion of the Christian martyr cult and in his writings,[148] Cyril sought to define the Coptic church's identity over against pagan beliefs and practices. Linked in spirit with this anti-pagan agenda were the numerous letters and treatises Cyril wrote against forms of Christian belief that he viewed as heretical or schismatic. In the introduction to his *Letter to the Monks of Scetis*, Cyril consciously frames his condemnation of Origenist and Arian beliefs in terms of anti-pagan rhetoric: "Those who side with Origen are following the aberration of the pagans and the madness of the Arians."[149] In this letter, one sees again how Cyril emulated Theophilus in opposing certain Origenist ideas and seeking to enforce theological orthodoxy among the monks living in the area around Nitria and Scetis. In this case, however, Cyril's concern with Origen's influence among the monks hinges not so much on a defense of anthropomorphite ideas about God, but on a defense of the resurrection of the flesh over against Origenist ideas about the dissolution of body and soul when they come into union with God.[150] In fact, even while he maintains a hard public line against certain forms of Origenist belief in the area around Scetis, in his correspondence with other monastic communities he actually reverses course and condemns extreme anthropomorphite doctrines. This can be seen in his correspondence with a Palestinian monastic community headed by a deacon-priest named Tiberias, as well as in his short *Letter to Calosirius* in which he concerns himself with heterodox beliefs circulating among the monks at Mount Calamon in the Egyptian Fayûm.[151]

The letter addressed to Calosirius is especially instructive as it gives a picture of the mechanisms by which Cyril stayed informed about the inner workings in Egyptian monasteries and how he used personal letters to urge the re-drawing of theological boundaries. The patriarch apparently made use of monastic informants who provided him with information about those with divergent theological and ecclesiastical viewpoints in the monastery at Mount Calamon—not only those holding to extreme anthropomorphite views, but also Melitian monks as well. The picture painted is that of a monastery not sharply differentiated along doctrinal or sectarian lines. This picture of monasticism in the Fayûm is confirmed by another source from this period— the *Sayings of the Desert Fathers*—that tells the story of how a famous orthodox monk named Sisoes settled in the Fayûm and lived there peaceably amidst a community of Melitian ascetics.[152] Cyril's interest in writing his letter to Calosirius, the bishop of the region, was to urge him to "put a stop to" those who were voicing errant beliefs and to forbid those he recognized as orthodox from associating with Melitians.[153]

Despite the fact that his specific theological concerns are diametrically different in this case, Cyril follows Theophilus in his attempts to bring the monastic leadership more directly under his own authority. He does so by urging them to draw firmer, more exclusive lines of community identity by separating themselves from (or suppressing) monks who espouse theological and ecclesiastical views that differ from his own.

The Christological Conflict with Constantinople (Part One)

On the international front, Cyril also followed Theophilus in his turbulent relations with the church of Constantinople and its leadership. Early in Cyril's episcopacy, this was most evident in the hard line he took with regard to the legacy of John Chrysostom, the former bishop of Constantinople. Theophilus' conflict with Chrysostom had ended with the latter's exile from office (and his ensuing death in 407). At the time of his exile, Chrysostom's name had been stricken from the Alexandrian church diptychs—that is, the official ecclesiastical registers that recorded the names of bishops in good standing. Now, just over a decade later, there was a move afoot in some sees to restore his name to the official list of bishops; indeed, the bishoprics of Rome, Constantinople, and Antioch did just that. However, Cyril, who had himself been present with Theophilus to witness Chrysostom's condemnation at the Synod of the Oak (403), adamantly refused, and he remained resolute even after Atticus, the new bishop of Constantinople (the second successor to Chrystostom), wrote him a letter appealing for clemency in the matter.[154] Over the course of his thirty-three years in office, Cyril gradually moderated his stance toward Chrysostom,[155] but the tensions between Alexandria and Constantinople remained.

These tensions erupted into full-blown theological warfare shortly after a man named Nestorius took office as bishop of Constantinople in the year 427. The opening salvo in this renewed conflict was Nestorius' public proclamation against the doctrine that the Virgin Mary was the "Mother of God" (*Theotokos*—literally, "God-bearer").[156] Nestorius disagreed with this phrase: for him, it raised a series of troubling questions. How could Mary, only a human being, give birth to the transcendent God? Was that not a confusion of terms? Would it not be better to say that Mary gave birth to the human being, Jesus Christ? Therefore, Nestorius proposed an alternative title for Mary— the "Mother of Christ" (*Christotokos*): "That God passed through from the Virgin *Christotokos* I am taught by the divine Scripture, but that God was born from her I have not been taught anywhere." In his lectures on the subject, he went so far as to condemn those who continued to call the Virgin *Theotokos*.[157]

Nestorius' rejection of *Theotokos* provoked immediate indignation among the Egyptian church leadership. Prior to the fifth century, the term had had a long history of usage in Egypt; indeed, it seems to have been a distinctive feature of Alexandrian theology. Origen, Peter, Alexander, Athanasius, and Didymus the Blind—all either popes or prominent Alexandrian theological instructors—had employed this title for the Virgin Mary in their writings.[158] For Cyril himself, this term additionally served as a crucial theological tool in his efforts to combat the Isis cult in Egypt. Isis was known as the "great virgin" and as the "mother of the god" among her devotees: in Egyptian mythology, she was credited with giving birth to the Egyptian solar deity Horus. By representing Mary as the Virgin and Mother of God *(Theotokos)* in literature, liturgy, and art, Cyril and the fifth-century Egyptian church tried to appeal to the sensibilities of Isis worshippers and to redirect such devotion to the Christian cult of Mary.[159] Thus, it should not be surprising that when Cyril got wind of Nestorius' teachings he immediately felt the need to defend this long-held tenet of Alexandrian belief in writing.

The nature of Cyril's reaction is significant for understanding the role Egyptian monasticism continued to play in relation to the Alexandrian patriarchate. In the face of another theological dispute with Constantinople, Cyril turned to the Egyptian monasteries in an effort to consolidate this traditional base of support. Thus, even before writing to Nestorius directly, he composed a general *Letter to the Monks of Egypt*. In that letter, his primary concern was to root out potential seeds of doubt or division planted by the news of Nestorius' teaching. He writes,

> But I am disturbed beyond measure because I have heard that certain troublesome rumors have reached you, and that certain men go about destroying your simple faith, spewing out a multitude of useless pet phrases, making close inquiries, and saying that it is necessary to specify clearly whether or not the Holy Virgin Mary is to be called the Mother of God.[160]

Sociologically, Cyril's aim was to solidify the bonds of group loyalty under his own leadership: he did so by defining such loyalty on the basis of theological adherence and seeking to separate the community from teachings perceived to be false.[161] Over against

Nestorius' claims that the doctrine of *Theotokos* was unscriptural, Cyril appealed to apostolic tradition and the "holy Fathers" of the faith—those who were thought to have interpreted Scripture rightly—in order to defend the use of that title for Mary.[162] Here, the *History of the Patriarchs* properly recognizes how Cyril's rhetorical agenda was tied to the construction of Egyptian ecclesiastical identity: "Cyril availed himself of the weapons of the fathers, Alexander and Athanasius, and put on the breastplate of faith which his predecessors had handed down in the Church of Saint Mark the Evangelist."[163]

In his *Letter to the Monks of Egypt*, Cyril appeals especially to Athanasius' precedent, citing two places where Athanasius himself referred to Mary as the "Mother of God."[164] At the outset of this emerging christological debate with Nestorius, Cyril's recollection of Athanasius' example would have functioned on at least two levels. First, by situating himself as Athanasius' spiritual successor in his correspondence with Egyptian monks, Cyril was laying claim to the role of monastic patron (and the benefits of monastic patronage) that Athanasius had established nearly one hundred years before. Second, by invoking Athanasius' name, Cyril also laid claim to his mantle as orthodox defender of the Nicene faith: in his *Letter to the Monks of Egypt*, immediately after citing Athanasius, Cyril prominently quotes the text of the famous creed.[165] Later, when Nestorius also tried to align himself with Nicaea, Cyril would complain that the bishop of Constantinople had "not understood" and had "not interpreted rightly" the theology of that council.[166]

Cyril's dependence on Athanasius also helps elucidate the deeper theological reasons for his opposition to Nestorius. At the end of his *Letter to the Monks of Egypt*, Cyril emphasizes the *unity of Christ* (as both human and divine) as justification for calling Mary the Mother of God:

> Because, therefore, he is truly God and king according to nature, and because the one crucified has been called the Lord of glory, how could anyone hesitate to call the Holy Virgin the Mother of God? Adore him as one, without dividing him into two after the union.[167]

Elsewhere, Cyril describes this union of divinity and humanity in Christ as a "*hypostatic* union"—that is, a union of two "substantial realities" (Greek, *hypostaseis*) in the person of Christ.

> We do not say that the nature of the Word was altered when he
> became flesh. Neither do we say that the Word was changed into
> a complete man of soul and body. We say rather that the Word
> by having united to himself hypostatically flesh animated by a
> rational soul, inexplicably and incomprehensibly became man.[168]

For Cyril, it was this complete union of the divine and human in
Christ that made it possible to call Mary the Mother of God.
According to the "economy" of the Incarnation, what was attributable
to Christ's humanity was also attributable to his divinity, and vice
versa.[169] The nature of this union also had profound implications for
human salvation. Here, Cyril's Christology relied heavily on
Athanasius' doctrine of the Incarnation. According to Athanasius,
the life-giving Word, by uniting itself with a human body and by
divinizing that body, salvifically transformed all of human nature.
For Cyril as well as Athanasius, human access to salvation was made
possible only by participation in the divine (or divinized) body of
Christ.[170]

This christological logic, so tied to soteriology ("the science of
salvation"), helps explain what was at stake for Cyril in his opposition
to Nestorius. Cyril complained that Nestorius' doctrine divided Christ
into two persons, or alternatively, that it merely suggested a loose
conjunction of two persons in Christ. Cyril's fundamental concern was,
ultimately, that such a Christology might undermine the essential unity
of Christ and thereby jeopardize human access to salvation.[171]

Cyril pressed his case against Nestorius in numerous letters and
treatises addressed to Leo, the bishop of Rome, to other Eastern bishops,
to the imperial court, and to Nestorius himself.[172] Indeed, his attacks
against the bishop of Constantinople quickly grew more and more
vehement: his third and final letter to Nestorius, which was backed by
an Alexandrian synod, included a series of twelve scathing statements
condemning Nestorius' views—the "Twelve Anathemas."[173] Cyril's
vocal protests soon prompted the emperor Theodosius II, in June of 431,
to call a church council at Ephesus to resolve the matter. At this Council
of Ephesus, Nestorius would be condemned, but the proceedings were
not without complications.

As senior bishop, Cyril presided over the council. He arrived in
Ephesus accompanied by an entourage of loyal supporters, including
the Coptic monk Shenoute, head of the White Monastery in Upper
Egypt.[174] Some Egyptian monks were even commissioned as Cyril's

"agents" in Constantinople, where they tried to drum up opposition against Nestorius. Once again, an Alexandrian patriarch would benefit from Egyptian monastic support in a time of theological crisis.[175] Buoyed by the enthusiasm of his supporters, Cyril was eager to start the proceedings. The council was already delayed two weeks past its appointed starting date. So, with the representatives from Antioch still almost a week's journey away, with the Roman delegation delayed even longer, and with Nestorius himself refusing to attend, Cyril decided to call the council to order. The decision of the council came quickly: within twenty-four hours, Nestorius was deposed by a unanimous vote of the 197 bishops present.[176]

However, Cyril's decision to go ahead without the Antiochene party, while technically within his rights, ended up creating a serious rift between the two sees. When John, the bishop of Antioch, and his supporters arrived a few days later, they were enraged by Cyril's decision and adamantly dissented from the decision taken at the council. In reaction, they held their own session and condemned Cyril and his "Twelve Anathemas." When the news of this rift reached the emperor Theodosius, he decided "to annul everything that had taken place in a partial manner" at the two separate gatherings, and called for a new theological consultation near the capital at Chalcedon.[177] For the next three months, the emperor Theodosius tried to resolve the differences between the two parties, but met with no success. In the end, it would take almost two years before Alexandria and Antioch were officially reconciled in a Formulary of Reunion (433).

Despite the equivocal outcome of the Council of Ephesus, the public fates of Nestorius and Cyril could not have been more different. Nestorius, desiring to leave public life and return to his original monastic retreat, relinquished his episcopal chair after the Council.[178] Five years later, he would be summarily exiled by the emperor to the frontiers of the Roman world (first to Petra, and then to the Great Oasis in the Western Desert of Egypt).[179] As for Cyril, he returned to Egypt a hero: in subsequent generations he would be lauded in Greek and Coptic monastic literature as a pastor and patron of Egyptian monks and as a defender of the true faith against Nestorius.[180] For the time being, with a less controversial person occupying the bishop's chair at Constantinople (Maximian), the tensions between Alexandria and Constantinople were temporarily defused. During the next decade and a half, an uneasy peace would exist between the two sees.

The Christological Conflict with Constantinople (Part Two)

This theological détente between Alexandria and Constantinople was decisively broken at the second Council of Ephesus in 449. There, many of the same christological issues would be revisited, albeit with a new cast of principals: Dioscorus (444–454) was named bishop of Alexandria after Cyril's death in 444, and in Constantinople a man named Flavian now occupied the episcopal throne. The initial spark for this renewed controversy, however, came from an influential monk named Eutyches, who was the head of a monastery in the imperial capital, Constantinople. In the two years prior to this second Ephesian Council, Eutyches had begun to attract negative attention among church leaders in Asia Minor and Syria, who raised vocal objections to his teaching on the "one nature" of Christ.

Eutyches' teaching (and the controversy it engendered) was not new. Cyril of Alexandria himself had commonly used the phrase, "one nature" *(mia physis)*, in order to describe the "hypostatic" unity of Christ. Indeed, already in the 430s, this phrase had proven to be controversial not only with Nestorius, but also with bishop John of Antioch and his constituency, who feared that such a "one-nature" Christology would effectively do away with Christ's humanity. In the face of such concerns voiced by the Antiochene party, Cyril moved to clarify and temper his language. First, he explained that he taught the "one *enfleshed* nature of the Word" *(mia physis tou logou sesarkômenê)* in order to highlight his central concern that the incarnate Word be recognized as the privileged *subject*—the singular, life-giving source—of God's redemptive action on behalf of humanity.[181] At the same time, even while employing this "one-nature" language to guarantee the unity of Christ's person, Cyril was willing to seek common ground with his Antiochene critics by acknowledging that the particularity of both Christ's humanity and his divinity was somehow still present in their "synthesis."[182] In the end, Cyril's careful rearticulation and refinement of his Christology played a key role in facilitating the aforementioned Formulary of Reunion signed by the churches of Alexandria and Antioch in 433.

While the monk Eutyches adhered to Cyril in his emphasis upon the "one nature" of Christ, he demonstrated less aptitude for subtlety in theological expression and far less willingness to compromise in his strict interpretation of "one nature" doctrine. To him, anyone who suggested that there might be "two natures" in Christ after the union was simply guilty of christological innovation (a cardinal sin in early Christian theological circles). In support of this claim, he pointed out—correctly, in this case—that there was no ancient precedence for "two-nature" language: it was used neither in Scripture nor at the ecumenical councils of Nicaea (325) and Ephesus (431). Over against such perceived innovation, Eutyches continued to repeat his "one nature" formula like a mantra.[183]

For their part, Eutyches' opponents (including the bishops Theodoret of Cyrus, Flavian of Constantinople, and Leo of Rome) suspected that his "one-nature" views inevitably caused Christ's human nature to be "swallowed up" *(katapothênai)* by his divinity.[184] Thus, at a "Home Synod" at Constantinople in 448, Flavian had him condemned for misreading and distorting Cyril's theology, a judgment that was echoed by Pope Leo, the bishop of Rome, who dismissed Eutyches as "exceedingly foolish and thoroughly ignorant" *(multum imprudens et nimis imperitus)*.[185]

At this point, in opposition to Flavian and Leo, the Egyptian pope, Dioscorus, decided to weigh in on behalf of Eutyches. It proved to be a fateful decision for the future of the Egyptian church. While some modern historians have accused Dioscorus of opportunism,[186] the reasons for his intervention were not simply political. On the theological level, he seems to have shared Eutyches' rigid interpretation of the "one-nature" formula, as well as a profound dissatisfaction with some of the christological concessions made by Cyril in his conversations with the Antiochenes leading up to their Formulary of Reunion in 433.[187] In any event, regardless of his motivations, Dioscorus was able to take advantage of a favorable political climate at the time. Because Eutyches had an influential patron in the imperial court (the court chamberlain Chrysaphius), Dioscorus quickly garnered the emperor Theodosius' support for a second council at Ephesus to review the case.[188]

Like Cyril at the previous council at Ephesus eighteen years before, Dioscorus was granted the privilege to preside as the representative of the Alexandrian see. He wielded his authority with an even more assertive hand than his predecessor. With an overwhelming majority of the bishops attending the conference in his own camp, and with imperial troops present to squelch dissent, Dioscorus quickly pushed through his agenda: in the end, Eutyches was exonerated, and Flavian, the bishop of Constantinople, was deposed. Once again Egyptian monks played a key role in the course of events: just as the voting was about to begin, a group of them (along with a throng of other militant activists) streamed into the meeting hall, clamoring for the participants to support their bishop. Throughout the council, there were flare-ups of violence, and the rough tactics of the military guard left a number of participants bruised, among them Flavian himself. Within a year, he would be dead, having been "unable to endure the hardship of (his) journey" into exile.[189]

Dioscorus returned to Alexandria in triumph, but it was a short-lived and costly victory. In the process of defending Eutyches, he had alienated not only Constantinople, but also the formidable Roman see. Leo of Rome himself had not been able to attend the council: in his stead, he had sent a papal delegation with a detailed letter to Flavian opposing Eutyches' views. This document, known as the *Tome of Leo*,[190] was never read at the council: it did not fit into Dioscorus' plans and was accordingly suppressed. This obviously did not please Leo, who was so angered by Dioscorus' leadership tactics that he labeled the second Council of Ephesus a *latrocinium*—a "Council of Robbers."[191] Thus, when the emperor Theodosius died a year later in 450 (as a result of a freak riding accident), the Alexandrian bishop found himself suddenly vulnerable, bereft of his most powerful international advocate and ally.

Following the emperor Theodosius' death, the backlash against Dioscorus was swift and uncompromising. The new empress Pulcheria, sympathetic to Leo, moved to invalidate the actions of the second Council of Ephesus and called for a new council to meet the next year at Chalcedon, near the capital of Constantinople. At this Council of Chalcedon (451), Dioscorus was deposed (allegedly for his attempts to excommunicate Leo at Ephesus), Eutyches' Christology was once again condemned, and a compromise solution based on three primary documents—Leo's *Tome*, Cyril's Second *Letter to Nestorius*, and the Alexandrian-Antiochene Formulary of Reunion—was approved. The language of the Chalcedonian Creed was significant: even while it affirmed the Virgin Mary as the "Mother of God" *(Theotokos)*, it spoke about Christ "in two natures, without confusion, without change, without division, without separation."[192] To most in the Egyptian delegation, the emphasis on Christ's "two natures" smacked too much of Nestorius' thought. The statement was seen as a betrayal of Cyril's legacy. The Council's refusal to accept Cyril's *Twelve Anathemas* against Nestorius only seemed to confirm that impression.

In the end, the majority of the Egyptian delegation resolutely rejected the council's authority to depose Dioscorus. After the Council, even when Dioscorus was sent into exile to Gangra (Paphlagonia) and a pro-Chalcedonian appointment (Proterius) was installed in his place,

Coptic Christians continued to recognize Dioscorus as their legitimate patriarch. Among the Egyptian faithful—especially among Coptic monks—his forcible expulsion from office only seems to have reinforced his popularity as "an embattled ascetic leader," the latest in a long line of patriarchs (including Dionysius, Peter, and Athanasius) who had experienced exile at the hands of hostile adversaries.[193] Indeed, Dioscorus' reputation as an exiled patriarch and monastic favorite would be celebrated by later generations of anti-Chalcedonian monastic writers[194] and artists[195] in Egypt (see Figs. 6 and 7).

Thus, what emerged from the Council of Chalcedon was not a christological compromise that was amenable to all parties, but a formal schism between the church in Egypt and the churches at Rome and Constantinople. For the next two centuries, this schism had profound implications for the social, political, and religious landscape of Egypt, as the anti-Chalcedonian church there continued to resist the hegemony of the Byzantine state. Marginalized under the political rule of Constantinople, the Coptic church and its patriarchs soon became exiles in their own land.

Four

Contesting the Alexandrian Papacy
Ecclesiastical "Colonialism" and
the Egyptian Church from 451 to the Rise of Islam
(Dioscorus I to Benjamin I)

Despite his permanent banishment at the Council of Chalcedon in 451, the patriarch Dioscorus (444–454) proved to be a pivotal figure for the shaping of Egyptian ecclesiastical identity. *The History of the Patriarchs* commemorates his legacy in hagiographic terms, lauding him as one who "preserved the orthodox faith, which persists in the see of the evangelist Saint Mark to this day and forever" and who "received the crown of martyrdom" while in exile.[1] In so doing, this Coptic chronicle reads the contours of Dioscorus' experience in light of earlier papal models, especially as they were informed by the discourses of apostolicity and martyrdom.

At the same time, however, Dioscorus' biography in the *History of the Patriarchs* also shows the immense significance of his banishment for the subsequent history of the Egyptian patriarchate, and for the relationship of the Coptic Church both to the Byzantine state and to the imperial (pro-Chalcedonian) church. According to that account, the Council of Chalcedon and its aftermath marked a profound disjuncture in the historical identity and practice of the Egyptian church. Following the council, the work of recording the history of the Egyptian patriarchs was reportedly disrupted:

> But at that time the creeds were separated, and the sees were torn asunder, so that none was left to write histories of the patriarchs, and the practice of composing them was interrupted. . . . In this way no biography of the holy patriarch Dioscorus after his banishment has been found.[2]

Dioscorus' banishment also brought about a radical change in the way that many Egyptian Christians viewed the imperial state in Constantinople. The *History of the Patriarchs* emphasizes that Dioscorus had been persecuted and banished "at the hands of the prince (emperor) Marcian and his wife" and through the agency of a council that was seen to be subservient to imperial will. Indeed, in the two centuries following the Council of Chalcedon, the Coptic Church and other anti-Chalcedonian communities would begin labeling their opponents, the "Melkite" (or "Imperial") Church.[3]

Dioscorus' banishment signaled a decisive shift in the relationship between the Egyptian church and the imperial state, but for Egyptian Christians with long-term memories it would also have evoked vivid images from the experience of earlier Egyptian patriarchs. A century before, the Roman emperor Constantius II had acted to expel Athanasius from his see and to replace him (on two separate occasions) with Arian-appointed bishops. Now, with Dioscorus physically removed from the scene, the emperor Marcian and his Chalcedonian loyalists moved quickly to appoint a replacement—an Egyptian bishop named Proterius who had left Dioscorus' side to support the Chalcedonian cause. In this way, the Chalcedonian hierarchy sought to silence Egyptian opposition by endorsing their own imperially-sanctioned representative as patriarch.

As a result of these actions, during much of the next two centuries, from 451 to 642, the Egyptian papacy was sharply contested between (at least) two parties. While the majority of the Egyptian bishoprics recognized Dioscorus and a line of anti-Chalcedonian successors as the legitimate patriarchs, their validity was only infrequently recognized by the Byzantine (pro-Chalcedonian) church at Constantinople. Instead, the pro-Chalcedonians often chose to promote their own claimants to the episcopal throne in Alexandria, reinforcing their authority through state-sponsored military intervention. These pro-Chalcedonian bishops installed at Alexandria were also backed by new forms of imperial legislation—legislation that granted the episcopal office an unprecedented degree of civil authority over Alexandrian economic and political affairs.[4] Finally, the intrusion of Proterius and his successors into the Alexandrian see was also coordinated with an official campaign of theological propaganda (led primarily by the churches of Rome and Constantinople) that sought to move the anti-Chalcedonian opposition to the margins of Byzantine public discourse. Leo, the bishop of Rome, spearheaded this campaign: in his letters, he proclaimed that the church in Egypt was in a state of "deplorable captivity" from which the emperor was called to set it free so that "the dignity of the fathers and the sacerdotal right" might be restored.[5]

This intervention by the imperial, pro-Chalcedonian church functioned, I would argue, as a form of ecclesiastical colonialism. The military, legal, economic, and rhetorical policies of Constantinople and Rome were specifically designed to displace and disenfranchise the Coptic opposition, and to secure a pro-Chalcedonian outpost at Alexandria.[6] And yet, in the modern study of this period, Western ecclesiastical historians—themselves heirs to Chalcedonian tradition—have often unwittingly echoed and perpetuated the colonialist biases of their Roman and Byzantine forebears. As an obvious example, many scholars continue to use the term Monophysite ("one-naturist") to refer to the anti-Chalcedonian Coptic community, despite the fact that in later centuries it was only used as a pejorative epithet by their theological adversaries and is rejected as a self-designation by most modern Copts.[7] Other scholars, when listing the Alexandrian patriarchs, enumerate them according to the lines of succession officially recognized by the Chalcedonian imperial authority.[8] In this chapter I offer a corrective to this trend by re-reading this period of history from the perspective of the colonized—the predominantly anti-Chalcedonian Egyptian church—in order to understand how the social and theological identity of the Egyptian papacy was conditioned by "imperialist" discourses of power and by the complications of political resistance.[9]

The phenomenon of resistance is not simply the antithesis of colonial domination. Rather, resistance has been shown to be a multi-faceted process of cultural negotiation,[10] which inevitably involves forms of *compromise and complicity*.[11] Thus, a variegated mixture of social dynamics is to be expected in a colonized community. Among these are: (1) the formation of new elite systems in the contestation of local, institutional leadership; (2) internal divisions and social stratification based on ethnic, linguistic, and religious distinctions, and (3) discourses and practices that attempt to redraw lines of community identity by contesting assumed boundaries between center and periphery/margin, or those that seek to forge a larger sense of collective consciousness among a colonized people, as in the case of nationalism or movements of ethnic solidarity.

In different ways, each of these paradigmatic aspects of colonial resistance manifests itself in the history of the Coptic patriarchate during the two centuries following the Council of Chalcedon. In the aftermath of the council, the Alexandrian patriarchate became a site of institutional contestation between the imperially sponsored Chalcedonian bishop Proterius and his anti-Chalcedonian counterparts—namely, the exiled Dioscorus and his eventual successor Timothy II Aelurus. As we shall see, however, the historical legacy of that resistance in the decades that followed was not without its twists and turns. Even in their public theological opposition to Chalcedon, later Coptic patriarchs did not always fully give up their hope for imperial patronage, nor did they reject the possibility of theological compromise, a fact that would inevitably bring some of them into conflict (and even schism) with more stringent anti-Chalcedonian factions in their own Egyptian churches. This fourth and final chapter will trace the circuitous history of this papal resistance up to the Arab conquest of Egypt in 642, an event that ultimately reshuffled the political landscape for Egyptian Christians and posed new possibilities and new challenges for Coptic papal leadership.

The Politics of Resistance and Compromise: Early Conflicts with the "Imperial" (Chalcedonian) Church

A Cat and a Wobble-Hat: A Tale of Two Timothies

After the death of the exiled Dioscorus in 454, Coptic resistance to the ecclesiastical policy of the imperial church soon crystallized around the figure of Timothy II Aelurus (457–477).[12] His nickname Aelurus—most often translated as "the Cat"—seems to have been a reference to his skinny physique;[13] however, as an icon of Egyptian ecclesiastical opposition to Chalcedon, he has enjoyed a considerably more robust stature in the eyes of Copts. Formerly a monk and presbyter under Cyril, and a member of Dioscorus' retinue at the second Council of Ephesus in 449, he had been exiled from Alexandria along with Dioscorus in 451.[14] Their physical absence cleared the ecclesiastical landscape for the Chalcedonians' election and insertion of Proterius that same year.

Riots and protests broke out immediately following Proterius' election in 451, and local unrest continued throughout the latter's time in office.[15] And yet, for three years after Dioscorus' death in 454, with his principal rivals still in exile, Proterius was able to maintain his position in Alexandria, largely because he enjoyed the political patronage of the emperor Marcian. With Marcian's death in 455, the situation changed: the Chalcedonian hegemony over Alexandrian ecclesiastical politics began to weaken. Within two years, Timothy "the Cat" had been smuggled into Alexandria by anti-Chalcedonian monks and was ordained as Dioscorus' successor (457).[16] Timothy's installation in one of the large Alexandrian churches ("the great church from which he had been forcibly removed") established him publicly as a rival to Proterius and as a rallying point for renewed unrest over the presence of the Chalcedonian bishop.[17] Within the span of a month, this unrest boiled over into violence. Proterius was murdered, the victim either of mob action or of a military coup.[18]

The allegedly clandestine nature of Timothy's election and Proterius' subsequent murder made "the Cat" a target for numerous accusations from Proterius' Chalcedonian supporters in Egypt and from Leo, the bishop of Rome. Each sent letters of protest to the new emperor (Leo I), claiming that Timothy's election was invalid and accusing Timothy of conspiring in the murder of Proterius.[19] In the letters written by Pope Leo of Rome, he goes so far as to call Timothy a "parricide" and compares him to the brother-murdering, biblical Cain.[20] Behind such incendiary language, the Roman bishop was doggedly pursuing a rhetorical agenda starkly reminiscent of modern colonial ideologies. Using terms that a modern colonial writer might apply to a renegade Third World dictator, Leo portrays Timothy as a "raging tyrant" and describes the church in Egypt as in a state of "deplorable captivity," with the only possibility for emancipation being the prospect of imperial intervention.[21] In political terms, Leo of Rome's letter-writing campaign was successful. The emperor responded by canvassing the opinions of pro-Chalcedonian bishops and monks in the East, an action that gave Leo of Rome the occasion to drum up further opposition to Timothy.[22] In the face of such mounting pressure from church leaders, the emperor Leo I in 459 banished Timothy to the town of Gangra on the Black Sea, the very place where his predecessor Dioscorus had languished during the final years of his life.

In exile (first in Gangra, and then later on at the town of Chersonesus in the Crimea), Timothy established "rival assemblies,"[23] and began to produce what might be called a theological literature of resistance. In a treatise *Against Chalcedon*, written while in exile, Timothy rebuts Leo's *Tome* in a point-by-point commentary, condemns the "blasphemy" of the council, and criticizes his opponents for "currying favor with the sovereign at that time."[24] Elsewhere in his letters, he warns his followers about "the unknown and foreign religious" who come to Egypt to teach the "heresy of the Diphysites (i.e.,

Chalcedonian doctrine)."[25] Here, we can see how Timothy begins to construct a way of speaking that incorporates certain ambivalent terms and dichotomies typical of resistance rhetoric. In particular, he echoes his opponents' use of terms such as "blasphemy" and "heresy" and uses the label "diphysite" as a counter to Chalcedonian criticisms of so-called "monophysite" doctrine (thus underwriting binary conceptions of communal affiliation). On the other hand, the complexity and complicity of Timothy's resistance can be observed in his posture toward imperial power: his effort to portray his opponents as political toadies "currying favor with the sovereign" does not prevent him from emphasizing in another letter how the emperor had specially summoned him from exile "to offer advice on the tumultuous problems of the church."[26] Finally, in characterizing the Chalcedonian clerical hierarchy in Egypt as "unknown and foreign," and in contrasting them to the "people" of Egypt,[27] Timothy demonstrates an early move to shape Egyptian Christian identity in something approximating populist terms.

One of the things that strikes the modern reader about Timothy's writing during this period is its profoundly theological character. Large portions of his treatise *Against Chalcedon* and his letters to churches consist of *florilegia* from the church fathers. These collections or chains of quotations were utilized systematically to refute detailed points of Chalcedonian doctrine. And yet, at the same time, they tell us a lot about the way that Timothy was representing himself to his constituency while in exile. It is especially noteworthy that Timothy, in assembling his *florilegia*, quotes most liberally from his predecessors Athanasius, Theophilus, and Cyril. In doing so, he links his own theological resistance against Chalcedon to a long and illustrious lineage of Alexandrian christological reflection, and implicitly underscores what he viewed as his rightful claim upon the office they held.

Such rhetorical aims become explicit in Timothy's treatise *Against Chalcedon*. After repeatedly citing Cyril in order to refute Leo's *Tome*, Timothy goes on to extol Cyril's successor (and his own predecessor) Dioscorus as "the mighty guardian of the faith and the canons of the fathers."[28] Then, drawing an analogy between his own experience of exile and that of Dioscorus, Timothy defends the validity of his succession as the bishop of Alexandria:

> Now I myself, having been found worthy by the invocation of the Holy Ghost to succeed (Dioscorus), on profession of the same faith as he had, the faith which has come to us from the

holy apostles and blessed fathers, pray that I may imitate him in his struggle. For this reason I endure these things to the point of exile and imprisonment.[29]

The theme of endurance in the face of persecution is central to Timothy's letters as well, where he uses the language of shared suffering to highlight his solidarity with the Egyptian faithful: "A mighty storm has come upon the church of God, dear brethren, and we must suffer in company with one another."[30] For Timothy, this discourse of solidarity and suffering was crucially connected to fundamental christological concerns that lay at the root of the Chalcedonian controversy—specifically, concerns about the nature of human participation in Christ. Thus, he wrote to Faustinus the Deacon: "And although we are physically distant from one another yet we are mutually joined by the spirit of unity and with the bond of Christ's love; since our Lord Christ, who is persecuted with us, is in our midst and abides in us with the heavenly Father and the Holy Spirit."[31] Ultimately, by portraying himself, his church, and (by extension) the person of Christ as victims of a new wave of persecution, the exiled patriarch Timothy was once again, like Theophilus and Cyril before him, consciously drawing on the Egyptian church's legacy of resistance as a church of the martyrs.[32]

For the next sixteen years (A.D. 459–475), Timothy the Cat would remain in exile, forced to oversee the anti-Chalcedonian majority in Egypt from afar. In the meantime, the pro-Chalcedonian church in Alexandria moved quickly to fill the vacancy left by his absence. In his place, they appointed their own representative as patriarch, a monk named Timothy Salofaciolus ("Wobble-Hat") from the Pachomian monastery at Canopus (which quickly emerged as a Chalcedonian enclave during this period).[33] From this Timothy we have no direct written testimony, but ancient historians describe his period of leadership (460–475 and 476–481) in terms that correspond remarkably to the social profile of latter-day colonial administrators. One recent post-colonialist scholar has pointed out how such administrators (colons) "quickly found themselves in-betweens: neither the centre, the metropolitan government, which could both protect them and oppress them, nor the colonized . . . from whose perspective the *colons* and the metropolitan government would be equated."[34]

Timothy Salofaciolus' public persona in many ways embodied the ambiguities of this liminal administrative figure in colonial society, as he sought to negotiate and keep in balance a complex set of social concerns (a juggling act that would earn him his unique nickname, "Wobble-Hat"). Specifically, even as he continued to cultivate and enjoy the financial and military patronage of the emperor and the churches in Constantinople and Rome,[35] he made a concerted effort to foster local Egyptian support for his leadership. Yet, at the same time, he also tried to seek more autonomy from Constantinople in his own regional authority over the Egyptian dioceses. Thus, he is described by one ancient historian as "a man who sought popularity" and who was "soft and feeble in his actions" toward the dissenting Egyptian church. This capitulating policy was epitomized in his decision to restore Dioscorus' name to the *diptychs* (the list of Alexandrian bishops—in this case, those officially recognized by the Chalcedonian hierarchy). While this drew praise from anti-Chalcedonian Egyptians, it quickly produced tensions with the church in Rome, especially drawing the ire of Pope Simplicius, who pronounced a sentence of excommunication upon Timothy Salofaciolus until the latter defused the situation by apologizing and publicly reiterating his support for the Council of Chalcedon.[36]

At the same time that he adopted a conciliatory policy toward anti-Chalcedonian Egyptian Christians, Timothy "Wobble-Hat" occasionally took a firmer stance in relation to the see of Constantinople as he tried to maneuver for more independence in his exercise of authority over Alexandrian ecclesiastical affairs. Indeed, in a public disputation before the emperor, he went so far as to deny the right of primacy claimed by Constantinople over Alexandria (a right granted at the Council of Constantinople in 381): "I do not accept the Synod which would make your see the next in importance to Rome, and cast contempt upon the honour of my see."[37]

In 475, a change in imperial fortunes would temporarily interrupt Timothy Salofaciolus' efforts to carve out a political niche that would allow him more autonomy as Chalcedonian bishop of Alexandria. Early that year, the emperor Zeno, who had acceded to the throne a few short months before, was forced into exile by a coup led by a naval commander named Basiliscus (the brother-in-law of the former emperor Leo I).[38] Zeno's removal from office would prove short-lived, lasting little more than a year; but, in the meantime, Basiliscus' rise to power caused a sudden shift in imperial lines of religious patronage. He immediately professed his opposition to the Council of Chalcedon, and opened the door for Timothy Aelurus ("the Cat") to return from exile and reclaim the Alexandrian patriarchate.

Timothy the Cat would live for only about two more years, but his actions during that short period show how he continued to pursue his policy of anti-Chalcedonian resistance in ecumenical and local contexts. On his way back to Alexandria, Timothy immediately organized a gathering of like-minded eastern bishops at a synod in Ephesus to repudiate the Chalcedonian canon.[39] From his place of exile, he carried with him "the bones of Dioscorus." Once in the Egyptian capital, he ceremoniously buried the remains of his predecessor in a silver coffin, "laying him in the place of the bishops, and honouring him as a confessor (i.e., martyr)."[40] Through such actions, Timothy was publicly seeking to restore and defend the legacy of Dioscorus as a defender of the faith at the second Council of Ephesus in 449 and as a martyr who died in exile. In the process, he was also consciously representing himself as one who stood in solidarity and continuity with his venerated predecessor.

For his part, Timothy Salofaciolus ("Wobble-Hat") put up little resistance to the return of his namesake rival: suddenly out of political favor, he seemed content simply to retreat to his former monastery outside Alexandria at Canopus. However, when Zeno rallied his forces in 476 and retook the imperial throne from Basiliscus, the political landscape shifted again and the tale of the two Timothies took another turn. Facing the very real possibility of another exile, Timothy the Cat died in July, 477. Within a couple months of his death, Timothy Wobble-Hat reemerged from his monastic retirement and laid claim once again to the Alexandrian bishopric, but not before the anti-Chalcedonian church elected their own candidate as the Cat's successor—a man named Peter Mongus ("the Stammerer").[41] The seesaw battle for control of the Alexandrian see continued into the next generation.

The Politics of Anti-Chalcedonian Compromise: Peter Mongus and His Successors

Peter III Mongus (477–490) entered office with a long pedigree of anti-Chalcedonian resistance: according to sixth-century sources, he is supposed to have been exiled to Gangra with Dioscorus himself after the Council of Chalcedon, and to have headed up an underground resistance with Timothy II Aelurus ("the Cat") during the Chalcedonian episcopacy of Proterius.[42] Having served for over twenty years as Timothy's archdeacon, Peter would have been viewed as the natural choice to succeed him as bishop.

With the return of Timothy Salofaciolus from his retirement in 477 after the death of the Cat (a return sponsored by the emperor Zeno), the newly-consecrated Peter was forced once again to go underground in his leadership of the anti-Chalcedonian majority. However, even while he was in hiding, his influence remained palpable. For his part, Timothy Salofaciolus seems to have regarded Peter as a very real and present threat. The Chalcedonian bishop filed a complaint with the emperor, requesting that Peter be sentenced to exile "because he was hiding in Alexandria and plotting *(insidiabatur)* against the (Chalcedonian) church." However, such a sentence was never carried out.[43]

It should be noted that despite the underground status of its leadership, the anti-Chalcedonian church did not give up on the hope of garnering imperial patronage. Indeed, with Timothy Salofaciolus' health in decline, both parties began jostling over the issue of episcopal succession—namely, over which party would have the right to imperial patronage after Salofaciolus' death. While Peter's supporters sent a petition to Zeno defending his rights as "the lawfully-appointed bishop," Timothy's supporters drafted their own petition, which sought to deny Peter imperial recognition "in the event of the death of Timothy."[44]

When Timothy Salofaciolus finally died in 482, it appeared that the Chalcedonian faction was once more going to prevail in the battle for imperial patronage. One of their number, John Talaia, another Pachomian monk from Canopus, claimed the Alexandrian patriarchate. However, he immediately fell afoul of the emperor and the bishop of Constantinople (Acacius), who suspected him of duplicity, overweening ambition, and treasonous political alliances.[45] The fall of John Talaia caused the emperor Zeno to turn to Peter Mongus in the hope of reestablishing stability to the contentious see of Alexandria. For the previous thirty years, the anti-Chalcedonian patriarchate had been out of favor. Now, Peter Mongus was in the position to regain the very tangible benefits of imperial patronage and ecumenical partnership with Constantinople, but those benefits would come at a costly price—the price of theological compromise.

This compromise came in the form of a doctrinal statement prepared by Zeno and Acacius, the bishop of Constantinople. The statement was called the *Henoticon*, and (as the name suggests) it was meant to establish a basis for unity between the imperial capital and the dissenting churches in Egypt and Syria.[46] The document made overtures to these churches in two ways. First, it reaffirmed the Council of Nicaea, the (First) Council of Ephesus, Cyril's Twelve Chapters condemning Nestorius, and the oneness of the Word made flesh. Second, it anathematized "anyone who has thought, or thinks, any other opinion, either now or at any time, whether at Chalcedon or at any Synod whatsoever, and especially the aforesaid Nestorius and Eutyches."[47] In the process, the language of the new creed inextricably linked this "blameless faith" with the "power" of the empire and with "Roman affairs." By signing this statement of faith, Peter Mongus finally won the emperor's formal recognition of his papal status and made a tangible gesture toward ecumenical rapprochement. Indeed, for a time, the bishoprics of Constantinople, Ephesus, Antioch, Jerusalem, and Alexandria were reunited under Zeno's creed.[48]

However, at the same time, Peter's signing of the *Henoticon* left him open to vigorous criticism at home. The document, despite its condemnation of Nestorius and support for Cyril's Twelve Chapters, used vague language in speaking about the Council of Chalcedon; in fact, it never explicitly condemned the decisions taken there. In the eyes of more radical anti-Chalcedonian Egyptians, Peter's signing of such a creed seemed an act of unforgivable capitulation, a betrayal of the legacy of resistance he had inherited from his predecessors, Dioscorus and Timothy the Cat. In protest, such groups, including a sizable cross-section of the monastic population, "seceded from the communion of Peter."[49] These dissidents came to be called the *Aposchistai* ("Separatists") or the *Akephaloi* ("Headless Ones" or "Leaderless Ones"), since they no longer recognized the authority of their elected patriarch.

Caught between his desire to ameliorate relations with Constantinople and the need to placate outbreaks of unrest among the Egyptian populace, Peter Mongus suddenly found himself "forced to balance on the tautest of tight-ropes."[50] In the face of accusations of betrayal lodged by the so-called Separatists, Peter publicly interpreted the *Henoticon* agreement as one that (1) overruled or usurped the decisions taken at Chalcedon and (2) was consistent with the theological aspirations of the anti-Chalcedonian resistance of his Alexandrian predecessors. Thus, shortly after his return to Egypt, before a large gathering of civic leaders, clergy, monastics, and laypersons, he explained that "this document further cancels and condemns the whole doctrine of Chalcedon and the Tome of Leo, *because Dioscorus and Timothy the Great also thought and expounded similarly*" (my italics).[51]

The public spin that Peter Mongus put on his signing of the *Henoticon* did not satisfy his more radical critics, who objected to the fact that Peter, even though he himself anathematized Chalcedon, was still willing to remain in communion with those who had not anathematized that same council.[52] During his remaining eighteen years in office, Peter would feel compelled to defend his anti-Chalcedonian credentials on numerous other occasions, including an address supposedly delivered before 30,000 people at the Martyr Church of Saint Euphemia in Alexandria.[53] Such public reiterations of his opposition to Chalcedon were motivated by a desire to win back the allegiance of the Separatists and other more radical constituencies of the Coptic church.[54]

And yet, even as he consistently reasserted this anti-Chalcedonian interpretation of the *Henoticon* before an Egyptian audience, Peter Mongus often took a more mollifying approach in his dealings with the Constantinopolitan church. Thus, in an early letter to Acacius, the bishop of Constantinople, Peter three times implies that he has no quarrel with the Council of Chalcedon, agreeing that "it concurred with, and ratified what had been done by, the holy Fathers at Nicaea" and that "nothing new was transacted at it."[55] Peter's ostensible goal was to pacify Acacius, who had heard news of Peter's anti-Chalcedonian reading of the *Henoticon* and who wanted to make a theological inquiry concerning such matters. The letter did help defuse a potential conflict with the bishop of Constantinople, but it also would have undoubtedly contributed to the Separatists' file of complaints against him. In fact, Peter Mongus' success in allaying Acacius' doubts apparently prompted the Separatist party to sponsor a separate inquiry to satisfy their own questions concerning the nature of Peter's theological allegiances.[56] In the end, the persistent pressure that the Separatists exerted may have had some effect: Peter Mongus' last surviving correspondence, a letter to the newly elected patriarch Fravitta of Constantinople written in 490 (the year of Peter's death), shows a marked increase in anti-Chalcedonian rhetoric. In the letter, Peter rejects the idea that the *Henoticon* stood in continuity with the Council of Chalcedon, instead stressing that it in fact "anathematized all the rash thoughts and words of Chalcedon and the Tome of Leo."[57]

Peter Mongus' seeming equivocation in policy has sometimes drawn harsh criticism from ancient and modern commentators: representative of this tendency, the sixth-century chronographer Evagrius labels him an "opportunist" and remarks on his "unstable" character.[58] However, such judgments fail to appreciate the complexity of the social and political situation that he faced as patriarch. In many ways his situation was quite similar to that of another famous Alexandrian "equivocator," his former Chalcedonian rival, Timothy Salofaciolus ("Wobble-Hat"). Both Peter Mongus and Timothy Salofaciolus were Egyptian leaders who sought to maintain or reestablish good relations with a trans-local imperial power, while still appealing to indigenous interest groups in their own region. The situations of the two men differed only in their respective postures toward that local constituency base. While Timothy Salofaciolus had no prior claim upon the tradition of theological resistance, Peter Mongus did have such a claim, and he made concerted efforts to retain his mantle as leader of that resistance even as he was seeking theological and political compromise with Constantinople.

As in the case of Timothy "Wobble-Hat," the social tensions inherent in Peter's leadership suggest cogent parallels to the liminal role of indigenous administrators in modern colonial societies. The aptness of this analogy to colonial cultures may be observed in another important area as well: the production of differentiated forms of theological and political resistance. Those who study colonial cultures have frequently called attention to the heterogeneity of resistance in such settings.[59] In this context, it should not be surprising that Peter's efforts to find a conciliatory middle ground in relation to Constantinopolitan imperial and ecclesial power structures ended up revealing the socially stratified lines of dissent and allegiance that existed among anti-Chalcedonian Egyptians.[60] The shifting nature of such lines of allegiance shows how each form of resistance carried with it elements of compromise and complicity: indeed, even the rigorous, anti-establishment stance of the *Aposchistai* (Separatists) did not prevent them from sending their own delegate to the emperor in order to seek redress in their dispute with Peter.[61]

In the four decades following the death of Peter Mongus (490), the ambiguities and complexities of Egyptian theological resistance did not cease to complicate life for the Alexandrian patriarchs. Peter's successors—Athanasius II (490–496), John I Hemula (496–505), John II Nicaiotes (505–516), and Dioscorus II (516–517)—maintained communion with Constantinople and continued to reap the benefits of imperial patronage.[62] However, the available sources paint an otherwise variegated, even inconsistent, picture of patriarchal policy during this period. On the one hand, Athanasius II and John I Hemula seem to have been reluctant to make Chalcedon an issue of debate with Constantinople, a reluctance that continued to draw the ire of Separatist groups who were still active in Egypt. On the other, John II Nicaiotes was bold enough to demand that the bishop of Constantinople condemn Chalcedon as a basis for ongoing agreement over the *Henoticon*.[63]

The sources also give evidence of further social stratification among Egyptians advocating theological and political resistance against Constantinople. In particular, the events surrounding

Dioscorus II's election in 516 show how, even among the patriarch's diehard supporters, there were those who were agitating against any imperial intrusion in church affairs. First, the clergy who had gathered to witness Dioscorus' consecration, upon noticing that imperial officials were in attendance, objected and demanded that there be another gathering free from the magistrates' intervention. As a result, Dioscorus was taken to another site (the Church of Saint Mark), where he was consecrated without the imperial authorities present. Then, when Dioscorus returned to the original church to celebrate Mass, a crowd "began to abuse the *augustalis* for praising the emperor," and in the violent riots that ensued, this same imperial prefect was killed.[64] The militant actions of the crowd may be contrasted to the views of Dioscorus himself, who would later take a more accommodating posture toward the emperor and toward reconciliation with those who upheld Chalcedon and the *Tome* of Leo.[65]

Therefore, such popular uprisings, even as they purported to endorse patriarchal authority, ultimately had a destabilizing function in relation to that authority. Along with sectarian groups like the *Aposchistai*, one sees in these rioters new lines of differentiation—subtle gradations in ideology and allegiance—within the Egyptian church. Within a generation, such hairline fractures in the Egyptian social structure would split open into gaping fissures. The church in Egypt—and in particular, the Coptic papacy—was about to enter a period of internal schism.

A Period of Internal and Inter-Regional Schism

Alexandria and Antioch, Part One:
An External Catalyst for Internal Division

By the second decade of the sixth century, internal lines of division were appearing in the anti-Chalcedonian church of Egypt;[66] however, it would take external factors to push the church in Egypt into a period of full-blown, internal schism. In particular, two related events in Constantinople and Antioch proved to be catalysts for the exacerbation of rifts in Egyptian ecclesiastical politics.

The first catalyst was a change in imperial rule and policy. Only one year after Timothy III (517–535) had succeeded Dioscorus II as pope of Egypt, the emperor Anastasius I died. During his reign (491–518), Anastasius I had been open in his attitude toward anti-Chalcedonian communities in the East, allowing them to recover and retain the bishoprics of Antioch and Alexandria. However, his successor, Justin I

(518–527), moved quickly to reverse this trend. Seeking rapprochement with the church in Rome, he dismissed a number of anti-Chalcedonian bishops and appointed prelates who were loyal to the Chalcedonian creed.[67] He also expelled anti-Chalcedonian monks from their communities.[68] This "Chalcedonian restoration" spearheaded by Justin I would later be adopted and developed by his nephew and successor, Justinian (527–565). During Justinian's thirty-eight year reign he would make Chalcedonian belief an integral component of imperial legislation and would reestablish (in 538) a Chalcedonian episcopal hierarchy in Alexandra that would survive until the rise of Islam in the mid-seventh century. But such intervention in Egyptian church affairs would not come for another twenty years. For the time being—during the entire reign of Justin I and the first decade of Justinian's rule—Timothy III and the anti-Chalcedonian leadership in Alexandria remained unscathed by this shift in imperial patronage.

The second catalyst for division in the Egyptian church was a direct consequence of the emperor Justin I's new Chalcedonian policies: namely, the exile of prominent anti-Chalcedonian church leaders from their dioceses in Syria and Asia Minor to Egypt. At the same time that this influx of visitors strengthened the ranks of the anti-Chalcedonian church in Egypt, emerging tensions among the visitors ended up creating serious rifts among their Egyptian hosts.

One of those exiled to Egypt was Severus of Antioch, who, during his six years as bishop of Antioch (512–518), had already carved out for himself a reputation as an outstanding exponent of Cyril of Alexandria's "one-nature" Christology and a controversialist who opposed any concessions to Chalcedonian belief. During his twenty-year exile in Egypt (518–538), Severus solidified his role as a leader of anti-Chalcedonian resistance in the East, playing an instrumental role in organizing a clerical hierarchy in opposition to those appointed by the emperors Justin and Justinian. In the process, Severus' interpretation of Cyril in defending the "one nature" *(mia physis)* of Christ[69] became immensely influential for the formation of Egyptian Christian theological identity in the sixth century and beyond. In the later Egyptian *History of the Patriarchs*, he is extolled as "God's champion" and is given more attention than the Alexandrian patriarch Timothy III himself.[70] Likewise, in a thirteenth-century wall painting at the Monastery of Saint Antony at the Red Sea, one finds Severus celebrated as the only non-Egyptian figure in an iconographic program otherwise dedicated to Egyptian popes.[71]

However, Severus' presence in Egypt did not come without its complications. Along with him came a retinue of other exiled Eastern bishops, including a man named Julian of Halicarnassus. For the previous decade, Julian and Severus had been allies for the anti-Chalcedonian cause, but after their arrival in Egypt, differences began to emerge in the details of their theology.[72] The origins of their dispute lay in Julian's teaching that the body of Christ was incorruptible, or uncorrupted (*aphthartos*)—in other words, that it was not subject to the necessity of suffering and death. He drew this conclusion on the basis of the "one-nature" Christology that he shared with Severus. His logic was as follows: if Christ's body was fully united with the divine Word, it must fully share the impassible qualities of that divine Word. Therefore, Christ's (divinized) body could not be fully subject to suffering.[73]

For his part, Severus was not willing to draw the same conclusion: he thought Julian's teaching threatened to obscure the true humanity of Christ in the incarnation. If Christ's body was not subject to suffering, how could one affirm that the Word had truly united itself with a human being? Severus began writing numerous treatises and letters attacking Julian's "erroneous fantasy" as a latter-day christological docetism (the view that Christ's humanity was not real, but only an appearance).[74] Julian responded in kind by accusing Severus of being a closet Nestorian, a secret supporter of a "two-nature" Christology.[75] To him, Severus was speaking of the humanity of Jesus in a way that distinguished it too much from his divine qualities. Of course, as in many theological disputes in antiquity, the accusations hurled in each direction inevitably distorted the views held by the other side.

Thus, while the quarrel between Severus and Julian, in fact, hinged on a fairly technical distinction concerning their use of the term "incorruptible" (*aphthartos*), it soon grew into a "civil war" that involved nearly all sectors of the church in Egypt, including the monasteries and the patriarchate itself. It appears that Pope Timothy III initially welcomed all the theological fugitives without discrimination, offering them refuge within Egyptian monasteries, especially at the famous Enaton monastery, located nine miles west of Alexandria.[76] However, with the outbreak of dissension between the followers of Severus and Julian, the patriarch Timothy was forced to take sides. One ancient witness claims that Timothy vacillated in his support, "sometimes agreeing with one, but at other times agreeing with the other."[77] However, the few fragments that survive from his homilies indicate that he ultimately sided with Severus. Indeed, his language echoes

Severus' writings against Julian: "(Christ) himself was truly human, and he did not want this to be unknown, precluding those who suffer from a fantasy *(phantasia)*."[78] Timothy's choice of words is significant here: the followers of Julian came to be known by their critics as "Phantasiasts" (i.e., those who treat Christ's body as a fantasy, or illusion).[79]

Despite the fact that he faced opposition from the Alexandrian patriarch, Julian gained a vocal following within Egyptian monasteries. The editor of *History of the Patriarchs* describes how many "monks of the desert" became enamored of his teaching, while others (led by those at the Monastery of Saint Macarius) refused to accept it. The result was violent turmoil within such desert communities.[80] Thus, a dispute that originally arose between two fugitive Asian bishops ultimately engulfed the Egyptian church.[81] After the death of Timothy III in 535, the threat that this Severan-Julianist controversy posed to monastic unity would ultimately prove a destabilizing influence on the Egyptian papacy as well.

Social Fragmentation and Internal Schism in Egypt

The forty-two year period spanning the reigns of the Egyptian popes Theodosius (536–566) and Peter IV (575–579) was a time of social and theological fragmentation. If one were to trace a "genealogy" or "family tree" of the Alexandrian patriarchate and anti-Chalcedonian resistance during this period, the result would be a tangled web of now-intersecting, now-diverging branches. (For the brave of heart, I have attempted such a "genealogy" in Appendix 3.)[82] As we shall see, rival factions hotly contested the elections of both Theodosius and Peter IV, and the two patriarchs spent large portions of their tenures physically removed from their seat of authority in the Egyptian capital.

The initial challenge to Theodosius' election in 536 arose as a consequence of the Severan-Julianist division that had already been agitating the Egyptian church for almost two decades. As the secretary to Timothy III, Theodosius had aligned himself publicly with Severus, and his election as patriarch received the endorsement of Severus' loyalists. Thus, when news of his consecration reached the ears of Julian's numerous supporters in Alexandria, it triggered an uprising in the city. The success of this popular revolt attests to the strength of the Julianist movement and to the tenuous status of Severus' following in Egypt at that time. According to the writer Ps.-Leontius, the base of Severan support in Alexandria was primarily limited to those of high social station *(hoi megaloi tês poleôs)*.[83] Almost immediately,

Theodosius was forced out of the city, and a Julianist candidate, Gaianus, the former archdeacon of Timothy III, was put forward in his place. In his sudden rise to office, Gaianus also seems to have drawn on the support of the Separatists *(Aposchistai)*, whose history of dissent traced its roots to the time of Peter Mongus (see above).[84]

The tide would turn quickly. Little more than one hundred days after he had been compelled to flee Alexandria, Theodosius returned and was reinstalled with the aid of an armed legion commissioned by the empress Theodora.[85] As a result, Gaianus' occupation of the patriarchal chair proved short-lived: he was summarily exiled, first to Carthage and then later to Sardinia. However, the patriarchal rift that came to be named after him—the Gaianite Schism—would last much longer. His followers would continue to make rival claims upon Egyptian bishoprics at least into the eighth century A.D.[86]

Back in office, Theodosius made an immediate effort to reconsolidate his authority by convening a local synod and proclaiming his unwavering commitment to the conciliar legacy of his Alexandrian predecessors: the Council of Nicaea, the first Council at Ephesus (against Nestorius), Cyril's *Twelve Chapters*, and Zeno's *Henoticon*. In so doing, he continued to solicit—and receive—Severus of Antioch's support. After the synod was adjourned, Theodosius wrote to Severus to communicate the results and to decry "those who teach an illusion and a fantasy" (i.e., the Gaianites/Julianists). The exiled Antiochene bishop responded in kind by defending Theodosius' "divine designation to the evangelical seat" of Alexandria. In his reply, Severus also used biblical metaphors that strategically cast Theodosius as a persecuted, but faithful, leader of the church, comparing him to the apostle Paul, who was called to suffer for the name of Christ (Acts 9:15), and to Moses' brother, the priest Aaron, who withstood the opposition of the wayward Israelites (Numbers 16).[87]

This image of Theodosius as an apostolic-priestly figure beset by troubles was a rhetorical attempt to reframe his contested authority in biblical terms; however, the picture Severus presented was also grounded in an acute awareness of the ongoing challenges that Theodosius faced in maintaining his position of leadership. Even after the exile of Gaianus, a large cross-section of the populace continued to recognize him (and not Theodosius) as their legitimate patriarch. In this divisive climate, violent riots broke out once again, and in the military clampdown that followed perhaps as many as three thousand of the rioters were killed. Finally, in the midst of such turmoil, and after only one year and four months back in Alexandria, Theodosius was forced to leave the city a second time.[88] As circumstances had it, he would never return—the final thirty years of his life (536–566) he spent in Constantinople, a patriarch in perpetual exile.

In being forced to leave Alexandria a second time, Theodosius weathered pointed accusations from his Gaianist/Julianist opponents that he "shared the sentiments of the emperor."[89] For them, the exiled Gaianus embodied the true Egyptian legacy of resistance, while Theodosius had simply become a pawn in a larger game of Constantinopolitan politics. To be honest, such accusations may have held more than just a grain of truth. During his short time occupying the Alexandrian episcopal throne, Theodosius had found himself increasingly dependent on the imperial arm in trying to maintain his own ecclesiastical authority. The empress Theodora, famous for her anti-Chalcedonian sympathies, had originally lent her considerable influence to support his candidacy for archbishop; and he had relied heavily upon imperial military backing for his safety while in office.[90] For this reason, one modern scholar has referred to Theodosius as a "new Proterius."[91] Proterius had been the original Chalcedonian appointee to fill the Alexandrian bishopric after the Council of Chalcedon in 451—someone who likewise had (unsuccessfully) relied on imperial military aid to bolster his claim to authority.

This comparison to Proterius may seem odd, since Theodosius had long been a staunch opponent of Chalcedonian doctrine. How did he find himself in this position, accused by other anti-Chalcedonians of being in the pocket of the emporer? Part of the reason, of course, may be traced to the nature of the theological divisions that had plagued the Egyptian church since the time of Peter Mongus. Since that time, the Alexandrian patriarchs had largely pursued a politics of conciliation that proved unsatisfactory to more radical anti-Chalcedonians (who, by Theodosius' time, may actually have comprised the majority of the Egyptian population). However, another important factor contributed to Theodosius' quandary as well: namely, the complex theological politics of the emperor Justinian (527–565) and his wife, the empress Theodora (d. 548).

As mentioned earlier, Justinian generally followed his uncle, the Emperor Justin I in pursuing a policy of Chalcedonian restoration; however, his application of that policy during the early years of his reign was often inconsistent. One of the reasons for this was Justinian's pragmatic concern to promote unity among the churches in the Roman

Empire: to that end, he employed a wide variety of means (from coercion to compromise) to bring the dissenting communities together.[92]
Another reason for the emperor's shifting theological politics was
the empress Theodora, whose quiet (and sometimes not-so-quiet)
activism on behalf of anti-Chalcedonian causes offset Justinian's own
theological biases and provided the political patronage that sustained
Theodosius (at least temporarily) in the Alexandrian see. Indeed, for a
short time in 535, she even was successful in maneuvering for
Justinian's "tacit assent" to the election of an anti-Chalcedonian
patriarch at Constantinople as well.[93] This bishop (Anthimus), along
with Theodosius, briefly formed a Severan "axis" in the East before the
Roman Pope Agapetus intervened and convinced Justinian to renew his
campaign against those who opposed Chalcedon.[94] Within the space of
a year, the emperor acted to anathematize and depose Anthimus. The
same fate awaited Theodosius. After Theodosius' escape from the rioting
in Alexandria and arrival in Constantinople in the autumn of 536, the
emperor tried for a year to persuade the Alexandrian patriarch to
endorse the Chalcedonian definition. When Theodosius refused,
Justinian formally deposed him as bishop (the first time an emperor had
unilaterally removed a Christian bishop from office), and installed in
his place a Chalcedonian monk named Paul Tabennesiota.[95]

Thus, with the insertion of Paul Tabennesiota, there were, in fact,
now three rival parties contesting the Egyptian patriarchate: 1) the
Severan churches who continued to recognize Theodosius, 2) the
Gaianite/Julianist communion that retained allegiance to Gaianus and
his successors, and 3) the renewed Chalcedonian hierarchy with Paul
at its head. Angered by this tension-filled atmosphere with many
Alexandrians refusing to recognize Paul's leadership, the emperor
Justinian decided to lock the doors to the city churches. They
remained locked for a year before Justinian reopened them and placed
them in the exclusive hands of the Chalcedonian hierarchy.[96]

With Justinian's sanction, Paul and his successors enacted a policy
of repression against the other parties. The Chalcedonian leadership,
now endowed with even more civil and military power than
Theodosius had previously enjoyed, assumed the role of "soldier-
patriarchs."[97] The effect of this repressive policy can be vividly seen in
the case of the Gaianite community. When the Gaianites elected a man
named Elpidios as bishop in 565, he was summarily arrested by
Justinian and sent into exile (in fact, he ended up dying on the journey
to his destination).[98] Emblematic of this new breed of Chalcedonian

bishop was Apollinaris (551–570), a patrician who had formerly served as a state official under Justinian. Apollinaris arrived in Alexandria with an army escort, which he would later employ to suppress religious dissent by means of force.[99]

The exile of Theodosius (which lasted from 537 to 566), came as a result of this reimposition of a strict Chalcedonian religious policy by Justinian, and yet the shape his exile took was far from conventional. Originally sent away to nearby Thrace (30 miles from Constantinople), Theodosius actually spent most of his "exile' back in the imperial capital itself. It was there, hidden away in the Palace of Hormisdas under the protective eye of his imperial patroness Theodora,[100] that Theodosius began to reshape his image in relation to other anti-Chalcedonian leaders in the eastern Mediterranean.

Indeed, after the death of Severus in 538, Theodosius was able to assume his mantle as the ecumenical head of the anti-Chalcedonian churches through his concerted attempts to reorganize theological resistance among such churches in Syria and Arabia. First, in letters to eastern bishops, he emphasized his indebtedness to Severus (whom he calls "our father" and "ecumenical light") and interpreted the *Henoticon* as an agreement designed "to overthrow the Council of Chalcedon."[101] One of these letters attests his support for "our blessed brother and colleague," Paul, the new bishop of Antioch, whom he would commission as his representative in Egypt during his absence.[102] Second, still claiming his prerogative as Alexandrian patriarch, Theodosius moved to quell further theological divisions that were arising in the anti-Chalcedonian churches of Egypt. In particular, he directed a treatise against the teachings of an Alexandrian deacon named Themistius who claimed that if Jesus fully shared our human nature he must have experienced ignorance in the body.[103] Themistius' adherents— nicknamed by their opponents the *Agnoetai* (derived from the Greek verb, *agnoeô*, meaning "to be ignorant")—remained active into the seventh century.[104] Third, despite the fact that he was effectively under house arrest, Theodosius was able to consecrate new anti-Chalcedonian bishops to serve in Syria and Arabia—respectively, Jacob Baradaeus, the metropolitan of Edessa, and Theodore, the metropolitan of Bostra. Similar attempts to install twelve new bishops in Upper Egypt were thwarted by the Chalcedonian leadership in Alexandria, but the appointments in Syria and Arabia were highly significant, especially in the case of Jacob Baradaeus (sometimes called James Baradai), who went on to become famous for his successful missionary work on behalf of the anti-Chalcedonian churches.[105] On the frontiers of the Roman Empire, missionary activism became a form of ecclesiastical-political resistance.

In a variety of ways, the picture we get of Theodosius' experience in exile overturns traditional binary conceptions of "center" and "margin," and as such, is instructive as we continue to draw analogies between modern forms of colonialism and the role of the early Byzantine church and state in Egyptian ecclesiastical affairs. It has often been observed that the rhetoric of colonial powers has typically sought to accentuate the difference between the imperial "center" and the colonized "margin."[106] This same kind of link between rhetoric and imperial politics can be identified in sixth-century Byzantium as well.

For Justinian, the frontiers of the eastern Roman Empire seemed all-too-permeable and insecure—like partially-drawn pencil lines on a map that are ever in danger of being erased altogether. His international policy was thoroughly committed to plugging the gaps, to redrawing the boundary lines in bold, indelible ink. Egypt was just one of several border regions where the margins threatened to intrude upon Byzantine centrism.[107] The "desert fringes to the west of the Nile"— including the monastic territories of Scetis and the more far-flung Kharga and Dakhla oases—suffered from repeated attacks by nomadic tribes during the fifth and sixth centuries: indeed, during this period, the Byzantine government effectively lost control over their outposts in the southern oases.[108] The island of Philae, a pilgrimage destination connected with the Isis cult at the first cataract of the Nile (just south of modern day Aswan), was another contested border site: there, Justinian moved to suppress indigenous worship of the Egyptian goddess and to replace it with a Christian church (ca. 537). The inscription that was carved at the entrance to the converted temple—"The cross has conquered! It ever conquers!"—was meant to forestall "pagan spirits that might try to creep back into their old sanctuary,"[109] but it also represented an attempt to demarcate cognitive boundaries between the "civilized world" *(oikoumenê)* and its periphery.

Of course, such boundaries were themselves by no means solid or constant. In the case of Philae, after Justinian had suppressed the Isis cult, a conflict arose between his Chalcedonian representatives and the anti-Chalcedonian leadership in Egypt over who would have the right to conduct missions in this border zone among the local Nubian tribes—that is, over who would control the theology of this "civilized world" and who would patrol its borders. The anti-Chalcedonians (secretly aided by Theodora) prevailed in this skirmish, but the skirmish itself unmasks the way that such symbolic boundaries were constantly contested and destabilized.[110]

Theodosius' experience of exile likewise shows how discursive (colonial) categories like "margin" and "center" could be subverted or deconstructed. While still in office at the Egyptian "margins" of Byzantine rule, Theodosius had nonetheless retained intimate access to imperial power, especially in the form of military aid. Later, however, at Constantinople, he found himself disenfranchised of that power—in exile, banished from office, but nonetheless at the "center" of imperial life. In the context of a similar modern confusion over "margin" and "center," one scholar has noted that "the colonized subject who travels to the colonizing center will remain in terms of power and political status on the periphery."[111] And yet, Theodosius, when read as this colonized subject who inhabits a marginalized center, was still able to appropriate the tools of power available to him—most notably, Theodora's beneficent patronage—in shaping a rhetoric and practice of theological resistance.[112]

Theodosius died in 566, only a year after Justinian. However, neither Theodosius' efforts to organize the anti-Chalcedonian movement in the East, nor the change in imperial regime (under Justin II, 565–578), provided a solution for the multi-layered schism that wracked the Egyptian church. If anything, the schism grew worse.[113] The election of Peter IV followed an extended interregnum of ten years during which the Chalcedonian hierarchy successfully thwarted attempts by the anti-Chalcedonian community to name a successor to Theodosius.[114] Furthermore, during Peter's short tenure (576–577), as many as *four* separate patriarchal claimants vied for precedence in Alexandria (see Appendix 3), a situation that would continue for almost another decade under Peter's successor, Damian (578–607). These rival claimants included not only the Chalcedonian bishop John (570–581) and the Gaianite-Julianist bishop Dorotheus (565–after 580), but also another Severan-Theodosian candidate named Theodore.[115]

How did it come to be that Peter IV and Theodore both put themselves forth as Theodosius' legitimate successor? In 575, Theodosius' former proxy, Paul of Antioch, faced with a gaping leadership void among the Severan anti-Chalcedonian community in Egypt, decided to intervene and nominated Theodore (a Syrian monk from one of the monasteries at Scetis) as bishop. Paul's intervention was not received well: three years earlier (571), he had made an aborted attempt to reach a theological compromise with the Chalcedonian emperor Justin II, and in the process had severely wounded his reputation in anti-Chalcedonian circles. The majority of Alexandrians refused to accept Theodore's election. Instead, they elected their own candidate, Peter IV (who also happened to be from a monastic background).[116]

Peter IV moved quickly to consolidate his support both internationally and domestically. First, through a synodical letter written in 576, he was able to secure official recognition of his election from Theodosius' famous protégé, the Syrian missionary Jacob Baradaeus.[117] Second, he appointed seventy new bishops to fill previously vacant dioceses in Egypt, thereby strengthening his own local support up and down the Nile.[118] Finally, Peter also sought to communicate his solidarity with Egyptian monastic communities: with Chalcedonian priests still occupying the churches in Alexandria, he situated his patriarchal headquarters at the Enaton, the monastery located nine miles west of the Egyptian capital.[119]

Such constructive measures helped reconsolidate the anti-Chalcedonian hierarchy in Egypt, but they did not immediately solve the internal schism that plagued the Severan-Theodosian leadership. This internecine feud with the followers of Theodore would last into the papacy of Damian (578–607).[120] And yet, the fragmentation of the anti-Chalcedonian leadership was not limited to internal Egyptian matters. In addition, an equally vexing challenge to anti-Chalcedonian unity would arise on the international stage, and it took the form of a new conflict between the church of Alexandria and the church of Antioch.

Alexandria and Antioch, Part Two: Schism Between Two Anti-Chalcedonian Sees

This conflict between Alexandria and Antioch was fueled by events that took place under the leadership of Pope Damian (578–607),[121] but tensions had already been brewing between the two sees for several years by the time of Damian's election. Indeed, the political roots of this emerging ecclesiastical schism may be traced back to the year 575 and Paul of Antioch's attempt to intervene in the Alexandrian electoral process (see above). Paul's decision to sponsor the Syrian monk Theodore as pope of Egypt (and the Alexandrians' counter-election of Peter IV) had exascerbated the divisions within the anti-Chalcedonian leadership and had added to the growing reservoir of ill feelings toward Paul himself. In the end, Peter IV, along with Jacob Baradaeus and other anti-Chalcedonian leaders in the East, moved to depose Paul from office on account of the fact that he "had entered into communion with the Synodites (i.e., the Chalcedonians)" and "had ordained a certain Theodore of Rhamnis as a patriarch for the Alexandrians without the Alexandrians having been informed."[122]

Now the tables were turned. For the next five years (while Paul of Antioch was still alive, but in exile), there would be a struggle over who was the rightful occupant of the Antiochene episcopal chair, and it was the Alexandrian patriarch, Damian (himself of Syrian background), who made efforts to extend his influence over the process of selecting a successor to the controversial Paul.[123] In 579, on a tour of the eastern Mediterranean, Damian visited Syrian monasteries and stopped in Antioch, where he secretly arranged to have a monk named Severus elected as bishop. However, his plans were foiled when the Chalcedonian bishop of Antioch got wind of his presence and sent his guard to seize him. Damian managed to escape only by sneaking out of the church through the underground sewer system.[124] In the end, Damian's own attempt to intervene in Antiochene affairs only added to the tensions between the two sees. In 580, a young monk named Peter of Callinicum finally assented to become the Antiochene patriarch (he had previously declined on at least three other occasions due to his reluctance to intrude upon that office while Paul was still alive).[125] After his election, it would only take one year before a disagreement between Peter and Damian escalated into formal schism between Antioch and Alexandria.

The nature of their disagreement shows that this schism had not only political roots (as mentioned above in relation to Paul of Antioch), but also theological foundations within the context of the anti-Chalcedonian factionalism that continued to plague the churches in Syria and in Egypt. During the 550's and 560's in Syria and eastern Asia Minor, some anti-Chalcedonian church leaders began to advocate a view of the Trinity that saw God not as consisting of one substance or nature, but of three substances *(ousiai)* or natures *(physeis)*. While exiled in Constantinople, Pope Theodosius of Alexandria wrote a treatise against this viewpoint, condemning it as a form of polytheism that made the Trinity into three separate gods. In this vein, later opponents would dub the proponents of this doctrine "Tritheists."[126]

After Theodosius' death in 566, this so-called "Tritheism" made inroads in Egyptian ecclesiastical and philosophical circles. During the interregnum before the election of Peter IV as pope, the Alexandrian philosopher John Philoponos became its most articulate spokesperson, providing a distinctively Aristotelian basis for the doctrine of three consubstantial substances ("divinities") within the Trinity (see Appendix 3).[127] His writings met staunch opposition among other anti-Chalcedonianists in Egypt: for example, in 567, Bishop John of the monastic settlement Kellia, along with "the entire clergy of the great city of Alexandria," condemned him with a written decree of anathema.[128] Despite this action, the influence of the "Tritheist" movement was still keenly felt a few decades later during Damian's papal reign (A.D. 578–607).[129] Indeed, the dispute between Damian and Peter the bishop of Antioch seems to have been an unexpected result of Damian's efforts to combat Tritheism in his own diocese and in the eastern Roman Empire generally.

From the first years of his patriarchate, the Alexandrian archbishop had begun writing against "Tritheist" doctrine. In doing so, he (like his fourth and fifth century predecessors) worked to cultivate monastic support for his campaign against this perceived theological threat. Damian himself was reportedly trained as a monk in the Wadi al-Natrun, and indeed his memory seems to have been commemorated there in later monastic art (see Fig. 8).[130] This ascetic pedigree may have proved valuable as Damian sought to bring Egyptian monks in line with his anti-Tritheist stance. His success in this endeavor is vividly attested in the archaeological record: a portion of his *Synodical Letter* against the Tritheists is preserved in inscriptional form on a wall in one of the monastic cells at the Monastery of Epiphanius at Thebes (modern day Luxor) (see Fig. 9).[131]

A few years after he wrote this *Synodical Letter*, Damian—who by this time had gained at least informal recognition as the international head of the anti-Chalcedonian churches—composed another work against Tritheism, a *Refutation of Tritheist Chapters* (ca. 586). He sent a copy of this treatise to the bishop of Antioch, Peter of Callinicum, "so that he might examine it and correct in it what was necessary." However, when Peter responded with reservations about "strange expressions" in the treatise that he found "out of key with the Doctors (i.e., the Church Fathers)," Damian took offense and communication between the two sees quickly broke down.[132] While Peter made over-tures to heal the breach, Damian remained decidedly aloof. Soon, both church leaders began venting their displeasure in a public forum. Damian had two letters delivered to Peter in which he accused the latter of being a Tritheist sympathizer; Peter responded with a large-scale treatise *Against Damian* (in three books), in which he declared Damian's theology a brand of Sabellianism (an early Christian heresy that collapsed the distinctions between the persons of the Trinity).[133] Neither accusation was really accurate, but the rhetorical posturing on both sides tangibly heightened the tensions between the sees and led to a formal suspension of communion between the churches in Alexandria and Antioch that would last for almost thirty years.[134]

It would not be until 616—under the leadership of Damian's successor Anastasius of Alexandria (607–619) and Peter's successor Athanasius of Antioch—that the two regional churches would resolve their differences. According to the *History of the Patriarchs*,[135] the Egyptian Pope Anastasius initially broached the subject of repairing relations in a synodical letter addressed to his Syrian counterpart, Athanasius. The conciliatory letter was well-received, and Athanasius (along with his clerical entourage from Antioch) journeyed by ship to Alexandria for an ecclesiastical summit, which took place in one of the Egyptian monasteries along the Mediterranean coast (probably at the Enaton or one of the other monasteries located west of the capital city). There, Anastasius and Athanasius shared a kiss of peace, and issued a joint statement announcing their reunion. This statement, preserved by chronographer Michael the Syrian, emphasizes the common theological heritage celebrated by the two churches, specifically citing the councils at Nicaea (325), Constantinople (381), and Ephesus (431), and the writings of the "divinely inspired" Severus of Antioch as markers of anti-Chalcedonian "orthodoxy." Meanwhile, the rancorous dispute between their predecessors Damian and Peter was deftly swept under the table: "If any heterodox person enquires, 'How do you interpret what was written in the time of difficulty between the blessed archbishops?' we respond: 'The writers have gone to God; as for us, we are united in accord with the presently effected doctrinal agreement.'"[136] With these words, the three-decade-long schism between Alexandria and Antioch was finally healed.

However, the agreement between Anastasius of Alexandria and Athanasius of Antioch did not come with unanimous support. It was no secret that a vocal Egyptian minority opposed the reunion: in one of his letters, Athanasius actually records the names of these dissenters.[137] Counted among those who resisted the idea of a settlement were diehard loyalists to the former Pope Damian, who were not quite so willing to forgive and forget the fact that the Antiochenes had previously anathematized their beloved patriarch. These "intransigents" within the Egyptian anti-Chalcedonian camp may have even taken steps to elect their leader, a man named John, as an "anti-Pope," a new papal rival to Anastasius.[138]

Thus, despite his success in reestablishing a bond of unity with
Antioch, the patriarch Anastasius still faced a divided communion at
home. Splinter groups like this party of "Damianite" dissenters and the
by-now eighty-year-old Gaianite faction were lingering signs of anti-
Chalcedonian disunity in Egypt. In addition to these groups, the
imperially-sponsored Chalcedonian church leadership in Alexandria
also continued to make rival claims on the Egyptian papacy, and
backed those claims with the military and economic power of the
Byzantine state and its interests. Early in his tenure as Pope,
Anastasius endured the seizure of his churches by the Chalcedonian
bishop Eulogius.[139] Later, he faced a more congenial, but equally formidable rival in Eulogius' successor, John "the Almsgiver," whose
lavish forms of public beneficence (e.g., the building of hospitals and
shelters for the poor) competed with and inevitably disrupted traditional anti-Chalcedonian lines of episcopal patronage.[140] Physically
displaced from his churches, faced with the military and economic
enforcement of Chalcedonian hegemony over Alexandria, Anastasius
was forced to take refuge in a monastery outside the city.[141] It was
there, in 616, that he would have to host Athanasius, the bishop of
Antioch, to craft their formula of reunion. And yet, within the space
of three years, the political climate would radically shift and the
Byzantine-Chalcedonian control of Alexandria would be undermined.
A storm was brewing on the eastern horizon: the Persian army was
about to invade Egypt.

New Colonial Rivals and the
End of Byzantine Rule in Egypt

The Period of Persian Occupation (619–629)

The three decades of Egyptian history leading up to the arrival of the
Persian army were marked by episodic fits of social turbulence and
political upheaval. The seventh-century chronicler John of Nikiu (ca.
690) describes the situation in the Egyptian Delta during the reign of
the Emperor Maurice (582–602) as one akin to civil war. At the Delta
city of Aikêlah (Zâwjâ), leading residents of the city led an armed
rebellion in which they commandeered ships plying the Nile grain
trade and intercepted tax payments bound for Constantinople.[142] This
rebellion was made more complicated by the party politics of the local
hippodrome factions, the Greens and the Blues. These factions had
originated as business sponsors and partisan supporters for athletes

competing in the hippodrome chariot races, but had evolved to exert an increasing influence over early Byzantine politics. As a result of their public responsibility for leading the chants of acclamation honoring the emperor in the arena, the Greens and the Blues were privileged recipients of imperial patronage. However, at the same time, they resolutely resisted complete state control of their activities. In the last decades of the sixth century, their resistance to state control sometimes came to expression in the form of local uprisings.[143]

The insurrection in the Delta was not an isolated case. Around the same time, a similar uprising took place at Akhmîm in Upper Egypt under "a rebel named Azarias . . . who mustered a large force of Ethiopian slaves and brigands and seized the imperial taxes."[144] Such localized revolts continued in Egypt during the reign of the usurper Phocas, who in 602 deposed the emperor Maurice and put him to death as part of an imperial coup in Constantinople.[145] Finally, in the years 609 and 610, Alexandria and the Delta served as a pivotal battleground for the would-be-emperor Heraclius (610–641), who funded a military campaign to reclaim the Byzantine throne from Phocas. Heraclius' success in this struggle was determined in part by his ability to regain control once again of revenues from taxation and the grain trade, and to pacify the still-restive hippodrome factions in Egypt.[146] However, by the time the Persians arrived on the banks of the Nile in 618 or 619, this history of civil unrest and political skirmishing had taken its toll. In the clash between Phocas and Heraclius—two pro-Chalcedonian contenders for the imperial throne—the lines of imperial allegiance for the Egyptian Chalcedonian leadership had become quite thorny (there were hazards in lending one's support to the wrong side), and as a result, the Byzantine administrative grip on Egypt was loosened, if ever so slightly.

In fact, the imperial power struggle triggered by Phocas' coup in 602 seems to have been one of the primary catalysts that incited Persians to invade the eastern Roman territories in 603. The emperor Maurice, deposed and assassinated by Phocas and his loyalists, had been a political ally of the Persian shah, Chosroes II. According to one early Byzantine historian,[147] Chosroes II was indebted to Maurice for helping him ascend to the throne in the face of political opposition. When news reached Chosroes II of Maurice's death at Phocas' hands, the Persian ruler decided to initiate what turned out to be a decade-long campaign against Roman settlements in Mesopotamia and Syria (603–613).

Whether Chosroes II's declaration of war against Phocas was due to his sense of loyalty to Maurice, to crass opportunism, or to some combination of the two,[148] it is clear that the Persian aggression was not an isolated incident. Tensions between the Romans and the Sassanian dynasty in Persia had been long in the making. Periodic border crises between the two empires had begun to erupt already in the third century.[149] In the sixth century, Persian incursions on the Mesopotamian frontier early in Justinian's reign had led to a series of ineffectual peace treaties (in 533, 545, 551, and 561) and to the Byzantine practice of making large, regular tribute payments to the Persians in an equally vain attempt to secure their borders.[150]

By 613, after ten years of systematic Persian attacks on eastern Roman installations around the Euphrates river basin and into Syria, and after Heraclius had expended considerable resources in wresting imperial power back from Phocas, the Byzantine Empire had grown vulnerable, and the Persians took advantage. In the space of three years, they captured Damascus (613), Caesarea (613), Jerusalem (614), and Chalcedon (615), advancing to the doorstep of the imperial capital, Constantinople. Four years later, Alexandria fell, and by 620 all of Egypt was in Persian hands.[151]

What effect did this Persian invasion have on the Alexandrian patriarchate and on Egyptian Christian communities? Unfortunately, this question is not easy to answer, since we have relatively little contemporaneous information about the thirteen-year period of Persian rule in Egypt.[152] A handful of Greek and Coptic letters preserved on papyri and ostraca (pottery shards) provide us with only fleeting glimpses of the disruptions and dislocations suffered by Egyptians during the Persian invasion.[153] Later Coptic (or Copto-Arabic) sources that refer to this period tend to put special emphasis on the violent character of the Persian conquests. For example, the ancient editor of the *History of the Patriarchs* laments the Persians' mistreatment of Christians, describing in great detail their destruction of numerous monasteries, including their slaughter of monks living at the Enaton monastery west of Alexandria.[154] The expanded Arabic *Life of Shenoute* (based on a Coptic version that was redacted in the late seventh century) has the Savior appear to Shenoute and prophesy about the coming of the Persians to Egypt—with an emphasis on their "great butchery, . . . (their) persecution and their tyranny."[155]

However, the question remains as to how one should interpret these accounts of Persian violence. While the seventh-century papyrological record would seem to confirm that certain Egyptians did in fact suffer violence during the initial Persian invasions, other evidence suggests that such brutal tactics did not truly characterize the subsequent period of Persian rule. Indeed, one scholar has argued that, once it was established, the Persian administration in Egypt pursued a more general policy of conciliation and sought to maintain the status quo in social and economic affairs.[156] One example of this is the way that the Persians adopted the system of Byzantine administration that was already in place: tax records preserved on early seventh-century papyri from Oxyrhynchus show that the taxation machinery continued to operate as usual throughout this period. The Persians also continued to promote the longstanding Egyptian grain trade, although they re-channeled it away from Constantinople and toward their own war efforts.[157]

The evidence for a Persian public policy of conciliation—at least in the case of Egyptian anti-Chalcedonian Christians—lies in the ability of Popes Andronicus (619–626) and Benjamin (626–665) to remain in Alexandria and to exercise their leadership from their patriarchal seat there throughout the entire period of Persian rule (619–629).[158] Of course, for the Chalcedonian leadership, with its links to Byzantine state authority, the situation was quite different: with the Persian army threatening Alexandria, the Chalcedonian patriarch John the Almsgiver was forced to flee to his native country of Cyprus.[159] In this way, the Persian conquest of Egypt brought about a discernible shift in religious patronage. While the new presence of the Persians disrupted Chalcedonian claims to authority, it ultimately (despite the devastating effect of the Persian invasion on some Egyptian monastic communities) provided an unexpected window of opportunity for the anti-Chalcedonian leadership in Alexandria. However, this window of opportunity would soon slam shut in 629 when the Byzantine emperor Heraclius, fresh from an astonishingly successful military counterattack deep in Persian territory, retook Egypt and reclaimed it for Constantinople.[160]

The Byzantine Recovery in Egypt (629–642)

In the aftermath of his victories over Persia, the emperor Heraclius remained, more than ever, a stauch patron of the Chalcedonian church. During the war, the Byzantine patriarch Sergius had "placed his Church treasure at the disposal of the emperor" in an effort to help fund Heraclius' military "crusade" against the Persians.[161] Now, Heraclius repaid the favor by reestablishing Chalcedonian bishops in the dissenting provinces and equipping them with the economic and military wherewithal to enforce doctrinal adherence. In the case of Egypt, he appointed a man named Cyrus from the Caucasus as his archbishop (631).

Cyrus' appointment was coordinated with theological and social policies designed to bring anti-Chalcedonians back into line with Constantinople, or, failing that, to suppress forms of dissent by force. This two-pronged effort to implement doctrinal uniformity was part of a larger "politics of survival" pursued by the Byzantine state in the face of external threats.[162]

The first tactic took the form of a christological "solution" originally proposed by the emperor Heraclius and Sergius, the patriarch of Constantinople. Their solution, ostensibly designed to appeal to anti-Chalcedonian sensibilities, emphasized the "one will" of Christ. As a result, it later came to be known as "Monotheletism," from the Greek stems *mon(o)-* ("only, single") and *thel-* ("will"). For Chalcedonians like Heraclius, Sergius, and Cyrus, this provided a way of affirming the unity of the human and divine in Christ without abandoning their affirmation of Christ's two natures. Cyrus was charged with the task of promoting the "one will" doctrine in Alexandria, and his efforts seem to have been at least partially successful. There is evidence that a number of anti-Chalcedonians embraced this christological solution in a formal *Charter of Union between the Melkite Patriarch Cyrus of Alexandria and the Theodosians* (although they themselves probably interpreted the "one will" formula as consonant with "one nature" rather than "two nature" belief).[163] However, the majority of Christians in Egypt rejected Monotheletism. By this time, they had come to see any doctrine sponsored by Chalcedonian patriarchs as theologically suspect.[164] Later in the seventh century, Monotheletism would also founder on the rocks of controversy within Chalcedonian circles (e.g., in Rome), where it began to be viewed as too much of a concession to so-called "Monophysite" belief.[165] In the end, despite their numerous areas of intersecting belief, the Chalcedonians and anti-Chalcedonians were politically as far apart as ever, especially in the ranks of leadership.

With the failure of such attempts to forge a christological agreement, the Byzantine government and the Chalcedonian patriarch Cyrus increasingly turned to military force, economic disenfranchisement, and social displacement as a means to suppress anti-Chalcedonian resistance in Egypt. Later Coptic sources excoriate Cyrus for his repressive tactics—tactics that had severe consequences for the anti-Chalcedonian church in Egypt under Pope Benjamin (626–665). The seventh-century *Chronicle* of John, bishop of Nikiu, reports how Cyrus "robbed the (anti-Chalcedonian) church of large possessions in the time of the persecution, without any authorization on the part of the magistrates."[166] Along these lines, a Coptic homily attributed to Pope Benjamin himself labels Cyrus as "the criminal" or "the lawless one" *(paranomos)*.[167] In addition to the confiscation of churches, Cyrus (in close association with the emperor Heraclius) is accused by Coptic authors of initiating a new wave of persecution, including methods of terror and physical torture, against the anti-Chalcedonian community.

The monastic *Life of Samuel of Kalamun*,[168] a work preserved in a ninth-century manuscript but with elements that possibly trace back to the seventh century, describes Cyrus' attempts to impose his authority over the monks of Scetis and the Fayûm, and at the same time the monastic resistance to Cyrus that the monk Samuel spearheaded in these areas. The author of the *Life* pointedly portrays Samuel's resistance in anti-Chalcedonian terms. First, the "Monothelite" edict that Cyrus had delivered to Scetis is erroneously (or perhaps quite purposefully) identified with the *Tome* of Leo. Then, when Samuel hears the edict read, he publically rejects it by taking the text and ripping it up in the presence of the magistrate: "We do not accept this Tome or that which is written in it, nor yet do we accept the Council of Chalcedon, nor do we have any archbishop but our father Apa Benjamin . . . Anathema to this Tome. Anathema to the Council of Chalcedon . . ."[169] Within the context of the story, the mention of "Apa Benjamin" is not random. Cyrus had originally sent emissaries to the monasteries in order to find and arrest Pope Benjamin, who had been forced to go into hiding outside Alexandria. Thus, in Samuel's demonstrative speech and actions, one observes once again how the rejection of Chalcedonian doctrine among Egyptian monks remained intimately connected with their sense of solidarity with their archbishop.

In reaction to Samuel's public rejection of Monothelite doctrine (and by extension, Cyrus' authority), the magistrate resorted to violence.

> He (the magistrate) caused ten soldiers to flog him (Samuel) at once, until everyone said that he was already dead. . . . After this he made them bind his feet and suspend him. Then they fixed him on stakes and tortured him until his blood flowed like

water. A thong which an attendant held slipped from his hand and fell on his right eye, whereupon his pupil immediately burst and spilled down upon his cheek.[170]

After the magistrate "returned to his senses" and granted Samuel a reprieve (on account of his horrific eye injury), Samuel was driven out of town by the soldiers and ended up resettling at Mount Kalamun (= Calamon) in the Fayûm (approximately 150 kilometers south of Scetis).[171] However, after a short while, Cyrus renewed his "persecution" of anti-Chalcedonian monks, and took Samuel into custody once again. Again he was chained, flogged, and beaten to within an inch of his life. Throughout the ordeal, Samuel is said to have stood firm, equating Cyrus' civil rule with the temporal rule of the devil and castigating him as a "son of Satan," a "deceiving Antichrist," and a "Chalcedonian heretic."[172]

Regardless of whether or not one accepts this account as historical,[173] what is important to note here is the way that Coptic self-identity was being framed anew through the production of a new generation of "martyr literature." Even though Samuel does not succumb to death as a result of his injuries, he is nonetheless celebrated as a "confessor and athlete of the orthodox faith" and "one who became a martyr many times without losing his life."[174] Indeed, the narration of his story bears three important hallmarks of ancient Christian martyrologies: (1) a confrontation and verbal exchange with a governmental magistrate (here identified with the Chalcedonian hierarchy), (2) vivid descriptions of bodily tortures that are heroically endured, and (3) specific, coded metaphors, such as Samuel's worthiness of the three "crowns" (of martyrdom) as a result of his struggle.[175] One sees the production of martyr accounts in other contexts as well. For example, the *History of the Patriarchs* contains a brief account of the brutal torture and martyrdom of Pope Benjamin's brother Mennas at the hands of the emperor Heraclius and Cyrus.

> And Heraclius seized the blessed Mennas, brother of the Father Benjamin, the patriarch, and brought great trials upon him, and caused lighted torches to be held to his sides until the fat of his body oozed forth and flowed upon the ground, and knocked out his teeth because he confessed the faith; and finally commanded that a sack should be filled with sand, and the holy Mennas placed within it and drowned in the sea. . . .

> For they took the sack, and conveyed him to a distance of seven
> bowshots from the land, and said to him: 'Say that the council
> of Chalcedon is good and not otherwise, and we will release
> thee.' But Mennas would not do so. And they did this with him
> three times; and when he refused they drowned him. Thus
> they were unable to vanquish this champion, Mennas, but he
> conquered them by his Christian patience.[176]

Here again one observes the same constituent elements of ancient
martyrologies: an encounter with the authorities (in this case the martyr remains silent in the face of their threats), graphic depictions of the
tortures inflicted upon the martyr, and stock metaphors describing the
martyr as the true victor or "champion" in the struggle—the one who
overturns imperial pretensions to power, who ultimately "vanquishes"
those who sought to vanquish him. It is noteworthy that in both
cases—in the *Life of Samuel of Kalamun* as well as in the account of
Mennas' martyrdom in the *History of the Patriarchs*—these Coptic
writers employ the conventions of early Christian martyrology to subvert (and yet at the same time they also reproduce) the kinds of rhetorical oppositions that were being utilized by their Chalcedonian
"oppressors."[177]

In this literature, Pope Benjamin is inextricably linked to this
martyr legacy on several levels: through his role as the monastic patron
of Egyptian monks who suffered in allegiance to him, through his own
blood ties with his martyred brother, but also through his own suffering
as a displaced patriarch, a leader exiled in his own land. In the *History
of the Patriarchs*, an angelic messenger reveals to him the necessity of
his facing what would turn out to be a decade-long flight from Cyrus'
persecution: "Flee thou . . . for great troubles will come upon you. But
take comfort, for this conflict will last only ten years." It is in this
immediate context—the necessity of taking on the hardship of such a
flight—that the editor grants Benjamin the status of "the confessor, the
militant by the power of our Lord Jesus Christ."[178]

Benjamin's exile within Egypt, his time of hiding out in the
Egyptian monasteries of the Fayûm and Upper Egypt,[179] and the
remembrance of that exile in later Coptic literature, were crucial factors in the formation of Coptic social and religious identity, an identity that was conditioned by and grew out of colonial social dynamics.
In the eyes of Copts during the seventh-century and later, Benjamin's
counterpart and adversary Cyrus became the embodiment of the ever-

deepening alliance of Chalcedonian religious interests and Byzantine imperial policy. In this light, the *History of the Patriarchs* describes the Chalcedonian patriarch as a "governor *(wâlî)* to the land of Egypt," a "prefect *(wâlî)* and patriarch at the same time."[180] Given the still-valid provisions of Justinian's legislation (538) on the administrative organization of Egypt, one must recognize such statements as tendentious: Cyrus legally could not have been able to serve as the "prefect" over all of Egypt.[181] And yet, despite its apparent "unhistorical" basis, this account in the *History of the Patriarchs* speaks volumes about Coptic *perceptions* of Chalcedonian influence.

In this context, the origins of this tradition about Cyrus as "prefect and patriarch" prove significant. On the basis of a manuscript variant in a text entitled *The Book of the Consecration of the Sanctuary of Benjamin*, one scholar has argued convincingly that this tradition originated in Upper Egypt.[182] Such a provenance might correlate this tradition with Benjamin's decade of exile in Upper Egypt, during which Chalcedonian and anti-Chalcedonian sentiments became increasingly polarized. In that region, Cyrus' public image contrasted sharply with that of Benjamin. Over against Cyrus' perceived investment in imperial mechanisms of power, the exiled Pope Benjamin is represented as a disenfranchised "colonial subject"—a figure who is marginalized and divested of certain forms of religious-political power, but who nonetheless functions as an icon of resistance.[183]

This heightened sense of displacement among Egyptian anti-Chalcedonian Christians (of which Benjamin became the primary symbol) also helped produce a religious self-consciousness that was increasingly framed in ethnic terms.[184] In both the *Life of Samuel of Kalamun* and the *History of the Patriarchs*, the Chalcedonian patriarch Cyrus is repeatedly referred to not by his given name, but by an epithet that indicated his conspicuously foreign, ethnic origins—"the Colchian," or in other words, "the Caucasian."[185] This rhetorical strategy may be starkly contrasted with other statements in the *History of the Patriarchs* that explicitly seek to underscore the native Egyptian character of the anti-Chalcedonian resistance to Cyrus. Most notably, the editor of the *History of the Patriarchs* praises a certain monastery, the Monastery of Metras, as (reportedly) the only monastery that remained faithful to the anti-Chalcedonian cause, and attributes this to the fact that "the inmates of it were exceedingly powerful, being Egyptians by race and all of them natives *('ahl)*, without a stranger *(gharîb)* among them."[186]

To identify such rhetoric as an incipient political "nationalism" would be anachronistic: the Copts did not voice aspirations of supplanting the Byzantine emperor with their own form of government. Revolution was simply not in the realm of possibilities.[187] Nonetheless, a new kind of self-constructed identity was emerging. During the last period of Byzantine rule in Egypt and in its aftermath, the anti-Chalcedonian majority began to talk about themselves as a distinctive people (in Arabic, *'ahl*). In this way, a type of populist "national culture" was constructed,[188] a shared community defined in terms of religious-ethnic solidarity and created through the production of "minority discourse" (although in the present case it was actually the majority of Egyptian Christians who employed this minoritarian way of talking and thinking).[189] This discourse operated as follows. First, the dominant, imperial church was increasingly labeled as foreign (despite the fact that some members of the Chalcedonian church in Egypt were Copts).[190] And second, native Egyptian identity was implicitly identified with anti-Chalcedonian opposition.[191] The cultural production of this "minority discourse" underscores the fact that the social dynamics produced by Chalcedonian imperialism and ecclesiastical colonialism continued to play an enormous role in shaping perceptions of the Egyptian papacy and of Coptic religious identity on the eve of the Arab invasion.

From Byzantine to Arab Rule: Continuity of Identity in the Midst of Change (642–)

This volume will end with a brief look at the transition from Byzantine to Arab rule in Egypt. What were the factors that led to the Arab invasion? What were the social and political implications for the Coptic patriarchate? And finally, how was Egyptian Christian identity shaped in the early years of Arab rule?

Since the fourth century A.D., the Arab tribes living on the Roman-Persian frontier had played a vital military and political role as vassal clients of those two major powers. Most notably, the Lakhmids were crucial military allies of the Persians, while the Ghassanids headed a semi-autonomous, pro-Byzantine federation of Arab tribes. For over two centuries, these tribes operated in the military "buffer-zone" between the two empires, providing security for their respective imperial patrons in exchange for payment.[192] However, when Heraclius' defeat of the Persian army in the late 620s "upset the internal Persian equilibrium," a power vacuum was created—one that would quickly be filled by the Arabs, united under the common creed of Islam.[193]

When it came, the Arab invasion of Persia and the eastern Roman territories advanced rather swiftly. Only four years after the death of the prophet Muhammad (632), the Arabs celebrated a victory over the Persians at al-Qâdisiya (635–636). Within the space of ten more years, the Arab armies took Jerusalem, occupied Alexandria and much of the Egyptian Delta (640–642), and began military forays into Libya (645). A brief Byzantine recapture of Alexandria in 645 was quickly reversed, and by 646 the Arabs had solidified their control over the Egyptian capital.

The significance of the Arab conquest for Egyptian Christians has been much debated. According to the traditional view—still often cited—the coming of the Arabs marked a decisive turning point for Christians living in the eastern Mediterranean. Scholars studying the history of Christianity in Egypt have often characterized the Arab victory over the Byzantines as having a "drastic impact" and as the cause of "profound and lasting changes" to the political and religious landscape.[194] Along these lines, one Byzantine historian has asserted that Islam effectively sealed "the end of Late Antiquity."[195]

Linked with this theory of sweeping cultural change is a corollary emphasis upon the ways in which the fortunes of anti-Chalcedonian Christians, once subjugated under Byzantine rule, were radically improved under the Arabs. Indeed, historians have routinely attributed the rapid and overwhelming success of the Arab campaigns (at least in part) to the religious dissension and mutual antagonism that existed between the Chalcedonians and anti-Chalcedonians, interreligious tensions that are seen to have made the eastern Roman territories more vulnerable to an external threat. On the basis of references in later Arabic literature, many have assumed that anti-Chalcedonian Christians were united in seeing the Arabs as liberators, and that its leadership even collaborated with the Arabs in overthrowing Byzantine rule.

In recent decades, however, scholars of late antique Christianity and early Islam have begun to reassess such assumptions. With regard to the reception of the Arabs by Egyptian Christians, a broader survey of the available evidence shows a decidedly mixed range of perspectives. While the ninth-century Muslims historians Ibn 'Abd al-Hakam (d. 871) and al-Baladhuri (d. 892) and the tenth-century Christian writer Eutychius (d. 940) all claim that the Copts offered aid to the Muslims,[196] earlier Coptic authors writing in the seventh century evince fairly negative reactions to the Arab invasion.[197] A *Homily on the Child Saints of Babylon*, composed and delivered in Egypt shortly after the arrival of the Arabs, describes them as "oppressors" who "lead into captivity the sons of men."[198] Another Coptic writer, John of Nikiu (writing ca. 698), at one point compares the Arabs' heavy "yoke" unfavorably to that of the biblical Pharaoh (though it must be conceded that almost immediately thereafter he explicitly praises the Arab commander, 'Amr ibn al-'Âs, for preserving the churches).[199] The evidence for Christian attitudes toward their Muslim conquerors, even within individual authors, varies considerably.

Another claim made by later writers—that Pope Benjamin himself had worked out with 'Amr in advance an agreement for the surrender of Egypt[200]—also proves misleading. In fact it was Cyrus, the Chalcedonian patriarch who originally negotiated such a truce, only to die shortly thereafter and to have the truce dissolve.[201] During the early years of the Arab invasion, Benjamin was simply not in the position to negotiate terms of surrender, as he was still in hiding. Both John of Nikiu and the *History of the Patriarchs* make clear that Benjamin did not return from his self-imposed exile in Upper Egypt until after the Arab army had finally secured Alexandria.[202]

In the end, the recent reassessment of available sources produces a strangely disunified picture. While the Arab armies benefited at times from local forms of cooperation (as in the case of the Alexandrian governor Sanutius reported in the History of the Patriarchs),[203] there is also evidence that they met initial native Coptic resistance in some quarters (such as at Sakha and Damietta in Lower Egypt, and at Antinoe in Upper Egypt).[204] Unquestionably, the dissension between the Chalcedonians and the anti-Chalcedonians influenced the way that many Egyptian Christians interpreted the military incursions that were reshaping the political landscape: Coptic writers (regard-less of their attitude toward the new Arab presence) frequently attribute the Arab victories in battle to God's judgment upon the wayward faith of the Byzantine emperor and the Chalcedonian church.[205] However, to what extent such dissession facilitated Arab military success remains a debatable point. Perhaps the most one can say is that intercommunal conflict among Christians was one of sev-eral negative factors (including inferior Byzantine military strategy and intelligence, inadequate human resources, unstable supply lines, and some measure of "fatigue" after the Persians wars) that set the conditions for a swift and successful Arab invasion.[206] In short, Egyptian Christian attitudes toward the Arabs were quite mixed. Such a range of different responses among anti-Chalcedonian Copts should not be surprising, for historians have learned to expect heterogeneity in the resistance and complicity practiced by colonized peoples.

Finally, how might we assess the question of social and cultural change under this nascent Arab rule? As I mentioned above, most scholars studying this period have accentuated the discontinuities brought about by the coming of the Arabs and the rise of Islam in Egypt (and in the Middle East as a whole). Indeed, it would be folly to deny that there were changes. On a geopolitical level, the Arab invasions had the effect of breaking down internal borders and reshuffling political alliances, and the result was an inevitable increase in "human interaction across social, ethnic, and religious lines," as well as in "the circulation of ideas and information."[207] In the case of the Egyptian papacy, the establishment of Arab rule brought about a reversal in the pattern of disruption and displacement experienced under previous Byzantine administrations during the seventh century. For the preceding forty years, the geographical fortunes of the Egyptian popes had ebbed and flowed in relation to the vicissitudes of imperial rule. The anti-Chalcedonian patriarch Anastasius (607–619) had been forced out of Alexandria under the emperor Phocas (602–610) and remained there at least during the first nine years of Heraclius' imperial reign. Popes Andronicus (619–626) and Benjamin were able to maintain their office within the city during the eleven years of Persian occupation (619–629). However, Benjamin was forced out yet again with the reimposition of Byzantine rule in 629. It was only with the Arab ouster of the Byzantine government that Benjamin was able to return from hiding and take up his chair in Alexandria once more.

And yet, in the midst of such changes, one can identify important lines of continuity in the experience of the Coptic church and its leadership. The Arabs inherited a world in flux, and in establishing their own governance they advanced larger cultural and political trends already in evidence under the Byzantines. In particular, they contributed to the ongoing shift of geopolitical power to the eastern Mediterranean (as represented by Constantinople, Persia, and now Arabia); they participated with the Byzantines in a movement toward more centralized and authoritarian rule; and they promoted the continued linking of religious and state interests. In addition, the Arabs borrowed much from the Byzantine administrative structure: the Arabs retained Egyptian civil servants in their positions, and—at least until around the year 700—they continued to use Greek as the official language for imperial account books and minted coinage very similar to that of the Byzantine emperors.[208]

How, then, might we describe the mix of social change and continuity that accompanied the arrival of the Arabs, while taking into account the varying and sometimes contradictory assessments of the Arab invasions espoused by Egyptian Christian writers? One solution is to see the establishment of the new Arabic administration in Egypt as *the replacement of one form of colonial rule by another.* Thus, even as the presence of the Arabs produced a shift in colonial allegiances, familiar forms of economic and religious patronage continued to mark the relationship between the Arabs (as colonizing power) and the Copts, who still found themselves in the role of colonized subject.

One can observe how such patronage relationships were reframed in the case of Pope Benjamin and in the circumstances surrounding his return from exile within Egypt. According to the *History of the Patriarchs,* Benjamin's return (ca. 644–645) was facilitated by an agreement worked out with the Arab commander 'Amr ibn al-'Âs after the death of Benjamin's rival Cyrus (the Chalcedonian patriarch) and after the Arab armies had taken "full possession of the city of Alexandria." 'Amr granted Benjamin "protection and security" and the freedom to administer the affairs of the Egyptian churches; he also returned to Benjamin property formerly controlled by the Chalcedonian bishopric in Egypt. In exchange, he requested intercessory prayer on behalf of the Arab troops in their upcoming Libyan campaign.[209] Of course, the Arabs' expectation of allegiance and loyalty from their Coptic clients was not limited to spiritual intercession: they also soon implemented a special poll tax *(jizya),* which was obligatory for non-Muslim citizens in order for them to retain their status of "protected persons" *(dhimmî or 'ahl al-dhimma).*[210]

Under the protection of Arab patronage, Pope Benjamin was free to begin renovating and rebuilding churches confiscated or neglected under Byzantine rule. Such building projects were one way that the Egyptian papacy attempted to stamp its historical identity on the panorama of Egyptian culture under the new Muslim administration. In architectural adaptation, artistic patronage, and the production of narratives that linked such activity to the past, one recognizes by now familiar practices and discursive strategies through which the Coptic (anti-Chalcedonian) church renewed its claims upon local sacred space.

First, there are suggestions in the *History of the Patriarchs* that Benjamin's return to office was coordinated with the miraculous preservation and rediscovery of the head of Saint Mark after the church dedicated to the evangelist had been burned during the Arab-Byzantine battle that raged in Alexandria. In that account, a ship captain under the anti-Chalcedonian duke Sanutius (= Shenoute) enters the church after it was plundered and secretly rescues "the head of the holy Mark." Later, Benjamin himself has a dream-vision in which a man "dressed in the garments of the disciples *(thiyâb al-talâmîdh)*" appears to him and requests that he "make a place for me with you, in order that I may abide therein this day." Immediately following this vision, the precious relic is "rediscovered" when the sea captain's ship refuses to sail until the captain divulges his secret. In the midst of the subsequent celebrations, the duke Sanutius offers the patriarch money to "rebuild the church of the Holy Mark." These reported events—the original rescue of the relic of Saint Mark's head and its miraculous rediscovery—function as narrative elements that bracket and highlight the account of Benjamin's pact with 'Amr and his return to Alexandria.[211]

If this story goes back to the time of Benjamin's reign (and I think it probably does), it would likely represent an attempt by Benjamin, newly reinstated in Alexandria, to lay claim once again to the apostolic legacy of Saint Mark through the promotion of his relics. The *History of the Patriarchs* reports that he made plans (and acquired sources of funding) for the rebuilding of Saint Mark's church, but never indicates that this work was completed on his watch. Benjamin may have also sought to promote the veneration of Mark's relics in conjunction with other building projects, such as the construction and consecration of a new church at the Monastery of Saint Macarius in the Wadi al-Natrun (ancient Scetis). One of the chapels of the seventh-century church was originally dedicated to Saint Mark, and the head of the evangelist may have been temporarily transferred to that site and housed there during this period.[212]

Benjamin's architectural patronage of the Saint Macarius monastery was another way that he was able to represent himself as heir to a rich monastic and patriarchal past. His consecration of the new sanctuary at the monastery (a sanctuary that to this day remains dedicated in his name) is celebrated in a work entitled *The Book of the Consecration of the Sanctuary of Benjamin*, which survives in at least five different manuscripts from the monastic library at Saint Macarius, as well as in the *History of the Patriarchs*.[213] The earliest manuscript (in Coptic) dates to the tenth century, but internal textual evidence (especially the extensive use of Greek terms, and specific social and topographical details) suggest that the original text traces back much earlier, perhaps to within a generation of Benjamin's life. The *Book* itself purports to be based on Benjamin's own testimony but recorded by his protégé and successor, Pope Agathon.[214]

In the narrative, Benjamin experiences a private vision of Saint Macarius while consecrating the church. As he is contemplating "the people and the monks and the priests" gathered around him, he sees one whose face "shone brightly," and after recognizing him as the saint, he lauds him as "the father of the patriarchs and bishops" and "the spirit-bearing father of all the monks."[215] Later, after the consecration is over, he conveys the news of his vision in similar terms: "I have seen the father of the patriarchs and the bishops and all the doctors of orthodoxy standing in our midst today."[216]

It may very well be possible that this description of Benjamin's vision was actually inspired by the iconographic program commissioned for the church. Another Coptic manuscript (preserved in Paris) actually provides details about the interior decoration of the seventh-century church in which Benjamin was supposed to have had his vision. According to this manuscript, images of famous Egyptian monks and patriarchs originally graced the walls of the sanctuary, and Macarius was featured prominently in one of the iconographic pairings arrayed around the worship space: Antony and Paul, Pachomius and Macarius, Mark and Peter (the Alexandrian bishop and martyr), Athanasius and Liberius (a fourth-century Roman pope who was deposed for refusing to accept the condemnation of Athanasius), Cyril and Dioscorus.[217] These figures (with the exception of Liberius) constitute a virtual pantheon of Egyptian monastic and ecclesiastical heroes—revered saints who appear regularly in the iconographic programs of later Egyptian monastic churches.[218]

The monks at Saint Macarius who preserved this consecration tradition would have been intimately familiar with this visual program. In this context, one wonders whether the representation of Pope Benjamin consecrating the church in the ecstatic presence of Macarius—along with the patriarchs, bishops, and monks in his company—was in fact meant to highlight for this monastic readership not only Benjamin's apostolic and martyrological pedigree (represented by Mark and Peter of Alexandria),[219] but also his solidarity with the Egyptian monks (represented by Antony, Paul, Pachomius, and Macarius) and his faithfulness to a legacy of christological teaching that was read through the lens of anti-Chalcedonian resistance (represented by Athanasius, Cyril, and Dioscorus).[220]

This imaginative reconstruction of the way that ancient monks would have "read" the figure of Benjamin in the *Book of the Consecration* reveals how, on the cusp of a new era, the Egyptian popes continued to function as living metaphors for local piety and practice. In the person of Benjamin, one can see finally how the discourses that so vitally shaped the self-perceptions of the Egyptian church and its leadership over the previous centuries—apostolicity, martyrdom, monastic patronage, christological resistance—remained defining markers of identity for Copts as they adjusted to the new realities of Arab rule and to the rise of Islam.

Epilogue
The Making of the Coptic Papacy

During the first six and a half centuries A.D., the social identity of the Egyptian church and its leadership was shaped by a diverse set of discursive practices. In this book, I have called attention to four recurrent strategies of representation that proved determinative for the cultural construction of the Coptic papacy in late antiquity: apostolicity, martyrdom, monastic patronage, and theological resistance.

These discourses were by no means ideologically neutral: all of them originated in situations of conflict where they were used to negotiate contested claims of authority surrounding the role of the Egyptian papacy. In the second and third centuries, the discourses of apostolicity and apostolic succession played a key role in cultural disputes between intellectual and institutional models of authority. In these disputes, a rising class of Alexandrian bishops increasingly moved to bring the teaching office of the church under their purview. Later, in the third and early fourth centuries, a rhetoric of solidarity with the martyrs emerged in the midst of ecclesiastical debates over the proper response to the threat of persecution and to the dilemmas raised by lapsed Christians. By identifying themselves as friends of the martyrs, bishops and other church leaders sought to appropriate the *charisma*—the spiritual power—of those who had suffered for the faith, and redirect that power in the exercise of their own clerical policies. The fourth and early fifth centuries marked the rise to prominence of monastic communities in Egypt, communities that offered a powerful (and sometimes quite volatile) base of grassroots support for Alexandrian episcopal authority. In the midst of doctrinal controversy at home and abroad, Alexandrian patriarchs like Alexander, Athanasius, Theophilus, and Cyril consistently portrayed themselves as privileged monastic patrons and offered material forms of benefaction to monasteries in an effort to win the allegiance of Egyptian monks away from theological rivals. Finally, during the final two centuries of Byzantine rule in Egypt, an ethos of theological resistance gripped the Coptic church. Often politically disenfranchised and geographically displaced, the Egyptian popes in this period produced a complex rhetoric of resistance that was crafted as a response to colonial models of ecclesiastical control and often deployed as a standard for adjudicating internal disputes.

And yet, even though these strategies of representation were each forged in the midst of specific conflicts, it was their adaptability to different times and to different social settings that allowed them to exert such a profound influence over the ways that ancient Copts perceived themselves and their leadership. As discursive "events," they became etched in Egyptian cultural memory and were eminently "open to repetition, transformation, and reactivation."[1] One example of this is the way that Alexandrian popes recycled the discourses of apostolic succession and martyrdom, and utilized them in new contexts. Thus, while the concept of apostolicity was originally applied as a mark of pedigree in second- and third-century disputes over the intellectual authority of teachers and the institutional prerogatives of bishops, it could also be used in the early fourth century by Peter I of Alexandria to justify his actions in the face of persecution, and in the fifth century by Timothy II Aelurus ("the Cat") to defend the legitimacy of his theological resistance to the Council of Chalcedon. Late ancient discourses of martyrdom proved equally malleable. Well after the era of Roman persecution had ended, the Alexandrian bishop Athanasius self-consciously employed martyr rhetoric as part of his campaign to cultivate monastic support for his leadership,[2] and his successors Theophilus and Cyril invoked the spirit of martyrdom to stir up anti-pagan activism among the monks. Later, under Byzantine oppression, exiled Egyptian popes cast themselves in solidarity with the martyrs, and the Coptic church produced a new generation of martyr literature.

A final example of this adaptability is the way that such representational strategies could be combined—interwoven, if you will—in discrete social settings. For instance, in historical and theological literature, the phenomenon of exile or physical displacement could simultaneously be rendered as a venue for solidarity with the suffering of the martyrs, a context for the renewal and deepening of monastic patronage ties, and a locus for redefining that displacement as a necessary corollary of faithful theological resistance.

As we have seen, this potential for the interweaving of cultural discourses is also evident in Coptic art and liturgy where the Alexandrian
patriarchs were visually displayed—and ritually re-imagined—in the
company of apostles, martyrs, and monks. A further, striking illustration
of this is found in an eleventh-century wall painting at the Monastery
of the Archangel Gabriel (Deir al-Malâk) on the desert outskirts of the
Fayûm Oasis, where the image of the patriarch Peter I is actually
assimilated to that of the apostle Peter (see Fig. 10). In the apse of the
monastic church, the figure in question stands in a row of twelve apostles and carries a biblical roll marked in Coptic lettering as "the Epistle
of Peter." At first glance, this would appear to be a conventional representation of Saint Peter the apostle. However, the dress of the figure
distinguishes him from the other apostles depicted in the church: Peter
wears the robe of a bishop and a monk's hood. Two accompanying
Coptic inscriptions identify him as both "the apostle Peter" and "Peter
the archbishop." In this painted image, Peter I of Alexandria, the
famous martyr pope, is re-visualized in the roles of monk, bishop, and
apostle.[3] Such iconography vividly demonstrates how the public image
of the early Egyptian popes was, in effect, "made" through the creative
intersection of selected cultural discourses, almost as the design on a
piece of fabric is woven together by different colored strands.[4]

Ultimately, through their reiteration (and recombination) in
Coptic literature and art, the discourses of apostolicity, martyrdom,
monastic patronage, and theological resistance became inextricably
linked with the institutional memory of the Alexandrian papacy. The
production of such rhetoric—and the ways that such rhetoric was put
into practice—reveals much about how the lines of Egyptian papal
authority were continually drawn, contested, and redrawn in late
antiquity. Indeed, as we shall see in the next volume, these discourses
remained vital and enduring markers of social and religious identity for
the Coptic church under Islamic rule.

Appendix 1
A List of the Egyptian Popes
up to the Rise of Islam

1. Mark
2. Anianus (Ananius)
3. Abilius
4. Cerdon (Cerdo)
5. Primus
6. Justus   **DATES UNCERTAIN**
7. Eumenius (Eumenes)
8. Marcianus (Mark)
9. Celadion
10. Agrippinus
11. Julian

12. Demetrius I	189–231
13. Heraclas	231–247
14. Dionysius	247–264
15. Maximus	264–282
16. Theonas	282–300
17. Peter I	300–311
18. Achillas	312
19. Alexander I	312–328
20. Athanasius I	328–373
21. Peter II	373–380
22. Timothy I	380–385
23. Theophilus	385–412
24. Cyril I	412–444
25. Dioscorus I	444–454
26. Timothy II Aelurus ("the Cat")	457–477

Appendix 2
The Election of the Alexandrian Patriarchs
in the Early Church

In antiquity, the early church in Alexandria gained a reputation for its distinctive method of episcopal election: a number of ancient and medieval sources attest to the fact that, for at least the first two and a half centuries, the election and consecration of the Alexandrian patriarch lay in the hands of a group of presbyters (priests).[1]

Ancient and medieval sources give conflicting accounts of when the Alexandrian church might have changed its policy and begun the current practice of having the new patriarch consecrated by a council of bishops. However, the reigns of Heraclas (231–247) and Dionysius (247–264) may have played a pivotal role in this process. In one of his letters,[2] the church father Jerome (ca. 347–419/20) notes that, in the Alexandrian church, a group of presbyters used to elect the new bishop from their own ranks, and that this practice continued up until the time of Heraclas and Dionysius. Severus of Antioch (ca. 465–538), who spent most of his later years as a theological exile in Egypt, also attests the early role presbyters played in the election of the patriarch: "The bishop also of the city renowned for its orthodox faith, the city of the Alexandrians, used in former days to be appointed by presbyters, but in later times in accordance with the canon which has prevailed everywhere the solemn institution of their bishop has come to be performed by the hand of bishops."[3] However, Severus gives no indication as to the timing of this change of policy.

Some other sources suggest that presbyterial election of the Alexandrian patriarch may have continued into the early fourth century;[4] however, it is certain that the practice must have been discontinued by the time Athanasius I was elected in 328.[5] Unfortunately, the nature of the sources does not allow us to answer with any certainty the question of when regular presbyterial involvement in the election of the Alexandrian patriarch was suspended.

The reason for this early electoral practice is easier to discern: during the first two centuries of the church in Egypt, there simply would have been no other bishops available for the task.[6] In fact, Pope Demetrius (189–231) may have been the first to consecrate other bishops to serve Egyptian dioceses outside Alexandria: the medieval historian Eutychius (Sa'id Ibn Batriq) claims that, prior to Demetrius' reign at the end of the second century, there were no other bishops in Egypt. According to Eutychius, Demetrius tried to remedy this situation by ordaining three new bishops; his successor Heraclas is then said to have ordained twenty more. As a historian, Eutychius is often viewed as unreliable ("blundering and incompetent" in the words of one author);[7] however, on this point he has received some support from modern scholars.[8] If Demetrius, in fact, was the first to ordain other Egyptian bishops, this would at least provide an explanation for why the church had previously entrusted the election of the patriarch to a committee of presbyters. In addition, the presence of a new cadre of bishops ordained under Demetrius and Heraclas would give an indication of why the Egyptian church, starting in the early third century, had the opportunity to reform its practice of patriarchal election. In any case, whenever the actual change in policy took place, the election of the new patriarch by a council of bishops has remained a canonical practice to the present day.[9]

Appendix 3

The Anti-Chalcedonian Patriarchate of Alexandria (477–577)

Other Theological Factions in Egypt	Separatist Anti-Chalcedonian Communions in Egypt	Influence of the Anti-Chalcedonian Patriarchate of Antioch	The Anti-Chalcedonian Patriarchate of Alexandria (477–577)	The Chalcedonian Hierarchy in Egypt (Reestablished under the emperor Justinian in 538)
			Peter III Mongus (477–490)	
			Athanasius II (490–496)	
	Separatists (Aposchistai) Also known as the Akephaloi (ca. 482– early seventh century)		John I Hemula (496–505)	
			John II Nicaiotes (505–516)	
			Dioscorus II (516–517)	
			Timothy III (517–535)	
		Anti-Chalcedonian fugitives from Antioch and Asia Minor		
	Julian of Halicarnassus (exiled to Egypt, 518–?)	Severus of Antioch (exiled to Egypt, 518–538)		
	Julianists			Paul Tabennesiota (538–540)
	Gaianus (535)			Zoilus (540–551)
	Gaianites			Apollinaris (551–570)
	Elpidius (?–565)		Theodosius (536–566)	
Themistius and the Agnoetai (ca. 537–early seventh century)				*John* (570–581) (Chalcedonian patriarch of Alexandria, and rival to Peter IV)
			(10 year lapse)	
	Dorotheus (565–after 580) (Gaianite anti-Chalcedonian patriarch of Alexandria, and rival to Peter IV) Paul of Antioch (564–577)	Paul of Antioch (564–577)	*Peter IV* (576–577)	
John Philoponos and the Tritheists (ca. 567–early seventh century)		*Theodore* (575–after 587) (Anti-Chalcedonian patriarch of Alexandria originally endorsed by Paul of Antioch, and rival to Peter IV)		

Key

Vertical dotted lines: Lines of patriarchal succession

Curved dotted lines: Lines of ecclesiastical alliance and patronage

Black Bordered Text: Anti-Chalcedonian fugitives from Antioch and Asia Minor, exiled to Egypt in 518

Underlined: Contestants for the Alexandrian Patriarchate, ca. 535–540

Italics: Contestants for the Alexandrian Patriarchate. ca. 575–580

The one-hundred-year period from 477 to 577 was a time of social and theological fragmentation. The authority of the anti-Chalcedonian patriarchs of Alexandria was contested in successive generations not only by their Chalcedonian rivals, but also by a bewildering variety of anti-Chalcedonian factions within the Egyptian church—separatists who believed themselves to be more faithful to the theology of Cyril (412–444) and the legacy of resistance represented by Dioscorus (444–454). The ecclesiastical politics of Egypt during this period were also complicated by two other factors: namely, shifting lines of imperial patronage, and a series of rifts and reconciliations with the anti-Chalcedonian leadership of the church in Antioch.

This chart is designed to depict in visual terms the complex networks of contestation and allegiance during this period of Egyptian church history. Vertical dotted lines represent direct lines of succession within particular ecclesiastical communities in Egypt. For example, the succession of anti-Chalcedonian patriarchs of Alexandria (the one still recognized by the Coptic church today) is represented in column four. By contrast, the chain of anti-Chalcedonian bishops loyal to Gaianus is represented in column three, and the lineage of the Chalcedonian hierarchy in Alexandria is represented in column five. Curved dotted lines represent significant relationships of alliance and patronage that crossed community-based and/or geographical boundaries. Black bordered text highlights two anti-Chalcedonian figures—Severus of Antioch and Julian of Halicarnassus—who were exiled from Antioch and Asia Minor to Egypt in 518, and whose presence contributed further to Egyptian theological factionalism in the sixth century. Underlined text highlights the names of three contemporaneous rivals for the Alexandrian patriarchate during the late 530s. Italicized text highlights the names of four contemporaneous rivals for the Alexandrian patriarchate during the late 570s.

Works Cited
Primary Sources and Collections

Acta Conciliorum Oecumenicorum (= ACO). Volume 1.1.1–8. Concilium Universale Ephesenum. Acta Graeca. Indices. Edited by Eduard Schwartz. Berlin and Leipzig: Walter de Gruyter, 1927–1930.

Acta Conciliorum Oecumenicorum (= ACO). Volume 1.2. Concilium Universale Ephesenum. Collectio Veronensis. Edited by Eduard Schwartz. Berlin and Leipzig: Walter de Gruyter, 1925–1926.

Acta Conciliorum Oecumenicorum (= ACO). Volume 1.3–4. Concilium Universale Ephesenum. Collectionis Casinensis. Edited by Eduard Schwartz. Berlin and Leipzig: Walter de Gruyter, 1927–1930.

Acta Conciliorum Oecumenicorum (= ACO). Volume 1.5. Concilium Universale Ephesenum. Collectio Palatina, et al. Edited by Eduard Schwartz. Berlin and Leipzig: Walter de Gruyter, 1927–1930.

Acta Conciliorum Oecumenicorum (= ACO). Volume 2.1.1–3. Concilium Universale Chalcedonense. Epistularum Collectiones. Epistularum Collectio B. Edited by Eduard Schwartz. Berlin and Leipzig: Walter de Gruyter, 1933–1935.

Acta Conciliorum Oecumenicorum (= ACO). Volume 2.2. Concilium Universale Chalcedonense. Versiones Particulares, Pars Prior. Collectio Novariensis de Re Eutychis. Edited by Eduard Schwartz. Berlin and Leipzig: Walter de Gruyter, 1932.

Acta Conciliorum Oecumenicorum (= ACO). Volume 2.3.1–3. Concilium Universale Chalcedonense. Epistularum ante Gesta Collectio. Edited by Eduard Schwartz. Berlin and Leipzig: Walter de Gruyter, 1935–1937.

Acta Conciliorum Oecumenicorum (= ACO). Volume 2.4. Concilium Universale Chalcedonense. Leonis Papae I Epistularum

Collectiones. Edited by Eduard Schwartz. Berlin and Leipzig: Walter de Gruyter, 1932.

Acta Conciliorum Oecumenicorum (= ACO). Volume 2.5. Concilium Universale Chalcedonense. Collectio Sangermanensis. Edited by Eduard Schwartz. Berlin and Leipzig: Walter de Gruyter, 1936.

Acta Conciliorum Oecumenicorum (= ACO). Volume 2.6. Concilium Universale Chalcedonense. Prosopographia et Topographia. Indices. Edited by Eduard Schwartz. Berlin and Leipzig: Walter de Gruyter, 1938.

Acta Conciliorum Oecumenicorum (= ACO). Volume 3. Collectio Sabbaitica. Contra Acephalos et Origeniastas Destinata. Insunt Acta Synodorum Constantinopolitanae et Hierosolymintanae A. 536. Edited by Eduard Schwartz. Berlin and Leipzig: Walter de Gruyter, 1940.

Acta Conciliorum Oecumenicorum, Second Series (= ACO[2]). Volume 1. Concilium Lateranense a. 649 celebratum. Edited by R. Riedinger. Berlin: Walter de Gruyter, 1984.

Acta Conciliorum Oecumenicorum, Second Series (= ACO[2]). Volume 2. Parts 1–3. Concilium Universale Constantinopolitanum Tertium. Edited by R. Riedinger. Berlin: Walter de Gruyter, 1990–1995.

Acts of Mark (Coptic). Edited by P. Hubai, in "The Legend of St. Mark: Coptic Fragments." In *Studia Aegyptica XII*, 165–234. Studia in Honorem L. Fóti; Budapest: Chaire d'Égyptologie, l'Université Eötvös Loránd de Budapest, 1989.

Acts of Mark (Greek). PG 115:164–169. *Acta Sanctorum*. Revised edition. Volume 12 (April 3), XXXVIII–XL. Paris: Palmé, 1863–1940. Translated by A.D. Callahan, in "The Acts of Saint Mark: An Introduction and Translation," *Coptic Church Review* 14 (1993), 3–10.

Alexander of Alexandria, *Deposition of Arius and his Followers*. Edited by H.-G. Opitz, in *Athanasius: Werke*, Volume 3, 6 (no. 4a).

Alexander of Alexandria, *Encomium on Saint Peter*. Edited by H. Hyvernat, in *Les actes des martyrs de l'Égypte*, 247–262. Hildesheim and New York: Georg Olms Verlag, 1977. Translated by T. Vivian, in *St. Peter of Alexandria: Bishop and Martyr*, 78–84. Philadelphia: Fortress, 1988.

Alexander of Alexandria, *Letter to Alexander of Thessalonica*. Edited by H.-G. Opitz, in *Athanasius: Werke*, Volume 3, 19–29 (no. 14). Translated by W. Rusch, in *The Trinitarian Controversy*, 33–44.

Alexander of Alexandria, *Letter to Bishops*. Edited by H.-G. Opitz, in *Athanasius: Werke*, Volume 3, 29–31 (no. 15).

Alexander of Alexandria, *Letter to Sylvester of Rome* (fragment). Edited by H.-G. Opitz, in *Athanasius: Werke*, Volume 3, 31 (no. 16).

Ambrosiaster, *Commentary on Ephesians*. Edited by A. Souter, in *A Study of Ambrosiaster*. Texts and Studies 7.4. Cambridge: Cambridge University Press, 1905. Repr. Nendeln: Kraus Reprint, 1967.

Anastasius Bibliothecarius, *Acta Sincera Sancti Petri*. PG 18.451–466. ANF 6.261–268.

Anastasius of Sinai, *Viae dux* (= *Hodegos*). Edited by K.-H. Uthemann. Corpus Christianorum Series Graeca 8. Turnout: Brepols, 1981. Also PG 89.35–310.

Apocrypha and Pseudepigrapha of the Old Testament. Edited by R.H. Charles. 2 volumes. Oxford: Clarendon Press, 1913.

Apophthegmata Patrum (Greek alphabetical version). PG 65.72–440. Translated by Benedicta Ward, in *The Desert Christian: Sayings of the Desert Fathers. The Alphabetic Collection*. New York: Macmillan, 1975.

Arius, *Letter to Alexander of Alexandria*. Edited by H.-G. Opitz, in *Athanasius: Werke*, Volume 3, 12–13 (no. 6). Translated by W. Rusch, in *The Trinitarian Controversy*, 31–32.

Arius, *Letter to Eusebius of Nicomedia*. Edited by H.-G. Opitz, in *Athanasius: Werke*, Volume 3, 1–3 (no. 1). Translated by W. Rusch, in *The Trinitarian Controversy*, 29–30.

Asterius, *Fragments*. Edited by G. Bardy, in *Recherches sur Lucien d'Antioche et son École*, 339–354. Paris: Beauchesne, 1936.

Athanasius of Alexandria, *Against the Arians*. PG 26.12–468.

Athanasius of Alexandria, *De synodis*. Edited by H.-G. Opitz, *Athanasius: Werke*, Volume 2.1, 231–278.

Athanasius of Alexandria, *Festal Letters*. Edited by F. Larsow, in *Die Fest-Briefe des heiligen Athanasius, Bischofs von Alexandrien. Aus dem Syrischen übersetzt und durch Anmerkungen erläutert*. Leipzig: F.C.W. Vogel, 1852.

Athanasius of Alexandria, *Festal Letters*. Edited by L. Th. Lefort, in *Lettres festales et pastorals en copte*. 2 volumes. CSCO 150–151. Louvain: L. Durbecq, 1955. Translated by A. Robertson, in NPNF, Second series, Volume 4, 500–553.

Athanasius of Alexandria, First *Letter to Virgins*. Edited by L. Th. Lefort, in *S. Athanase: Lettres festales et pastorals en copte*, 73–99. Louvain: L. Durbecq, 1955. Translated by D. Brakke, in *Athanasius and the Politics of Asceticism*, 274–291.

Athanasius of Alexandria, *History of the Arians*. Edited by H.-G. Opitz, in *Athanasius Werke*, volume 2.1, 183–230. Berlin: De Gruyter, 1940.

Athanasius of Alexandria, *Letter to Amun*. PG 26.1169–1176 (Greek text). NPNF, series 2, vol. 4, 556–557 (English translation).

Athanasius of Alexandria, *Letter to Dracontius*. PG 25.523–534. NPNF, series 2, vol. 4, 557–560 (English translation).

Athanasius of Alexandria, *Life of Antony*. Edited by G.J.M. Bartelink, in SC 400. Paris: Cerf, 1994. Also PG 26.835–976. Translated by R.C. Gregg, in *The Life of Antony and the Letter to Marcellinus*. New York: Paulist Press, 1980.

Athanasius of Alexandria, *On Virginity*. Armenian text edited and translated by R. Casey, in "Der dem Athanasius zugeschriebene Traktat PERI PARTHENIAS," *Sitzungsberichte der preussischen Akademie der Wissenschaften* 33 (1935), 1026–1045. Syriac text edited by J. Lebon, in "Athanasiana Syriaca I: Un LOGOS PERI PARTHENIAS attribué à saint Athanase d'Alexandrie," *Muséon* 40 (1927), 205–248; translated by D. Brakke, in *Athanasius and the Politics of Asceticism*, 303–309.

Athanasius of Alexandria, Second *Apology*. Edited by H.-G. Opitz, in *Athanasius Werke*, Volume 2.1, 87–168. Berlin: De Gruyter, 1940. Also PG 25.247–410.

Athanasius of Alexandria, Second *Letter to Monks*. PG 26.1185–1188. Translated by A. Robertson, in NPNF, second series, vol. 4, 564 (Letter LIII).

Athanasius of Alexandria, *Werke*. Edited by H.-G. Opitz. 3 volumes. Berlin and Leipzig: Walter de Gruyter, 1934–1940.

Augustine of Hippo, *Confessions*. Edited by M. Skutella, H. Jürgens, and W. Schaub, in *S. Aureli Augustini Confessionum libri XIII*. Stuttgart: B. G. Teubner, 1969. Translated by R.S. Pine-Coffin. London and New York: Penguin, 1961.

al-Baladhuri, *Kitab futuh al-buldan* (*The Origins of the Islamic State*). 2 volumes. Translated by P. Hitti. New York: AMS Press, 1968.

Barhebraeus, *Chronicle*. Edited by J.-B. Abbeloos and Th. J. Lamy. 3 volumes. Paris: Maisonneuve, 1872–1877.

2 Baruch. Edited and translated by R.H. Charles, in *Apocrypha and Pseudepigrapha of the Old Testament*, Volume 2, 470–526. Oxford: Clarendon Press, 1913.

Benjamin of Alexandria, *Sixteenth Festal Letter*. Edited and translated by C.D.G. Müller, in *Die Homilie über die Hochzeit zu Kana und weitere Schriften des Patriarchen Benjamin I. von Alexandrien*, 302–351. Heidelberg: Carl Winter; Universitätsverlag, 1968.

Besa, *Life of Shenoute*. Edited by J. Leipoldt and W.E. Crum, in *Sinuthii Archimandritae Vita et Opera Omnia*, CSCO 41. Scriptores Coptici, Series Secunda, Tomus II. Paris: Typographeo reipublicae, 1906. Translated by David N. Bell. Kalamazoo, MI: Cistercian Publications, 1983.

Canons of the First Council of Constantinople (A.D. 381). Translated by H. Percival, in NPNF, Second series, Volume 14, 172–186.

Chronicle of 846. Edited by E.W. Brooks and J.-B. Chabot. CSCO 3, 157–242 (Syriac text). CSCO 4, 121–182 (Latin translation). Scriptores Syri 3, 4. Paris: Typographeo reipublicae, 1903.

Chronicle of 1234. Edited by J.-B. Chabot. 2 volumes. CSCO 81–82, Scriptores Syri 36–37. Paris: Typographeo reipublicae, 1916–1920. Repr. Louvain: L. Durbecq, 1953.

Clement of Alexandria, *Stromata*. Edited by O. Stählin, L. Früchtel, and U. Treu, in *Clemens Alexandrinus*, Volumes 2 and 3. Fourth edition. GCS. Berlin: Akademie-Verlag, 1985. Translated by W. Wilson, in ANF 2.299–567.

Codex Vaticanus gr. 1431: Eine antichalkedonische Sammlung aus der Zeit Kaiser Zenos. Edited by E. Schwartz. Abhandlungen der Bayerischen Akademie der Wissenschaften philosophisch-philologisch und historische Klasse, Vol. 32. Abhandlung 6. Munich: Verlag der Bayerischen Akademie der Wissenschaften, 1927.

Codex Veronensis LX. Edited by C.H. Turner, in *Ecclesiae Occidentalis Monumenta Iuris Antiquissima*. 2 volumes. Oxford: Clarendon Press, 1899–1939.

Consecration of the Sanctuary of Benjamin. Edited by R.G. Coquin. Bibliothèque d'études coptes 13. Cairo: Institut français d'archéologie orientale, 1975.

Constantine, *Letter to Alexander and Arius*, preserved in Eusebius, *Life of Constantine* 2.64. Edited by H.-G. Opitz, *Athanasius: Werke*, Volume 3, 32–35 (no. 17).

Constantine, *Letter to Arius and his Companions*. Edited by H.-G. Opitz, in *Athanasius: Werke*, Volume 3, 69–75 (no. 34).

Cyprian of Carthage, *On the Lapsed*. Edited by W. Hartel, in CSEL 3, 1 (1868), 235–264. Translated by M. Bévenot, in Ancient Christian Writers 25. Westminster, MD: Newman Press, 1957.

Cyril of Alexandria, *Against Julian*. Edited by P. Burguière and P. Evieux, *Contre Julien*, volume 1. SC 322 (books 1–2). Paris: Cerf,

1985. PG 76.613–1064 (books 3–10). Excerpts of this work have been translated into English by N. Russell, in *Cyril of Alexandria*, 190–203.

Cyril of Alexandria, *Against Nestorius*. Edited by E. Schwartz, in ACO 1.1.6, 13–106. Excerpts translated by N. Russell, in *Cyril of Alexandria*, 130–174.

Cyril of Alexandria, *Answers to Tiberias*. Syriac text edited by R.Y. Ebied and L.R. Wickham, in "The Letter of Cyril of Alexandria to Tiberias the Deacon," *Le Muséon* 83 (1970), 433–482.

Cyril of Alexandria, *Homiliae Diversae*. PG 77.981–1116.

Cyril of Alexandria, *Letter to Acacius of Beroea (Ep. 33)*. Edited by E. Schwartz, in ACO 1.1.7, 147–156. Translated by J.A. McGuckin, in *St. Cyril of Alexandria: The Christological Controversy*, 336–342. Leiden: E.J. Brill, 1994.

Cyril of Alexandria, *Letters 1–50*. Translated by J. McEnerney, in The Fathers of the Church, Vol. 76. Washington, D.C.: The Catholic University of America Press, 1987.

Cyril of Alexandria, *Letters 51–100*. Translated by J. McEnerney, in The Fathers of the Church, Vol. 77. Washington, D.C.: The Catholic University of America Press, 1987.

Cyril of Alexandria, *Paschal Letters*. Edited by W.H. Burns, in *Lettres Festales*, 3 volumes. SC 372, 392, 434. Paris: Cerf, 1991–1998. PG 77.401–982.

Cyril of Alexandria, *Select Letters*. Translated by L. Wickham. Oxford: Clarendon Press, 1983.

Damascius, *Life of Isidore*. Edited by C. Zintzen, in *Vitae Isidori Reliquiae*. Hildesheim, Georg Olms Verlag, 1967.

Dionysius of Alexandria, *Letters*. Edited by W.A. Biernert, in *Dionysius von Alexandrien, Das erhaltene Werk*. Bibliothek der griechischen Literatur, Bd. 2. Stuttgart: Hiersemann, 1972. Translated by C.L. Feltoe, in *Letters and Treatises*. Translations of Christian Literature, series 1: Greek Texts. New York: Macmillan Co., 1918.

Documents Illustrating Papal Authority, A.D. 96–454. Edited by E. Giles. London: SPCK, 1952.

Elias of Nisibis, *Opus Chronologicum*. Edited by E.W. Brooks and J.-B. Chabot, in CSCO 62–63. Louvain : Secrétariat du CorpusSCO, 1954–1962.

Epiphanius, *Panarion*. Edited by K. Holl. 3 volumes. GCS 25, 31, and 37. Leipzig and Berlin: Hinrichs, 1915–1933. Second edition by K.

Holl and J. Dummer. Berlin: Akademie-Verlag, 1980–1985. Also PG 41–42. Translated by F. Williams. 2 volumes. Nag Hammadi Studies 35–36. Leiden and New York: E.J. Brill, 1987–1994. Excerpts translated by P. Amidon, S.J., in *The 'Panarion' of St. Epiphanius of Salamis: Selected Passages.* New York and Oxford, Oxford University Press, 1990.

Eunapius, *The Lives of the Sophists.* Edited by J. Giangrande, in *Eunapii vitae sophistarum*, 1–101. Rome: Polygraphica, 1956. Translated by W.C. Wright, in *Philostratus and Eunapius: The Lives of the Sophists.* London, W. Heinemann; New York, G.P. Putnam's Sons, 1922.

Eusebius of Caesarea, *Chronicle* (preserved in Jerome's Latin translation). Edited by R. Helm. Third edition. GCS. Berlin: Akademie-Verlag, 1984.

Eusebius of Caesarea, *HE.* Edited by E. Schwartz and T. Mommsen. 3 volumes. GCS 9.1–3. Leipzig: J.C. Hinrichs, 1903–1909. Second edition, by F. Winkelmann. Berlin: Akademie Verlag, 1999. Translated by G.A. Williamson. New York: Penguin, 1965.

Eusebius of Caesarea, *Life of Constantine.* Edited by F. Winkelmann, in *Eusebius Werke, Band 1.1: Über das Leben des Kaisers Konstantin.* GCS. Berlin: Akademie-Verlag, 1975.

Eusebius of Caesarea, *Martyrs of Palestine.* Edited by G. Bardy, in *Histoire ecclésiastique.* Volume 3. SC 55, 121–174. Paris: Cerf, 1958; repr. 1967.

Eusebius of Caesarea, *Oration in Praise of the Emperor Constantine.* Edited by I.A. Heikel, in *Eusebius Werke*, Volume 1. GCS 7, 195–259. Leipzig: Hinrichs, 1902.

Eutychius (Saîd ibn Batrîq), *Annales.* Edited by L. Cheikho. CSCO 50–51. Beirut: Typographeo Catholico, 1906–1909. Also PG 111.907–1156.

Evagrius Ponticus, *Letter to Melania.* Edited by W. Frankenburg, in *Opera. Euagrius Ponticus.* Abhandlungen der königlichen Gesellschaft der Wissenschaften zu Göttingen, philologisch-historische Klasse, n. f. 13.2. Berlin: Weidmann, 1912. Translated by M. Parmentier, "Evagrius of Pontus' 'Letter to Melania,'" *Bijdragen, tijdschrift voor filosofie en theologie* 46 (1985), 2–38.

Evagrius Scholasticus, *HE.* Edited by J. Bidez and L. Parmentier. Amsterdam: Adolf M. Hakkert, 1964. Translated by M. Whitby, in *Translated Texts for Historians*, Volume 33. Liverpool: Liverpool University Press, 2000.

George the Monk ("Hamartolos"), *Chronicon*. PG 110.41–1285.

Gregory of Nazianzus, *Poems on Himself* (*De seipso*). PG 37.969–1452.

Gregory of Nazianzus, *Orations*. PG 35.395–1252 and PG 36.9–664.

History of the Patriarchs of the Coptic Church of Alexandria. Edited by B. Evetts, in PO 1.2, 1.4, 5.1, 10.5. Paris: Firmin-Didot, 1904–1914. Edited by Y. 'Abd al-Masîh, O.H.E. Burmeister, A.S. Atiya, and A. Khater. Cairo: Société d'archéologie copte, 1943–1974.

Homily on the Child Saints of Babylon. Edited and translated by H. de Vis, in *Homélies coptes de la Vaticane*. 2 volumes. Coptica 5. Hauniae: Gyldendal, 1922–29. Repr. in *Cahiers de la bibliothèque copte* 5–6. Louvain and Paris: Peeters, 1990.

Ibn 'Abd al-Hakam, *Futûh Misr wa-akhbâruhâ* (*The History of the Conquest of Egypt*). Edited by C.C. Torrey. New Haven: Yale University Press, 1922.

Irenaeus, *Against Heresies*, Book 3. Edited by J. Sagnard. SC. Paris: Cerf, 1974. Translated in ANF 1.315–567.

Isidore of Pelusium, *Epistles*. PG 78.177–1646.

Jerome, *Letters*. Edited by I. Hilberg, in CSEL 54–56. Second edition. Vindobonae: Verlag der Österreichischen Akademie der Wissenschaften, 1996.

Jerome, *Life of Paul the Hermit*. PL 23.17–28.

Jerome, *Lives of Illustrious Men*. Edited by E.C. Richardson, 1–56. Leipzig: J. C. Hinrichs, 1896. Translated by T. Halton, in Fathers of the Church, Volume 100. Washington, D.C.: Catholic University of America Press, 1999.

John Cassian, *Conferences*. Edited by M. Petschenig, in CSEL 13. Vindobonae: C. Geroldi filium, 1886. Translated by C. Luibheid. New York: Paulist Press, 1985.

John Chrysostom, *Homilies on Matthew*. PG 57. Translated by S.G. Prevost (revised by M.B. Riddle), in NPNF 10 (1889).

John of Ephesus, *HE*, Part Three. Edited and translated by E.W. Brooks, in CSCO 105–106. Paris: Typographeo reipublicae, 1935–1936.

John of Ephesus, *Lives of the Eastern Saints*. Edited by E.W. Brooks, in PO 17–19. Paris: Firmin-Didot, 1923–1925.

John of Nikiu, *Chronicle*. Translated by R.H. Charles, in *The Chronicle of John (c. 690 A.D.) Coptic Bishop of Nikiu*. Text and Translation Society 3. London and Oxford: William & Norgate, 1916.

John Philoponos, *Tritheist Fragments*. Edited by A. Van Roey, in "Les fragments trithéites de Jean Philopon," *Orientalia Lovaniensia Periodica* 11 (1980), 135–163.

Josephus, *Antiquities*. Edited and translated by H. St. J. Thackeray. Loeb Classical Library. 5 volumes. Cambridge, MA: Harvard University Press; London: Heinemann, 1930–1969.

Julian of Halicarnassus, *Fragments*. Edited and translated by R. Draguet, in *Julien d'Halicarnasse et sa controverse avec Sévère d'Antioche sur l'incorruptibilité du corps du Christ*. Louvain: Imprimerie P. Smeesters, 1924.

Lactantius, *On the Deaths of the Persecutors*. Edited by S. Brandt and G. Laubmann, in CSEL 27.2. Venice: F. Tempsky, 1897. Translated by M.F. McDonald, O.P., in The Fathers of the Church 54. Washington, D.C.: The Catholic University of America Press, 1965.

Leo of Rome, *Epistles*. Edited by E. Schwartz, in ACO 2.4. Berlin and Leipzig: Walter de Gruyter, 1932.

Leo of Rome, *Tome* (= *Ep.* 28, to Flavian of Constantinople). Edited by E. Schwartz, in ACO 2.2, 24–33. Translated by R.A. Norris, in *The Christological Controversy*, 145–155. Philadelphia: Fortress Press, 1980.

Libanius, *Pro Templis*. Edited by R. Van Loy, in "Le 'Pro Templis' de Libanius," *Byzantion* 9 (1933), 7–39, 388–404.

Liberatus, *Brevarium*. Edited by E. Schwartz, in ACO 2.5, 98–141. Berlin and Leipzig: Walter de Gruyter, 1936.

Life and Martyrdom of the Holy and Glorious "Holy Martyr" of Christ, Peter Archbishop of Alexandria. Edited by P. Devos, in "Une passion grecque inédite de S. Pierre d'Alexandrie et sa traduction par Anastase le Bibliothècaire," *Analecta Bollandiana* 83 (1965), 157–187. Translated by T. Vivian, in *St. Peter of Alexandria*, 70–78.

Life of John the Almsgiver. Translated by E. Dawes and N.H. Baynes, in *Three Byzantine Saints*, 199–262. Crestwood, NY: St. Vladimir's Seminary Press, 1977.

Life of Pachomius (Bohairic). Edited by L. Th. Lefort, in *S. Pachomii vita bohairice scripta*. CSCO 89, Scriptores Coptici 7. Paris: E typographeo reipublicae, 1925. Repr. Louvain: Secrétariat du CSCO, 1965.

Life of Pachomius (First Greek *Life*). Edited by F. Halkin, in *Sancti Pachomii Vitae Graecae*. Subsidia Hagiographica 19. Brussels: Société des Bollandistes, 1932.

Life of Samuel of Kalamun (Coptic). Edited and translated by A. Alcock, in *The Life of Samuel of Kalamun by Isaac the Presbyter.* Warminster, England: Aris & Phillips, Ltd., 1983.

Life of Samuel of Kalamun (Ethiopic). Edited by F.M.E. Pereira, in *Vida do Abba Samuel do mosteiro do Kalamon.* Lisbon: Imprensa Nacional, 1894.

Life of Shenoute (Arabic text). Edited by E. Amélineau, in *Monuments pour server à l'histoire de l'Égypte chrétienne*, Volume 1. Paris: Ernest Leroux, 1888.

Life of St. Onnophrius. Translated by T. Vivian, in *Journeying into God: Seven Monastic Lives*, 172–187. Minneapolis: Fortress Press, 1996.

Life of Theodore. Edited by E. Amelineau, in *Histoire de St. Pakhôme et de ses communautés: Documents coptes et arabes inédits*, 215–334. Annales du Musée Guimet, Volume 17. Paris: Ernest Leroux, 1889.

London Papyrus 1914. Edited by H.I. Bell, in *Jews and Christians in Egypt*, 58–61 (Greek text), 61–63 (English translation). Oxford: Clarendon Press, 1924.

al-Maqrizi, *El-Mawâ'iz wa'l-i'tibâr fî dhikr el-khitat wa'l-âthâr* (*Topographical Description of Egypt*). Edited by G. Wiet, in *Mémoires publiés par les members de la Mission archéologique française.* Volume 30. Paris: Institut français d'archéologie orientale, 1911.

Martyrdom of St. Coluthus. Edited and translated by E.A.E. Raymond and J.W.B. Barns, in *Four Martyrdoms from the Pierpont Morgan Coptic Codices.* Oxford: Clarendon Press, 1973.

Mena of Nikiou, *The Life of Isaac of Alexandria.* Translated by D.N. Bell. Kalamazoo: Cistercian Publications, 1988.

Michael the Syrian, *Chronicle.* Edited by J.-B. Chabot. 4 volumes. Paris, 1899–1910. Repr. Brussels: Culture et Civilisation, 1963.

Monuments from Lycaonia, the Pisido-Phrygian borderland, Aphrodisias. Edited by W.M. Calder and J.M.R. Cormack, in Monumenta Asiae Minoris Antiqua, Volume 8. Manchester: Manchester University Press, 1962.

Nestorius, *The Bazaar of Heracleides.* Translated by G.R. Driver and L. Hodgson. Oxford: Clarendon Press, 1925.

Origen of Alexandria, *Against Celsus.* Edited by M. Borret. 4 volumes. SC 132, 136, 147, 150. Paris: Cerf, 1967–1969.

Origen of Alexandria, *Commentary on John.* 3 volumes. Edited by C. Blanc, in SC 120, 157, 222. Paris: Cerf, 1966, 1970, 1975. Excerpts translated by J. Trigg, in *Origen*, 103–178. London: Routledge, 1998.

Origen of Alexandria, *Exhortation to Martyrdom*. Edited by P. Koetschau, in *Origenes Werke*, volume 1. GCS 2, 3–47. Leipzig: Hinrichs, 1899. Translated by R. Greer, 41–79. The Classics of Western Spirituality. New York: Paulist Press, 1979.

Origen of Alexandria, *Homily on Leviticus*. Edited by W.A. Baehrens, in *Origenes Werke*, volume 6. GCS 29, 332–334, 395, 402–407, 409–416. Leipzig: Teubner, 1920.

Origen of Alexandria, *On First Principles*. Edited by H. Görgemanns and H. Karpp. Darmstadt: Wissenschaftliche Buchgesellschaft, 1976. Translated by G.W. Butterworth. Gloucester, MA: Peter Smith, 1973.

Oxyrhynchus Papyri. Volumes 51 and 58. Edited by J.R. Rea. London: Egypt Exploration Society, 1984, 1991.

Palladius, *Dialogue on the Life of Chrysostom*. Edited by P.R. Coleman-Norton. Cambridge: Cambridge University Press, 1928. Translated by H. Moore. Translations of Christian Literature. Series I. Greek Texts. London and New York: Macmillan, 1921.

Palladius, *Lausiac History*. Edited by G.J.M. Bartelink. Verona: Fondazione Lorenzo Valla, 1974. Translated by R. Meyer, in Ancient Christian Writers, Volume 34. Westminster, MD: The Newman Press; London: Longmans, Green and Co., 1965.

Passions des Saints Ecaterine et Pierre d'Alexandrie, Barbara et Anysia. Publiée d'après les manuscrits grecs de Paris et de Rome. Edited by J. Viteau. Paris: E. Bouillon, 1897.

Paulinus of Nola. *Carmina*. Edited by W. Hartel, in CSEL 30. Vienna: F. Tempsky, 1894. Second edition supplemented by M. Kamptner. Vienna: Verlag der Österreichischen Akademie der Wissenschaften, 1999.

Peter I of Alexandria. *Canonical Letter*. PG 18.468–508. Translated by T. Vivian, in *St. Peter of Alexandria*, 185–192.

Peter IV of Alexandria, *Synodical Letter to Jacob Baradaeus*. Excerpt edited by J.-B. Chabot, in *Documenta ad origins monophysitarum illustrandas*. CSCO 17, 230 (Syriac text). CSCO 103, 161 (Latin translation). Louvain: L. Durbecq, 1952, 1955.

Peter of Callinicum. *Against Damian*. Edited by R.Y. Ebied, A. Van Roey, and L.R. Wickham, in *Petri Callinicensis Patriarchae Antiocheni Tractatus contra Damianum*, Volume 1. CSCO, Series Graeca, 29, 1–367. Turnhout: Brepols; Leuven: University Press, 1994.

Philo, *On the Contemplative Life* (*De vita contemplative*). Edited and translated by F.H. Colson. Loeb Classical Library. Works of Philo, Volume 9, 103–169. Cambridge, MA: Harvard University Press; London: William Heinemann, 1985.

Philostorgius, *HE*. Edited by J. Bidez. Third edition, revised by F. Winkelmann. GCS. Berlin: Akademie-Verlag, 1981.

Photius, *Bibliotheca*. Edited by R. Henry. 9 volumes. Paris: Société d'édition les Belles Lettres, 1959–1991.

Ps.-Athanasius, *Apocalypse*. Edited and translated by F.J. Martinez, in *Early Christian Apocalyptic in the Early Muslim Period: Pseudo-Methodius and Pseudo-Athanasius*, Chapter three. Ph.D. thesis, Catholic University of America; Washington, D.C., 1985.

Ps.-Augustine, *Quaestiones Veteris et Novi Testamenti CXXVII*. Edited by A. Souter, in CSEL 50. New York: Johnson Reprint Corporation, 1963.

(Ps.-)Benjamin, *Homily on the Wedding at Cana*. Edited and translated by C.D.G. Müller, in *Die Homilie über die Hochzeit zu Kana und weitere Schriften des Patriarchen Benjamin I. von Alexandrien.* Heidelberg: Carl Winter; Universitätsverlag, 1968.

(Ps.-)Clement of Alexandria, *Letter to Theodore*. Edited by M. Smith, in *Clement of Alexandria and a Secret Gospel of Mark*. Cambridge: Harvard University Press, 1973.

Ps.-Dioscorus, *Panegyric on Macarius, Bishop of Tkôw*. Edited and translated by D. W. Johnson, in CSCO 415–416, Scriptores Coptici 41–42. Louvain: Secrétariat du CorpusSCO, 1980.

Ps.-Leontius, *De sectis*. PG 86.1193–1268.

Ptolemy, *Letter to Flora*. Edited by G. Quispel, in SC 24. Paris, Le Cerf, 1966. Translated by B. Layton, in *Gnostic Scriptures*, 308–315. Garden City, NY: Doubleday & Co., 1987.

The Qur'ân. Arabic text and English translation in *The Meaning of the Glorious Qur'ân*. Translated by M.M. Pickthall. Beirut: Dar al-Kitab Allubnani, 1970.

Rufinus, *HE*, Books 10 and 11. Edited by T. Mommsen. Second edition. GCS, Neue Folge, Band 6.2, 957–1040. Berlin: Akademie Verlag, 1999. Translated by P. R. Amidon, in *The Church History of Rufinus, Books 10 and 11*. New York: Oxford University Press, 1997.

Severus of Antioch, *Critique of the Tomus*. Edited and translated by R. Hespel, in CSCO 244, 20–205 (Syriac text), and CSCO 245, 15–158 (Latin translation). Louvain: Secrétariat du CSCO, 1964.

Severus of Antioch, *Letters*. Edited and translated E.W. Brooks, in *The*

Sixth Book of the Select Letters of Severus. 2 volumes. London: Williams & Norgate, 1904.

Severus of Ashmunein (Sawirus ibn al-Muqaffa), *Refutation of Eutychius (Book of the Councils)*. 2 volumes. Edited by P. Chébli, in PO 3.2, 121–242, and PO 6.4, 469–640. Paris: Firmin-Didot, 1909.

Shenoute, *On the Modesty of Clerics*. Edited by J. Leipoldt and W.E. Crum, in CSCO 42, 33–37. Translated by H. Wiesmann, in CSCO 96, 15–18. Louvain: L. Durbecq, 1953, 1955.

Sibylline Oracles. Edited and translated by H.C.O. Lanchester, in *Apocrypha and Pseudepigrapha of the Old Testament*, Volume 2, 368–406. Oxford: Clarendon Press, 1913.

Simplicius, *Letter to Acacius*. Edited by O. Guenther, in CSEL 35.1, 142–144. Venice: F. Tempsky, 1895.

Socrates, *HE*. PG 67.29–872. Translated by A.C. Zenos, in NPNF, Second Series. Volume 2, 1–178. New York: The Christian Literature, 1890. Repr. Grand Rapids, MI: William B. Eerdmans, 1952.

Sophronius, *Laudes in Ss. Cyrum et Joannem*. PG 87.3380–3424.

Sozomen, *HE*. PG 67.844–1630. Translated by C. Hartranft, in NPNF, Second Series, Volume 2, 236–427. New York: The Christian Literature Company, 1890. Repr. Grand Rapids, MI: William B. Eerdmans, 1952.

Strabo, *Geography*. Edited and translated by H.L. Jones. 8 volumes. Loeb Classical Library. London: W. Heinemann; New York: G.P. Putnam's Sons, 1917–1933. Repr. London: W. Heinemann; Cambridge, MA: Harvard University Press, 1960–1969.

Synaxarium Alexandrinum. Edited by J. Forget, in CSCO 47–49, 67, 78, 90. Rome: Catholicus, 1905–1926.

Synaxaire arabe jacobite. 6 volumes. Edited by R. Basset, in PO 1.3, 3.3, 11.5, 16.2, 17.3, 20.5. Paris: Firmin-Didot, 1904–1929.

Theodoret of Cyrus, *Eranistes*. PG 83.27–336.

Theodoret of Cyrus, *HE*. Edited by L. Parmentier. GCS 19. Third edition, by G. C. Hansen. Berlin: Akademie-Verlag, 1998. Translated by B. Jackson, in NPNF, Second Series, Volume 3, 1–348.

Theodosius of Alexandria, *Against the Tritheists*. Edited and translated by J.-B. Chabot, in CSCO 17, 40–79 (Syriac text), and CSCO 103, 26–55 (Latin translation). Louvain: L. Durbecq, 1952, 1955.

Theodosius of Alexandria, *Letter to Eastern Orthodox Bishops*. Edited and translated by J.-B. Chabot, in CSCO 17, 96–98 (Syriac text), and CSCO 103, 66–68 (Latin translation). Louvain: L. Durbecq, 1952, 1955.

Theodosius of Alexandria, *Tome to Empress Theodora*. Edited and translated by A. Van Roey and P. Allen, in *Monophysite Texts of the Sixth Century*, 23–41 (Syriac text), 42–56 (Latin translation). Leuven: Peeters, 1994.

Theophanes Confessor, *Chronicle*. Edited by C. de Boor. 2 volumes. Leipzig: B.G. Teubner, 1883–1885. Translated by C. Mango and R. Scott. Oxford: Clarendon Press, 1997.

Theophylact Simocatta, *History*. Translated by Michael Whitby and Mary Whitby. Oxford: Clarendon Press, 1986.

Timothy Aelurus, "A Collection of Unpublished Syriac Letters of Timothy Aelurus." Edited and translated by R.Y. Ebied and L.R. Wickham, in *Journal of Theological Studies* 21 (1970), 321–369.

Timothy Aelurus, *Against Chalcedon*. Edited and translated by R.Y. Ebied and L.R. Wickham, in *After Chalcedon: Studies in Theology and Church History*, edited by C. Laga, J.A. Munitiz, and L. Van Rompay, 120–142 (Syriac text), 143–166 (English translation).

Timothy Aelurus, *Histoire*. Edited by F. Nau, in *Documents pour servir à l'histoire de l'Èglise nestorienne : Textes syriaques*. PO 13.2, 202–217. Paris: Firmin-Didot, 1919.

Timothy III of Alexandria, *Fragmenta Dogmatica*. PG 86.265–276.

Transcript of a Written Statement of Anathema. Edited and translated by J.-B. Chabot, in CSCO 17, 160–161 (Syriac text), and CSCO 103, 111–112 (Latin translation). Louvain: L. Durbecq, 1952, 1955.

Zacharias Rhetor, *HE*. Edited and translated by E.W. Brooks, in CSCO 83–84, 87–88. Louvain: L. Durbecq, 1953. Translated by F.J. Hamilton and E.W. Brooks, *The Chronicle of Zachariah of Mitylene*. London: Methuen & Co., 1899.

Works Cited

Secondary Sources

Allen, Graham. *Intertextuality*. London: Routledge, 2000.

Allen, Pauline. *Evagrius Scholasticus the Church Historian*. Leuven: Spicilegium Sacrum Lovaniense, 1981.

Altheim, Franz, and Ruth Stiehl. *Christentum am Roten Meer*. 2 volumes. Berlin: Walter de Gruyter & Co., 1971–1973.

Altheim-Stiehl, Ruth. "Persians in Egypt (619–629)." In *The Coptic Encyclopedia*. Edited by A.S. Atiya, Volume 6, 1938–1941. New York: Macmillan, 1991.

Altheim-Stiehl, Ruth. "The Sasanians in Egypt – Some Evidence of Historical Interest," *Bulletin de la Société d'archéologie copte* 31 (1992), 87–96.

Altheim-Stiehl, Ruth. "Wurde Alexandreia im Juni 619 n. Chr. durch die Perser erobert: Bermerkungen zur zeitlichen Bestimmung der sâsânidischen Besetzung Ägyptens unter Chosrau II. Parwêz," *Tyche* 6 (1991), 3–16.

Amélineau, Emile. *Monuments pour server à l'histoire de l'Egypte Chrétienne aux IVe et Ve siècles*. Mémoires publies par les membres de la Mission archéologique française au Caire 4.1. Paris: Ernest Leroux, 1888.

Anderson, Benedict. *Imagined Communities: Reflections on the Origins and Spread of Nationalism*. Revised edition. London and New York: Verso, 1991.

Ashcroft, Bill, Gareth Griffiths, and Helen Tiffin. *The Post-Colonial Studies Reader*. London and New York: Routledge, 1995.

Atiya, Aziz S. *A History of Eastern Christianity*. London: Methuen & Co., Ltd., 1968.

Atiya, Aziz S., ed. *The Coptic Encyclopedia*. New York: Macmillan Publishing Company, 1991.

Atiya, Aziz S. "Patriarch." In *The Coptic Encyclopedia*. Edited by A.S. Atiya, Volume 6, 1909. New York: Macmillan, 1991.

Atiya, Aziz S. "Patriarchs, Dates and Succession of." In *The Coptic Encyclopedia*. Edited by A.S. Atiya, Volume 6, 1913–20. New York: Macmillan, 1991.

Ayres, Lewis, and Gareth Jones, eds. *Christian Origins: Theology, Rhetoric and Community*. London and New York: Routledge, 1998), 68–93.

Bacht, Heinrich, S.J. "Die Rolle des orientalischen Mönchtums in den kirchenpolitischen Auseinandersetzungen um Chalkedon (431–519)." In *Das Konzil von Chalkedon*, Volume 2, edited by A. Grillmeier and H. Bacht, 193–314. Würzburg: Echter-Verlag, 1953.

Bagnall, Roger S. "Alexandria: Library of Dreams," *Proceedings of the American Philosophical Society* 146.4 (2002), 348–362.

Bagnall, Roger S., and Klaas A. Worp. *Chronological Systems of Byzantine Egypt*. Second edition. Leiden: Brill, 2003.

Bardy, Gustave. "Aux origines de l'école d'Alexandrie," *Recherches de science religieuse* 27 (1937), 65–90.

Bardy, Gustave. "Pour l'histoire de l'École d'Alexandrie." In *Vivre et Penser*, Second series (1942), 80–109.

Bardy, Gustave. *Recherches sur saint Lucien d'Antioche et son École*. Paris: Beauchesne, 1936.

Barker, John W. "Justinian." In *Late Antiquity: A Guide to the Postclassical World*, edited by G.W. Bowersock, P. Brown, and O. Grabar, 531. Cambridge, MA: The Belnap Press of Harvard University Press, 1999.

Barnard, L.W. "Athanasius and the Melitian Schism in Egypt," *Journal of Egyptian Archaeology* 59 (1973), 181–189.

Barnard, L.W. "Two Notes on Athanasius: 1. Athanasius' Election as Archbishop of Alexandria. 2. The Circumstances Surrounding the Encyclical Letter of the Egyptian Bishops (Apol. C. Ar. 3.1–19.5)," *Orientalia Christiana Periodica* 41 (1975), 344–356.

Barnes, Robert. "Cloistered Bookworms in the Chicken-Coop of the Muses: The Ancient Library in Alexandria." In *The Library of Alexandria*, edited by R. MacLeod, 61–77. Cairo: The American University in Cairo Press, 2002.

Barnes, Timothy D. *Athanasius and Constantius: Theology and Politics in the Constantinian Empire*. Cambridge, MA: Harvard University Press, 1993.

Barnes, Timothy D. *Constantine and Eusebius.* Cambridge, MA: Harvard University Press, 1981.

Barnes, Timothy D. "Legislation Against the Christians," *Journal of Roman Studies* 58 (1968), 32–50. Repr. in T.D. Barnes, *Early Christianity and the Roman Empire*, Article II. London: Variorum Reprints, 1984.

Barnes, Timothy D. "Sossianus Hierocles and the Antecedents of the Great Persecution," *Harvard Studies in Classical Philology* 80 (1976), 239–252.

Barthes, Roland. "Theory of the Text." In *Untying the Text: A Post-Structuralist Reader*, edited by R. Young, 31-47. Boston: Routledge & Kegan Paul, 1981.

Barns, John, and Henry Chadwick. "A Letter Ascribed to Peter of Alexandria," *Journal of Theological Studies* 24, new series (1973), 443–455.

Basilios, Archbishop. "Patriarch, Consecration of." In *The Coptic Encyclopedia.* Edited by A.S. Atiya, Volume 6, 1909–11. New York: Macmillan Publishing Company, 1991.

Bauer, A., and J. Strzygowski. *Eine alexandrinische Weltchronik: Text und Miniaturen eines griechischen Papyrus des Sammlung W. Goleniscev.* Denkschriften der kaiserlichen Akademie der Wissenschaften in Wien, Phil.-hist. Klasse. Band 51, Abhandlung 2. Vienna: Alfred Hölder, 1905.

Bauer, Walter. *Orthodoxy and Heresy in Earliest Christianity.* Philadelphia: Fortress Press, 1971.

Bedjan, P. *Acta Martyrum et Sanctorum.* 7 volumes. Leipzig: Otto Harrassowitz, 1890–1897.

Bell, David N. "Introduction," to Besa, *Life of Shenoute*, 1–35. Kalamazoo, MI: Cistercian Publications, 1983.

Bell, H.I. *Cults and Creeds in Graeco–Roman Egypt.* New York: Philosophical Library, 1953.

Bell, H.I. "Evidences of Christianity in Egypt during the Roman Period," *Harvard Theological Review* 37 (1944) 185–208.

Bell, H.I. *Jews and Christians in Egypt: The Jewish Troubles in Alexandria and the Athanasian Controversy Illustrated by Texts from Greek Papyri in the British Museum.* London: British Museum and Oxford University Press; Milan: Cisalpino-Goliardica, 1924.

Bhabha, Homi. "Of Mimicry and Man: The Ambivalence of Colonial Discourse," *October* 28 (Spring 1984), 125–133.

Bilaniuk, Petro. "Pope in the Coptic Church." In *The Coptic Encyclopedia*. Edited by A.S. Atiya, Volume 6, 1998–2000. New York: Macmillan, 1991.

Bobertz, Charles A. "Cyprian of Carthage: A Social Historical Study of the Role of Bishop in the Ancient Christian Community of North Africa." Ph.D. dissertation, Yale University, 1988.

Bobertz, Charles A. "Patronage Networks and the Study of Ancient Christianity." In *Studia Patristica* 24, 20–27. Leuven: Peeters Press, 1993.

Bolman, Elizabeth, ed. *Monastic Visions: Wall Paintings in the Monastery of St. Antony at the Red Sea*. New Haven: Yale University and the American Research Center in Egypt, 2002.

Bosworth, C. E. "The Concept of Dhimma in Early Islam." In *Christians and Jews in the Ottoman Empire: The Functioning of a Plural Society*, Volume 1, edited by B. Braude and B. Lewis, 37–51. London and New York: Holmes and Meier, 1982.

Boularand, E. *L'Hérésie d'Arius et la Foi de Nicée*. Paris: Letouzey & Ané, 1972.

Bovon, François, Ann Graham Brock, and Christopher R. Matthews, eds. *The Apocryphal Acts of the Apostles: Harvard Divinity School Studies*. Cambridge, MA: Harvard University Center for the Study of World Religions, 1999.

Bowder, Diana. *The Age of Constantine and Julian*. London: Paul Elek, 1978.

Bowersock, G.W. "The Arabs Before Islam." In *The Genius of Arab Civilization: Source of Renaissance*. Third edition, edited by John R. Hayes, 15–34. New York and London: New York University Press, 1992.

Bowersock, G.W., Peter Brown, and Oleg Grabar. *Late Antiquity: A Guide to the Postclassical World*. Cambridge, MA: The Belnap Press of Harvard University Press, 1999.

Bowman, Alan K. *Egypt After the Pharaohs: 332 B.C.– A.D. 642*. Berkeley: University of California Press, 1986.

Brakke, David. *Athanasius and the Politics of Asceticism*. Oxford: Clarendon Press, 1995. Reprinted as *Athanasius and Asceticism*. Baltimore: The Johns Hopkins University Press, 1998.

Brakmann, H. "Zum Pariser Fragment angeblich des koptischen Patriarchen Agathon: Ein neues Blatt der Vita Benjamin I," *Muséon* 93 (1980), 299–309.

Breccia, Evaristo. *Alexandria ad Aegyptum: Guide de la ville ancienne et moderne et du Musée gréco-romain*. Bergamo: Istituto italiano d'arti grafiche, 1914.

Brennan, Timothy. "The National Longing for Form." In *Nation and Narration*, edited by Homi K. Bhabha, 44–70. London: Routledge, 1990.

Bright, W. "Petrus I, St." In *A Dictionary of Christian Biography and Literature to the End of the Sixth Century* A.D. Edited by H. Wace and W.C. Piercy. Volume 4, 331–334. London: J. Murray, 1911. Repr. Peabody, MA: Hendrickson, 1994.

Broek, Roelof van den. "The Christian 'School' of Alexandria in the Second and Third Centuries." In *Centers of Learning: Learning and Location in Pre-Modern Europe and the Near East*. Edited by J.W. Drijvers and A.A. MacDonald, 39–47. Leiden: E.J. Brill, 1995. Reprinted in *Studies in Gnosticism and Alexandrian Christianity*. Edited by R. van den Broek, 197–205. Leiden: E.J. Brill, 1996.

Broek, Roelof van den. "Jewish and Platonic Speculations in Early Alexandrian Theology: Eugnostus, Philo, Valentinus, and Origen." In *The Roots of Egyptian Christianity*. Edited by B.A. Pearson and J.E. Goehring, 190–203. Philadelphia: Fortress, 1986.

Brooks, E.W. "The Ordination of the Early Bishops of Alexandria," *Journal of Theological Studies* 2 (1901), 612–613.

Brooks, E.W. "The Patriarch Paul of Antioch and the Alexandrian Schism of 575," *Byzantinische Zeitschrift* 30 (1929–1930), 468–476.

Brown, Peter. *The Cult of the Saints*. Chicago: University of Chicago Press, 1981.

Brown, Peter. *The Making of Late Antiquity*. Cambridge, MA: Harvard University Press, 1978.

Brown, Peter. *Power and Persuasion in Late Antiquity*. Madison: University of Wisconsin Press, 1992.

Budge, E.A.W. *The Book of the Saints of the Ethiopian Church: A Translation of the Ethiopic Synaxarium*. 4 volumes. Cambridge: Cambridge University Press, 1928.

Buell, Denise. *Making Christians: Clement of Alexandria and the Rhetoric of Legitimacy*. Princeton: Princeton University Press, 1999.

Burns, J. Patout. *Cyprian the Bishop*. London: Routledge, 2002.

Burrus, Virginia. *'Begotten, Not Made': Conceiving Manhood in Late Antiquity*. Stanford: Stanford University Press, 2000.

Butler, Alfred J. *The Arab Conquest of Egypt and the Last Thirty Years of the Roman Dominion*, Second edition. Edited by P.M. Fraser. Oxford: Clarendon Press, 1978.

Butterworth, G.W. "Introduction." In *Origen, On First Principles*, xxiii–lviii. Gloucester, MA: Peter Smith, 1973.

Cahen, Claude. "Dhimma. In *The Encyclopedia of Islam*. Second edition. Volume 2, 227–231. Leiden: E.J. Brill, 1954–.

Cahen, Claude. "Djizya." In *The Encyclopedia of Islam*. Second edition. Volume 2, 559–562. Leiden: E.J. Brill, 1954–.

Callahan, Allen Dwight. "The *Acts of Mark*: Tradition, Transmission, and Translation of the Arabic Version." In *The Apocryphal Acts of the Apostles: Harvard Divinity School Studies*, edited by F. Bovon, A.G. Brock, and C.R. Matthews, 62–85. Cambridge, MA: Harvard University Center for the Study of World Religions, 1999.

Cameron, Alan. *Circus Factions: Blues and Greens at Rome and Byzantium*. Oxford: Clarendon Press, 1976.

Cameron, Averil. *Christianity and the Rhetoric of Empire: The Development of Christian Discourse*. Berkeley: University of California Press, 1991.

Cameron, Averil. "Eusebius of Caesaria and the Rethinking of History." In *Tria Corda: Scritti in onore di Arnaldo Momigliano*, edited by E. Gabba, 71–88. Como: Edizioni New Press, 1983.

Cameron, Averil. *The Mediterranean World in Late Antiquity*, A.D. 395–600. London and New York: Routledge, 1993.

Chadwick, Henry. "The Exile and Death of Flavian of Constantinople: A Prologue to the Council of Chalcedon," *Journal of Theological Studies*, new series, 6.1 (1955), 17–34.

Chitty, Derwas J. *The Desert a City*. Crestwood, NY: St. Vladimir's Seminary Press, 1966.

Choksy, Jamsheed K. "Sassanians." In *Late Antiquity: A Guide to the Postclassical World*, edited by G.W. Bowersock, P. Brown, and O. Grabar, 682–685. Cambridge, MA: The Belknap Press of Harvard University Press, 1999.

Christophilopoulou, Aikaterina. *Byzantine History*. 2 volumes. Translated by W. W. Phelps. Amsterdam: Adolf M. Hakkert, 1986.

Chuvin, Pierre. *A Chronicle of the Last Pagans*. Translated by B.A. Archer. Cambridge, MA: Harvard University Press, 1990.

Clark, Elizabeth. *The Origenist Controversy: The Cultural Construction of an Early Christian Debate*. Princeton: Princeton University Press, 1992.

Clark, Elizabeth. "Thinking with Women: The Uses of the Appeal to 'Woman' in Early Christian Propaganda Literature." Paper presented at the Symposium on the Expansion of Christianity in the First Four Centuries, Columbia University, New York, March 30, 2003.

Cody, Aelred, O.S.B. "Calendar, Coptic." In *The Coptic Encyclopedia*. Edited by A.S. Atiya, Volume 2, 433–436. New York: Macmillan, 1991.

Coquin, René-Georges, ed. *Livre de la consecration du sanctuaire de Benjamin*. Bibliothèque d'études copte 13. Cairo: Institut français d'archéologie orientale du Caire, 1975.

Coquin, René-Georges. "Patriarchal Residences." In *The Coptic Encyclopedia*. Edited by A.S. Atiya, Volume 6, 1912–1913. New York: Macmillan, 1991.

Countryman, L.W. *The Rich Christian in the Church of the Early Empire: Contradictions and Accommodations*. New York and Toronto: Edwin Mellen Press, 1980.

Cramer, Maria, and Heinrich Bacht. "Der antichalkedonische Aspekt im historisch-biographischen Schrifttum der koptischen Monophysiten (6.–7. Jahrhundert): Ein Beitrag zur Geschichte der Entstehung der monophysitischen Kirche Ägyptens." In *Das Konzil von Chalkedon*, Volume 2, edited by A. Grillmeier and H. Bacht, 315–338. Würzburg: Echter-Verlag, 1953.

Criddle, Andrew H. "On the Mar Saba Letter Attributed to Clement of Alexandria," *Journal of Early Christian Studies* 2 (1995), 215–220.

Crouzel, Henri. *Origen*. Translated by A.S. Worrell. Edinburgh: T. & T. Clark, 1989.

Crum, W.E. *Catalogue of the Coptic Manuscripts in the British Museum*. London: British Museum, 1905.

Crum, W.E., ed. *The Monasteries of the Wâdi 'n Natrûn*. 3 volumes. New York: The Metropolitan Museum of Art, 1926, 1932, 1933.

Crum, W.E. "Review of *Ein Mani-Fund in Aegypten*, by Carl Schmidt and H.J. Polotsky," *Journal of Egyptian Archaeology* 19 (1933), 196–199.

Crum, W.E. "Texts Attributed to Peter of Alexandria," *Journal of Theological Studies* 4 (1902–3), 387–397.

Crum, W.E., and H.G. Evelyn White, eds. *The Monastery of Epiphanius at Thebes*. 2 volumes. New York: Metropolitan Museum of Art, 1926.

Daniélou, Jean. *Origen*. Translated by W. Mitchell. London and New York: Sheed and Ward, 1955.

Davis, Stephen J. *The Cult of Saint Thecla: A Tradition of Women's Piety in Late Antiquity.* Oxford: Oxford University Press, 2001.

Davis, Stephen J. "Patronage and Architectural Adaptation in the Roman Cult of the Martyrs," *Anistoriton* 3 (1999), on the web at http://users.hol.gr/~ianlos/e993.htm.

Dawson, David. *Allegorical Readers and Cultural Revision in Ancient Alexandria.* Berkeley, CA: University of California Press, 1992.

Devos, P. "Une passion grecque inédite de S. Pierre d'Alexandrie et sa traduction par Anastase le Bibliothécaire," *Analecta Bollandiana* 83 (1965), 157–187.

Diels, Hermann. *Doxographi Graeci.* Second edition. Berlin: Walter de Gruyter, 1929.

Dillon, John. *The Middle Platonists.* Ithaca, NY: Cornell University Press, 1977.

Dörrie, Heinrich. "Die Erneuerung des Platonismus im ersten Jahrhundert vor Christus." In *Le Néoplatonisme.* Colloque international sur le néoplatonisme, 17–33. Paris: Éditions du Centre national de la recherche scientifique, 1971.

Douglas, Mary. *Natural Symbols.* New York: Random House, 1970.

Draguet, René. *Julien d'Halicarnasse et sa controverse avec Sévère d'Antioche sur l'incorruptibilité du corps du Christ.* Louvain: Imprimerie P. Smeesters, 1924.

Drake, Harold. "Models for Understanding the Success of Christianity." Paper presented at the Symposium on the Expansion of Christianity in the First Four Centuries, Columbia University, New York, March 30, 2003.

Drioton, Etienne. "La discussion d'un moine anthropomorphite Audien avec le patriarche Théophile d'Alexandrie en l'année 399," *Revue de l'Orient Chrétien* (2ᵉ ser.) 10 (= 20) (1915–1917), 92–100, 113–128.

Duffy, Eamon. *Saints and Sinners: A History of the Popes.* New Haven: Yale University Press, 1997.

Dzielska, Maria. *Hypatia of Alexandria.* Translated by F. Lyra. Cambridge, MA: Harvard University Press, 1995.

Ebied, R.Y., A. Van Roey, and L.R. Wickham. *Peter of Callinicum: Anti-Tritheist Dossier.* Orientalia Lovaniensia Analecta 10. Leuven: Departement Oriëntalistiek, 1981.

Ebied, R.Y., A. Van Roey, and L.R. Wickham, eds. *Petri Callinicensis Patriarchae Antiocheni Tractatus contra Damianum.* Volume 1. CSCO, Series Graeca, 29. Turnhout: Brepols; Leuven: University Press, 1994.

Ebied, R.Y., and L.R. Wickham. "A Collection of Unpublished Syriac Letters of Timothy Aelurus," *Journal of Theological Studies* 21 (1970), 321–369.

Ebied, R.Y., and L.R. Wickham. "Timothy Aelurus: Against the Definition of the Council of Chalcedon." In *After Chalcedon: Studies in Theology and Church History*, edited by C. Laga, J.A. Munitiz, and L. Van Rompay, 115–166. Leuven: Departement Oriëntalistiek, 1985.

Ehrman, Bart. *Lost Christianities: The Battles for Scripture and the Faiths We Never Knew*. New York and Oxford: Oxford University Press, 2003.

Ehrman, Bart. "Response to Charles Hedrick's Stalemate," *Journal of Early Christian Studies* 11:2 (2003), 155–163.

Ehrman, Bart. "Too Good to Be False? A Text Critic Looks at the Secret Gospel of Mark." Paper presented at the SBL Annual Meeting, Toronto, Canada, November 25, 2002.

Elm, Susanna. "The Dog That Did Not Bark: Doctrine and Patriarchal Authority in the Conflict Between Theophilus of Alexandria and John Chrysostom of Constantinople." In *Christian Origins: Theology, Rhetoric and Community*, edited by L. Ayres and G. Jones, 68–93. London and New York: Routledge, 1998.

Emmel, Stephen. "Shenoute's Literary Corpus." 5 volumes. Ph.D. dissertation, Yale University, 1993.

Emmel, Stephen, Martin Krause, Siegfried G. Richter, and Sofia Schaten, eds. *Ägypten und Nubien in spätantiker und christlicher Zeit*. Akten des 6. Internationalen Koptologenkongresses, Münster, 20.–26. Juli 1996. Band 1: Materielle Kultur, Kunst und religiöses Leben. Sprachen und Kulturen des christlichen Orients 6.1. Wiesbaden: Reichert, 1999.

Evans, James Allen. *The Age of Justinian: The Circumstances of Imperial Power*. London and New York: Routledge, 1996.

Evans, James Allen. *The Empress Theodora: Partner of Justinian*. Austin: University of Texas Press, 2002.

Everett Ferguson, ed. *Encyclopedia of Early Christianity*. New York and London: Garland, 1990.

Eyer, Shawn. "The Strange Case of the Secret Gospel According to Mark: How Morton Smith's Discovery of a Lost Letter by Clement of Alexandria Scandalized Biblical Scholarship." *Alexandria: The Journal for the Western Cosmological Traditions* 3

(1995), 103–129. Reprinted on the web at http://www-user.uni-bremen.de/~wie/Secret/secmark-engl.html.

Fanon, Frantz. *The Wretched of the Earth*. New York: Grove Press, 1968.

Fedalto, G. *Hierarchia Ecclesiastica Orientali. Series episcoporum ecclesiarum christianarum orientalium II. Patriarchatus alexandrinus, antiochenus, hierosolymitanus*. 2 volumes. Padua: Messaggero, 1988.

Foucault, Michel. *The Archaeology of Knowledge*. Translated by A.M. Sheridan Smith. New York: Pantheon Books, 1972.

Foucault, Michel. "On the Archaeology of the Sciences: Response to the Epistemology Circle." In *Aesthetics, Method, and Epistemology*, edited by J.D. Faubion. Essential Works of Foucault, Volume 2, 297-333. New York: The New Press, 1998.

Frankfurter, David, ed. *Pilgrimage and Holy Space in Late Antique Egypt*. Leiden: E.J. Brill, 1998.

Frankfurter, David. *Religion in Roman Egypt: Assimilation and Resistance*. Princeton: Princeton University Press, 1998.

Frankfurter, David. "'Things Unbefitting Christians': Violence and Christianization in Fifth-Century Panopolis," *Journal of Early Christian Studies* 8:2 (2000), 273–295.

Frend, W.H.C. *The Archaeology of Early Christianity: A History*. Minneapolis: Fortress Press, 1996.

Frend, W.H.C. "Athanasius as an Egyptian Christian Leader in the Fourth Century," *New College Bulletin* 8.1 (1974), 20–37. Repr. in *Religion Popular and Unpopular in the Early Christian Centuries*, Article XVI. London: Variorum Reprints, 1976.

Frend, W.H.C. *The Early Church*. Philadelphia: Fortress Press, 1982.

Frend, W.H.C. "The Failure of the Persecutions in the Roman Empire," *Past and Present* 8 (1959), 10–27. Repr. in *Town and Country in the Early Christian Centuries*, Article X. London: Variorum Reprints, 1980.

Frend, W.H.C. *Martyrdom and Persecution in the Early Church*. London: Basil Blackwell, 1965. Repr. Grand Rapids, MI: Baker Book House, 1981.

Frend, W.H.C. *Religion Popular and Unpopular in the Early Christian Centuries*. London: Variorum Reprints, 1976.

Frend, W.H.C. *The Rise of Christianity*. Philadelphia: Fortress, 1984.

Frend, W.H.C. *The Rise of the Monophysite Movement: Chapters in the History of the Church in the Fifth and Sixth Centuries*. Cambridge: Cambridge University Press, 1972.

Frend, W.H.C. "Severus of Antioch and the Origins of the Monophysite Hierarchy," *Orientalia Christiana Analecta* 195 (1973), 261–275. Reprinted in *Religion Popular and Unpopular in the Early Christian Centuries*, Article XIX. London: Variorum Reprints, 1976.

Frend, W.H.C. *Town and Country in the Early Centuries.* Repr. London: Variorum Reprints, 1980.

Gabra, Gawdat. *Coptic Monasteries: Egypt's Monastic Art and Architecture.* Cairo: American University in Cairo Press, 2002.

Gabra, Gawdat, and Anthony Alcock. *Cairo: The Coptic Museum and Old Churches.* Cairo: Egyptian International Publishing Company – Longman, 1993.

Gellner, Ernst. "The Mighter Pen? Edward Said and the Double Standards of Inside-out Colonialism," *The Times Literary Supplement* (February 19, 1993), 3–4.

Gibbon, Edward. *The History of the Decline and Fall of the Roman Empire.* 5 volumes. Philadelphia: Porter and Coates, 1845.

Godlewski, Wlodzimierz. "Deir el Naqlun: Topography and Tentative History." In *Archeologia e papiri nel Fayyum: Storia della ricerca, problemi e prospettive.* Atti del convegno internazionale, 123–145. Syracuse: Istituto Internazionale del Papiro, 1997.

Godlewski, Wlodzimierz. "Naqlun 1993–1996." In *Ägypten und Nubien in spätantiker und christlicher Zeit.* Akten des 6. Internationalen Koptologenkongresses, Münster, 20.–26. Juli 1996. Band 1: Materielle Kultur, Kunst und religiöses Leben. Edited by S. Emmel, M. Krause, S.G. Richter, and S. Schaten. Sprachen und Kulturen des christlichen Orients 6.1, 157–162. Wiesbaden: Reichert, 1999.

Godlewski, Wlodzimierz. "Les peintures de l'église de l'archange Gabriel à Naqlun," *Bulletin de la Société d'archéologie copte* 39 (2000), 89–101.

Goehring, James E. *Ascetics, Society, and the Desert: Studies in Early Egyptian Monasticism.* Studies in Antiquity and Christianity. Harrisburg, PA: Trinity Press International, 1999.

Goehring, James E. "Monastic Diversity and Ideological Boundaries in Fourth-Century Christian Egypt," *Journal of Early Christian Studies* 5.1 (1997), 61–84. Repr. in J. E. Goehring, *Ascetics, Society, and the Desert: Studies in Early Egyptian Monasticism*, 196–218. Studies in Antiquity and Christianity. Harrisburg, PA: Trinity Press International, 1999.

Goehring, James E. "Monasticism." In *Encyclopedia of Early Christianity*, edited by E. Ferguson, 612–619. New York and London: Garland Publishing, Inc., 1990.

Goehring, James E., "New Frontiers in Pachomian Studies." In *The Roots of Egyptian Christianity*, edited by B.A. Pearson and J.E. Goehring, 236–257. Reprinted with an addendum in J.E. Goehring, *Ascetics, Society, and the Desert*, 162–186.

Gore, Charles. "On thè Ordination of the Early Bishops of Alexandria," *Journal of Theological Studies* 3 (1902), 278–282.

Graf, Georg. "Zwei dogmatische Florilegien der Kopten," *Orientalia Christiana Periodica* 3 (1937), 49–77, 345–402.

Grant, Robert M. "The New Testament Canon." In *The Cambridge History of the Bible*. Volume 1, 284–308. Cambridge: Cambridge University Press, 1970.

Grant, Robert M. "The Oldest Gospel Prologues," *Anglican Theological Review* 23 (1941), 231–245.

Greenslade, S.L. *Schism in the Early Church*. London: SCM Press, 1953.

Gregg, Robert C., ed. and trans. *The Life of Antony and the Letter to Marcellinus*. New York: Paulist Press, 1980.

Gregg, Robert C., and Dennis E. Groh. *Early Arianism—A View of Salvation*. Philadelphia: Fortress Press, 1981.

Griggs, C. Wilfred. *Early Egyptian Christianity: From Its Origins to 451 C.E.* Second edition. Leiden: E.J. Brill, 1991.

Grillmeier, Aloys, S.J. *Christ in Christian Tradition. Volume One: From the Apostolic Age to Chalcedon (451)*. Translated by J. Bowden. Second edition. Atlanta: John Knox Press, 1975.

Grillmeier, Aloys, S.J. *Christ in Christian Tradition. Volume Two, Part One: From Chalcedon to Justinian I*. Translated by P. Allen and J. Cawte. Atlanta: John Knox, 1987.

Grillmeier, Aloys, S.J., with Theresia Hainthaler. *Christ in Christian Tradition. Volume Two, Part Two: From the Council of Chalcedon (451) to Gregory the Great (590–604), The Church of Constantinople in the Sixth Century*. Translated by P. Allen and J. Cawte. London: Mowbray; Louisville: Westminster / John Knox Press, 1995.

Grillmeier, Aloys, S.J., with Theresia Hainthaler. *Christ in Christian Tradition. Volume Two, Part Four: From the Council of Chalcedon (451) to Gregory the Great (590–604), The Church of Alexandria with Nubia and Ethiopia*. Translated by O.C. Dean. London: Mowbray; Louisville: Westminster John Knox, 1996.

Grossmann, Peter, Charles Le Quesne, and Peter Sheehan. "Zur römischen Festung von Babylon – Alt-Kairo," *Archäologischer Anzeiger* (1994), 271–287.

Guelich, Robert A. *Mark 1—8:26*. Word Biblical Commentary, Volume 34A. Dallas: Word Books, 1989.

Guha, Ranajit. "On Some Aspects of the Historiography of Colonial India," *Subaltern Studies* 1 (1982), 1–8.

Haacke, Rhaban. "Die kaiserliche Politik in den Auseinandersetzungen um Chalkedon (451–553)." In *Das Konzil von Chalkedon*, Volume 2, edited by A. Grillmeier and H. Bacht, 95–177. Würzburg: Echter-Verlag, 1953.

Haas, Christopher. *Alexandria in Late Antiquity: Topography and Social Conflict*. Baltimore: The Johns Hopkins University Press, 1997.

Haas, Christopher. "The Arians of Alexandria," *Vigiliae Christianae* 47 (1993), 234–245.

Haase, Felix. *Patriarch Dioskur I. von Alexandria: Nach monophysitischen Quellen*. Kirchengeschichtliche Abhandlungen, Band 6, 141–236. Breslau, G.P. Aderholz, 1908.

Haldon, J.F. *Byzantium in the Seventh Century: The Transformation of a Culture*. Cambridge: Cambridge University Press, 1990.

Hanson, R.P.C. "Was Origen Banished from Alexandria?" In *Studia Patristica* 17.2, 904–906. New York: Pergamon Press, 1982.

Hanson, R.P.C. *The Search for the Christian Doctrine of God*. Edinburgh: T. & T. Clark, 1988.

Hardy, E.R. *Christian Egypt: Church and People*. New York: Oxford University Press, 1952.

Hardy, E.R., ed. *Christology of the Later Fathers*. Library of Christian Classics 3. Philadelphia: Westminster Press, 1954.

Hardy, E.R. "Damian." In *The Coptic Encyclopedia*. Edited by A.S. Atiya, Volume 3, 688–689. New York: Macmillan, 1991.

Harvey, Susan Ashbrook. *Asceticism and Society in Crisis: John of Ephesus and the Lives of the Eastern Saints*. Berkeley: University of California Press, 1990.

Hawley, John C., ed. *Encyclopedia of Postcolonial Studies*. Westport, CT; London: Greenwood Press, 2001.

Hayes, John R., ed. *The Genius of Arab Civilization: Source of Renaissance*. Third edition. New York and London: New York University Press, 1992.

Hedrick, Charles W. "The Secret Gospel of Mark: Stalemate in the Academy," *Journal of Early Christian Studies* 11:2 (2003), 133–145.

Hefele, C.J. *History of the Councils of the Church*. Translated by H. Oxenham. Edinburgh: T. & T. Clark, 1896.

Heijer, Johannes den. "History of the Patriarchs of Alexandria." In *The Coptic Encyclopedia*. Edited by A.S. Atiya, Volume 4, 1238–1242. New York: Macmillan Publishing Company, 1991.

Heijer, Johannes den. *Mawhûb ibn Mansûr ibn Mufarrig et l'historiographie copte-arabe. Etude sur la composition de l'Histoire des Patriarches d'Alexandrie*. CSCO 513. Louvain: Peeters, 1989.

Heijer, Johannes den. "Mawhûb ibn Mansûr ibn Mufarrij al-Iskandarâni." In *The Coptic Encyclopedia*. Edited by A.S. Atiya, Volume 5, 1573–1574. New York: Macmillan Publishing Company, 1991.

Heisey, Nancy. *Origen the Egyptian*. Nairobi: Paulines Publications Africa, 2000.

Hengel, Martin. *Studies in the Gospel of Mark*. Trans. J. Bowden. Philadelphia: Fortress, 1985.

Herrin, Judith. *The Formation of Christendom*. Princeton: Princeton University Press, 1987.

Hoek, Annewies van den. "The 'Catechetical' School of Early Christian Alexandria and Its Philonic Heritage," *Harvard Theological Review* 90.1 (1997), 59–87.

Hoek, Annewies van den. "Origen and the Intellectual Heritage of Alexandria: Continuity or Disjunction." In *Origeniana quinta*. Edited by R.J. Daley, 46–50. Leuven: Peeters, 1992.

Hondelink, Hans, ed. *Coptic Art and Culture*. The Netherlands Institute for Archaeology and Arabic Studies in Cairo. Cairo: Shouhdy Publishing House, 1990.

Hooker, Morna D. *The Gospel According to Mark*. London: A & C Black, 1991.

Hoyland, Robert G. *Seeing Islam as Others Saw It: A Survey and Evaluation of Christian, Jewish and Zoroastrian Writings on Early Islam*. Princeton: Darwin Press, 1997.

Hubai, P. "The Legend of St. Mark: Coptic Fragments." In *Studia Aegyptica XII*. Studia in Honorem L. Fóti, 165–234. Budapest: Chaire d'Égyptologie, l'Université Eötvös Loránd de Budapest, 1989.

Humphreys, R. Stephen. *Islamic History: A Framework for Inquiry*. Princeton: Princeton University Press, 1991. Repr. Cairo: The American University in Cairo Press, 1992.

Hunzinger, C.H. "Babylon als Deckname für Rom und die Datierung des 1. Petrusbriefes." In *Gottes Wort und Gottes Land*, edited by H.G. Reventlow, 67–77. Göttingen: Vandenhoeck & Ruprecht, 1965.

Hyvernat, H., ed. *Les Actes des Martyrs de l'Égypte*. Hildesheim and New York: Georg Olms Verlag, 1977.

Inglisian, Vahan. "Chalkedon und die armenische Kirche." In *Das Konzil von Chalkedon*, Volume 2, edited by A. Grillmeier and H. Bacht, 361–417. Würzburg: Echter-Verlag, 1953.

Innemée, Karel C. "The Iconographical Program of Paintings in the Church of al-'Adra in Deir al-Sourian: Some Preliminary Observations." In *THEMELIA: Spätantike und koptologische Studien Peter Grossmann zum 65. Geburtstag*, edited by M. Krause and S. Schaten, 143–155. Wiesbaden: Reichert Verlag, 1998.

Innemée, Karel C., and Lucas Van Rompay. "Deir al-Surian (Egypt): New Discoveries of 2001–2002." In *Hugoye: Journal of Syriac Studies* 5.2 (July 2002), on the web at http://syrcom.cua.edu/Hugoye/Vol5No2/HV5N2InnemeeVan Rompay.html.

Jarry, Jacques. *Hérésies et factions dans l'Empire byzantin du IVe au VIIe siècle*. Cairo: L'Institut français d'archéologie orientale, 1968.

Johnson, David W., S.J. "Anti-Chalcedonian Polemics in Coptic Texts, 451–641," in *The Roots of Egyptian Christianity*. Edited by B.A. Pearson and J.E. Goehring, 216–234. Philadelphia: Fortress Press, 1986.

Johnson, David W., S.J. "Pope Peter III Mongus: Conflicts within Egypt." Paper presented at the Seventh International Congress of Coptic Studies, Leiden, Holland, August 2000.

Johnson, David W., S.J. "Pope Timothy II Aelurus: His Life and His Importance for the Development of Christianity in Egypt," *Coptica* 1 (2002), 77–89.

Johnson, Patricia Cannon. "The Neoplatonists and the Mystery Schools of the Mediterranean." In *The Library of Alexandria*. Edited by R. MacLeod, 143–161. Cairo: The American University in Cairo Press, 2002.

Johnson, Sherman E. *A Commentary on the Gospel According to St. Mark*. Second edition. London: Adam & Charles Black, 1972.

Jones, A.H.M. *The Later Roman Empire, 284–602*. 2 volumes. London: Basil Blackwell, Ltd., 1964. Repr. Baltimore: The Johns Hopkins University Press, 1986.

Jones, A.H.M. "Were the Ancient Heresies National or Social Movements in Disguise?" *Journal of Theological Studies* 10, new series (1959), 280–298.

Joplin, Patricia K. "Ritual Work on Human Flesh: Livy's Lucretia and the Rape of the Body Politic," *Helios* 17 (1990), 51–70.

Joshel, Sandra. "The Body Female and the Body Politic: Livy's Lucretia and Verginia." In *Pornography and Representation in Greece and Rome*, ed. A. Richlin, 112–130. Oxford: Oxford University Press, 1992.

Jülicher, Adolf. "Die Liste der alexandrinischen Patriarchen im 6. und 7. Jahrhundert." In *Festgabe von Fachgenossen und Freunden Karl Müller zum siebzigsten Geburtstag dargebracht*, 7–23. Tübingen: J.C.B. Mohr (Paul Siebeck), 1922.

Kaegi, Walter. "Heraclius." In *Late Antiquity: A Guide to the Postclassical World*, edited by G.W. Bowersock, P. Brown, and O. Grabar, 488. Cambridge, MA: The Belknap Press of Harvard University Press, 1999.

Kaegi, Walter. *Byzantium and the Early Islamic Conquests.* Cambridge: Cambridge University Press, 1992.

Kannengiesser, Charles, S.J. "Athanasius of Alexandria vs. Arius: The Alexandrian Crisis," in *The Roots of Egyptian Christianity*, edited by B.A. Pearson and J.E. Goehring, 204–215. Philadelphia: Fortress Press, 1986.

Kelly, J.N.D. *A Commentary on the Epistles of Peter and Jude.* New York: Harper & Row; Grand Rapids, MI: Baker Book House, 1969.

Kelly, J.N.D. *Early Christian Creeds.* Third edition. London: Longman, 1972.

Kelly, J.N.D. *Early Christian Doctrines.* Revised edition. San Francisco: HarperCollins Publishers, 1978.

Kemp, Eric Waldram. "Bishops and Presbyters at Alexandria," *Journal of Ecclesiastical History* 6 (1955), 125–142.

King, Karen L. *What is Gnosticism?* Cambridge, MA: The Belknap Press of Harvard University Press, 2003.

Knipfing, J.R. "The Libelli of the Decian Persecution," *Harvard Theological Review* 16 (1923), 345–390.

Koester, Helmut. *Ancient Christian Gospels: Their History and Development.* Philadelphia: Trinity International Press, 1990.

Koester, Helmut. "GNÔMAI DIAPHORAI: The Origin and Nature of Diversification in the History of Early Christianity." In *Trajectories Through Early Christianity*. Edited by J.M. Robinson and H. Koester, 114–157. Philadelphia: Fortress Press, 1971.

Koester, Helmut. *Introduction to the New Testament.* 2 volumes. Philadelphia: Fortress Press, 1982.

Kraft, Robert A., and Janet A. Timbie. "Review of James M. Robinson, *The Nag Hammadi Library in English.*" In *Religious Studies Review* 8 (1982), 32–52.

Krawiec, Rebecca. *Shenoute and the Women of the White Monastery: Egyptian Monasticism in Late Antiquity.* New York: Oxford University Press, 2002.

Kuhn, K.H. "Shenute, Saint." In *The Coptic Encyclopedia.* Edited by A.S. Atiya, Volume 7, 2131–2133. New York: Macmillan, 1991.

Lampe, G.W.H. *A Patristic Greek Lexicon.* Oxford: Clarendon Press, 1961.

Lane Fox, Robin. *Pagans and Christians.* New York: Alfred A. Knopf, Inc., 1987.

Langener, Lucia. *Isis lactans – Maria lactans: Untersuchungen zur koptischen Ikonographie.* Altenberge: Oros Verlag, 1996.

Larsow, F. *Die* Fest-Briefe *des heiligen Athanasius Bischofs von Alexandrien aus dem Syrischen übersetzt und durch Anmerkungen erläutert.* Leipzig: F.C.W. Vogel, 1852.

Layton, Bentley. *The Gnostic Scriptures.* Garden City, NY: Doubleday, 1987.

Layton, Bentley. "Prolegomena to the Study of Gnosticism." In *The Social World of the First Christians: Essays in Honor of Wayne A. Meeks.* Edited by L. Michael White and O. Larry Yarbrough, 334–350. Minneapolis: Fortress Press, 1995.

Layton, Bentley. "The Significance of Basilides in Ancient Christian Thought," *Representations* 28 (1989), 135-151.

Leclercq, Henri. "Alexandrie, Archéologie." In *Dictionnaire d'archéologie chrétienne et de liturgie.* Edited by F. Cabrol. Volume 1, 1098–1182. Paris: Letouzey et Ané, 1907.

Lee, G.M. "Eusebius on St. Mark," *Studia Patristica* 12 (TU 115), 422–431. Berlin: Akademie-Verlag, 1973.

Lefort, L. Th. "Théodore de Tabennese et la letter de S. Athanase sur le canon de la Bible," *Muséon* 29 (1920), 205–216.

Leitzmann, Hans. *A History of the Early Church.* 2 volumes (4 parts). Translated by B.L. Woolf. Cambridge: James Clarke & Co., 1951, 1993.

Leroy, Jules. *Les peintures des couvents du desert d'Esna.* La peinture murale chez les coptes, vol. 1. Cairo: L'Institut français d'archéologie orientale du Caire, 1975.

Lilla, Salvatore R.C. *Clement of Alexandria: A Study in Christian Platonism and Gnosticism.* Oxford: Oxford University Press, 1971.

MacLeod, Roy. "Introduction: Alexandria in History and Myth." In *The Library of Alexandria*, edited by R. MacLeod, 1–15. Cairo: The American University in Cairo Press, 2002.

MacLeod, Roy, ed. *The Library of Alexandria*. Cairo: The American University in Cairo Press, 2002.

MacMullen, Ramsay. *Christianizing the Roman Empire, A.D. 100–400*. New Haven and London: Yale University Press, 1984.

Mai, Angelo, ed. *Spicilegium Romanum*. 10 volumes. Rome: Typis Collegii Urbani, 1839–1844.

Marrou, Henri-Irénée. "L'Arianisme comme phénomène alexandrine." In *Patristique et humanisme*. Edited by Henri-Irénée Marrou, 321–330. Patristica Sorbonensia 9. Paris: Éditions du Seuil, 1976.

Martin, Annik. *Athanase d'Alexandrie et l'église d'Égypte au IVe siècle (328–373)*. Collection de l'École française de Rome 216. Rome: École française de Rome, 1996.

Martin, Annik, ed., with Micheline Albert. *Histoire 'acéphale' et index syriaque des letters festales d'Athanase d'Alexandrie*. SC 317. Paris, Cerf, 1985.

Martin, Ralph P. "Mark, John." In *The International Standard Bible Encyclopedia*, Volume 3. Revised edition, 259–260. Grand Rapids, MI: William B. Eerdmans, 1986.

Maspero, Jean. *Histoire des patriarches d'Alexandrie depuis la mort l'empereur Anastase jusqu'a la reconciliation des églises jacobites (518–616)*. Paris: Librairie ancienne Édouard Champion, 1923.

Mathison, Ralph W. "Persecution." In *Encyclopedia of Early Christianity*. Edited by E. Ferguson, 712–717. New York and London: Garland, 1990.

McGuckin, John A. "The Influence of the Isis Cult on St. Cyril of Alexandria's Christology." In *Studia Patristica* 24, 291–299. Leuven: Peeters Press, 1993.

McGuckin, John A. *St. Cyril of Alexandria, The Christological Controversy: Its History, Theology, and Texts*. Leiden; New York; Köln: E.J. Brill, 1994.

Michaels, J. Ramsey. *1 Peter*. Word Biblical Commentary, Volume 49. Waco, Texas: Word Books, 1988.

Miles, Richard, ed. *Constructing Identities in Late Antiquity*. London and New York: Routledge, 1999.

Minh-ha, Trinh T. *When the Moon Waxes Red: Representation, Gender and Cultural Politics*. New York and London: Routledge, 1991.

Monks, George R. "The Church of Alexandria and the City's Economic Life in the Sixth Century," *Speculum* 28 (1953), 349–362.

Montserrat, Dominic. "Pilgrimage to the Shrine of SS Cyrus and John at Menouthis in Late Antiquity." In *Pilgrimage and Holy Space in Late Antique Egypt*, ed. D. Frankfurter, 257–279. Leiden: E.J. Brill, 1998.

Moore-Gilbert, Bart. *Postcolonial Theory: Contexts, Practices, Politics*. London and New York: Verso, 1997.

Moorhead, John. *Justinian*. London and New York: Longman, 1994.

Moussa, Mark. "The Anti-Chalcedonian Movement in Byzantine Egypt: An Evaluation of Past Scholarship and Current Interpretations." In *Ägypten und Nubien in spätantiker und christlicher Zeit*. Akten des 6. Internationalen Koptologenkongresses, Münster, 20.–26. Juli 1996. Band 1: Materielle Kultur, Kunst und religiöses Leben. Edited by S. Emmel, M. Krause, S.G. Richter, and S. Schaten. Sprachen und Kulturen des christlichen Orients 6.1, 504–510. Wiesbaden: Reichert, 1999.

Müller, Caspar Detlef Gustav. "Damian, Papst und Patriarch von Alexandrien," *Oriens Christianus* 70 (1986), 118–142.

Müller, Caspar Detlef Gustav, ed. *Die Homilie über die Hochzeit zu Kana und weitere Schriften des Patriarchen Benjamin I. von Alexandrien*. Heidelberg: Carl Winter; Universitätsverlag, 1968.

Naghibi, Nima. "Colonial Discourse." In *Encyclopedia of Postcolonial Studies*, edited by John C. Hawley, 102–107. Westport, CT; London: Greenwood Press, 2001.

Nautin, Pierre. "La conversion du temple de Philae en église chrétienne," *Cahiers Archéologique* 17 (1963), 1–43.

Nautin, Pierre. *Lettres et écrivains chrétiens des IIe et IIIe siècles*. Paris: Editions du Cerf, 1961.

Nautin, Pierre. *Origène: Sa vie et son oeuvre*. Paris: Beauchesne, 1977.

Neale, J.M. *The Patriarchate of Alexandria*. 2 volumes. London: Joseph Masters, 1847.

Neuschäfer, Bernhardt. *Origenes als Philologe*. 2 volumes. Schweizerische Beiträge zur Altertumswissenschaft 18. Basel: Friedrich Reinhardt, 1987.

Nineham, D.E. *St. Mark*. Harmondsworth: Penguin Books, 1963.

Norris, Richard A. *The Christological Controversy*. Philadelphia: Fortress Press, 1980.

Northcote, J.S., and W.R. Brownlow. *Roma Sotteranea, or Some Account of the Roman Catacombs, especially of the Cemetery of San Callisto*. London: Longmans, Green, Reader, and Dyer, 1869.

Opitz, Hans-Georg, ed. *Athanasius*: Werke. Auftrage der Kirchenväter-Kommission der Preussischen Akademie der Wissenschaften. 3 volumes. Berlin and Leipzig: Walter de Gruyter, 1934–1940.

Opitz, Hans-Georg. "Die Zeitfolge der arianischen Streites von den Anfang bis zum Jahre 328," *Zeitschrift für Neutestamentliche Wissenschaft und die Kunde der älteren Kirche* 33 (1934), 131–159.

Orlandi, Tito. "Un frammento copto Teofilo di Alessandria," *Rivista degli studi orientali* 44 (1969), 23–26.

Orlandi, Tito. "Richerche su una storia ecclesiastica alessandrina del IV sec.," *Vetera Christianorum* 11 (1974), 269–312.

Orlandi, Tito. "Uno scritto di Teofilo di Alessandria sulla distruzione del Serapeum?" *La Parola del passato* 23, fasc. 121 (1968), 295–304.

Orlandi, Tito. "Theophilus of Alexandria in Coptic Literature." In *Studia Patristica* 16 (= TU 129), 100–104. Berlin: Akademie-Verlag, 1985.

Parry, Benita. "Problems in Current Theories of Colonial Discourse," *Oxford Literary Review* 9.1–2 (1987), 27–58.

Partrick, Theodore Hall. *Traditional Egyptian Christianity: A History of the Coptic Orthodox Church.* Greensboro, NC: Fisher Park Press, 1996.

Pearson, Birger A. "Earliest Christianity in Egypt: Some Observations," in *The Roots of Egyptian Christianity*, edited by B.A. Pearson and J.E. Goehring, 132–159. Philadelphia: Fortress Press, 1986.

Pearson, Birger A., and James E. Goehring, eds. *The Roots of Egyptian Christianity.* Philadelphia: Fortress Press, 1986.

Pelikan, Jaroslav. *The Spirit of Eastern Christendom (600–1700).* The Christian Tradition, Volume 2. Chicago and London: The University of Chicago Press, 1974.

Perkins, Judith. *The Suffering Self: Pain and Narrative Representation in the Early Christian Era.* London and New York: Routledge, 1995.

Perkins, Pheme. "Docetism." In *Encyclopedia of Early Christianity*, ed. E. Ferguson, 272–273. New York and London: Garland Publishing, Inc., 1990.

Prasad, Madhava. "The 'Other' Worldliness of Postcolonial Discourse: A Critique," *Critical Quarterly* 34.3 (1992), 74–89.

Quasten, J. *Patrology.* 4 volumes. Utrecht: Spectrum, 1950–1986. Repr. Westminster, MD: Christians Classics, Inc., 1992.

Quesnell, Quentin. "The Mar Saba Clementine: A Question of Evidence," *Catholic Biblical Quarterly* 37 (1975), 48–67.

Rahner, Karl. "La doctrine d'Origène sur le penitence," *Recherches de science religieuse* 37 (1950), 47–97, 252–286.

Raval, Shilpa. "Boys to Men: Erotic and Political Violence in Livy's Rape of Lucretia." Paper presented at the Greco–Roman Lunch, Yale University, November 4, 2002.

Reicke, Bo. *The Roots of the Synoptic Gospels.* Philadelphia: Fortress, 1986.

Reventlow, H.G., ed. *Gottes Wort und Gottes Land.* Göttingen: Vandenhoeck & Ruprecht, 1965.

Riad, Henri, Youssef Hanna Shehata, and Youssef al-Gheriani. *Alexandria: An Archeological Guide to the City.* Second edition. Alexandria: The Regional Authority for Tourism Promotion, 1996.

Roberts, C.H. "Early Christianity in Egypt: Three Notes," *Journal of Egyptian Archaeology* 40 (1954) 92–96.

Roberts, C.H. *Manuscript, Society, and Belief in Early Christian Egypt.* London: Oxford University Press, 1979.

Roncaglia, Martiniano. *Histoire de l'Eglise Copte.* 4 Volumes. Beirut: Dar al-Kalima, 1966–1973.

Roueché, Charlotte. "Factions." In *Late Antiquity: A Guide to the Postclassical World,* edited by G.W. Bowersock, P. Brown, and O. Grabar, 442. Cambridge, MA: The Belknap Press of Harvard University Press, 1999.

Rougé, Jean. "Les débuts de l'épiscopat de Cyrille d'Alexandrie et le Code Théodosien." In *ALEXANDRINA: Hellenisme, judaisme et christianisme à Alexandrie. Mélanges offerts au P. Claude Mondesert,* 339–349. Paris: Cerf, 1987.

Rousseau, Philip. *Ascetics, Authority, and the Church in the Age of Jerome and Cassian.* Oxford: Oxford University Press, 1978.

Routh, M. J. *Reliquae Sacrae.* 5 volumes. Second edition. Oxford: Typographeo Academico, 1846–1848. Repr. Hildesheim; New York: Georg Olms Verlag, 1974.

Rubenson, Samuel. *The Letters of St. Antony: Monasticism and the Making of a Saint.* Minneapolis: Fortress Press, 1995.

Rusch, William G. *The Trinitarian Controversy.* Philadelphia: Fortress, 1980.

Russell, Norman. "Bishops and Charismatics in Early Christian Egypt." In *Abba: The Tradition of Orthodoxy in the West*. Edited by J. Behr, A. Louth, and D. Conomos, 99–110. Crestwood, NY: St. Vladimir's Seminary Press, 2003.

Russell, Norman. *Cyril of Alexandria*. London: Routledge, 2000.

Rutherford, Ian. "Island of the Extremity: Space, Language and Power in the Pilgrimage Traditions of Philae." In *Pilgrimage and Holy Space in Late Antique Egypt*, ed. D. Frankfurter, 229–256. Leiden: E.J. Brill, 1998.

Saad, Saad Michael, and Nardine Miranda Saad. "Electing Coptic Patriarchs: A Diversity of Traditions," *Bulletin of Saint Shenouda the Archimandrite Coptic Society* 6 (2001), 20–32.

Said, Edward. *Culture and Imperialism*. New York: Vintage Books, 1993.

Said, Edward. *Orientalism*. New York: Vintage Books, 1978.

Saller, Richard P. *Personal Patronage under the Early Empire*. Cambridge: Cambridge University Press, 1982.

Santos Otero, Aurelio de. "Later Acts of the Apostles (9.1. Martyrium Marci)." In *New Testament Apocrypha*. Revised edition. Volume 2. Edited by W. Schneemelcher, 461–464. Louisville: Westminster / John Knox Press, 1992.

Schneider, Annedith M. "Center/Periphery." In *Encyclopedia of Postcolonial Studies*, edited by John C. Hawley, 85–86. Westport, CT; London: Greenwood Press, 2001.

Schroeder, Caroline. "Disciplining the Monastic Body: Asceticism, Ideology, and Gender in the Egyptian Monastery of Shenoute of Atripe." Ph.D. dissertation, Duke University, 2002.

Schwartz, Eduard. *Cyrill und der Mönch Viktor*. Sitzungsberichte der Akademie der Wissenschaften in Wien, Philosophisch-historische Klasse 208, 4. Vienna: Hölder-Pichler-Tempsky, 1928.

Schwartz, Eduard. *Gesammelte Schriften*. 5 volumes. Berlin: Walter de Gruyter, 1959.

Schwartz, Eduard. *Publizistische Sammlungen zum Acacianische Schisma*. Abhandlungen der Bayerischen Akademie der Wissenschaften, Philosophisch-historische Abteilung, Neue Folge, Heft 10. München: Verlag der Bayerischen Akademie der Wissenschaften, 1934.

Schwartz, Eduard. *Zur Geschichte des Athanasius*. Gesammelte Schriften. Band 3. Berlin: Walter de Gruyter, 1959.

Schwartz, Eduard. "Zur Geschichte des Athanasius," *Nachrichten von der Gesellschaft der Wissenschaften zu Göttingen (Phil-hist-Klasse)* (1905), 164–187.

Sellers, R. V. *The Council of Chalcedon.* London: SPCK Press, 1953.

Selwyn, E. G. *The First Epistle of Peter.* London: Macmillan & Co., Ltd., 1964.

Sharpe, Jenny. "Figures of Colonial Resistance," *Modern Fiction Studies* 35:1 (1989), 137–155.

Shoucri, Mounir. "Patriarchal Election." In *The Coptic Encyclopedia.* Edited by A.S. Atiya, Volume 6, 1911–1912. New York: Macmillan, 1991.

Slemon, Stephen. "Unsettling the Empire: Resistance Theory for the Second World," *World Literature Written in English* 30.2 (1990), 30–41.

Smith, Morton. *Clement of Alexandria and a Secret Gospel of Mark.* Cambridge: Harvard University Press, 1973.

Smith, Morton. "Clement of Alexandria and Secret Mark: The Score at the End of the First Decade." *Harvard Theological Review* 75.4 (1982), 449–461.

Smith, Morton. *The Secret Gospel: The Discovery and Interpretation of the Secret Gospel According to Mark.* New York: Harper & Row, 1973.

Souter, Alexander. *A Study of Ambrosiaster.* Texts and Studies 7.4. Cambridge: Cambridge University Press, 1905. Repr. Nendeln: Kraus Reprint, 1967.

Spanel, Donald B. "Timothy II Aelurus." In *The Coptic Encyclopedia.* Edited by A.S. Atiya, Volume 7, 2263–2268. New York: Macmillan, 1991.

Spanel, Donald. "Two Fragmentary Sa'idic Coptic Texts Pertaining to Peter I, Patriarch of Alexandria," *Bulletin de la Société d'Archéologie Copte* 24 (1979–82), 85–102.

Spivak, Gayatri. "Can the Subaltern Speak?" In *Marxism and the Interpretation of Culture,* ed. C. Nelson and L. Grossberg, 271–313. London: Macmillan, 1988.

Spivak, Gayatri. *In Other Worlds: Essays in Cultural Politics.* London: Routledge, 1987.

Spivak, Gayatri. "Subaltern Studies: Deconstructing Historiography." In *In Other Worlds: Essays in Cultural Politics,* edited by G. Spivak, 197–221. London: Routledge, 1987.

Starowieyski, M. "Le titre *theotokos* avant le concile d'Ephese." In *Studia Patristica* 19, 236–242. Leuven: Peeters, 1989.

Stevenson, J., ed. *The New Eusebius: Documents Illustrating the History of the Church to* A.D. *337*. London: SPCK, 1957.

Stratos, A.N. *Byzantium in the Seventh Century*. 4 volumes. Amsterdam: Adolf M. Hakkert, 1972.

Stroumsa, Gedaliahu A.G. "Comments on Charles Hedrick's Article: A Testimony," *Journal of Early Christian Studies* 11:2 (2003), 147–153.

Suleri, Sara. *The Rhetoric of English India*. Chicago: University of Chicago Press, 1992.

Telfer, William. "Episcopal Succession in Egypt," *Journal of Ecclesiastical History* 3 (1952), 1–13.

Telfer, William. "Melitius of Lycopolis and Episcopal Succession in Egypt." *Harvard Theological Review* 48 (1955), 227–237.

Telfer, William. "St. Peter of Alexandria and Arius," *Analecta Bollandiana* 67 (1949), 117–130.

Telfer, William. "When Did the Arian Controversy Begin?" *Journal of Theological Studies* 47 (1946), 129–142.

Thompson, Herbert. "Dioscorus and Shenoute." In *Recueil d'études égyptologique*. Bibliothèque de l'École des haute etudes, IVe section, Sciences historiques et philologiques. Fascicule 234, 367–376. Paris: E. Champion, 1922.

Treadgold, Warren. *A History of the Byzantine State and Society*. Stanford: Stanford University Press, 1997.

Trigg, Joseph W. *Origen*. London and New York: Routledge, 1998.

Trigg, Joseph W. *Origen: The Bible and Philosophy in the Third-Century Church*. Atlanta: John Knox Press, 1983.

Vallance, John. "Doctors in the Library: The Strange Tale of Apollonius the Bookworm and Other Stories." In *The Library of Alexandria*, edited by R. MacLeod, 95–113. Cairo: The American University in Cairo Press, 2002.

Van Roey, Alfred. "Les débuts de l'église jacobite." In *Das Konzil von Chalkedon*, Volume 2, edited A. Grillmeier and H. Bacht, 339–360. Würzburg: Echter-Verlag, 1953.

Van Roey, Alfred. "Les fragments trithéites de Jean Philopon," *Orientalia Lovaniensia Periodica* 11 (1980), 135–163.

Van Roey, Alfred, and Pauline Allen. *Monophysite Texts of the Sixth Century*. Leuven: Uitgeverij Peeters en Departement Oriëntalistiek, 1994.

Veilleux, Armand. "Monasticism and Gnosis in Egypt." In *The Roots of Egyptian Christianity*, edited by B.A. Pearson and J.E. Goehring, 271–306.

Viteau, Joseph. *Passions des Saints Ecaterine et Pierre d'Alexandrie, Barbara et Anysia. Publiée d'après les manuscrits grecs de Paris et de Rome.* Paris: E. Bouillon, 1897.

Vivian, Tim. *Journeying into God: Seven Monastic Lives.* Minneapolis: Fortress Press, 1996.

Vivian, Tim. *St. Peter of Alexandria, Bishop and Martyr.* Philadelphia: Fortress, 1988.

Volbach, W. F. *Elfenbeinarbeiten der Spätantike und des frühen Mittelalters,* 3. Auflage. Mainz: Verlag Philipp von Zabern, 1976.

Wade-Hampton Arnold, Duane. *The Early Episcopal Career of Athanasius of Alexandria.* Notre Dame and London: University of Notre Dame Press, 1991.

Wagner, Guy. *Les oasis d'Égypte à l'époque grecque, romaine et Byzantine d'après les documents grecs.* Cairo: Institut français d'archéologie orientale du Caire, 1987.

Walters, C.C. "Christian Paintings from Tebtunis," *Journal of Egyptian Archaeology* 75 (1989), 191–209, and plates XVI–XXIX.1.

Ward, Benedicta. *The Desert Christian: Sayings of the Desert Fathers. The Alphabetic Collection.* New York: Macmillan, 1975.

Watts, Edward Jay. "City and School in Late Antique Athens and Alexandria." Ph.D. dissertation, Yale University, 2002.

Weitzmann, Kurt. *Age of Spirituality: Late Antique and Early Christian Art.* New York: Metropolitan Museum of Art, 1979.

Weitzmann, Kurt. "The Ivories of the So-called Grado Chair," *Dumbarton Oaks Papers* 26 (1972), 45–91.

White, L. Michael. *Building God's House in the Roman Word: Architectural Adaptation among Pagans, Jews, and Christians.* Baltimore and London: The Johns Hopkins University Press, 1990.

Whittow, Mark. *The Making of Orthodox Byzantium, 600–1025.* Houndmills, Basingstoke, Hampshire, and London: Macmillan Press, 1996.

Williams, Michael A. *Rethinking "Gnosticism": An Argument for Dismantling a Dubious Category.* Princeton: Princeton University Press, 1996.

Williams, Rowan. *Arius: Heresy and Tradition.* London: Darton, Longman, and Todd, 1987. Second edition. London: SCM, 2001.

Winkelmann, Friedhelm. "Ägypten und Byzanz vor der arabischen Eroberung," *Byzantinoslavica* 40:2 (1979), 161–182.

Winkelmann, Friedhelm. *Der monenergetisch-monotheletische Streit.* Frankfurt am Main: Peter Lang, 2000.

Winkelmann, Friedhelm. "Die Stellung Ägyptens im oströmisch-byzantinischen Reich." In *Graeco-Coptica: Griechen und Kopten im byzantinischen Ägypten*, edited by P. Nagel, 11–35. Wissenschaftliche Beiträge 48 (I 29). Halle: Martin-Luther-Universität, 1984.

Wipszycka, E. "La christianisation de l'Égypte aux IVe–Ve siècles. Aspects sociaux et ethniques," *Aegyptus* 58 (1988), 117–165.

Yang, John. "Representation and Resistance: A Cultural, Social, and Political Perplexity in Post-Colonial Literature." On the web at http://www.scholars.nus.edu.sg/landow/post/poldiscourse/yang/1.html.

Young, Frances M. *From Nicaea to Chalcedon: A Guide to the Literature and its Background.* Philadelphia: Fortress Press, 1983.

Young, Robert J.C. *Postcolonialism: An Historical Introduction.* Oxford: Blackwell Publishers, 2001.

Notes

Author's Preface

1. J.M. Neale, *The Patriarchate of Alexandria* (2 volumes; London: Joseph Masters, 1847).
2. Edward R. Hardy, *Christian Egypt: Church and People. Christianity and Nationalism in the Patriarchate of Alexandria* (New York: Oxford University Press, 1952). Hardy is somewhat heavy-handed in his broad thesis of an Egyptian "nationalism" that prevailed in the fourth through seventh centuries. For a more nuanced treatment of this subject, see chapter four in this book.
3. Jean Maspero's fine monograph, *Histoire des patriarches d'Alexandrie depuis la mort l'empereur Anastase jusqu'à la reconciliation des églises jacobites (518–616)* (Paris: Édouard Champion, 1923), focuses only on a century's worth of material in the sixth and early seventh centuries.
4. See, e.g., C. Wilfrid Griggs, *Early Egyptian Christianity from its Origins to 451 CE* (Leiden: E.J. Brill, 1990) who, while touching frequently on the leadership role of the Alexandrian bishops, has dedicated himself to the much broader task of narrating the "history of Christianity in Egypt from its earliest recorded origins to the Council of Chalcedon in 451 C.E." (p. 1).
5. On the "performative" and "enunciative" functions of discursive speech, see Michel Foucault, *The Archaeology of Knowledge*, trans. A.M. Sheridan Smith (New York: Pantheon Books, 1972), esp. 79–117. A pioneering work in the application of "discourse analysis" to the study of Christianity in late antiquity was Averil Cameron's *Christianity and the Rhetoric of Empire: The Development of Christian Discourse* (Berkeley: University of California Press, 1991). On the relationship of discourse and identity in late antiquity, see also Richard Miles, "Introduction," in *Constructing Identities in Late Antiquity* (London and New York: Routledge, 1999), 1–15.

Chapter 1: The Succession of St. Mark

1. Ivory relief, Musée du Louvre, inv. OA.3317; W.F. Volbach, *Elfenbeinarbeiten der Spätantike und des frühen Mittelalters,* Third edition (Mainz: Verlag Philipp von Zabern, 1976), 96–97, no. 144; K. Weitzmann, *Age of Spirituality: Late Antique and Early Christian Art* (New York: Metropolitan Museum of Art, 1979), 544–546, no. 489; Christopher Haas, *Alexandria in Late Antiquity: Topography and Social Conflict* (Baltimore and London: The Johns Hopkins University Press, 1997), 200–201, figs. 21a–b, and 247; H. Leclercq, "Alexandrie, Archéologie," in

Dictionnaire d'archéologie chrétienne et de liturgie, ed. F. Cabrol (Paris: Letouzey et Ané, 1907), I.1119–1120, fig. 273.

2. As early as the third century A.D., the title "Pope" (in Greek, *papas*, meaning "father") was used to refer to the bishop of Alexandria: the earliest extant example of its usage appears in the writings of Dionysius of Alexandria (A.D. 247–264), as preserved in Eusebius, *HE* 7.7.4 (ed. E. Schwartz and T. Mommsen, GCS 9.2 (1908), 644). Over the first six and a half centuries of the Egyptian church, the terms "Pope" and "Patriarch" came to be virtually interchangeable honorific titles for the Alexandrian archbishop.

3. See, for example, Acts 12:12 and 12:25 ("John, whose other name was Mark"), Acts 15:37 ("John called Mark"), and Acts 15:39 ("Mark"). In Acts 13:5 and 13:13, he is simply referred to as "John."

4. In one of his authentic letters (Philemon 24), Paul himself identifies Mark as one of his "co-workers." In addition, two letters attributed to Paul but probably written by second-generation disciples (Colossians 4:10–11 and 2 Timothy 4:11) commend Mark as someone who was helpful to Paul in his ministry

5. Due to the popularity of the name Mark in the ancient Roman world, some scholars have questioned whether the Mark in 1 Peter was the same Mark that was mentioned in the book of Acts (see, e.g., D.E. Nineham, *St. Mark* (Harmondsworth: Penguin Books, 1963), 39). This issue is difficult to resolve based on the scant information provided by the New Testament sources.

6. Robert A. Guelich, *Mark 1—8:26* (Word Biblical Commentary, Volume 34A; Dallas: Word Books, 1989), xxvii–xxviii. From ancient Christian papyrological evidence, Martin Hengel and Bo Reicke both argue that the gospel title "according to Mark" probably dates back at least to the early second century A.D. (M. Hengel, *Studies in the Gospel of Mark*, trans. J. Bowden (Philadelphia: Fortress, 1985), 64–72; B. Reicke *The Roots of the Synoptic Gospels* (Philadelphia: Fortress, 1986), 150–157, 161–166).

7. Papias of Hieropolis, *The Sayings of the Lord Explained*, cited by the fourth-century historian Eusebius, *HE* 3.39.15 (ed. E. Schwartz and T. Mommsen, GCS 9.1 (1903), 290–292.

8. The Alexandrian Christian philosopher and gnostic Basilides (active ca. A.D. 132–135) also claimed that his teacher Glaucias was "the interpreter of Peter" (*hermêneus Petrou*; Clement of Alexandria, *Stromata* VII.17.106.4 (ed. O. Stählin, L. Früchtel, and U. Treu, Fourth edition, volume 3 (Berlin: Akademie-Verlag, 1985), 75); also Bentley Layton, "The Significance of Basilides in Ancient Christian Thought," *Representations* 28 (1989), 135-151.

9. For a summary of different opinions on Papias' testimony, see R. Guelich, *Mark*, xxvii.

10. R.P. Martin, "Mark, John," in *The International Standard Bible Encyclopedia*, Volume 3, revised edition (Grand Rapids, MI: William B. Eerdmans, 1986) 260. Martin believes that Papias was simply drawing an inference from information found in the New Testament concerning Mark's association with Peter (see, for example, Acts 12:12, where Peter visits the house of Mark's mother; and 1 Peter 5:13).

11 Irenaeus, *Against Heresies* 3.1.1; ed. N. Brox (Fontes Christiani 8.3; Freiburg: Herder, 1993), 24 (Greek and Latin).

12. This tradition from Clement of Alexandria is preserved in Eusebius, *HE* 6.14.5–7.

13. Morna D. Hooker, *The Gospel According to Mark* (London: A & C
Black, 1991), 7. The *Anti-Marcionite Prologue to Mark* (ed. and trans.
R.M. Grant, "The Oldest Gospel Prologues," in *Anglican Theological
Review* 23 (1941) 231–245, esp. 235–236) also used to be cited as a second-
century source that mentions Mark's reputation as "the interpreter of
Peter" (Sherman E. Johnson, *A Commentary on the Gospel According to
St. Mark*, Second edition (London: Adam & Charles Black, 1972), 14).
However, it has been shown more recently that the *Anti-Marcionite
Prologue to Mark* was in fact produced during the second half of the
fourth century (Helmut Koester, *Ancient Christian Gospels: Their
History and Development* (Philadelphia: Trinity Press International,
1990), 243). The writer of this *Prologue* adds a colorful detail about Mark
not found in the other sources: he relates that the evangelist was called
"Stumpfinger" on account of the fact that "for the size of the rest of his
body he had fingers that were too short."
14. See, for example, Franz Altheim and Ruth Stiehl, *Christentum am Roten
Meer*, volume 2 (Berlin: Walter de Gruyter & Co., 1973), 297–299.
15. The existence of this garrison town in antiquity is attested by Josephus
(*Antiquities* 2.315; ed. and trans. H. St. J. Thackeray, volume 1, 302–303) and
Strabo (*Geography* 17.1.30; ed. and trans. H.L. Jones, volume 8, 84–87).
16. For a discussion of some of the problems related to the interpretation of
Babylon as the Egyptian site, see C. Wilfred Griggs, *Early Egyptian
Christianity: From its Origins to 451 c.e.* (Leiden: E.J. Brill, 1991), 17–18; and
J.N.D. Kelly, *A Commentary on the Epistles of Peter and Jude* (New York:
Harper & Row; Grand Rapids, MI: Baker Book House, 1969), 218–220).
17. H.I. Bell, "Evidences of Christianity in Egypt during the Roman Period,"
Harvard Theological Review 37 (1944), 187–188.
18. Peter Grossmann, Charles Le Quesne, and Peter Sheehan, "Zur römischen
Festung von Babylon – Alt-Kairo," *Archäologischer Anzeiger* (1994),
271–287.
19. For examples from ancient Jewish apocalyptic literature, see *2 Baruch*
(11.1; 67.7) and the *Sibylline Oracles* (5.143, 159). On the use of Babylon
as a code name for Rome in ancient Jewish literature and in 1 Peter, see
C.H. Hunzinger, "Babylon als Deckname für Rom und die Datierung
des 1. Petrusbriefes," in *Gottes Wort und Gottes Land*, ed. H.G.
Reventlow (Göttingen: Vandenhoeck & Ruprecht, 1965), 67–77.
20. On Babylon as an image of exile in 1 Peter, see E.G. Selwyn, *The First
Epistle of Peter* (London: Macmillan & Co., Ltd., 1964), 303–305; J.N.D.
Kelly, *Commentary on the Epistles of Peter and Jude*, 219–220; and J.
Ramsey Michaels, *1 Peter* (Word Biblical Commentary, Volume 49;
Waco, Texas: Word Books, 1988), 310–311.
21. Eusebius, *HE* 2.16.1 (ed. E. Schwartz and T. Mommsen, GCS 9.1 (1903),
140).
22. Eusebius, *HE* 2.15 (ed. E. Schwartz and T. Mommsen, GCS 9.1 (1903),
140).
23. Eusebius' *Chronicle* survives in a Latin version that was reworked by
Jerome: ed. R. Helm, in *Eusebius Werke* (GCS 47; rev. ed.; Berlin:
Akademie-Verlag, 1956).
24. The *Paschal Chronicle* (PG 92.560A) dates Mark's arrival two years before
the accession of Claudius (A.D. 39), while the tenth-century historian
Eutychius of Alexandria (Saîd ibn Batrîq, PG 111.982A) claims that Mark
came to the city in the ninth year of Claudius' reign (A.D. 49–50). On the
various sources related to the dating of Mark's arrival in Alexandria, see
B.A. Pearson, "Earliest Christianity in Egypt: Some Observations," in *The

Roots of Egyptian Christianity, edited by B.A. Pearson and J.E. Goehring (Philadelphia: Fortress Press, 1986), 139, note 30.

25. *History of the Patriarchs of the Coptic Church of Alexandria*, ed. B. Evetts, in PO 1.2 (Paris: Firmin-Didot, 1948), 140.

26. G.M. Lee ("Eusebius on St. Mark," *Studia Patristica* 12 (TU 115; Berlin: Akademie-Verlag, 1973), 425–27) has argued from the usage of the verb *phasi* in Greek literature that Eusebius may be referring to a written source. Along the same lines, Morton Smith (*Clement of Alexandria and a Secret Gospel of Mark* (Cambridge: Harvard University Press, 1973), 27) has tried to argue for the possibility that the verb *phasi* here is not used impersonally, and instead refers to the writers Clement and Papias, whom Eusebius mentions in the preceding paragraph. On Eusebius' use of previously existing traditions about Mark, see also C.W. Griggs, *Early Egyptian Christianity*, 19ff., and B.A. Pearson, "Earliest Christianity in Egypt," 138–39).*

27. Eusebius, *HE* 2.16.1–2 (ed. E. Schwartz and T. Mommsen, GCS 9.1 (1903), 140–142).

28. Philo, *On the Contemplative Life* (*De vita contemplative*); ed. and trans. F.H. Colson (Loeb Classical Library; Cambridge, MA: Harvard University Press; London: William Heinemann, 1985) IX.103–169.

29. For an example of such skepticism, see Hans Lietzmann (*A History of the Early Church*, Volume 1, Part 2 (Cambridge: James Clarke & Co., 1951, 1993), 543), who, in commenting on the lack of early sources for Christianity in Egypt, notes that early Christians "tried, though clumsily, to fill the blanks of knowledge from a fictitious list of bishops of Alexandria, and a legend that Mark founded the Church."

30. Morton Smith gives an account of his 1958 discovery of this text at the Monastery of Mar Sabas in Palestine in his book, *The Secret Gospel: The Discovery and Interpretation of the Secret Gospel According to Mark* (New York: Harper & Row, 1973). For the Greek text with critical commentary, published the same year, see Morton Smith, *Clement of Alexandria and a Secret Gospel of Mark* (Cambridge: Harvard University Press, 1973). For an English translation, see M. Smith, *The Secret Gospel*, 14–17; and http://www-user.uni-bremen.de/~wie/Secret/letter-engl.html.

31. John Chrysostom, *Homily on Matthew* 1.3 (PG 57.17); B.A. Pearson, "Earliest Christianity," 138, note 28.

32. Morton Smith (*Clement of Alexandria*, 67–85) argued for the authenticity of Clement's authorship on the basis of the language, style, and contents of the letter. For summaries of various positive and negative responses to Smith's arguments, see M. Smith, "Clement of Alexandria and the Secret Mark: The Score at the End of the First Decade," *Harvard Theological Review* 75.4 (1982), 449–61; and Shawn Eyer, "The Strange Case of the Secret Gospel According to Mark: How Morton Smith's Discovery of a Lost Letter by Clement of Alexandria Scandalized Biblical Scholarship," *Alexandria: The Journal for the Western Cosmological Traditions* 3 (1995), 103–129; reprinted on the web at http://www-user.uni-bremen.de/~wie/Secret/secmark-engl.html. For access to ongoing scholarly conversations about this document, see the website http://www-user.uni-bremen.de/~wie/Secret/secmark_home.html.

33. Quentin Quesnell, "The Mar Saba Clementine: A Question of Evidence," *Catholic Biblical Quarterly* 37 (1975), 48–67; Andrew H. Criddle, "On the Mar Saba Letter Attributed to Clement of Alexandria," *Journal of Early Christian Studies* 2 (1995), 215–220. In a paper presented at the 2002 SBL Annual Meeting in Toronto, Bart Ehrman enumerated the

objections of various scholars to the letter's authenticity and pointed out the circumstantial oddities of the work's discovery (along with its subsequent disappearance) and its manuscript setting (B. Ehrman, "Too Good to Be False? A Text Critic Looks at the Secret Gospel of Mark," November 25, 2002). A revised version of this paper is included in a special issue of the *Journal of Early Christian Studies* (Summer 2003) that features a three-way discussion on the Secret Gospel of Mark: see Charles W. Hedrick, "The Secret Gospel of Mark: Stalemate in the Academy," *Journal of Early Christian Studies* 11:2 (2003), 133–145; Gedaliahu A.G. Stroumsa, "Comments on Charles Hedrick's Article: A Testimony," *Journal of Early Christian Studies* 11:2 (2003), 147–153; and B. Ehrman, "Response to Charles Hedrick's Stalemate," *Journal of Early Christian Studies* 11:2 (2003), 155–163. Most recently, Ehrman presents a fuller analysis of issues surrounding the discovery of the *Secret Gospel of Mark* in his book, *Lost Christianities: The Battles for Scripture and the Faiths We Never Knew* (New York and Oxford: Oxford University Press, 2003), 67–89.

34. (Ps.-)Clement of Alexandria, *Letter to Theodore* I.15—II.2; ed. M. Smith, *Clement of Alexandria*, 19–44; trans. M. Smith, *The Secret Gospel*, 15.

35. B.A. Pearson, "Earliest Christianity," 144.

36. The *Acts of Mark* was originally written in Greek or Coptic, but the work is also extant in Latin, Arabic, and Ethiopic translations. The Greek text is preserved in two complete versions: an eleventh century Paris manuscript printed in PG 115:164ff. (cod. Paris gr. 881), and an eleventh or twelfth century Vatican manuscript printed the *Acta Sanctorum* (rev. ed.; Paris: Palmé, 1863–1940) 12: April, 3, XXXVIII–XL (cod. Vatican gr. 866). For a translation of the latter version, see Allen Dwight Callahan, "The Acts of Saint Mark: An Introduction and Translation," *Coptic Church Review* 14 (1993), 3–10. The Coptic text only survives in fragments: see P. Hubai, "The Legend of St. Mark: Coptic Fragments," in *Studia Aegyptica XII* (Studia in Honorem L. Fóti; Budapest: Chaire d'Égyptologie, l'Université Eötvös Loránd de Budapest, 1989) 165–234. For references to the Latin, Arabic, and Ethiopic text traditions, see P. Hubai, "The Legend of St. Mark," 187, note 1; B.A. Pearson, "Earliest Christianity in Egypt," 140, note 37; Aurelio de Santos Otero, "Later Acts of the Apostles (9.1. Martyrium Marci)," in *New Testament Apocrypha*, rev. ed., volume 2, edited by W. Schneemelcher (Louisville: Westminster/ John Knox Press, 1992), 461–464; and Allan Dwight Callahan, "The *Acts of Mark*: Tradition, Transmission, and Translation of the Arabic Version," in *The Apocryphal Acts of the Apostles: Harvard Divinity School Studies*, edited by F. Bovon, A.G. Brock, and C.R. Matthews (Cambridge, MA: Harvard University Center for the Study of World Religions, 1999), 62–85.

37. The Latin monk Paulinus of Nola (A.D. 353–431) provides the earliest external witness to the tradition about Mark's martyrdom: in one of his poems, he mentions Mark's conflict with the cult of Serapis in Alexandria, a conflict that led to his imprisonment and death in the *Acts of Mark* (Paulinus of Nola, *Carmen* XIX.84–86; ed. W. Hartel, CSEL 30 (Vienna: F. Tempsky, 1894), 121). For other references to the story of Mark's martyrdom from the sixth and seventh centuries, see Aurelio de Santos Otero, "Later Acts of the Apostles (9.1. Martyrium Marci)," 462. The fact that a Latin writer was aware of this tradition (probably via a Latin translation) around the end of the fourth century would suggest that the Greek (or Coptic) original dated from somewhat earlier. Regarding the tradition about Mark's founding of the Alexandrian

church, Eusebius of Caesarea identifies Anianus as Mark's successor in his *History of the Church* (completed A.D. 325), but does not mention any details from the story of Mark's encounter with Anianus found in the *Martyrdom*.

38. Unless otherwise noted, in my summary of the story I will be making reference to the version in PG 115:164ff. (cod. Paris gr. 881).

39. This story about Mark's construction of an Alexandrian church in the first century is an anachronistic detail in the later *Acts of Mark*. The earliest Christians in Egypt (and elsewhere) did not build their own churches, but met in the homes of believers—i.e., in house churches. On the evidence for such house churches and its place in the development of early Christian architecture, see L. Michael White, *Building God's House in the Roman Word: Architectural Adaptation among Pagans, Jews, and Christians* (Baltimore and London: The Johns Hopkins University Press, 1990).

40. B.A. Pearson, "Earliest Christianity in Egypt," 132–159, esp. 144ff.

41. Eusebius, *HE* 2.24.1 (ed. E. Schwartz and T. Mommsen, GCS 9.1 (1903), 174).

42. The text of the *History of the Patriarchs* was originally edited by B. Evetts in *Patrologia Orientalis* 1.2; 1.4; 5.1; 10.5 (Paris: Firmin-Didot, 1904–1914), and then continued by Y. 'Abd al-Masîh, O.H.E. Burmeister, A.S. Atiya, and A. Khater (Cairo: Société d'archéologie copte, 1943–1974).

43. While the famous Copto-Arabic theologian Sawirus ibn al-Muqaffa (tenth century A.D.) has traditionally been credited with editing the *History of the Patriarchs*, recent analysis has shown that an Alexandrian deacon named Mawhûb ibn Mansûr Mufarrig was responsible for redacting the text in the eleventh century. In compiling his material, he relied on a number of earlier Coptic sources. The first series of biographies, from Anianus up to the time of Cyril I (412–444), traces to the work of an otherwise unknown scribe named Menas, who was perhaps a monk of the White Monastery (Deir Anba Shenoute) near Sohag. The second group of biographies, covering the period from Cyril I to the life of Simon I (692–700) at the end of the seventh century, was authored by a certain George the Archdeacon, who lived at the end of the seventh century and served as a scribe under Simon I. The material on the life and martyrdom of Saint Mark derived from a separate textual tradition in the Coptic sources. For an accessible account of the redaction of the *History of the Patriarchs*, with bibliography, see J. den Heijer, "History of the Patriarchs of Alexandria," *Coptic Encyclopedia* 4.1238–1242. For a more detailed treatment of this subject, see his monograph entitled, *Mawhûb ibn Mansûr ibn Mufarrig et l'historiographie copte-arabe. Etude sur la composition de l'Histoire des Patriarches d'Alexandrie* (Louvain: Peeters, 1989).

44. W. Volbach, *Elfenbeinarbeiten der Spätantike*, 139–140, nos. 237–241; K. Weitzmann, "The Ivories of the So-called Grado Chair," *Dumbarton Oaks Papers* 26 (Washington, D.C.: Dumbarton Oaks, 1972), nos. 7–11. Weitzmann argues persuasively for an eighth-century dating over against previous polarized attempts at dating the ivories either to the late sixth century or to the eleventh century (K. Weitzmann, "Ivories," 45–81).

45. K. Weitzmann, "Ivories," 82–85.

46. W. Volbach, *Elfenbeinarbeiten der Spätantike,* 139, no. 237; K. Weitzmann, "Ivories," no. 7.

47. W. Volbach, *Elfenbeinarbeiten der Spätantike*, 140, no. 239; K. Weitzmann, "Ivories," no. 8; T. Vivian, "Plaque with scene from life of St. Mark," in K. Weitzmann, *Age of Spirituality*, 508–509, no. 456.

48. W. Volbach, *Elfenbeinarbeiten der Spätantike*, 139, no. 238; K. Weitzmann, "Ivories," no. 9.
49. W. Volbach, *Elfenbeinarbeiten der Spätantike*, 140, no. 240; K. Weitzmann, "Ivories," no. 10.
50. W. Volbach, *Elfenbeinarbeiten der Spätantike*, 140, no. 241; K. Weitzmann, "Ivories," no. 11.
51. K. Weitzmann, "Ivories," 87–88.
52. Edward R. Hardy (*Christian Egypt*, 11) argues that when Eusebius (*HE* 5.22) refers to Demetrius' responsibility for the districts (*paroikiai*) at Alexandria, one may discern the beginnings of an early parish-based system, "the organization of the Alexandrian Church in separate communities under their respective presbyters." While he shares other historians' suspicion of the Alexandrian succession list prior to Demetrius, Hardy argues that the existence of such a local church organization at the time of Demetrius' election would increase the likelihood that Demetrius' predecessor Julian was a historical figure. However, Hardy's argument is weakened by the fact that the same word, *paroikiai*, is used in reference to earlier Alexandrian bishops like Anianus (Ananius). Eusebius' choice of terminology probably derives from his knowledge of the fourth-century ecclesiastical situation in Egypt, and not from the first- or second-century milieu.
53. W. Bauer, *Orthodoxy and Heresy in Earliest Christianity*, second edition, English text edited by R.A. Kraft and G. Krodel (Philadelphia: Fortress Press, 1971), 45.
54. C.H. Roberts, *Manuscript, Society, and Belief in Early Christian Egypt* (London: Oxford University Press, 1979), 1.
55. W. Bauer, *Orthodoxy and Heresy*, 53. While he grants that "orthodox" believers existed prior to this time, Bauer notes that their number must have been small, especially given the fact that at the time of his accession Demetrius was the only ordained bishop in Egypt.
56. W. Bauer, *Orthodoxy and Heresy*, 45. Bauer's judgment concerning the origins of Christianity in Egypt has been echoed by some other scholars, including R.M. Grant, who states that "in the second century, as far as our knowledge goes, Christianity in Egypt was exclusively heterodox" (R.M. Grant, "The New Testament Canon," in *The Cambridge History of the Bible*, Volume 1 (Cambridge: Cambridge University Press, 1970), 298). For a similar viewpoint, see Helmut Koester, "GNÔMAI DIAPHORAI: The Origin and Nature of Diversification in the History of Early Christianity," in *Trajectories Through Early Christianity*, ed. J.M. Robinson and H. Koester (Philadelphia: Fortress Press, 1971), 114; and also Koester's more recent book, *Introduction to the New Testament* (2 vols.; Philadelphia: Fortress Press, 1982), 2:220.
57. C.H. Roberts, *Manuscript, Society and Belief*, 13–14, 52–53. For a discussion of these different papyri, see C.W. Griggs, *Early Egyptian Christianity*, 23–34.
58. See, e.g., Bentley Layton, "Prolegomena to the Study of Gnosticism," in *The Social World of the First Christians: Essays in Honor of Wayne A. Meeks*, edited by L. Michael White and O. Larry Yarbrough (Minneapolis: Fortress Press, 1995), 334–350, esp. 335; Michael A. Williams, *Rethinking "Gnosticism": An Argument for Dismantling a Dubious Category* (Princeton: Princeton University Press, 1996); and Karen L. King, *What is Gnosticism?* (Cambridge, MA: The Belknap Press of Harvard University Press, 2003).
59. C.H. Roberts, *Manuscript, Society and Belief*, 54, 60.
60. *P. Oxy.* III.405 (= H. 671). Grenfell and Hunt, the original editors,

assigned the papyrus a late second- or early third-century date. H.I. Bell ("Evidences of Christianity in Egypt During the Roman Period," *Harvard Theological Review* 37 (1944), 202) concurred, estimating for the papyrus a date around A.D. 200.

61. C.W. Griggs, *Early Egyptian Christianity*, 33–34; C.H. Roberts, "Early Christianity in Egypt: Three Notes," *Journal of Egyptian Archaeology* 40 (1954), 94. The discovery in Egypt of Greek and Coptic manuscripts from the third and fourth centuries preserving the apologetic works of Melito of Sardis may point to the continued process of orthodox self-definition and anti-Gnostic polemic during that period (C.H. Roberts, *Manuscript, Society and Belief*, 63).

62. Bentley Layton, *per litt.*, July 25, 2003. For a classic study of how intellectual pedigrees functioned in ancient Greek doxography (i.e., the collection and systematization of philosophical teachings on a variety of topics), see Hermann Diels, *Doxographi Graeci*, Second edition (Berlin: Walter de Gruyter, 1929).

63. Clement of Alexandria, *Stromata* VII.17.106.4; ed. O. Stählin, L. Früchtel, and U. Treu, Fourth edition, volume 3 (Berlin: Akademie-Verlag, 1985), 75.

64. Clement of Alexandria, *Stromata* VII.17.106.4–107.1; ed. O. Stählin, L. Früchtel, and U. Treu, Fourth edition, volume 3 (Berlin: Akademie-Verlag, 1985), 75.

65. Ptolemy, *Letter to Flora*; ed. G. Quispel, Second edition (SC 24; Paris: Le Cerf, 1966), 72; trans. B. Layton, *The Gnostic Scriptures*, 314.

66. Irenaeus, *Against Heresies* 3.3.1; ed. N. Brox, Fontes Christiani 8.3 (Freiburg: Herder, 1993), 28 (Latin). On the apostolic succession list Irenaeus provides for the early Roman Papacy, see E. Duffy, *Saints and Sinners: A History of the Popes* (New Haven: Yale University, 1997), 9–11.

67. W. Telfer ("Episcopal Succession in Egypt," *Journal of Ecclesiastical History* 3 (1952), 2) portrays Demetrius who initiated a new age for Alexandrian Christianity, and who deserves to be recognized as the "Second Founder of the church of Alexandria."

68. Clement of Alexandria, *Stromata* I.1.11.3; ed. O. Stählin, L. Früchtel, and U. Treu, Fourth edition, volume 2 (Berlin: Akademie-Verlag, 1985), 9. Denise Buell, in her book, *Making Christians: Clement of Alexandria and the Rhetoric of Legitimacy* (Princeton: Princeton University Press, 1999), highlights the discursive function of such kinship language in the genealogical construction of early Christian authority, especially in the promotion and promulgation of teaching lineages.

69. Origen of Alexandria, *On First Principles* (*De principiis*) I, Preface 2; ed. H. Crouzel and M. Simonetti (SC 252; Paris: Cerf, 1978), 78; trans. G.W. Butterworth (Gloucester, MA: Peter Smith, 1973), 2.

Chapter 2: Bishops, Teachers, and Martyrs

1. Alan K. Bowman, *Egypt After the Pharaohs: 332 b.c.–A.D. 642* (Berkeley: University of California Press, 1986), 223–233.

2. Roger S. Bagnall, "Alexandria: Library of Dreams," *Proceedings of the American Philosophical Society* 146.4 (2002), 348–362, esp. 351–356.

3. For a recent, wide-ranging study of the Alexandrian Library and its importance in antiquity, see Roy MacLeod, ed., *The Library of Alexandria* (Cairo: The American University in Cairo Press, 2002), especially the articles by the editor ("Introduction: Alexandria in History and Myth," 1–15), by Robert Barnes ("Cloistered Bookworms in the

Chicken-Coop of the Muses: The Ancient Library in Alexandria," 61–77), and by John Vallance ("Doctors in the Library: The Strange Tale of Apollonius the Bookworm and Other Stories," 95–113). On the remains of the library at the Serapeum, see Henri Riad, Youssef Hanna Shehata, and Youssef al-Gheriani, *Alexandria: An Archeological Guide to the City*, Second edition (Alexandria: The Regional Authority for Tourism Promotion, 1996), 66. On the Museum and its relation to the Library, see Edward Jay Watts, "City and School in Late Antique Athens and Alexandria" (Ph.D. dissertation, Yale University, 2002), 259-266.

4.   For a comprehensive and detailed treatment of Middle Platonism, see John Dillon, *The Middle Platonists* (Ithaca, NY: Cornell University Press, 1977). Heinrich Dörrie has argued that the resurgence of Platonism in the first century B.C. was directly connected with the emerging role of Alexandria as a philosophical center (H. Dörrie, "Die Erneuerung des Platonismus im ersten Jahrhundert vor Christus," in *Le Néoplatonisme* (Paris: Éditions du Centre national de la recherche scientifique, 1971), 17–33). On the influence of Platonic philosophy in the writings of Alexandrian Christian theologians, see Salvatore R. C. Lilla, *Clement of Alexandria: A Study in Christian Platonism and Gnosticism* (Oxford: Oxford University Press, 1971); and Roelof van den Broek, "Jewish and Platonic Speculations in Early Alexandrian Theology: Eugnostus, Philo, Valentinus, and Origen," in *The Roots of Egyptian Christianity*, 190–203.

5.   Eusebius, *HE* 5.10.1 (ed. E. Schwartz and T. Mommsen, GCS 9.1 (1903), 450).

6.   Ibid. Pantaenus' writings are now lost.

7.   Clement, *Stromata* I.1.31–38; Eusebius, *HE* 5.11; 6.6.

8.   Eusebius, *HE* 6.6; cf. 6.3.

9.   Origen does mention Pantaenus in one of his letters preserved by Eusebius (*HE* 6.19.12–14; ed. E. Schwartz and T. Mommsen, GCS 9.2 (1908), 562). In it he holds up Pantaenus as one who set an example of philosophical expertise that "helped many before us." Origen's language seems to suggest that he gained knowledge of Pantaenus through his philosophical writings, and not that his concern was with emphasizing some sort of direct lineage of succession in the teaching office. If that had been the case, one would have expected him to mention Clement's example as well. Despite Origen's lack of explicit references to Clement, Annewies van den Hoek has argued that certain allusions in Origen's writing serve as possible evidence for a continuity of instruction: see A. van den Hoek, "Origen and the Intellectual Heritage of Alexandria: Continuity or Disjunction," in *Origeniana quinta*, ed. R.J. Daley (Leuven: Peeters, 1992), 46–50. For a summary of scholarship on the problematic relationship between Origen and Clement, see Nancy Heisey, *Origen the Egyptian* (Nairobi: Paulines Publications Africa, 2000), 24–25.

10.   Henri Crouzel, *Origen*, trans. A.S. Worrell (Edinburgh: T. & T. Clark, 1989), 7.

11.   Pierre Nautin, *Origène: Sa vie et son oeuvre* (Paris: Beauchesne, 1977), 54; Martiniano Roncaglia, *Histoire de l'Eglise Copte*, Second edition, Volume 2 (Beirut: Librairie St. Paul, 1987), 125.

12.   Clement's flight from Alexandria during the Severan persecution would not have sat well with Origen, who became well-known for his fervency for martyrdom and his support of Christians imprisoned during the persecution (see Eusebius, *HE* 6.1–5).

13. For a recent example of this critical appraisal of Eusebius' account, see Roelof van den Broek, "The Christian 'School' of Alexandria in the Second and Third Centuries," in *Centers of Learning: Learning and Location in Pre-Modern Europe and the Near East*, ed. J.W. Drijvers and A.A. MacDonald (Leiden: E.J. Brill, 1995), 39–47; repr. in R. van den Broek, *Studies in Gnosticism and Alexandrian Christianity* (Leiden: E.J. Brill, 1996), 197–205. For a more positive assessment of Eusebius' account, see Annewies van den Hoek, "The 'Catechetical' School of Early Christian Alexandria and Its Philonic Heritage," *Harvard Theological Review* 90.1 (1997), 59–87.

14. Eusebius, *HE* 6.3.8 (ed. E. Schwartz and T. Mommsen, GCS 9.2 (1908), 526); Gustave Bardy, "Aux origins de l'école d'Alexandrie," *Recherches de science religieuse* 27 (1937), 65–90; ibid., "Pour l'histoire de l'École d'Alexandrie," *Vivre et Penser*, Second series (1942), 80–109. On the early history of the Alexandrian catechetical school, see also David Dawson, *Allegorical Readers and Cultural Revision in Ancient Alexandria* (Berkeley, CA: University of California Press, 1992), 219–222.

15. G. Bardy, "Aux origins de l'école d'Alexandrie," *Recherches de science religieuse* 27 (1937), 78–79. In developing his concept of a succession of head teachers in Alexandria, Eusebius may have been relying on a letter written to Origen himself by bishop Alexander of Jerusalem. In that letter, Alexander writes, "For we know those blessed ones who preceded us as fathers. After a little while we will be with them—Pantaenus, the truly blessed master, and the holy Clement, who became my master and who gave me assistance, and whoever else is of this sort" (Eusebius, *HE* 6.14.9; ed. E. Schwartz and T. Mommsen, GCS 9.2 (1908), 552). Eusebius may have used Alexander's words as evidence for an institutional chain of leadership at the Alexandrian catechetical school, but in fact Alexander probably only met Clement after his departure from Alexandria and simply meant to highlight Origen's association with the "school of thought" or tradition of teaching that Alexander had learned about from his acquaintance with Clement (Pierre Nautin, *Lettres et écrivains chrétiens des IIe et IIIe siècles* (Paris: Editions du Cerf, 1961), 129–132).

16. Eusebius, *HE* 6.3.1 (ed. E. Schwartz and T. Mommsen, GCS 9.2 (1908), 524).

17. Ibid.; Joseph W. Trigg, *Origen* (London and New York: Routledge, 1998), 14. Christopher Haas (*Alexandria in Late Antiquity*, 183) notes that the growing fame of Origen was a crucial factor in attracting interested pagans and leading them to conversion during this period.

18. On Origen's tension with and eventual break from Demetrius, see J. Trigg, *Origen: The Bible and Philosophy in the Third-Century Church* (Atlanta: John Knox Press, 1983), 130–140.

19. J. Trigg, *Origen* (1998), 5–7, 12–14; also *Origen: The Bible and Philosophy in the Third-Century Church* (1983), 31–38, 52–54, 66–75. On Origen's literary and philological training, see especially Bernhardt Neuschäfer, *Origenes als Philologe*, 2 volumes (Schweizerische Beiträge zur Altertumswissenschaft 18; Basel: Friedrich Reinhardt, 1987). The famous Greek philosopher Porphyry attests to the fact that he and Origen were both students of Ammonius Saccas (Eusebius, *HE* 6.19.4–8; ed. E. Schwartz and T. Mommsen, GCS 9.2 (1908), 558–560). On Ammonius Saccas' reputation as a Neoplatonic teacher in Alexandria, see Patricia Cannon Johnson, "The Neoplatonists and the Mystery Schools of the Mediterranean," in *The Library of Alexandria*, ed. R. MacLeod (Cairo: The American University in Cairo Press, 2002), 143–161, esp. 149–150.

20. Eusebius, *HE* 6.14.11 (ed. E. Schwartz and T. Mommsen, GCS 9.2 (1908), 552).

21. Eusebius, *HE* 6.15 (ed. E. Schwartz and T. Mommsen, GCS 9.2 (1908), 552).

22. Eusebius, *HE* 6.19.16 (ed. E. Schwartz and T. Mommsen, GCS 9.2 (1908), 564).

23. P. Nautin, *Origène*, 366–368; J. Trigg, *Origen: The Bible and Philosophy in the Third-Century Church* (1983), 130. Nautin shows that Eusebius' language in *HE* 6.19 was dependent on Origen's *Commentary on John*, where the Alexandrian theologian describes his conflict with Demetrius as the "storm at Alexandria" (*ho kata tên Alexandreian xeimôn*) and celebrates his move to Caesarea in biblical terms as his deliverance from Egypt: Origen, 6.1–2 (ed. C. Blanc, SC 157 (1970), 128–136); N. Heisey, *Origen the Egyptian*, 171; J. Trigg, *Origen* (1998), 16.

24. Eusebius, *HE* 6.19 (ed. E. Schwartz and T. Mommsen, GCS 9.2 (1908), 564).

25. Eusebius, *HE* 6.23.

26. Eusebius, *HE* 6.8. As a pretext for his protest, Demetrius argued that Origen should be disqualified from the priesthood because he had castrated himself earlier on during his time as teacher at the Alexandria catechetical school. According to Eusebius, Demetrius had originally approved of Origen's act of self-castration as a sign of his ascetic "enthusiasm," but later, motivated by jealousy at Origen's fame, used the same act as the basis of his charges against the validity of Origen's ordination. Origen himself alludes to Demetrius' letter-writing campaign against him in his *Commentary on John* (6.2.9; ed. C. Blanc, SC 157 (1970), 132) referring to Demetrius as an enemy who "waged a most bitter war against me by means of his new writings."

27. G.W. Butterworth, "Introduction," in *Origen: On First Principles* (Gloucester, MA: Peter Smith, 1973), xxiv. The medieval historian Photius (*Bibliotheca* 118; ed. R. Henry, volume 2 (Paris: Société d'édition les Belles Lettres, 1962), 90–92) claims that Origen was formally banished by an Alexandrian synod, but R.P.C. Hanson ("Was Origen Banished from Alexandria?" in *Studia Patristica* 17.2 (New York: Pergamon Press, 1982), 904–906) argues against this possibility in the early third century, casting doubt on Photius' account.

28. G. Bardy, Pour l'histoire de l'École d'Alexandrie," 80–109, esp. 100 and 109.

29. Eusebius (*HE* 6.29.4; ed. E. Schwartz and T. Mommsen, GCS 9.2 (1908), 584) reports that, after Heraclas had been promoted to the office of bishop, "Dionysius, who had been one of Origen's pupils, took over the leadership of the school for elementary instruction." Eusebius' language here seems to imply that only the program for "elementary instruction" (*katêxêsis*) was maintained.

30. Christopher Haas, *Alexandria in Late Antiquity*, 217.

31. Eusebius, *HE* 7.7.4 (ed. E. Schwartz and T. Mommsen, GCS 9.2 (1908), 644).

32. C.W. Griggs, *Early Egyptian Christianity*, 69; Petro Bilaniuk, "Pope in the Coptic Church," *Coptic Encyclopedia* 6.1998–2000. In the extant sources, the earliest, undisputed use of the title "Pope" to refer to the bishop of Rome appears in a catacomb inscription that dates to around the year A.D. 303 (J.S. Northcote and W.R. Brownlow, *Roma Sotteranea* (London: Longmans, Green, Reader, and Dyer, 1869), 93; E. Giles, ed., *Documents Illustrating Papal Authority, A.D. 96–454* (London: SPCK, 1952), xvii).

33. G.W.H. Lampe, *A Patristic Greek Lexicon* (Oxford: Clarendon Press, 1961), 1006.

34. Eusebius, *HE* 6.41.1–2 (ed. E. Schwartz and T. Mommsen, GCS 9.2 (1908), 600).

35. Eusebius, *HE* 6.41.3–8 (ed. E. Schwartz and T. Mommsen, GCS 9.2 (1908), 600–602). For a complete edition of Dionysius' letters, see W.A. Biernert, ed., *Dionysius von Alexandrien, Das erhaltene Werk* (Bibliothek der griechischen Literatur, Bd. 2; Stuttgart: Hiersemann, 1972); *Letters and Treatises*, trans. and ed. C.L. Feltoe (Translations of Christian Literature, series 1: Greek Texts; New York: Macmillan Co., 1918). Dionysius' accounts of Christian women who endured torture without abandoning their faith would have had a specific propagandistic use—namely as a "shaming device" directed at the culturally powerful who proved unable to sway the commitment of the supposedly "weaker sex" (Elizabeth Clark, "Thinking with Women: The Uses of the Appeal to 'Woman' in Early Christian Propaganda Literature," Paper presented at the Symposium on the Expansion of Christianity in the First Four Centuries, Columbia University, New York, March 30, 2003).

36. Eusebius, *HE* 6.41.9 (ed. E. Schwartz and T. Mommsen, GCS 9.2 (1908), 602).

37. The Alexandrian uprising against the Christians in 248 was not sponsored by the imperial government; in fact, the emperor at the time, Philip, was widely viewed as sympathetic to the Christians (Eusebius, *HE* 6.34, 36, 39, 41; Eusebius, *Chronicle* (preserved in Jerome's Latin translation; ed. R. Helm, Third edition (GCS; Berlin: Akademie-Verlag, 1984), 217–218); W.H.C. Frend, *Martyrdom and Persecution in the Early Church* (London: Basil Blackwell, 1965; repr. Grand Rapids, MI: Baker Book House, 1981), 404; T.D. Barnes, "Legislation Against the Christians," *Journal of Roman Studies* 58 (1968), 43–44; repr. in T.D. Barnes, *Early Christianity and the Roman Empire* (London: Variorum Reprints, 1984) Article II).

38. An inscription from Aphrodisias speaks of these sacrifices as a demonstration of "solidarity with the Romans" and support for "our empire" (*Monuments from Lycaonia, the Pisido-Phrygian borderland, Aphrodisias*, ed. W.M. Calder and J.M.R. Cormack (Monumenta Asiae Minoris Antiqua, vol. 7; Manchester: Manchester University Press, 1962), no. 424 (Oct–Nov 250); W.H.C. Frend, *The Rise of Christianity* (Philadelphia: Fortress, 1984), 320; W.H.C. Frend, *Martyrdom and Persecution*, 405).

39. J.R. Knipfing ("The Libelli of the Decian Persecution," *Harvard Theological Review* 16 (1923), 345–390) originally published 41 of these *libelli*, identifying their formulaic character. For a more recent accounting and discussion of these certificates, see Robin Lane Fox, *Pagans and Christians* (New York: Alfred A. Knopf, Inc., 1987), 455–458. Lane Fox argues that these *libelli* were actually only employed during a "second stage" of persecution "aimed only at suspect Christians." He supports this theory by observing that a general issuance of certificates for all citizens would have caused a bureaucratic nightmare.

40. Eusebius, *HE* 6.41.11–12 (ed. E. Schwartz and T. Mommsen, GCS 9.2 (1908), 604).

41. R. Lane Fox, *Pagans and Christians*, 457–458. For possible cases of slaves sacrificing on their master's behalf, see J. Knipfing, "The Libelli of the Decian Persecution," 374–375, no. 20; and Cyprian, *On the Lapsed* 25. On the occurrence of bribery as a way of obtaining a false certificate, see

L.W. Countryman, *The Rich Christian in the Church of the Early Empire: Contradictions and Accommodations* (New York and Toronto: Edwin Mellen Press, 1980), 191 and 203, note 22.

42. Eusebius, *HE* 6.41.
43. On the reconciliation offered by confessors to apostates in the North African church, see Charles A. Bobertz, "Cyprian of Carthage: A Social Historical Study of the Role of Bishop in the Ancient Christian Community of North Africa" (Ph.D. dissertation, Yale University, 1988), 198–201; and J. Patout Burns, *Cyprian the Bishop* (London: Routledge, 2002), 41–44. The confessors' authority to offer forgiveness was based in the understanding that they had earned the right to sit with Christ at the final judgment: see, e.g., Revelation 7:14; 20:4; Origen, *Exhortation to Martyrdom* 30; Eusebius, *HE* 6.42.5; C.A. Bobertz, "Patronage Networks and the Study of Ancient Christianity," in *Studia Patristica* 24 (Leuven: Peeters Press, 1993), 24, note 16.
44. W.H.C. Frend, *Martyrdom and Persecution*, 406, 409–410.
45 Cyprian, *Ep.* 20.1 (CSEL 8.2.527); English translation in *The New Eusebius*, edited by J. Stevenson (London: SPCK, 1957), 235.
46. Eusebius, *HE* 6.40.1–3 (ed. E. Schwartz and T. Mommsen, GCS 9.2 (1908), 596).
47. Eusebius, *HE* 6.40.8–9 (ed. E. Schwartz and T. Mommsen, GCS 9.2 (1908), 598).
48. Eusebius, *HE* 6.42.4–5 (ed. E. Schwartz and T. Mommsen, GCS 9.2 (1908), 610).
49. On the discourse of holy suffering in the early church, see Judith Perkins, *The Suffering Self: Pain and Narrative Representation in the Early Christian Era* (London and New York: Routledge, 1995). Peter Brown perceptively highlights the discursive link between the bishops and martyrs in the early church by comparing "the way in which the Christians idealized their martyrs as the special 'friends of God,'" and the way that bishops "claimed with increasing assertiveness to be 'friends of God' in a similar manner" (*The Making of Late Antiquity* (Cambridge, MA: Harvard University Press, 1978), 57).
50. Eusebius, *HE* 6.42.6 (ed. E. Schwartz and T. Mommsen, GCS 9.2 (1908), 612).
51. Cyprian, *Epistles* 38 and 39; C.A. Bobertz, "Patronage Networks and the Study of Ancient Christianity," in *Studia Patristica* 24 (Leuven: Peeters Press, 1993), 23–24.
52. Eusebius, *HE* 6.44.4 (ed. E. Schwartz and T. Mommsen, GCS 9.2 (1908), 624).
53. Eusebius, *HE* 6.44, 46. During his reign as patriarch, Dionysius worked to strengthen the ties between the Alexandrian see and the churches of Upper Egypt. He did so not just through correspondence, but also through personal visitation. In one case (Eusebius, *HE* 7.24; ed. E. Schwartz and T. Mommsen, GCS 9.2 (1908), 684–690, esp. 688), Dionysius visited the district of Arsinoe in the Fayûm, where he "called the priests and the teachers of the Christians living in the villages to a meeting," sitting with them for three days in order to resolve disagreements over the interpretation of Revelation. In Dionysius' account of his visit, we see how, by the middle of the third century, the Egyptian patriarch was exercising his authority over church teaching not just at the Alexandrian catechetical school, but also in the towns and villages of Upper Egypt. However, see C.W. Griggs (*Early Egyptian Christianity*, 88), who notes that, Dionysius "was not able to capture the loyalty and obedience of more than a portion of the members" during his visit to Arsinoe.

54. Eusebius, *HE* 7.11 (esp. 11.22–24); ed. E. Schwartz and T. Mommsen, GCS 9.2 (1908), 654–664, esp. 662.

55. W.H.C. Frend (*Martyrdom and Persecution in the Early Church*, 440–476) characterizes this period as "The Triumph of Christianity"; however, see the reservations expressed by Robin Lane Fox (*Pagans and Christians*, 556 and 767, note 19), who observes that "these years are notoriously obscure and the evidence is unusually scattered and indirect." This is certainly the case for the reigns of Maximus and Theonas, for whom we have very little reliable early information. The biographical legends about these two patriarchs in the medieval *History of the Patriarchs* have questionable historical value: see *History of the Patriarchs*, ed. B. Evetts, PO 1.2, 192–211. J.M. Neale (*The Patriarchate of Alexandria*, 2 vols. (London: Joseph Masters, 1847), I.86–88) has published a conciliatory letter attributed to Theonas and addressed to the emperor Diocletian; however, the authorship of the letter has been a source of debate.

56. Eusebius, *HE* 8.2.4–5 (ed. E. Schwartz and T. Mommsen, GCS 9.2 (1908), 742).

57. Eusebius, *HE* 8.1.

58. On Diocletian's skill as a government reformer, see A.H.M. Jones, *The Later Roman Empire, 284–602*, 2 volumes (Baltimore: The Johns Hopkins University Press, 1964) I.37–70.

59. T.D. Barnes, *Constantine and Eusebius* (Cambridge, MA: Harvard University Press, 1981), 17–19.

60. R. Lane Fox, *Pagans and Christians*, 594–595. On the dating of this edict, see T.D. Barnes, "Sossianus Hierocles and the Antecedents of the Great Persecution," *Harvard Studies in Classical Philology* 80 (1976), 239–252, esp. 246–250.

61. Lactantius, *On the Deaths of the Persecutors* 11–15 (ed. S. Brandt and G. Laubmann, CSEL 27.2, 185–189; trans. M.F. McDonald, FC 54, 150–154); Eusebius, *HE* 8.2, 8.6; and *Martyrs of Palestine*, Prologue, 1.4, and 3.1 (ed. G. Bardy, SC 55 (1958), 121–122, 123, 126). For a summary of these successive edicts, see Diana Bowder, *The Age of Constantine and Julian* (London: Paul Elek, 1978), 12–13; and Ralph W. Mathison, "Persecution," in *Encyclopedia of Early Christianity*, ed. E. Ferguson (New York and London: Garland, 1990), 712–717, esp. 716.

62. On Peter's places of exile, see William Telfer, "St. Peter of Alexandria and Arius," *Analecta Bollandiana* 67 (1949), 126; Alexander of Alexandria, *Encomium on Saint Peter*, ed. H. Hyvernat, *Les actes des martyrs de l'É-gypte* (Hildesheim and New York: Georg Olms Verlag, 1977), 258; trans. T. Vivian, *St. Peter of Alexandria: Bishop and Martyr* (Philadelphia: Fortress, 1988), 83.

63. Both Origen (*Against Celsus* 1.65–66; 8.44) and Cyprian of Carthage (*On the Lapsed* 10) also cited Matthew 10:23 as justification for those who fled during persecution. On Peter's flight from persecution, see T. Vivian, *St. Peter of Alexandria*, 19–20, 157–159, 200–202.

64. W. Telfer, "Melitius of Lycopolis and Episcopal Succession in Egypt," *Harvard Theological Review* 48 (1955), 227–228.

65. *Codex Veronensis* LX, ed. C.H. Turner, *Ecclesiae Occidentalis Monumenta Iuris Antiquissima* (Oxford: Clarendon, 1899), I.634–635; trans. J. Stevenson, *A New Eusebius: Documents Illustrative of the History of the Church to A.D. 337* (London: SPCK, 1957), 290.

66. *Codex Veronensis* LX, ed. C.H. Turner, *Ecclesiae Occidentalis Monumenta Iuris Antiquissima*, I.635–636; trans. J. Stevenson, *A New*

Eusebius: Documents Illustrative of the History of the Church to A.D. *337* (London: SPCK, 1957), 292.

67. *Codex Veronensis* LX, ed. C.H. Turner, *Ecclesiae Occidentalis Monumenta Iuris Antiquissima*, I.636; trans. J. Stevenson, *A New Eusebius: Documents Illustrative of the History of the Church to* A.D. *337* (London: SPCK, 1957), 293.

68. H. Idris Bell, *Jews and Christians in Egypt*, 39; see also S.L. Greenslade, *Schism in the Early Church* (London: SCM Press, 1953), 117; and L.W. Barnard, "Athanasius and the Melitian Schism in Egypt," *Journal of Egyptian Archaeology* 59 (1973), 181–189.

69. J. Barns and Henry Chadwick, "A Letter Ascribed to Peter of Alexandria," *Journal of Theological Studies* 24, new series (1973), 443–455, esp. 449; *Martyrdom of St. Coluthus*, 90.R.ii—90.V.i, in E.A.E. Raymond and J.W.B. Barns, *Four Martyrdoms from the Pierpont Morgan Coptic Codices* (Oxford: Clarendon Press, 1973), 26–27 (Coptic text), 147 (English translation); see also T. Vivian, *St. Peter of Alexandria*, 28ff.

70. Epiphanius, *Panarion* 68.1–3; ed. K. Holl and J. Dummer, GCS 37 (1933), 140–143; trans. F. Williams (Nag Hammadi and Manichaean Studies 36; Leiden and New York: E.J. Brill, 1994), 315–318. See also PG 42.184B–189B; trans. T. Vivian, *St. Peter of Alexandria*, 84–86.

71. See, e.g., W.H.C. Frend, *Martyrdom and Persecution*, 539; and "The Failure of the Persecutions in the Roman Empire," in *Town and Country in the Early Christian Centuries* (London: Variorum Reprints, 1980), X.280; and Robin Lane Fox, *Pagans and Christians*, 609–610.

72. T. Vivian, *St. Peter of Alexandria*, 32.

73. For the Greek text of Peter's *Canonical Letter*, see PG 468–508; trans. T. Vivian, *St. Peter of Alexandria*, 185–192 (text), 194–204 (commentary).

74. J.N.D. Kelley, *Early Christian Doctrines*, revised edition (San Francisco: HarperCollins Publishers, 1978), 216. In his *Letter to the Egyptians*, Dionysius of Alexandria is said to have "explained what he thought about those who had lapsed, and delineated categories of transgressions" (Eusebius, *HE* 6.46.1; ed. E. Schwartz and T. Mommsen, GCS 9.2 (1908), 626–628). Origen provides corroborating evidence for the practice of penance in mid-third-century Alexandria (*Homily on Leviticus* 2.4; K. Rahner, "La doctrine d'Origène sur le penitence," *Recherches de science religieuse* 37 (1950), 47–97, 252–286; J. Daniélou, *Origen* (London and New York: Sheed and Ward, 1955), 68–72). See T. Vivian, *St. Peter of Alexandria*, 146–173, for a study of Peter's *Canonical Letter* in the context of earlier penitential tradition.

75. While Peter provides a detailed set of policies regarding the *length* of penance assigned for different offenses, his canons do not seem to presume a full penitential system, with grades or ranks of penitents: see T. Vivian, *St. Peter of Alexandria*, 180–184, contra W. Bright, "Petrus I, St.," *Dictionary of Christian Biography* IV.331; W.H.C. Frend, *Martyrdom and Persecution*, 540; and E. Schwartz, *Zur Geschichte des Athanasius* (Gesammelte Schriften 3; Berlin: Walter de Gruyter, 1959), 87–116. esp. 94–97.

76. The evidence for Melitius' stance on this issue is found in Epiphanius, *Panarion* 68.2–3; ed. K. Holl and J. Dummer, GCS 37 (1933), 141–143; trans. F. Williams (Nag Hammadi and Manichaean Studies 36; Leiden and New York: E.J. Brill, 1994), 316–318.

77. It is noteworthy that Peter validates the efficacy of confessors' prayers only in the case of those who sacrificed while subjected to torture or imprisonment and not in the case of those who sacrificed without coercion.

78. Epiphanius, *Panarion* 68.3; ed. K. Holl and J. Dummer, GCS 37 (1933), 143.

79. Peter's canons were incorporated into the *Syntagma Canonum* of Photius, patriarch of Constantinople (ca. 810–ca. 895) (ed. A. Mai, *Spicilegium Romanum*, Volume 7 (Rome: Typis Collegii Urbani, 1842), esp. 444–455).

80. On the concentration of Melitian communities in Upper Egypt, see E.R. Hardy, *Christian Egypt: Church and People* (New York: Oxford University Press, 1952), 52–53. W.H.C. Frend (*The Rise of the Monophysite Movement* (Cambridge: Cambridge University Press, 1972), 81ff.) characterizes the Melitian church as a nationalistic movement based in Upper Egypt. The Coptic (as opposed to Greek) character of the Melitian church has been confirmed by papyrological evidence: see H.I. Bell, *Jews and Christians in Egypt*, 44.

81. For a recent account of Melitian involvement in the Arian Controversy, see C.W. Griggs, *Early Egyptian Christianity*, 117–130. In 1924, H.I. Bell (*Jews and Christians in Egypt*, 45–71) published two papyri from the British Museum (Papyri 1913 and 1914, dated ca. 330–340) that shed light on the conflict between the Melitians and bishop Athanasius from a Melitian perspective. On the strong monastic association of the Melitian movement, see James E. Goehring, "Monastic Diversity and Ideological Boundaries in Fourth-Century Christian Egypt," *Journal of Early Christian Studies* 5.1 (1997), 61–84; repr. in J.E. Goehring, *Ascetics, Society, and the Desert: Studies in Early Egyptian Monasticism* (Studies in Antiquity and Christianity; Harrisburg, PA: Trinity Press International, 1999), 196–218.

82. The *History of the Patriarchs* (PO 5.1, 198–199) mentions the fact that Patriarch Michael I (744–768) tried (unsuccessfully) to convert "the followers of Melitius," who are said to have remained "dissidents, some of them in the monasteries and some in the deserts."

83. Eusebius, *HE* 7.32; 9.6. In a list of leading martyrs of the church, Eusebius extols Peter as "an extraordinary teacher of piety in Christ" (*HE* 8.13.7; ed. E. Schwartz and T. Mommsen, GCS 9.2 (1908), 772).

84. For a discussion of these three recensions, see T. Vivian, *St. Peter of Alexandria*, 64–68.

85. The short version (S) has been reconstructed by W. Telfer ("St. Peter of Alexandria and Arius," *Analecta Bollandiana* 67 (1949), 117–130; trans. T. Vivian, *op. cit.*, 68–70.

86. The *History of the Patriarchs* contains elements of the short version, as well as elements of a longer version (L) that includes a description of Peter's visit to the shrine of St. Mark in Baucalis (Boukolou) while in custody and his death at that location (PO 1.4.383–400; cf. *Synaxaire Arabe Jacobite*, ed. R. Basset, PO 3 (1909), 353–359 (Arabic); and P. Bedjan, *Acta Martyrum et Sanctorum*, volume 5 (Leipzig: Otto Harrasowitz, 1895), 543–561 (Syriac)). The longest version (LL), which includes a narration of Peter's posthumous enthronement and burial, has been preserved in Greek, Latin, Coptic, and Ethiopic: see P. Devos, "Une passion grecque inédite de S. Pierre d'Alexandrie et sa traduction par Anastase le Bibliothécaire," *Analecta Bollandiana* 83 (1965), 157–187, esp. 162–177 (Greek; trans. T. Vivian, *op. cit.*, 70–78); J. Viteau, *Passions des Saints Ecaterine et Pierre d'Alexandrie* (Paris: E. Bouillon, 1897) (Greek); Anastasius Bibliothecarius, *Acta Sincera Sancti Petri* (Latin; ed. P. Devos, in "Une passion grecque," 177–187; also PG 18.451–466; Eng. translation in ANF 6.261–268); H.

Hyvernat, ed., *Les Actes des Martyrs de l'Égypte* (Hildesheim and New York: Georg Olms Verlag, 1977), 263–283 (Coptic); E.A.W. Budge, *The Book of the Saints of the Ethiopian Church* (Cambridge: Cambridge University Press, 1928), I.300–303. For additional fragments of the *Martyrdom* that survive in Coptic: see W.E. Crum, "Texts Attributed to Peter of Alexandria," *Journal of Theological Studies* 4 (1902–3), 394; and Donald Spanel, "Two Fragmentary Sa'idic Coptic Texts Pertaining to Peter I, Patriarch of Alexandria," *Bulletin de la Société d'Archéologie Copte* 24 (1979–82), 85–102.

87. Most scholars have rejected the *Martyrdom of Saint Peter* as pious fiction: see, e.g., J. Quasten, *Patrology* (Utrecht: Spectrum, 1950; repr. Westminster, MD: Christians Classics, Inc., 1992), II.117. However, Tito Orlandi ("Richerche su una storia ecclesiastica alessandrina del IV sec.," *Vetera Christianorum* 11 (1974), 269–312; cited by T. Vivian, *St. Peter of Alexandria*, 66) has argued that there may be historical reminiscences in the *Martyrdom*, especially in its emphasis on the secrecy surrounding Peter's death, and on his willingness to submit to martyrdom in order to protect the Christian community from further harassment.

88. *History of the Patriarchs* (PO 1.4, 397); see also *The Life and Martyrdom of the Holy and Glorious "Holy Martyr" of Christ, Peter Archbishop of Alexandria* 12 (ed. P. Devos, "Une passion grecque inédite de S. Pierre d'Alexandrie et sa traduction par Anastase le Bibliothècaire," *Analecta Bollandiana* 83 (1965), 171–172; trans. T. Vivian, *St. Peter of Alexandria*, 75).

89. *History of the Patriarchs* (PO 1.4, 399); *The Life and Martyrdom of the Holy and Glorious "Holy Martyr" of Christ, Peter Archbishop of Alexandria* 13; ed. P. Devos, "Une passion grecque inédite de S. Pierre d'Alexandrie et sa traduction par Anastase le Bibliothècaire," *Analecta Bollandiana* 83 (1965), 172; trans. T. Vivian, *St. Peter of Alexandria*, 75. The link between Peter of Alexandria and his apostolic namesake is vividly attested in an eleventh-century wall painting at the Monastery of the Archangel Gabriel (Deir al-Naqlûn) in the Fayûm (Fig. 10). In the apse of the church, Peter the bishop and martyr is visually conflated with Saint Peter the apostle. Included in an iconographic program of six apostles, the figure in question is depicted wearing a bishop's robe and monk's cap, and is identified by a Coptic inscription as "Archbishop Peter" (Gawdat Gabra, *Coptic Monasteries: Egypt's Monastic Art and Architecture* (Cairo and New York: The American University in Cairo Press, 2002), 70, plates 5.5 and 5.6).

90. *History of the Patriarchs*; PO 1.4, 398 (translation modified).

91. *The Life and Martyrdom of the Holy and Glorious "Holy Martyr" of Christ, Peter Archbishop of Alexandria* 16–18; ed. P. Devos, "Une passion grecque inédite de S. Pierre d'Alexandrie," 175–177; trans. T. Vivian, *St. Peter of Alexandria*, 77–78.

92. On Egyptian documentary evidence for the "era of Diocletian" and the "era of the Martyrs" as chronological systems of dating, see Roger S. Bagnall and Klaas A. Worp, *Chronological Systems of Byzantine Egypt*, Second edition (Leiden: Brill, 2003), ch. 8 ("The Era of Diocletian and the Martyrs"). I want to thank Roger Bagnall for providing me with a copy of the revised chapter prior to its publication.

93. On the Coptic calendar and the "era of the Martyrs," see also Aelred Cody, OSB, "Calendar, Coptic," *Coptic Encyclopedia* 2.433–436.

Chapter 3: Theological Controversy and the Cultivation of Monastic Support: The Alexandrian Patriarchate from 312 to 451 (Achillas to Dioscorus I)

1. Lactantius, *On the Deaths of the Persecutors* 44.3–6 (ed. S. Brandt and G. Laubmann, CSEL 27.2, 223–224; trans. M. F. McDonald, FC 54, 190–192); Eusebius, *Life of Constantine* 1.26–29.

2. Ramsey MacMullen, *Christianizing the Roman Empire, A.D. 100–400* (New Haven and London: Yale University Press, 1984), 43–51.

3. On Constantine's rise to power and his imperial patronage of Christian institutions and leaders, see Timothy D. Barnes, *Constantine and Eusebius* (Cambridge, MA: Harvard University Press, 1981), esp. 28–53.

4. Eusebius, *Oration in Praise of the Emperor Constantine* 1.6; ed. I.A. Heikel, *Eusebius Werke*, vol. 1, GCS 7 (Leipzig: Hinrichs, 1902): 199. On the construction of this imperial ideology in the writings of Eusebius, see Averil Cameron, "Eusebius of Caesaria and the Rethinking of History," in E. Gabba, ed., *Tria Corda: Scritti in onore di Arnaldo Momigliano* (Como: Edizioni New Press, 1983), 71–88. On the later development of this ideology, see J.A.S. Evans, *The Age of Justinian: The Circumstances of Imperial Power* (London and New York: Routledge, 1996), 58–65.

5. Eusebius, *Life of Constantine* 4.24; ed. F. Winkelmann, *Eusebius Werke, Band 1.1: Über das Leben des Kaisers Konstantin* (GCS; Berlin: Akademie-Verlag, 1975), 128.

6. In the case of the Arian schism, Christopher Haas (*Alexandria in Late Antiquity*, 268–277) has shown, for example, how urban social class divisions contributed to Alexandrian theological factionalism. On the role of geographical divisions in the Egyptian church during the same controversy, see W.H.C. Frend, "Athanasius as an Egyptian Christian Leader in the Fourth Century," *New College Bulletin* 8.1 (1974), 20–37; reprinted in his collection of essays, *Religion Popular and Unpopular in the Early Christian Centuries* (London: Variorum Reprints, 1976), XVI: 20–37. Frend argues that Athanasius' response to the Arian crisis was successful in bridging the theological and cultural divisions between Alexandria and Upper Egypt. More recent scholars, however, have questioned the assumption (held by Frend and others) that there was such a sharp dichotomy between the "Hellenistic" culture of Alexandria and the "native Coptic" culture of the Nile Valley, especially in the context of documentary evidence for bilingual or "dual language" communities and the presence of a Hellenized elite in the towns and cities of Upper Egypt (Roger S. Bagnall, *Egypt in Late Antiquity* (Princeton: Princeton University Press, 1993), 251–260; and David Brakke, *Athanasius and the Politics of Asceticism* (Oxford: Clarendon Press, 1995; repr. Baltimore: The Johns Hopkins University Press, 1998), 15).

7. On the rhetoric and social practice of patronage in the Roman period, see Richard P. Saller, *Personal Patronage under the Early Empire* (Cambridge: Cambridge University Press, 1982).

8. James E. Goehring, "Monasticism," *Encyclopedia of Early Christianity*, edited by E. Ferguson (New York and London: Garland Publishing, Inc., 1990), 613.

9. Early Christian literature abounds with the stories of monks who went into hiding to avoid unwanted calls to ordination: see, e.g., the *Sayings of the Desert Fathers* (= *Apophthegmata Patrum*, Greek alphabetical version), Theodore of Pherme 25 (PG 65.193B–C), Macarius of Egypt 1 (PG

65.258C–260B), Matoes 9 (PG 65.291C–293A), and Moses 4 (PG 65.284A–B). On the presence of ordained clergy in Egyptian monasteries and on the tensions that existed between monastic and ecclesiastical leaders, see Philip Rousseau, *Ascetics, Authority, and the Church in the Age of Jerome and Cassian* (Oxford: Oxford University Press, 1978), 56–67.

10. On the relationship between the Alexandrian patriarchs and Egyptian monks in late antiquity, see also Norman Russell, "Bishops and Charismatics in Early Christian Egypt," in *Abba: The Tradition of Orthodoxy in the West*, ed. J. Behr, A. Louth, and D. Conomos (Crestwood, NY: St. Vladimir's Seminary Press, 2003), 99–110.

11. Scholars continue to debate the chronological origins of the controversy between Arius and Alexander, with theories ranging from 318 to 323. The traditional date of 318 was upheld by H.-G. Opitz, in his article "Die Zeitfolge der arianischen Streites von den Anfang bis zum Jahre 328," *Zeitschrift für Neutestamentliche Wissenschaft* 33 (1934), 131–159. E. Schwartz (*Zur Geschichte des Athanasius*, (Gesammelte Schriften 3; Berlin: Walter de Gruyter, 1959), 165–167) and W. Telfer ("When Did the Arian Controversy Begin?" *Journal of Theological Studies* 47 (1946) 129–142) have argued for the later date of 323. Finally, E. Boularand (*L'Hérésie d'Arius et la Foi de Nicée* (Paris: Letouzey & Ané, 1972), 21–24) has proposed 320 as an alternative starting date for the controversy. For a thorough, and yet concise, analysis of these various theories, see R.P.C. Hanson (*The Search for the Christian Doctrine of God* (Edinburgh: T. & T. Clark, 1988), 129–138). Hanson essentially judges in favor of Opitz's chronology, a judgment that has since been reconfirmed by Rowan Williams, "Appendix 1: Arius Since 1987," in *Arius: Heresy and Tradition*, Second edition (London: SCM Press, 2001), 247–267, esp. 251–256. In this chapter, I will be largely following Opitz's (and Hanson's) reconstruction of events.

12. Epiphanius, *Panarion* 69.1; ed. K. Holl and J. Dummer GCS 37 (1933), 152; trans. F. Williams (Nag Hammadi and Manichaean Studies 36; Leiden and New York: E.J. Brill, 1994), 325. Arius himself also hints at his connection with Libya in a fragment of his writings preserved in Constantine's *Letter to Arius and his Companions* (ed. H.-G. Opitz, *Athanasius: Werke*, Volume 3 (Berlin and Leipzig: Walter de Gruyter, 1934), 72, no. 34.20).

13. Sozomen, *HE* 1.15 (PG 67.904–905). The *History of the Patriarchs* (PO 1.4, 401) attributes the shortness of Achillas' reign to his error of judgment in ordaining Arius.

14. Epiphanius (*Panarion* 69.3.1; ed. K. Holl and J. Dummer, GCS 37 (1933), 154; trans. F. Williams (Nag Hammadi and Manichaean Studies 36; Leiden and New York: E.J. Brill, 1994), 326) gives witness to Arius' charming skills as a public speaker.

15. Arius, *Letter to Alexander of Alexandria* (ca. 320), preserved in Athanasius, *De Synodis* 16, and Epiphanius, *Panarion* 69.7; ed. H.-G. Opitz, *Athanasius: Werke*, Volume 3, 12–13, no. 6.2–5; trans. W. Rusch, *The Trinitarian Controversy* (Philadelphia: Fortress Press, 1980), 31–32.

16. Robert C. Gregg and Dennis E. Groh have shown how Arius and his early followers cited various scriptural passages to argue for the "received" nature of the Son's authority, the limitations of his knowledge, his progress in virtue, and his posture of obedience to the Father (*Early Arianism—A View of Salvation* (Philadelphia: Fortress Press, 1981), chapter 1; cf. E. Boularand, *L'Hérésie d'Arius*, chapter 4).

17. In this context, Arius' claim that his teaching is in line with the tradition of "our ancestors" and Alexander's own example may be more than simply a rhetorical move; it may also offer some insight into Arius' perception of himself as a theological and scriptural traditionalist. For a perspective on Arius' "fundamentally conservative intentions," see Frances M. Young, *From Nicaea to Chalcedon: A Guide to the Literature and its Background* (Philadelphia: Fortress Press, 1983), 62–63.
18. R. Gregg and D. Groh, *Early Arianism*, esp. chapter 2.
19. Alexander of Alexandria, *Letter to Alexander of Thessalonica* (ca. 324); preserved in Theodoret, *HE* 1.4.1; ed. H.-G. Opitz, *Athanasius: Werke*, Volume 3, 19–29 (no. 14); trans. W. Rusch, *The Trinitarian Controversy*, 33–44. This letter was probably written in 324, on the eve of the Council of Nicaea.
20. Alexander of Alexandria, *Letter to Alexander of Thessalonica* 26; ed. H.-G. Opitz, *Athanasius: Werke*, Volume 3, 23 (no. 14.26); trans. W. Rusch, *The Trinitarian Controversy*, 38.
21. Origen, *On First Principles* I.2.2, 2.4, 2.9, 4.4; IV.4.1.
22. Alexander of Alexandria, *Letter to Alexander of Thessalonica* 31; ed. H.-G. Opitz, *Athanasius: Werke*, Volume 3, 24 (no. 14.31); trans. W. Rusch, *The Trinitarian Controversy*, 39.
23. In a circular letter written to the bishops of churches in the eastern Mediterranean, Alexander claims that almost 100 bishops from Egypt and Libya attended the council (Socrates, *HE* 1.6; PG 67.48).
24. Arius, *Letter to Eusebius of Nicomedia* (ca. 318–319); preserved in Epiphanius, *Panarion* 69.6, and Theodoret, *HE* 1.5; ed. H.-G. Opitz, *Athanasius: Werke*, Volume 3, 1–3 (no. 1); trans. W. Rusch, *The Trinitarian Controversy*, 29–30.
25. Sozomen, *HE* 1.15 (PG 67.908).
26. Alexander, *Letter to Bishops* (preserved in Socrates, *HE* 1.6 and Gelasius, *HE* 2.3.3–21); ed. H.-G. Opitz, *Athanasius: Werke*, Volume 3, 6–11 (no. 4b). Later, around the year 324, Alexander would also write two more letters seeking the support of other leaders: 1) a letter to other bishops, edited by H.-G. Opitz, *Athanasius: Werke*, Volume 3, 29–31 (no. 15); and 2) a *Letter to Sylvester of Rome*, which does not survive in its entirety. A fragment of this *Letter to Sylvester* is quoted by Hilary of Poitiers (*CSEL* 65.91.24) and edited by H.-G. Opitz, *Athanasius: Werke*, Volume 3, 31 (no. 16).
27. Alexander of Alexandria, *Deposition of Arius and his Followers*; ed. H.-G. Opitz, *Athanasius: Werke*, Volume 3, 6 (no. 4a); cf. J. Quasten, *Patrology*, volume 3, 16.
28. Constantine, *Letter to Alexander and Arius*; preserved in Eusebius, *Life of Constantine* 2.64; ed. H.-G. Opitz, *Athanasius: Werke*, Volume 3, 32–35 (no. 17).
29. On the use of the term *homoousios*, see J.N.D. Kelly, *Early Christian Creeds*, Third edition (London: Longman, 1972), 242–254.
30. The historian Socrates writes, "As we ourselves have discovered from various letters, which the bishops began writing to each other after the synod, the term *homoousios* was throwing some people into confusion" (*HE* 1.23; PG 67.141; cited by R.P.C. Hanson, *The Search for the Christian Doctrine of God: The Arian Controversy 318–381* (Edinburgh: T. & T. Clark, 1988), 274).
31. Rowan Williams, *Arius: Heresy and Tradition*, Second edition (London: SCM, 2001), 82–91; D. Brakke, *Athanasius and the Politics of Asceticism*, 58ff.

32. D. Brakke, *Athanasius and the Politics of Asceticism*, 63; Henri-Irénée Marrou, "L'Arianisme comme phénomène alexandrine," in *Patristique et humanisme* (Patristica Sorbonensia 9; Paris: Le Seuil, 1976), 321–330.
33. Arius, *Thalia*; preserved in Athanasius, *Against the Arians* 1.5; PG 26.20C–21A; trans. R.P.C. Hanson, *The Search for the Christian Doctrine of God*, 12–13.
34. Epiphanius, *Panarion* 69.2.6; ed. K. Holl and J. Dummer, GCS 37 (1933), 154; trans. F. Williams (Nag Hammadi and Manichaean Studies 36; Leiden and New York: E.J. Brill, 1994), 325.
35. Henri-Irénée Marrou, "L'Arianisme comme phénomène alexandrine," in *Patristique et humanisme*, 321–30.
36. Robert C. Gregg and Dennis E. Groh (*Early Arianism*, 163–164) have recognized the behavioral connection between this academic social model of instruction and Arian christology. Arius and his followers understood God as a "teacher of wisdom," and believed that Christ had "learned to create as from a teacher or a craftsman" (Arius, *Thalia*, preserved in Athanasius, *De synodis* 15.3; ed. H.-G. Opitz, *Athanasius: Werke*, Volume 2 (Berlin: Walter de Gruyter, 1940), 242; and Asterius, *Fragment 9*, in Athanasius, *Against the Arians* 2.28; ed. G. Bardy, *Recherches sur Lucien d'Antioche et son École* (Paris: Beauchesne, 1936), 345). In the same way, human beings were thought to receive salvation by imitating Christ as their instructor. Thus, when Alexander was opposing the academic model of Christianity practiced by Arius, he was at the same time opposing the theological perspective that undergirded that practice (see also D. Brakke, *Athanasius and the Politics of Asceticism*, 69–70).
37. Arius, *Letter to Eusebius of Nicomedia* 2; ed. H.-G. Opitz, *Athanasius: Werke*, Volume 3, 1–2 (no. 2.2); trans. W. Rusch, *The Trinitarian Controversy*, 29.
38. Alexander of Alexandria, *Letter to Alexander of Thessalonica* 10; ed. H.-G. Opitz, *Athanasius: Werke*, Volume 3, 21 (no. 14.10); trans. W. Rusch, *The Trinitarian Controversy*, 35.
39. Philostorgius, *HE* 2.2 (ed. J. Bidez (with revisions by F. Winkelmann), GCS (Berlin: Akademie-Verlag, 1981), 13); cf. Athanasius, *Against the Arians* 1.2; and *De synodis* 15.
40. R.P.C. Hanson, *The Search for the Christian Doctrine of God*, 10–11.
41. C. Haas, *Alexandria in Late Antiquity*, 271–272; see also his article, "The Arians of Alexandria," *Vigiliae Christianae* 47 (1993), 237–238.
42. Epiphanius, *Panarion* 69.3.2; ed. K. Holl and J. Dummer, GCS 37 (1933), 154.17–18; trans. F. Williams (Nag Hammadi and Manichaean Studies 36; Leiden and New York: E.J. Brill, 1994), 326.
43. Alexander of Alexandria, *Letter to Alexander of Thessalonica* 5; ed. H.-G. Opitz, *Athanasius: Werke*, Volume 3, 20 (no. 14.5); trans. W. Rusch, *The Trinitarian Controversy*, 34.
44. D. Brakke, *Athanasius and the Politics of Asceticism*, 66.
45. Athanasius, *First Letter to Virgins* 36–43; trans. D. Brakke, *Athanasius and the Politics of Asceticism*, 286–288.
46. David Brakke (*Athanasius and the Politics of Asceticism*, 17–79) details how Athanasius sought to foster a loyal following among monastic women in Alexandria amidst a social context of ecclesiastical, theological, and ascetic factionalism.
47. Elizabeth Bolman, ed., *Monastic Visions: Wall Paintings in the Monastery of St. Antony at the Red Sea* (New Haven: Yale University and the American Research Center in Egypt, 2002), 94, fig. 6.8.

48. Elizabeth Bolman, ed., *Monastic Visions*, 71; for a plan of the Church of St. Antony, see pages xxiv–xxv in the same volume.
49. C.C. Walters, "Christian Paintings from Tebtunis," *Journal of Egyptian Archaeology* 75 (1989), 192–193, pl. XVII; E. Bolman, ed., *Monastic Visions*, 93–94, fig. 6.7.
50. Other medieval Coptic wall paintings depicting Athanasius have been discovered at Esna and (probably) at Naqlûn. On the Esna painting, where Athanasius flanks an enthroned Christ, see Jules Leroy, *Les peintures des couvents du desert d'Esna* (La peinture murale chez les coptes, vol. 1; Cairo: L'Institut français d'archéologie orientale du Caire, 1975) pls. 5–7. In the Naqlûn painting, (dated to the eleventh century), the figure in question is not definitively identified as Athanasius, but nonetheless it suggests intriguing compositional parallels to other examples of Athanasius in Coptic art: in this case, he is again seated on a throne and paired with Saint Antony (Wlodzimierz Godlewski, "Deir el Naqlun: Topography and Tentative History," in *Archeologia e papiri nel Fayyum: Storia della ricerca, problemi e prospettive* (Syracuse: Istituto Internazionale del Papiro, 1997), 130; cited by E. Bolman, ed., *Monastic Visions*, 94–95, fig. 6.9).
51. Duane Wade-Hampton Arnold (*The Early Episcopal Career of Athanasius of Alexandria* (Notre Dame and London: University of Notre Dame Press, 1991), 25–36) lists and comments on the sources regarding the dispute over Athanasius' election. For other discussions of this so-called "Consecration Controversy," see L.W. Barnard, "Two Notes on Athanasius: 1. Athanasius' Election as Archbishop of Alexandria. 2. The Circumstances Surrounding the Encyclical Letter of the Egyptian Bishops (Apol. C. Ar. 3.1–19.5)," *Orientalia Christiana Periodica* 41 (1975), 344–356, esp. 344–352; R.P.C. Hanson, *The Search for the Christian Doctrine of God*, 247–249; and Annik Martin, *Athanase d'Alexandrie et l'église d'Égypte au IVe siècle (328–373)* (Collection de l'École française de Rome 216; Rome: École française de Rome, 1996), 321–339.
52. The alleged number of offending Athanasian bishops varies from one account to another. Sozomen (*HE* 2.17; PG 67.977) reports that seven bishops secretly elected Athanasius without the knowledge of the larger assembly. According to Philostorgius (HE 2.11; ed. J. Bidez (with revisions by F. Winkelmann), GCS (Berlin: Akademie-Verlag, 1981), 22–24), Athanasius himself arranged for two bishops to consecrate him in secret. In his Second *Apology* (6.4–5; ed. H.-G. Opitz, in *Athanasius Werke*, Volume 2.1, 92), Athanasius acknowledges that he was accused of being consecrated secretly by six or seven bishops, but offers a letter from a group of Egyptian bishops in defense of his election.
53. Epiphanius, *Panarion* 68.7.3 and 68.11.4; ed. K. Holl and J. Dummer, GCS 37 (1933), 147, 161; trans. F. Williams (Nag Hammadi and Manichaean Studies 36; Leiden and New York: E.J. Brill, 1994), 321, 332.
54. The Index of Athanasius' *Festal Letters*; ed. F. Larsow, *Die* Fest-Briefe *des heiligen Athanasius Bischofs von Alexandrien aus dem Syrischen übersetzt und durch Anmerkungen erläutert* (Leipzig: F.C.W. Vogel, 1852), 26–27; trans. A. Robertson, NPNF, second series, vol. 4, 503. For a further discussion of this delay, see R.P.C. Hanson, *The Search for the Christian Doctrine of God*, 248–249.
55. Epiphanius, *Panarion* 69.11.4–6; ed. K. Holl and J. Dummer, GCS 37 (1933), 161; trans. F. Williams (Nag Hammadi and Manichaean Studies 36; Leiden and New York: E.J. Brill, 1994), 332.

56. Sozomen *HE* 2.21 (PG 67.985–989); Epiphanius, *Panarion* 68.6.1–3 (ed. K. Holl and J. Dummer, GCS 37 (1933), 145–146; trans. F. Williams (Nag Hammadi and Manichaean Studies 36; Leiden and New York: E.J. Brill, 1994), 319–320); T.D. Barnes, *Athanasius and Constantius: Theology and Politics in the Constantinian Empire* (London and Cambridge, MA: Harvard University Press, 1993), 20–21, 247, note 2; D.W.-H. Arnold, *The Early Episcopal Career of Athanasius of Alexandria*, 104.
57. Sozomen, *HE* 2.22 (PG 67.989).
58. *London Papyrus* 1914; ed. H.I. Bell, in *Jews and Christians in Egypt* (Oxford: Clarendon Press, 1924), 58–61 (Greek text), 61–63 (English translation), 63–71 (textual commentary).
59. *London Papyrus* 1914, lines 41–48; ed. H.I. Bell, in *Jews and Christians in Egypt* (Oxford: Clarendon Press, 1924), 60 (Greek text), 62 (English translation).
60. For example, Eduard Schwartz (*Zur Geschichte des Athanasius* (Gesammelte Schriften 3; Berlin: Walter de Gruyter, 1959), 1, 192) called Athanasius "a politician through and through," and emphasized his overweening will to power. T.D. Barnes (*Constantine and Eusebius* (London and Cambridge: Harvard University Press, 1981), 230) has gone so far as to say that Athanasius' methods were like those of "a gangster."
61. Duane Wade-Hampton Arnold (*The Early Episcopal Career of Athanasius of Alexandria*, 20–21) lists a number of recent attempts to reconsider the life of Athanasius in a more positive light and situates his own book within this same tradition of Athanasian scholarship.
62. Athanasius, *History of the Arians* IV.30.4 and 34.3; ed. H.-G. Opitz, *Athanasius: Werke*, Volume 2.1, 199, 202. Athanasius explicitly forecasts that Constantius' fate will be like that of the biblical Pharaoh who "perished together with those who were of one mind with him." Here, Athanasius also writes Constantius' Arian supporters into the biblical script, casting them in the role of the Pharaoh's army.
63. In the federation of monasteries founded by Pachomius, this inaugural tour of Athanasius was later celebrated as the act that established a foundation of good will between the Alexandrian episcopate and the Pachomian monks (First Greek *Life of Pachomius* 30; ed. F. Halkin, ed., *Sancti Pachomii Vitae Graecae* (Subsidia Hagiographica 19; Brussels: Société des Bollandistes, 1932) 19.24—20.15; D. Brakke, *Athanasius and the Politics of Asceticism*, 114).
64. On Athanasius' patronage of Alexandrian monastic women in the context of the Arian conflict, see D. Brakke, *op. cit.*, 17–79; and Stephen J. Davis, *The Cult of Saint Thecla: A Tradition of Women's Piety in Late Antiquity* (Oxford: Oxford University Press, 2001), 83–112.
65. Two examples are Athanasius' *Letter to Amun* (dated A.D. 354; Greek text in PG 26.1169–1176; Eng. trans. in NPNF, series 2, vol. 4, 556–557), and his *Letter to Dracontius* (dated A.D. 354 or 355; Greek text in PG 25.523–534; Eng. trans. in NPNF, second series, vol. 4, 557–560). For a discussion of these two letters, see C. Wilfred Griggs, *Early Egyptian Christianity*, 146–148. .
66. Athanasius, First *Letter to Virgins* 36–48: the Coptic text of this letter has been edited by L. Th. Lefort, *S. Athanase: Lettres festales et pastorals en copte* (Louvain: L. Durbecq, 1955), 73–99; for an English translation, see D. Brakke, *Athanasius and the Politics of Asceticism*, 274–291.
67. Athanasius also may have spent some time hiding out among the monastic communities of the Alexandrian capital (Index to the Syriac version of

Athanasius' *Festal Letters* 30; ed. and trans. Annik Martin, with Micheline Albert, *Histoire 'acéphale' et index syriaque des letters festales d'Athanase d'Alexandrie* (SC 317; Paris, Cerf, 1985), 258–259).

68. Athanasius, Second *Letter to Monks*; PG 26.1185–1188; trans. A. Robertson, NPNF, second series, vol. 4, 564 (=Letter LIII; translation slightly altered).

69. To emphasize this point, Athanasius writes, "We are specially bound to fly from the communion of men whose opinions we hold in execration" (Second *Letter to Monks*; PG 26.1188B; trans. A Robertson, NPNF, second series, vol. 4, 564).

70. Athanasius, *History of the Arians* VII.55; VIII.70–72 (ed. H.-G. Opitz, *Athanasius: Werke*, Volume 2.1, 214, 221–223).

71. *Werke*, Volume 2.1, 189–190.

72. T.D. Barnes, *Athanasius and Constantius*, 126. Barnes dates Athanasius' *History of the Arians* to "the closing months of 357" (ibid.).

73. Gregory of Nazianzus, *Oration* 21.5 (PG 35.1085D–1088A); Jerome, *Lives of Illustrious Men* 87–88, 125 (ed. E.C. Richardson, 45, 53); Augustine, *Confessions* 8.6 (ed. M. Skutella, H. Jürgens, and W. Schaub, in *S. Aureli Augustini Confessionum libri XIII* (Stuttgart: B.G. Teubner, 1969), 163–167. For examples of how the *Life of Antony* was received by other ancient authors, see Robert C. Gregg's "Introduction" to *Athanasius—The Life of Antony and the Letter to Marcellinus* (New York: Paulist Press, 1980), 13–17; and Samuel Rubenson, *The Letters of St. Antony: Monasticism and the Making of a Saint* (Minneapolis: Fortress Press, 1995), 163–191.

74. On the anti-Arian character of the *Life*, see especially Robert C. Gregg and Dennis E. Groh, *Early Arianism—A View of Salvation*, 131–159; and D. Brakke, *Athanasius and the Politics of Asceticism*, 201–265. On the question of literary genre, see the discussion in R.C. Gregg, "Introduction," in *Athanasius—The Life of Antony*, 4–6. Gregg argues that the *Life* is indebted to both biblical and classical Greek heroic models.

75. Athanasius, *Life of Antony* 68.3; ed. G.J.M. Bartelink, SC 400 (1994), 314; PG 26.940–941.

76. Athanasius, *Life of Antony* 69; ed. G.J.M. Bartelink, SC 400 (1994), 314–316; PG 26.941.

77. R.C. Gregg and D.E. Groh, *Early Arianism*, 131–159, esp. 142ff.

78. Athanasius, *Life of Antony* 5.7; ed. G.J.M. Bartelink, SC 400 (1994), 144–146; PG 26.849.

79. Athanasius, *Life of Antony* 7.1; ed. G.J.M. Bartelink, SC 400 (1994), 150; PG 26.852.

80. D. Brakke, *Athanasius and the Politics of Asceticism*, 203–244, esp. 216ff.

81. In his *Festal Letter* 39 (A.D. 367), Athanasius presents a list of biblical books he recognized as canonical. The critical edition of this text appears in L. Th. Lefort, *Lettres festales et pastorals en copte* (2 vols., CSCO 150–151; Louvain: L. Durbecq, 1955), 16–22, 58–62; for an English translation based upon this critical edition, see D. Brakke, *Athanasius and the Politics of Asceticism*, 326–332. The larger historical significance of this letter lies in the fact that it provides the first canon list from the early church to include the 39 Old Testament writings and 27 New Testament writings commonly recognized by churches today without any omissions or additions. The nature of Athanasius' list and its inclusion in a circular letter to Egyptian churches suggest that the Alexandrian bishop was trying to curb divergent uses of scripture under his jurisdiction.

Egyptian monks may have been among those who were reading "unapproved" works: the discovery of a Gnostic cache of documents at Nag Hammadi in 1945—a collection of non-canonical literature with possible geographical and papyrological connections with ancient Pachomian monasticism in the area—has sparked an ongoing debate about the reading habits of Coptic monks during the fourth century (James E. Goehring, "New Frontiers in Pachomian Studies," in B.A. Pearson and J.E. Goehring, eds., *The Roots of Egyptian Christianity*, 236–257, esp. 247–252; repr. in J.E. Goehring, *Ascetics, Society, and the Desert*, 162–186, esp. 173–179; see also Armand Veilleux, "Monasticism and Gnosis in Egypt," in *The Roots of Egyptian Christianity*, 271–306; and Robert A. Kraft and Janet A. Timbie, review of *The Nag Hammadi Library in English*, by James M. Robinson, *Religious Studies Review* 8 (1982), 34–35). In any case, it is clear that monks were among the original recipients of Athanasius' thirty-ninth *Festal Letter*. The letter was publicly read and posted in the Pachomian monasteries under the leadership of one of Pachomius' successors, Theodore (Bohairic *Life of Pachomius* 189; ed. L. Th. Lefort, *S. Pachomii vita bohairice scripta* (CSCO 89, Scriptores Coptici 7; Paris: E typographeo reipublicae, 1925; repr. Louvain: Secrétariat du CSCO, 1965), 175–178; *Life of Theodore*, ed. Emile Amelineau, *Histoire de St. Pakhôme et de ses communautés: Documents coptes et arabes inédits* (Annales du Museé Guimet 17; Paris: 1889), 238ff.; L. Th. Lefort, "Théodore de Tabennese et la letter de S. Athanase sur le canon de la Bible," *Muséon* 29 (1920), 205–216; C. W. Griggs, *Early Egyptian Christianity*, 175–176).

82. In the case of the Pachomian monastery at Tabennesi, Athanasius helped reconcile a schism in leadership (between Theodore and Horsiesius) after the death of Pachomius by means of a well-placed letter to Horsiesius (ca. 363–367). Later, a consolatory letter sent by Athanasius on the occasion of Theodore's death in 368 helped ease the transition of leadership once again. On Athanasius' role in these events, see D. Brakke, *Athanasius and the Politics of Asceticism*, 120–129.

83. T.D. Barnes, *Athanasius and Constantius*, 152.

84. Ibid., 164.

85. Socrates, *HE* 4.20–22, 24 (PG 67.505–509, 521–525); Sozomen, *HE* 6.20 (PG 67.1340–1344); Theodoret, *HE* 4.21 (ed. L. Parmentier, GCS 19, Third edition (1998), 247; translated as *HE* 4.18, in NPNF, second series, volume 3, 120–121).

86. Socrates, *HE* 5.8 (PG 67.576–581); Sozomen, *HE* 7.7 (PG 67.1429–1432); Theodoret, *HE* 5.6 (ed. L. Parmentier, GCS 19, Third edition (1998), 285–286).

87. Socrates, *HE* 5.8 (PG 67.576–581). The roots of this emerging tension between Constantinople and Alexandria actually may be traced to the reign of Peter, who in 379 had nominated a rival Egyptian candidate to replace Gregory of Nazianzus as the bishop of Constantinople (Gregory of Nazianzus, *De vita sua* 750–1056; esp. 844ff.). This attempt to intervene in Constantinopolitan church affairs may have helped precipitate the wording of the Second Canon at the Council of Constantinople, which urges, "The bishops are not to go beyond their dioceses to churches lying outside their bounds, nor bring confusion on the churches; but let the Bishop of Alexandria, according to the canons, alone administer the affairs of Egypt . . ."(Canon 2; trans. H.R. Percival, NPNF, series 2, vol. 14, 176; C.J. Hefele, *History of the Councils of the Church*, trans. H. Oxenham (Edinburgh: T. & T. Clark, 1896), 355). Peter's action itself may originally have been moti-

vated by a similar canonical concern about the perceived "irregularity" of Gregory's own election: his transfer from another diocese technically went against Canon 15 of the Council of Nicaea (W.H.C. Frend, *The Early Church* (Philadelphia: Fortress Press, 1982), 174). For a fuller analysis of these events, see C.W. Griggs, *Early Egyptian Christianity*, 183–185.

88. John of Nikiu, *Chronicle* 79 (ca. A.D. 690); trans. R.H. Charles, *The Chronicle of John (c. 690 A. D.) Coptic Bishop of Nikiu* (Text and Translation Society 3; London and Oxford: William & Norgate, 1916), 75–76.

89. A. Bauer and J. Strzygowski, *Eine alexandrinische Weltchronik: Text und Miniaturen eines griechischen Papyrus des Sammlung W. Goleniscev* (Denkschriften der kaiserlichen Akademie der Wissenschaften in Wien, Phil.-hist. Klasse, Bd. 51, Abh. 2; Vienna: Alfred Hölder, 1905), 56–58, 152, pl. VI (recto and verso); C. Haas, *Alexandria in Late Antiquity*, 180, fig. 17.

90. On the *pallium* as a symbol of episcopal rule, see Annik Martin, *Athanase d'Alexandrie et l'église d'Égypte au IVe siècle*, 327, note 20.

91. In later Coptic tradition, this connection between Theophilus' war against paganism and the theme of patriarchal succession also comes to expression in a story about how Athanasius disclosed to Theophilus (who was then Athanasius' scribe) his hope to "build upon these mounds (i.e., the site of the Serapeum) a church to John the Baptist and Elisha the prophet" (*History of the Patriarchs*; PO 1.4, 419). This story may actually go back to Theophilus himself, as it appears in a Coptic fragment attributed to him (T. Orlandi, "Un frammento copto Teofilo di Alessandria," *Rivista degli studi orientali* 44 (1969), 23–26).

92. A. Bauer and J. Strzygowski, *Eine alexandrinische Weltchronik*, 149–151, pl. III, VII (A and C).

93. In a letter to Jerome during the heat of the Origenist controversy (A.D. 400), Theophilus proclaims that he had cut down his opponents "with a prophet's sickle" (*prophetica falx*): Theophilus' letter is preserved as Jerome, *Ep.* 87; ed. I. Hilberg, CSEL 55 (1996), 140). Palladius (*Dialogue on the Life of Chrysostom 7*) reports that Theophilus was fond of calling himself "a second Moses."

94. On the events leading up to and surrounding the destruction of the Serapeum, see Rufinus, *HE* 11.22–30; ed. T. Mommsen, Second edition (GCS, Neue Folge, Band 6.2; Berlin: Akademie Verlag, 1999), 1025–1036; trans. P. Amidon, *The Church History of Rufinus, Books 10 and 11* (New York: Oxford University Press, 1997), 79–87. The historian Socrates specifically identifies the paraded objects of worship as phalli of Priapus (Socrates, *HE* 5.16–17; PG 67.604–609). For a critical account of these and other sources, see Elizabeth Clark, *The Origenist Controversy: The Cultural Construction of an Early Christian Debate* (Princeton: Princeton University Press, 1992), 52–56.

94. Rufinus, *HE* 11.23; ed. T. Mommsen, Second edition (GCS, Neue Folge, Band 6.2; Berlin: Akademie Verlag, 1999), 1026–1029; trans. P. Amidon, *The Church History of Rufinus, Books 10 and 11* (New York: Oxford University Press, 1997), 80–82.

96. *Sayings of the Desert Fathers* (= *Apophthegmata Patrum*, Greek alpha-betical version), Theophilus 3 (PG 65.200A). In another story from the same collection, the monk John of Lycopolis tells a fellow monk that God had revealed to him that the temples would be destroyed. The monk narrating this encounter emphasizes that his prediction was, of course, fulfilled (*Sayings of the Desert Fathers*, Bessarion 4; PG 65.140A–141A).

97. Libanius, *Pro Templis* 8 (ca. A.D. 390); ed. René Van Loy, "Le 'Pro Templis' de Libanius," 22 (text), 394–395 (commentary).

98. John of Nikiu, *Chronicle* 78.42–47; *History of the Patriarchs* 1.4, 419, 426; C. Haas, *Alexandria in Late Antiquity*, 163.
99. Rufinus, *HE* 11.27; ed. T. Mommsen, Second edition (GCS, Neue Folge, Band 6.2; Berlin: Akademie Verlag, 1999), 1033; trans. P. Amidon, *The Church History of Rufinus, Books 10 and 11* (New York: Oxford University Press, 1997), 85. In a Coptic fragment conceivably written by Theophilus himself, he describes the construction of this church on the site of the Serapeum and the subsequent miracles that took place there (T. Orlandi, "Uno scritto di Teofilo di Alessandria sulla distruzione del Serapeum?" *La Parola del passato* 23, fasc. 121 (1968), 295–304, esp. 300–301; ibid., "Un frammento copto Teofilo di Alessandria," *Rivista degli studi orientali* 44 (1969), 23–26; ibid. "Theophilus of Alexandria in Coptic Literature," in *Studia Patristica* 24 (1985), 100–104 (= TU 129).
100. In his writings, Theophilus' predecessor Athanasius identified both John the Baptist and Elijah as spiritual models for Egyptian ascetics (Athanasius, *On Virginity* 191–203; ed. R. Casey, "Der dem Athanasius zugeschriebene Traktat PERI PARTHENIAS," *Sitzungsberichte der preussischen Akademie der Wissenschaften* 33 (1935), 1033, 1044–1045; cf. *Life of Antony* 7; and D. Brakke, *Athanasius and the Politics of Asceticism*, 55, 169, 188, 250–251, 259). In Jerome's *Life of Paul the Hermit* 13 (PL 23.26C), the monk Antony reports on seeing his ascetic mentor Paul and exclaims, "I have seen Elijah, I have seen John in the desert." Finally, the hagiographer of Saint Onnophrius likewise invokes Elijah and John the Baptist as exemplars for the monastic life (*Life of St. Onnophrius* 11; trans. T. Vivian, *Journeying into God: Seven Monastic Lives* (Minneapolis: Fortress Press, 1996), 177). On episcopal patronage of the cult of the martyrs and the social relationship between patron bishops and their pilgrim clientele in late antiquity, see Peter Brown, *The Cult of the Saints* (Chicago: University of Chicago Press, 1981), 33–36; and Stephen J. Davis, "Patronage and Architectural Adaptation in the Roman Cult of the Martyrs," *Anistoriton* 3 (1999), on the web at http://users.hol.gr/~ianlos/e993.htm.
101. Haas, *Alexandria in Late Antiquity*, 262. On the monastic presence at Canopus, see *Sayings of the Desert Fathers* (= *Apophthegmata Patrum*, Greek alphabetical version), Arsenius 28, 42 (PG 65.96C–97B, 105D–108B).
102. Eunapius, *The Lives of the Sophists* 472 (written ca. A.D. 414); trans. W.C. Wright, *Philostratus and Eunapius: The Lives of the Sophists* (London, W. Heinemann; New York, G.P. Putnam's Sons, 1922), 425. For a critical edition of the Greek text, see J. Giangrande, *Eunapii vitae sophistarum* (Rome: Polygraphica, 1956), 1–101.
103. C. Haas, *Alexandria in Late Antiquity*, 206–207. This process of "Christianizing" the Egyptian landscape is also vividly illustrated in an anecdote reported by the historian Socrates (*HE* 5.17; PG 67.608–609): he relates how Alexandrian Christians, when they encountered a certain cruciform hieroglyph (undoubtedly the Egyptian *ankh*) among the inscriptional remains at the Serapeum, reinterpreted it as a sign of Christ's cross. The same symbolic connection is made by Egyptian Christians today. With regard to Theophilus' building projects, the vast scale of his investments actually drew criticism from several contemporary writers who accuse him of "lithomania" and "litholatry": see Palladius, *Dialogue on the Life of Chrysostom* 22; Isidore of Pelusium, *Ep.* I.152 (PG 78.284D–285A).

104. The names of these monasteries reflected their respective mile-markers—Pempton (five-mile), Enaton (nine-mile), and Oktokaidekaton (eighteen-mile). Palladius (*Lausiac History* 7; written ca. 419–420) visited the monasteries west of Alexandria and at Nitria during the last decade of the fourth century, and estimated the number of the monks in each of these areas at around 2000 and 5000 respectively.

105. For recent studies of Shenoute as a monastic leader and a Coptic author, see Stephen Emmel, "Shenoute's Literary Corpus," 5 volumes (Ph.D. dissertation, Yale University, 1993); Rebecca Krawiec, *Shenoute and the Women of the White Monastery: Egyptian Monasticism in Late Antiquity* (New York: Oxford University Press, 2002); and Caroline Schroeder, "Disciplining the Monastic Body: Asceticism, Ideology, and Gender in the Egyptian Monastery of Shenoute of Atripe" (Ph.D. dissertation, Duke University, 2002). For more general treatments, see David N. Bell, "Introduction," to Besa's *Life of Shenoute* (Kalamazoo, MI: Cistercian Publications, 1983), 9; and K.H. Kuhn, "Shenute, Saint," CE 7.2131–2133.

106. James E. Goehring, "New Frontiers in Pachomian Studies," in *Ascetics, Society, and the Desert*, 179-186. An even larger, five-aisled basilica (72 by 36 meters) was constructed at Pbow in the mid-fifth century. Completed in A.D. 459, it replaced the structure built in the late fourth or early fifth century.

107. Elizabeth Clark, *The Origenist Controversy*, 36, 45. As Clark argues, this late fourth-century defense of divine incorporeality reflects the way that Origen's theology was reinterpreted by writers like Evagrius Ponticus (ibid., 43–84).

108. Sozomen, *HE* 8.11 (PG 67.1544). On the theoretical connection between Theophilus' early anti-anthropomorphite stance and his anti-pagan agenda, see John Cassian, *Conferences* 10.5, where Cassian reports the comments of the monk Isaac concerning the anthropomorphite "error" prevalent in the Nitrian monasteries: "It is not a question, as you think, of a recent diabolical trick, but rather of an old pagan misapprehension. Paganism gave human shape to the demons which it adored. And nowadays it is thought that the incomprehensible and unspeakable majesty of the true God can be adored amid the limitations of some image or other. People believe they are holding on to nothing at all if they do not have some image in the mind, an image which is always there to be looked at." (ed. M. Petschenig, CSEL 13 (1886), 290–291); trans. C. Luibheid (New York: Paulist Press, 1985), 127–128).

109. John Cassian, *Conferences* 10.2 (ed. M. Petschenig, CSEL 13 (1886), 286–287); trans. C. Luibheid (New York: Paulist Press, 1985), 125–126. A Coptic document published by Etienne Drioton ("La discussion d'un moine anthropomorphite Audien avec le patriarche Théophile d'Alexandrie en l'année 399," *Revue de l'Orient Chrétien*, 2e ser., 10 (= 20) (1915–1917), 92–100, 113–128) describes the disturbed reaction of a monk from Pemdjé (Oxyrhynchus) to the same festal letter.

110. John Cassian, *Conferences* 10.3; ed. M. Petschenig, CSEL 13 (1886), 288–289; trans. C. Luibheid (New York: Paulist Press, 1985), 126–127.

111. Elizabeth Clark (*The Origenist Controversy*, 63–66) has shown how the debate over anthropomorphite views of God had profound implications for theories of "real presence" in the Eucharist, theories that undergirded Egyptian monastic worship practices.

112. Socrates, *HE* 6.7 (PG 67.684–688); Sozomen, *HE* 8.11 (PG 67.1544–1545). Theophilus' change of policy regarding the

"Anthropomorphites" may also have been influenced by the pressure being applied early on by Jerome in his letters to the Egyptian patriarch. As early as A.D. 397, Jerome was remonstrating Theophilus for his lenience toward "that nefarious heresy" (*Ep.* 63.3; ed. I. Hilberg, CSEL 54 (1996), 586). Two years later in 399, Jerome was still complaining about Theophilus' failure to take a strong stand against the Origenists (Jerome, *Ep.* 82; ed. I. Hilberg, CSEL 55 (1996), 107–119).

113. On Isidore, see Palladius, *Lausiac History* 1.1–5; trans. R. Meyer (Westminster, MD: The Newman Press; London: Longmans, Green and Co., 1965), 31–32. Early on, Isidore also seems to have functioned as a special emissary for Theophilus in his correspondence with other church leaders and was Theophilus' hand-picked candidate to fill the episcopal throne of Constantinople: Socrates, *HE* 6.2 (PG 67.661–664); Sozomen, *HE* 8.2 (PG 67.1517–1520); Jerome, *Ep.* 82.9 (ed. I. Hilberg, CSEL 55 (1996), 116); see also D. Chitty, *The Desert A City* (Crestwood, NY: St. Vladimir's Seminary Press, 1966), 54). On Theophilus' former friendship with the Tall Brothers, see Socrates, *HE* 6.7 (PG 67.684–685); cf. Sozomen, *HE* 8.12 (PG 67.1545).

114. Socrates, *HE* 6.7 (PG 67.684–688).

115. On the relationship between Theophilus' theological and political motivations in the ensuing conflict, see Susanna Elm, "The Dog That Did Not Bark: Doctrine and Patriarchal Authority in the Conflict Between Theophilus of Alexandria and John Chrysostom of Constantinople," in *Christian Origins: Theology, Rhetoric and Community*, edited by L. Ayres and G. Jones (London and New York: Routledge, 1998), 68–93, esp. 78–83.

116. A seventh-century Coptic manuscript contains a memorandum ascribed to Dioscorus in which he appeals to Shenoute, the head of the White Monastery in Upper Egypt, to help him coordinate a purge of Origenist belief in the vicinity of Panopolis (Herbert Thompson, "Dioscorus and Shenoute," in *Recueil d'études égyptologique* (Bibliothèque de l'École des haute etudes, IVe section, Sciences historiques et philologiques; Fasc. 234; Paris: E. Champion, 1922), 367–376).

117. Palladius (*Dialogue on the Life of John Chrysostom*, ch. 6–7) offers a decidedly unfriendly account of Theophilus' actions, portraying him as a mad despot.

118. Theophilus, *Letter to Jerome* (= Jerome, *Ep.* 87; A.D. 400; ed. I. Hilberg, CSEL 55 (1996), 140). In another letter to Jerome written in A.D. 400, Theophilus celebrates the fact that "the church of Christ . . . with the gospel sword has chopped apart the serpents of Origen who were slithering out of their caves, and has freed the holy company of monks at Nitria from their pestilential contagion" (Jerome, *Ep.* 90; ed. I. Hilberg, CSEL 55 (1996), 143–145, esp. 144).

119. Jerome, *Ep.* 97.1 (A.D. 402); ed. I. Hilberg, CSEL 55 (1996), 182–183.

120. Elizabeth Clark (*The Origenist Controversy*, 84) argues that this illogical disjuncture in Theophilus' "theory and praxis" points to the fact that "factors other than religion motivated Theophilus' behavior." However, at the same time, she does not at all dismiss the fact that religion and theology, even if inconsistently conceived, played a vital role in the Origenist controversy (ibid., 42).

121. This fact was recognized by Theophilus' contemporary Jerome: "The one whom Demetrius banished from the city of Alexander, Theophilus exiled from the whole world" (Jerome, *Ep.* 97.1; A.D. 402; ed. I. Hilberg, CSEL 55 (1996), 182).

122. Theophilus. *Letter to Epiphanius* (= Jerome, *Ep.* 90; A.D. 400; ed. I. Hilberg, CSEL 55 (1996), 145).

123. Theophilus, *Synodical Letter* (= Jerome, *Ep.* 92.3; ed. I. Hilberg, CSEL 55 (1996), 150–151).

124. Socrates, *HE* 6.2 (PG 67.661–664); Sozomen, *HE* 8.2 (PG 67.1517–1520).

125. Palladius, *Dialogue on the Life of John Chrysostom*, ch. 7–9; Sozomen, *HE* 8.13–17 (PG 67.1549–1561). Palladius accuses Theophilus of using well-placed gifts and favors to sway support in Constantinople away from Chrysostom. Chrysostom was, in fact, almost immediately recalled from exile due to popular protests over his condemnation, but his return would be short-lived. He was soon sent off into exile again, this time for good, in large part due to the continued maneuverings of Theophilus, who had returned to Egypt but still had active allies in Asia Minor (Palladius, *Dialogue* 9–11).

126. Sozomen, *HE* 8.17 (PG 67.1560); Socrates *HE* 6.16 (PG 67.712). Both of these historians believed that this reconciliation was due to political expediency on Theophilus' part rather than a sincere theological settlement.

127. Isidore of Pelusium, *Ep.* I.310 (PG 78.361C); John of Nikiu, *Chronicle* 79.2–14.

128. ACO 1.1.3, 22.7–9. Cyril makes a similar claim in his *Letter to Acacius of Beroea* (*Ep.* 33; ACO 1.1.7, 147–156; trans. J.A. McGuckin, *St. Cyril of Alexandria: The Christological Controversy* (Leiden: E.J. Brill, 1994), 336–342): "I have always been orthodox and was brought up (*etraphên*) in the care of an orthodox father" (33.7).

129. J.A. McGuckin, *St. Cyril of Alexandria*, 339, note 7; N. Russell, *Cyril of Alexandria* (London: Routledge, 2000), 5–6, 205–206, note 18.

130. Isidore of Pelusium, *Ep.* I.310; PG 78.361C.

131. N. Russell, *Cyril of Alexandria*, 6.

132. Socrates, *HE* 7.15 (PG 67.769).

133. Socrates, *HE* 7.13 (PG 67.760–765).

134. For an excellent account of Hypatia's life and death, and the various later interpretations of her legend, see Maria Dzielska, *Hypatia of Alexandria*, trans. F. Lyra (Cambridge, MA: Harvard University Press, 1995); cf. P. Chuvin, *A Chronicle of the Last Pagans*, trans. B. A. Archer (Cambridge, MA: Harvard University Press, 1990), 85–90. On "Hypatia and pagan philosophic culture in the later fourth century" (including an account of her conflict with Cyril), see Edward Jay Watts, "City and School in Late Antique Athens and Alexandria" (Ph.D. dissertation, Yale University, 2002), 327-354.

135. Damascius, *Life of Isidore*, Fragment 104; ed. C. Zintzen, *Damascii Vitae Isidori Reliquiae* (Hildesheim: Olms, 1967), 79.18ff.; Edward Gibbon, *The History of the Decline and Fall of the Roman Empire* (Philadelphia: Porter and Coates, 1845) V.119–120. For a discussion of these sources, see Maria Dzielska, *Hypatia of Alexandria*, 18–20.

136. Socrates, *HE* 7.7 (PG 67.749–752). For a discussion of Cyril's election and its immediate aftermath, see Jean Rougé, "Les débuts de l'épiscopat de Cyrille d'Alexandrie et le Code Théodosien," in *ALEXANDRINA: Hellenisme, judaisme et christianisme à Alexandrie. Mélanges offerts au P. Claude Mondesert* (Paris: Cerf, 1987), 339–349.

137, Socrates, *HE* 7.13–14 (PG 67.760–768).

138. Peter Brown, *Power and Persuasion in Late Antiquity* (Madison: University of Wisconsin Press, 1992), 115–117; for a further discussion of *parrhésia* and its social implications for the role of philosophers in late antiquity, see pages 61–70.

139. In ancient literature, women's bodies (both virginal and violated) often functioned as signifiers of civic institutions and the body politic: Patricia K. Joplin, "Ritual Work on Human Flesh: Livy's Lucretia and the Rape of the Body Politic," *Helios* 17 (1990), 51–70; Sandra Joshel, "The Body Female and the Body Politic: Livy's Lucretia and Verginia," in *Pornography and Representation in Greece and Rome*, ed. A. Richlin (Oxford: Oxford University Press, 1992), 112–130; Shilpa Raval, "Boys to Men: Erotic and Political Violence in Livy's Rape of Lucretia," Paper presented at the Greco–Roman Lunch, Yale University, November 4, 2002.

140. This may explain why the perpetrators of the crime went unpunished. Cyril would have been loath to lose the support of this more militant faction of the church: in fact, he would have had a vested interest in harnessing their energies. Of course, in doing so, Cyril had to tread lightly. After Hypatia's violent death, the imperial government published an edict reprimanding Cyril and forbidden bishops from overstepping their authority by involving themselves in the affairs of civil government. Cyril's subsequent anti-pagan policy was considerably more circumspect.

141. John of Nikiu, *Chronicle* 84.103; trans. R.H. Charles (Text and Translation Society 3; London: William & Norgate, 1916), 102.

142. On the perseverance of indigenous Egyptian religions in late antiquity, see David Frankfurter's book, *Religion in Roman Egypt: Assimilation and Resistance* (Princeton: Princeton University Press, 1998); and his article, "'Things Unbefitting Christians': Violence and Christianization in Fifth-Century Panopolis," *Journal of Early Christian Studies* 8:2 (2000), 273–295, esp. 274–281.

143. Some sculptural remains from the Isis shrine at Menouthis survive in the Graeco–Roman Museum in Alexandria (E. Breccia, *Alexandria ad Aegyptum: Guide de la ville ancienne et moderne et du Musée gréco-romain* (Bergamo: Istituto italiano d'arti grafiche, 1914), 138, 165–166).

144. Cyril, *Homiliae Diversae* 18; PG 77.1101. Fragments of homilies presented by Cyril either at Menouthis or at nearby Canopus are preserved in this collection by the seventh-century writer Sophronius.

145. J.A. McGuckin, "The Influence of the Isis Cult on St. Cyril of Alexandria's Christology," *Studia Patristica* 24 (1993), 291–299, esp. 293–295; also *St. Cyril of Alexandria*, 18–19. McGuckin has argued that Cyril founded the shrine of Saints Cyrus and John for the purpose of institutional competition with the Isis cult. E. Wipszycka ("La christianisation de l'Égypte aux IVe–Ve siècles. Aspects sociaux et ethniques," *Aegyptus* 58 (1988), 117–165, esp. 140–142) has argued for the possibility that the founding of this pilgrimage center actually took place in the seventh century; however, most scholars continue to support the dating of this sanctuary to the early fifth century under Cyril: for a recent discussion, see Dominic Montserrat, "Pilgrimage to the Shrine of SS Cyrus and John at Menouthis in Late Antiquity," in *Pilgrimage and Holy Space in Late Antique Egypt*, ed. D. Frankfurter (Leiden: E.J. Brill, 1998), 257–279, esp. 261–266.

146. Sophronius, *Laudes in Ss. Cyrum et Joannem*; PG 87.3380–3424.

147. In a sermon given at the shrine's dedication, Cyril refers to a "Church of the Holy Evangelists" that had already been established at the site: *Homiliae Diversae* 18 (PG 77.1101); see also Sophronius, *Laudes* 27 (PG 87.3413A).

148. At the end of his career (ca. 440 c.e.), Cyril composed a magisterial anti-pagan treatise *Against Julian*, in which he defended Christian belief against the attacks lodged against it in the fourth century by the emperor Julian in his work *Against the Galileans*. For the Greek text, see P.

Burguière and P. Evieux, eds., *Contre Julien*, vol. 1, SC 322 (Paris: Cerf, 1985) (books 1–2); and PG 76.613–1064 (books 3–10). Excerpts of the work have been translated into English by N. Russell, *Cyril of Alexandria*, 190–203.

149. Cyril, *Ep.* 81.1, *Letter to the Monks of Scetis*; ed. E. Schwartz, ACO 3.201; trans. J. McEnerney, in *St. Cyril of Alexandria: Letters 51–100* (FC 77; Washington, D.C.: The Catholic University of America Press, 1987), 105.

150. This idea, with its roots in Origen's treatise *On the Resurrection*, was rearticulated in the fourth century by Evagrius Ponticus (*Letter to Melania* 5; ed. W. Frankenburg, *Opera. Euagrius Ponticus* (Abhandlungen der königlichen Gesellschaft der Wissenschaften zu Göttingen, philologisch-historische Klasse, n. f. 13, 2 (Berlin: Weidmann, 1912), 616–617; trans. M. Parmentier, "Evagrius of Pontus' 'Letter to Melania,'" *Bijdragen, tijdschrift voor filosofie en theologie* 46 (1985), 11–12). Theophilus himself attacks this doctrine in his *Synodal Letter* of 400 (= Jerome, *Ep.* 92.2; ed. I. Hilberg, CSEL 55 (1996), 149). For a discussion of these sources, see E. Clark, *The Origenist Controversy*, 73 and 108.

151. For the Greek texts and English translations of these letters, see Cyril of Alexandria, *Select Letters*; trans. L. Wickham (Oxford: Clarendon Press, 1983), 132–179 (*Answers to Tiberias*), 180–213 (*Doctrinal Questions and Answers*), 214–221 (*Letter to Calosirius*). The Greek text of Cyril's *Answers to Tiberias* is fragmentary; however, the complete text survives in a Syriac version (R.Y. Ebied and L.R. Wickham, "The Letter of Cyril of Alexandria to Tiberias the Deacon," *Le Muséon* 83 (1970), 433–482).

152. *Sayings of the Desert Fathers* (= *Apophthegmata Patrum*, Greek alphabetical version), Sisoes 32 (PG 65.405; trans. B. Ward, *The Desert Christian: Sayings of the Desert Fathers. The Alphabetic Collection* (New York: Macmillan, 1975), 219); J. Goehring, "Monastic Diversity and Ideological Boundaries in Fourth-Century Christian Egypt," in *Ascetics, Society, and the Desert*, 196–218, esp. 200–208.

153. Cyril, *Letter to Calosirius*; ed. and trans. L. Wickham, *Select Letters*, 216–217, 220–221.

154. Cyril refers to himself as "one of the bystanders" at the Synod of the Oak (*Ep.* 33.7, *Letter to Acacius of Beroea*; ed. E. Schwartz, ACO 1.1.7, 148.34; trans. J. McEnerney, *St. Cyril of Alexandria: Letters 1–50* (FC 76; Washington, D.C.: The Catholic University of America Press, 1987), 131. For the critical text of Atticus' letter requesting the restoration of Chrysostom's name to the *diptychs* and Cyril's reply, see E. Schwartz, ed., *Codex vaticanus gr. 1431: Eine antichalkedonische Sammlung aus der Zeit Kaiser Zenos* (Abhandlungen der Bayerischen Akademie der Wissenschaften philosophisch-philologisch und historische Klasse, Vol. 32, Abhandlung no. 6; Munich, 1927), 23–24, 25–28. English translations of the two letters have been published by J. McEnerney, trans., *St. Cyril of Alexandria: Letters 51–100*, (FC 77; Washington, D.C.: The Catholic University of America Press, 1987), 83–85, 86–91.

155. J.A. McGuckin, *St. Cyril of Alexandria*, 5–6.

156. Socrates, *HE* 7.32 (PG 67.808–812).

157. ACO 1.1.6, 18.24–31 (excerpts from Nestorius' lectures are preserved in Cyril's later treatise *Against Nestorius*).

158. For a history of the usage of the term *Theotokos* among these and other patristic authors, see G.W.H. Lampe, *A Patristic Greek Lexicon*, 639–640; M. Starowieyski, "Le titre *theotokos* avant le concile d'Ephese," *Studia Patristica* 19 (1989), 236–242; and N. Russell, *Cyril of Alexandria*, 232, note 15.

159. On the use of the term *Theotokos* in its Egyptian theological context and in relation to the cult of Isis, see J.A. McGuckin, "The Influence of the Isis Cult on St. Cyril of Alexandria's Christology," *Studia Patristica* 24 (1993), 295–299. The depiction of Isis suckling Horus became the primary iconographic model for early Christian depictions of the Virgin Mary nursing the Christ child: see Lucia Langener, *Isis lactans – Maria lactans: Untersuchungen zur koptischen Ikonographie* (Altenberge: Oros Verlag, 1996).

160. Cyril, *Ep.* 1, *Letter to the Monks of Egypt*; ed. E. Schwartz, ACO 1.1.1, 11.12–15; trans. J. McEnerney, *St. Cyril of Alexandria, Letters 1–50* (FC 76), 14–15.

161. Through his theological rhetoric, Cyril was seeking to shape community identity along the lines of Mary Douglas' strong group model of sociological classification: see M. Douglas, *Natural Symbols* (New York: Random House, 1970).

162. Cyril, *Ep.* 1, *Letter to the Monks of Egypt*; ed. E. Schwartz, ACO 1.1.1, 11.27–30; trans. J. McEnerney, *St. Cyril of Alexandria, Letters 1–50* (FC 76), 15; cf. Cyril, *Against Nestorius*, Proem. 1; ed. E. Schwartz, ACO 1.1.6, 16.3–5; trans. N. Russell, *Cyril of Alexandria*, 132.

163. *History of the Patriarchs*; PO 1.4, 437.

164. Athanasius, *Against the Arians* 3.29, 33 (PG 26.385–388, 393–396); cited by Cyril, *Letter to the Monks of Egypt* (*Ep.* 1); ed. E. Schwartz, ACO 1.1.1, 11.27—12.20; trans. J. McEnerney, *St. Cyril of Alexandria, Letters 1–50* (FC 76), 15–16.

165. Cyril, *Ep.* 1, *Letter to the Monks of Egypt*; ed. E. Schwartz, ACO 1.1.1, 12.32—13.5; trans. J. McEnerney, *St. Cyril of Alexandria, Letters 1–50* (FC 76), 17.

166. Cyril, *Ep.* 17, Third *Letter to Nestorius*; ed. E. Schwartz, ACO 1.1.1, 34.14–20; trans. J. McEnerney, *St. Cyril of Alexandria, Letters 1–50* (FC 76), 81–82. L. Wickham (*Select Letters*, 15) also provides the Greek text with English translation. For an example of Nestorius' use of the Nicene Creed, see his Second *Letter to Cyril*; ed. E. Schwartz, ACO 1.1.1, 29.12–14; trans. J. McEnerney, *St. Cyril of Alexandria, Letters 1–50* (FC 76), 43.

167. Cyril, *Ep.* 1, *Letter to the Monks of Egypt*; ed. E. Schwartz, ACO 1.1.1, 23.11–13; trans. J. McEnerney, *St. Cyril of Alexandria, Letters 1–50* (FC 76), 33.

168. Cyril, *Ep.* 4, Second *Letter to Nestorius*; ed. E. Schwartz, ACO 1.1.1, 26.25–28; trans. J. McEnerney, *St. Cyril of Alexandria, Letters 1–50* (FC 76), 39; cf. J. Wickham, *Select Letters*, 4–7 (Greek text and English translation).

169. Cyril, *Against Nestorius*, Proem. 1 (ed. E. Schwartz, ACO 1.1.6, 16.3ff.; trans. N. Russell, *Cyril of Alexandria*, 132); cf. Cyril, *Paschal Letter* 17.2 (ed. W.H. Burns, in SC 434, 266–268; PG 77.776A–B). This mutual interchange of divine and human attributes in the unity of Christ would later come to be known as *communicatio idiomatum*.

170. See, e.g., Athanasius, *Against the Arians*, 2.70; cf. Cyril, *Against Nestorius* II.8; III.2; ed. E. Schwartz, ACO 1.1.6, 46.28–37; 58.6–13; trans. N. Russell, *Cyril of Alexandria*, 156–157, 161–162. For Cyril, this salvific participation in Christ's body was especially facilitated through the sacrament of the Eucharist: see especially Cyril, *Against Nestorius* IV.3–7, where he contests Nestorius' interpretation of John 6 (ed. E. Schwartz, ACO 1.1.6, 83.30—91.8; large excerpts of this section are translated by N. Russell, *Cyril of Alexandria*, 167–174).

171. Cyril, *Ep.* 4, Second *Letter to Nestorius*; ed. E. Schwartz, ACO 1.1.1, 28.3–25; trans. J. McEnerney, *St. Cyril of Alexandria, Letters 1–50* (FC

76), 40–41; also J. Wickham, *Select Letters*, 8–11. Nestorius' later attempts to explain his Christology more carefully have shown that at least some of Cyril's concerns were based on misconceptions of Nestorius' thought: see especially Nestorius, *The Bazaar of Heracleides*, trans. G. R. Driver and L. Hodgson (Oxford: Clarendon Press, 1925). The publication of this apologetic treatise in the twentieth century has led a number of Western scholars to revise their estimate of Nestorius and his conflict with Cyril.

172. For a catalogue of Cyril's anti-Nestorian writings, see J. Quasten, *Patrology*, volume 3, 126ff.

173. Cyril, *Ep.* 17, Third *Letter to Nestorius*; ed. E. Schwartz, ACO 1.1.1, 33–42; trans. J. McEnerney, *St. Cyril of Alexandria, Letters 1–50* (LC 76), 80–92; also J. Wickham, *Select Letters*, 12–33.

174. For evidence of Shenoute's participation in the Council of Ephesus, see Shenoute, *On the Modesty of Clerics* (ed. J. Leipoldt and W.E. Crum, CSCO 42.35; trans. J. Wiesmann, CSCO 96.16); and Besa, *The Life of Shenoute* 128–130 (ed. J. Leipoldt and W.E. Crum, in *Sinuthii Archimandritae Vita et Opera Omnia*, CSCO 41, 57–59; trans. D. Bell, 78–79). According to Besa's partially legendary account, Shenoute rebuked Nestorius at the council and punched him in the chest, after which Cyril promoted him to archimandrite (the title for a monastic superior in the Coptic Orthodox Church).

175. On Egyptian monks who served as Cyril's agents in Constantinople, see ACO 1.1.2, 66.10; and 1.1.4, 35.2; cited by E. Schwartz, *Cyrill und der Mönch Viktor* (Sitzungsberichte der Akademie der Wissenschaften in Wien, Philosophisch-historische Klasse 208, 4; Vienna: Hölder-Pichler-Tempsky, 1928), 8. Schwartz (op cit., *passim*) rightly points out that Egyptian monastic support for Cyril was not unanimous: Nestorius also recruited his own monastic loyalists, and there is evidence that there were some dissidents in Cyril's camp.

176. For a concise account of the proceedings at the Council of Ephesus in 431 and its immediate aftermath, see N. Russell, *Cyril of Alexandria*, 46–56. J.A. McGuckin (*St. Cyril of Alexandria*, 53–106) offers a more detailed account, albeit with a decidedly pro-Cyrillian bias.

177. ACO 1.1.7, 74.21–22.

178. ACO 1.1.7, 71.5–14; 76.41—77.1.

179. Socrates, *HE* 7.34 (PG 67.813–816); George the Monk ("Hamartolos"), *Chronicon* 105.6 (PG 110.741C). In two letters to the Egyptian governor of the Thebaid, Nestorius speaks of his time in the Kharga Oasis of the Western Desert and of his sufferings there during the raids of the Blemmyes tribe around the year A.D. 450 (Evagrius Scholasticus, *HE* 1.7.258–260).

180. See, e.g., *Sayings of the Desert Fathers* (= *Apophthegmata Patrum*, Greek alphabetical version), Daniel 8 (PG 65.160A–C; trans. B. Ward, *The Desert Christian*, 54); and Besa, *Life of Shenoute* 17–21, 128–130 (ed. J. Leipoldt and W.E. Crum, in *Sinuthii Archimandritae Vita et Opera Omnia*, CSCO 41, 15–18, 57–59; trans. D. Bell, 47–49, 78–79). In the seventh century, Anastasius, abbot of the Monastery of St. Catherine at Mount Sinai, refers to Cyril as "the seal of the Fathers" (*Viae dux* 7.1.101; ed. K.-H. Uthemann, Corpus Christianorum Series Graeca 8 (Turnout: Brepols, 1981), 107).

181. J.A. McGuckin, *St. Cyril of Alexandria*, 207–212.

182. Cyril, Second *Letter to Succensus*, *Ep.* 46.3 (ed. E. Schwartz, ACO 1.1.6, 160.5–7; trans. J. McEnerney, *St. Cyril of Alexandria, Letters 1–50* (LC 76), 201; cf. J. Wickham, *Select Letters*, 89).

183. R.V. Sellers, *The Council of Chalcedon: A Historical and Doctrinal Survey* (London: SPCK, 1961), 56–69.

184. Theodoret of Cyrus, *Eranistes* 2 (PG 83.153, 157); J.N.D. Kelly, *Early Christian Doctrines*, 330–334, esp. 331–332.

185. Leo, *Ep.* 28.1 (= *Tome of Leo*; ed. E. Schwartz, ACO 2.2, 24). On the condemnation of Eutyches at Constantinople in 448, see ACO 2.1.1, 100–145; A. Grillmeier, *Christ in Christian Tradition: Volume One, From the Apostolic Age to Chalcedon (451)*, trans. J. Bowden, Second edition (Atlanta: John Knox Press, 1975), 523–526. On Leo's response to Eutyches and the "Home Synod," see also Leo, *Ep.* 27 and 29 (ed. E. Schwartz, ACO 2.4, 9–10); and R.V. Sellers, *The Council of Chalcedon*, 73ff.

186. See, e.g., W.H.C. Frend, *The Rise of Christianity* (Philadelphia: Fortress Press, 1984), 764.

187. Heinrich Bacht, S.J., "Die Rolle des orientalischen Mönchtums in den kirchenpolitischen Auseinandersetzungen um Chalkedon (431–519)," in *Das Konzil von Chalkedon*, volume 2, edited by A. Grillmeier and H. Bacht (Würzburg: Echter-Verlag, 1953), 193–314; J.A. McGuckin, *St. Cyril of Alexandria*, 229.

188. Dioscorus may have also secured Theodosius' support through well-placed gifts: he would later be accused of diverting 1400 pounds of gold to the imperial court (ACO 2.1.2, 27). If this were the case, he would have been simply following the precedent of Cyril, who openly catalogues in one of his letters a staggering array of gifts that he had donated to members of the emperor's circle in order to win their favor in his dispute with Nestorius (Cyril, *Ep.* 96; ed. E. Schwartz, ACO 1.4, 224–225; trans. J. McEnerney, *St. Cyril of Alexandria, Letters 51–90* (FC 77), 151–153). Cyril's catalogue of gifts includes wool rugs, place covers, table cloths, curtains, caldrons, ivory chairs and stools, stool covers, tables, and hundreds of pounds of gold.

189. Nestorius, *The Bazaar of Heracleides* 2.2.490–496; trans. G.R. Driver and L. Hodgson (Oxford: Clarendon Press, 1925), 358–362. A number of ancient sources allege that Flavian's death was the result of injuries inflicted at the Council; however, these allegations appear to be unfounded (H. Chadwick, "The Exile and Death of Flavian of Constantinople: A Prologue to the Council of Chalcedon," *Journal of Theological Studies*, new series, 6.1 (1955), 17–34).

190. Leo, *Ep.* 28; ed. E. Schwartz, ACO 2.2.1, 24–33; trans. W. Bright, in E.R. Hardy, ed., *Christology of the Later Fathers* (Library of Christian Classics III; Philadelphia: Westminster Press, 1954), 359–370.

191. Leo, *Ep.* 95, *Letter to Pulcheria*; ed. E. Schwartz, ACO 2.4, 51.4.

192. On the actions taken at Chalcedon, see ACO 2.1–5; for the text of the Chalcedonian Creed, see ACO 2.1.2, 129–130; trans. R.V. Sellers, *The Council of Chalcedon*, 210–211.

193. W.H.C. Frend, *The Rise of the Monophysite Movement: Chapters in the History of the Church in the Fifth and Sixth Centuries* (Cambridge: Cambridge University Press, 1972), 141, 154; M. Cramer and H. Bacht, "Der antichalkedonische Aspekt im historisch-biographischen Schrifttum der koptischen Monophysiten (6.-7. Jahrhundert): Ein Beitrag zur Geschichte der Entstehung der monophysitischen Kirche Ägyptens," in *Das Konzil von Chalkedon*, vol. 2, 327. The *Chronicle of the Year 846* reports that "after Dioscorus was sent into exile, many of the monasteries still clung to him *(proclamabant)* secretly" (*Chronicle of 846*; ed. E.W. Brooks and J.-B. Chabot, in *Chronica Minora*, CSCO Syr. 3, 4 (Paris: Typographeo reipublicae, 1903), 163).

194. A Coptic *Panegyric on Macarius* attributed to Dioscorus (but undoubtedly by a later anti-Chalcedonian author) purports to record a speech he gave to a group of monastic and clerical visitors while he was in exile at Gangra: in the speech, he celebrates Macarius' and his own heroic resistance at Chalcedon and speaks about the sufferings he endured while in exile (Pseudo-Dioscorus, *Panegyric on Macarius, Bishop of Tkôw*; ed. and trans. D.W. Johnson, CSCO 415–416, Scriptores Coptici 41–42 (Louvain: Secrétariat du CorpusSCO, 1980)). The account in the *Panegyric* (ch. 9) of how Dioscorus took Leo's *Tome* at the council and "threw it away" may also have served as a literary model for later hagiographies of famous monks like Daniel of Scetis and Samuel of Calamon, both of whom were said to have shown their opposition to Chalcedonian doctrine by ripping Leo's *Tome* to shreds (M. Cramer and H. Bacht, "Der antichalkedonische Aspekt im historisch-biographischen Schrifttum der koptischen Monophysiten (6.–7. Jahrhundert)," in *Das Konzil von Chalkedon*, vol. 2, 320). For more information on anti-Chalcedonian works commemorating Dioscorus' role at Chalcedon, see Felix Haase, *Patriarch Dioskur I. von Alexandria: Nach monophysitischen Quellen* (Kirchengeschichtliche Abhandlungen, Band 6; Breslau, G.P. Aderholz, 1908), 141–236.

195. At the Monastery of the Syrians in the Wadi al-Natrun, Dioscorus is portrayed wearing a monastic hood: Karel Innemée, "The Iconographical Program of Paintings in the Church of al-'Adra in Deir al-Sourian: Some Preliminary Observations," in M. Krause and S. Schaten, eds., *THEMELIA: Spätantike und koptologische Studien Peter Grossmann zum 65. Geburtstag* (Wiesbaden: Reichert Verlag, 1998), 143–155, esp. 149 and 153, fig. 6). At Monastery of St. Antony at the Red Sea, he appears in an iconographic program of Egyptian monks and patriarchs, including his exiled predecessors Athanasius and Peter: Elizabeth S. Bolman, ed., *Monastic Visions: Wall Paintings in the Monastery of the St. Antony at the Red Sea* (New Haven: Yale University Press, 2002), 71, 76 (fig. 4.43), 112 (fig. 7.14).

Chapter 4: Contesting the Alexandrian Papacy

1. PO 1.4, 444.
2. Ibid.
3. On the social and ideological relationship between emperor and church in the aftermath of Chalcedon, see Rhaban Haacke, "Die kaiserliche Politik in den Auseinandersetzungen um Chalkedon (451–553)," in *Das Konzil von Chalkedon*, vol. 2, 95–177.
4. George R. Monks, "The Church of Alexandria and the City's Economic Life in the Sixth Century," *Speculum* 28 (1953), 349–362; J.F. Haldon, *Byzantium in the Seventh Century: The Transformation of a Culture* (Cambridge: Cambridge University Press, 1990), 283–285, 292.
5. Leo, *Ep.* 162, ACO 2.4, 107.13–16.
6. I follow Edward Said (*Culture and Imperialism* (New York: Vintage Books, 1993), 9) in his use of the terms of "imperialism" and "colonialism" and his recognition of their relationship: for him, the term "imperialism" refers to "the practice, the theory and the attitudes of a dominating metropolitan center ruling a distant territory," while "colonialism"— "the implanting of settlements on distant territory"—is understood as a common consequence of imperialist ideology and practice.
7. Note, for example, the title of one of the seminal works on this period in Western ecclesiastical scholarship, W.H.C. Frend's monograph, *The Rise*

of the Monophysite Movement: Chapters in the History of the Church in the Fifth and Sixth Century (Cambridge: Cambridge University Press, 1972). In more recent studies, David Johnson ("Anti-Chalcedonian Polemics in Coptic Texts, 451–641," in *The Roots of Egyptian Christianity*, ed. B.A. Pearson and J.E. Goehring, 218–219) and James Allen Evans (*The Empress Theodora: Partner of Justinian* (Austin: University of Texas Press, 2002), 131, note 1 for chapter 7) both admit that "it is somewhat anachronistic to speak of 'Monophysites'" even as late as the seventh century, but still choose to use the term anyway "for the sake of convenience."

8. Even in his treatment of the Christology of the anti-Chalcedonian patriarchs after Chalcedon, Aloys Grillmeier maintains a Western "accounting" of papal lineage at crucial points: note, for example, his designation of "Timothy IV," even though he acknowledges that "the Copts call him Timothy III, . . . (while) the Melkites say Timothy IV" (A. Grillmeier, with T. Hainthaler, *Christ in Christian Tradition*, volume 2.4, 42, note 52).

9. Throughout this chapter, I utilize the insights of post-colonialist theory in analyzing the social situation of the Egyptian church in the two centuries after the Council of Chalcedon. In simple terms, post-colonialism represents an approach to the study of culture that seeks to unmask forms of colonial (or imperialist) domination and to identify the different ways that colonized peoples have responded to such imbalances of power. From its roots in the work of Edward Said—especially his book, *Orientalism* (New York: Vintage, 1978)—post-colonialist theory has focused its attention often on the practice of cultural resistance, whether in the form of political action or literary performance. Some theorists in the field have questioned whether post-colonialism is applicable to the study of pre-modern history; however, Ernst Gellner ("The Mightier Pen? Edward Said and the Double Standards of Inside-out Colonialism," *The Times Literary Supplement* (February 19, 1993), 3–4) has critiqued the idea that post-colonialist theory is only applicable to the conditions of modern society. In discussing Gellner, Robert J.C. Young (*Postcolonialism: An Historical Introduction* (Oxford: Blackwell Publishers, 2001), 5, 11) notes the similarity of modern forms of colonialism to past forms of political domination, and goes on to argue that "interest in oppression of the past will always be guided by the relation of that history to the present."

10. Stephen Slemon, "Unsettling the Empire: Resistance Theory for the Second World," in *World Literature Written in English* 30.2 (1990), 30–41; Sara Suleri, *The Rhetoric of English India* (Chicago: University of Chicago Press, 1992), 3–4; Bill Ashcroft, Gareth Griffiths, and Helen Tiffin, "General Introduction," *The Post-Colonial Studies Reader* (London and New York: Routledge, 1995), 1–4. See also Nima Naghibi's critique of Edward Said in "Colonial Discourse," in *Encyclopedia of Postcolonial Studies* (Westport, CT; London: Greenwood Press, 2001), 102–107, esp. 102–103.

11. Stephen Slemon ("Unsettling the Empire: Resistance Theory for the Second World," 37) writes that resistance "is always *necessarily* complicit in the apparatus it seeks to transgress." That is to say, any act of resistance is, by definition, framed in relation to the terms set by the prevailing ideology or power. And yet, at the same time, it is only by "(mis)appropriating the terms of the dominant ideology" that the resisting community is able to redefine its own identity over against the colonial power (Benita Parry, "Problems in Current Theories of Colonial Discourse," *Oxford Literary Review* 9.1–2 (1987), 40; cf. John Yang, "Representation and Resistance:

A Cultural, Social, and Political Perplexity in Post-Colonial Literature,"
at http://www.scholars.nus.edu.sg/landow/post/poldiscourse/yang/1.html).

12. For a summary of Timothy's life and writings, see Donald B. Spanel,
"Timothy II Aelurus," *Coptic Encyclopedia* 7.2263–2268; and David
Johnson, "Pope Timothy II Aelurus: His Life and His Importance for
the Development of Christianity in Egypt," *Coptica* 1 (2002), 77–89.

13. In Syriac sources, he is called "Timothy the Weasel": R.Y. Ebied and L.R.
Wickham, "Timothy Aelurus: Against the Definition of the Council of
Chalcedon," in *After Chalcedon: Studies in Theology and Church
History*, ed. C. Laga, J.A. Munitiz, and L. Van Rompay (Leuven:
Departement Oriëntalistiek, 1985), 115.

14. On Timothy II Aelurus' background as a monk and presbyter: Zacharias
Rhetor, *HE* 4.1 (ed. E.W. Brooks, CSCO 83, 169 (Syriac text) and CSCO
87, 118 (Latin translation); trans. F.J. Hamilton and E.W. Brooks
(London: Methuen & Co., 1899), 64); Evagrius, *HE* 2.8 (ed. J. Bidez and
L. Parmentier (Amsterdam: Adolf M. Hakkert, 1964), 56.1–5). On his
accompaniment of Dioscorus to the synod at Ephesus: Timothy Aelurus,
Histoire, ed. Nau, PO 13, 205–209. On his deposition and exile: see the
History of the Patriarchs, PO 1.4, 445.

15. Evagrius, *HE* 2.5 (ed. Bidez and Parmentier, 50–51; trans. M. Whitby
(Liverpool: Liverpool University Press, 2000), 76–77; W.H.C. Frend,
The Rise of the Monophysite Movement, 149, 154.

16. On Timothy's consecration as bishop, see Zachariah Rhetor, *HE* 4.1 (ed.
E.W. Brooks, CSCO 83, 169–171 (Syriac) and CSCO 87, 117–119
(Latin); trans. F.J. Hamilton and E.W. Brooks, 64–66); Evagrius, *HE* 2.8
(ed. Bidez and Partmentier, 55–56; trans. Whitby, 85); and Michael the
Syrian, *Chronicle* 8.14 (trans. J.-B. Chabot, vol. 2 (Brussels: Culture et
Civilisation, 1963), 123). Theophanes Confessor, in an account hostile to
Timothy, claims that he used magical spells to win the allegiance of the
monks: "Timothy the Cat, having had recourse to magic, went round at
night to the cells of the monks, calling each of them by name, and when
there was a reply, he would say, 'I am an angel and I have been sent to tell
everyone to refrain from communion with Proterios and the party of
Chalcedon, and to appoint Timothy the Cat bishop of Alexandria'"
(*Chronicle* AM 5949; ed. C. de Boor, vol. 1 (Lipsius: B.G. Teubner,
1883), 109–110; trans. C. Mango and R. Scott, 169).

17. Zachariah Rhetor, *HE* 4.1 (ed. E.W. Brooks, CSCO 83, 171 (Syriac) and
CSCO 87, 118 (Latin); trans. F.J. Hamilton and E.W. Brooks, 65); *contra*
the pro-Chalcedonian account of Ps.-Leontius, *De sectis* V.1 (PG
86.1228C), who characterizes Timothy as a "secret" rival to Proterius.

18. Pro-Chalcedonian historians place the blame for Proterius' murder on an
unruly mob of Alexandrian citizens who supported Timothy: Evagrius,
HE 2.8 (ed. Bidez and Parmentier, 56; trans. Whitby, 85); Theophanes
Confessor, *Chronicle*, AM 5950 (ed. C. de Boor, vol. 1, 110–111; trans. C.
Mango and R. Scott, 170). Their anti-Chalcedonian counterparts attribute
the crime to a Roman soldier who had become angered by Proterius'
equivocation in his support for imperial policy: Zachariah Rhetor, *HE*
4.2 (ed. E.W. Brooks, CSCO 83, 171 (Syriac) and CSCO 87, 119 (Latin);
trans. F.J. Hamilton and E.W. Brooks, 66; Michael the Syrian, *Chronicle*
(trans. J.-B. Chabot, II, 124–125). Evagrius (*op. cit.*) himself acknowledges
this alternative explanation for Proterius' death, citing the earlier *Life of
Peter the Iberian* as his source.

19. For the Latin text of the *Letter to the Emperor Leo* from the
Chalcedonian hierarchy in Alexandria, see ACO 2.5, no. 7, 11–17.

Portions of this letter are cited by the historian Evagrius (*HE* 2.8; trans. Whitby, 86–88). For Leo of Rome's letters to the emperor (*Ep.* 156, 162, 164), see ACO 2.4, 101–104, 105–107, 110–112.

20. Leo of Rome, *Ep.* 162 and 164; ed. E. Schwartz, ACO 2.4, 107.10–13 and 112.6, 27.

21. Leo of Rome, *Ep.* 156 (ed. E. Schwartz, ACO 2.4, 104.1–2) and *Ep.* 162 (ibid., 107.12–15); A. Grillmeier, *Christ in Christian Tradition* 2.4, 11–12.

22. For the Latin text of this encyclical, see ACO 2.5, 9–11. A copy is also preserved in Evagrius, *HE* 2.9 (ed. Bidez and Parmentier, 59–61; trans. Whitby, 90–91). The letter is addressed to the archbishop of Constantinople, Anatolius, but among its other recipients were the famous Syrian monks Symeon (Stylites), Baradatos, and Jacob (the miracle worker): cf. Theophanes Confessor, *Chronicle* AM 5952 (ed. C. de Boor, vol. 1, 111; trans. C. Mango and R. Scott, 172).

23. Theophanes Confessor, *Chronicle*, AM 5952 (ed. C. de Boor, 112.6–8; trans. C. Mango and R. Scott, 172–173).

24. Timothy Aelurus, *Against Chalcedon*; ed. and trans. R.Y. Ebied and L.R. Wickham, in *After Chalcedon*, 120–142 (Syriac text); 143–166 (English translation)—for the quoted references, see fol. 60v: 141 (text) and 165 (translation).

25. Timothy Aelurus, *Letter to Egypt, Thebaid, and Pentapolis*, fol. 34a; ed. and trans. R.Y. Ebied and L.R. Wickham, "A Collection of Unpublished Syriac Letters of Timothy Aelurus," *Journal of Theological Studies* 21 (1970), 341 (text) and 362 (translation).

26. Timothy Aelurus, *Letter to Claudianus the Priest*; fol. 36b; ed. and trans. R.Y. Ebied and L.R. Wickham, "A Collection of Unpublished Syriac Letters," 346 (text) and 369 (translation).

27. Timothy Aelurus, *Letter to Egypt, Thebaid, and Pentapolis*, fol. 34a (ed. and trans. R.Y. Ebied and L.R. Wickham, "A Collection of Unpublished Syriac Letters," 341 and 362); *Letter to Faustinus the Deacon*, 35b (ibid., 344 and 365).

28. Timothy Aelurus, *Against Chalcedon*, fol. 51v; ed. and trans. R.Y. Ebied and L.R. Wickham, in *After Chalcedon*, 138 (text) and 163 (translation).

29. Timothy Aelurus, *Against Chalcedon*, fol. 60v; ed. and trans. R.Y. Ebied and L.R. Wickham, in *After Chalcedon*, 141 (text) and 165 (translation).

30. Timothy Aelurus, *Letter to Egypt, Thebaid, and Pentapolis*, fol. 34b; ed. and trans. R.Y. Ebied and L.R. Wickham, "A Collection of Unpublished Syriac Letters," 342 (text) and 364 (translation).

31. Timothy Aelurus, *Letter to Faustinus the Deacon*, fol. 35a; ed. and trans. R.Y. Ebied and L.R. Wickham, "A Collection of Unpublished Syriac Letters," 343 (text) and 365 (translation).

32. As part of this larger discursive strategy, Timothy casts his Chalcedonian opponents as those who had "lapsed," and who would therefore require a period of penance (one year) before readmission to the "orthodox": see, e.g., his *Letter to the City of Alexandria*, fol. 33b–34a; ed. and trans. R.Y. Ebied and L.R. Wickham, "A Collection of Unpublished Syriac Letters," 340–341 (text) and 361 (translation); and his *Letter to Egypt, Thebaid, and Pentapolis*, fol. 34b; ibid., 342 (text) and 363 (translation). By advocating a penance of only one year, Timothy was framing his policy in terms quite similar to that of his predecessor Peter I during the throes of the Diocletian Persecution. Timothy's moderate pastoral concern for the reestablishment of communion with his opponents would seem to belie Leo of Rome's one-sided, polemical characterization of him as a power-hungry tyrant.

33. H. Bacht, "Die Rolle des orientalischen Mönchtums," 259. Monastic patronage continued to play a large role in the contestation of Alexandrian episcopal authority: while the monastery of Canopus served as a stronghold for Chalcedonian belief, the Enaton monastery west of the city became a well-known center for the anti-Chalcedonian opposition (D. Chitty, *The Desert a City*, 92 and 99, notes 83–84).
34. Robert J.C. Young, *Postcolonialism: An Historical Introduction*, 19.
35. Zacharias Rhetor (*Chronicle* 4.10; ed. E.W. Brooks, CSCO 83, 183 (Syriac) and CSCO 87, 127 (Latin); trans. F.J. Hamilton and E.W. Brooks, 78) says that "because (Timothy) dreaded the fate of Proterius, he would not walk abroad without the Romans."
36. Zacharias Rhetor, *Chronicle* 4.10 (ed. E.W. Brooks, CSCO 83, 182–183 (Syriac) and CSCO 87, 127 (Latin); trans. F.J. Hamilton and E.W. Brooks, 78–79. On Timothy's temporary conflict with the church in Rome, see also Simplicius, *Letter to Acacius* (ed. O. Guenther, CSEL 35.1 (1895), 142–144); and Liberatus, *Brevarium* 16 (ACO 2.5, 126).
37. Zacharias Rhetor, *Chronicle* 4.10; ed. E.W. Brooks, CSCO 83, 183–184 (Syriac) and CSCO 87, 127 (Latin); trans. F.J. Hamilton and E.W. Brooks, 79.
38. Warren Treadgold, *A History of the Byzantine State and Society* (Stanford: Stanford University Press, 1997), 157; A.H.M. Jones, *The Later Roman Empire, 284–602*, volume 1 (London: Basil Blackwell, Ltd., 1964; repr. Baltimore: The Johns Hopkins University Press, 1986), 225.
39. Evagrius, *HE* 3.6 (ed. Bidez and Parmentier, 106; trans. Whitby, 140); Zacharias Rhetor, *Chronicle* 5.4 (ed. E.W. Brooks, CSCO 83, 216 (Syriac) and CSCO 87, 150 (Latin); trans. F.J. Hamilton and E.W. Brooks, 110).
40. Zacharias Rhetor, *Chronicle* 5.4 (ed. E.W. Brooks, CSCO 83, 218 (Syriac) and CSCO 87, 151 (Latin); trans. F.J. Hamilton and E.W. Brooks, 111–112). In the fourth and fifth centuries, the term "confessor" often came to be used as a synonym for "martyr." For a list of examples culled from Greek sources, see G.W.H. Lampe, *A Patristic Greek Lexicon*, 957.
41. The Chalcedonian historian Evagrius (*HE* 3.11; ed. Bidez and Parmentier, 109; trans. Whitby, 145) describes how the Alexandrians elected Peter Mongus "on their own authority" (i.e., independent of imperial sanction).
42. Pseudo-Dioscorus, *Panegyric on Macarius, Bishop of Tkôw* (ed. and trans. D.W. Johnson, CSCO 415.1 (text) and 416.1 (translation)); Liberatus, *Brevarium*, ACO 2.5, 124.2–4; D.W. Johnson, "Pope Peter III Mongus: Conflicts within Egypt," Paper presented at the Seventh International Congress of Coptic Studies, Leiden, Holland (August 2000).
43. Liberatus, *Brevarium*, ACO 2.5, 126.3–4. D.W. Johnson ("Pope Peter III Mongus") has surmised that Peter managed to evade such a sentence because the authorities were unable to find him.
44. Zachariah Rhetor, *HE* 5.6 (ed. E.W. Brooks, CSCO 83, 222 (Syriac) and CSCO 87, 154 (Latin); trans. F.J. Hamilton and E.W. Brooks, 116).
45. On the intrigues surrounding John Talaia, see E. Schwartz, *Publizistische Sammlungen zum Acacianische Schisma* (Abhandlungen der Bayerischen Akademie der Wissenschaften, Philosophisch-historische Abteilung, Neue Folge, Heft 10; München: Verlag der Bayerischen Akademie der Wissenschaften, 1934), 195–197. The original account appears in Zachariah Rhetor (*HE* 5.6–7; ed. E.W. Brooks, CSCO 83, 223–225 (Syriac) and CSCO 87, 154–156 (Latin); trans. F.J. Hamilton and E.W. Brooks, 116–118; cf. Evagrius, *HE* 3.12). Evagrius (*HE* 3.15, 18; ed. J. Bidez and L. Parmentier, 114, 117; trans. M. Whitby, 149–150, 153–154) provides additional reports on John's flight to Rome and his efforts to raise support for himself, and opposition to Peter Mongus, in that city.

46. For the text of the *Henoticon*, see E. Schwartz, *Codex Vaticanus gr. 1431, eine antichalkedonische Sammlung aus der Zeit Kaiser Zenos* (Abhandlungen der Bayerischen Akademie der Wissenschaften, philosophisch-philologische und historische Klasse 32.6; München: Verlag der Bayerischen Akademie der Wissenschaften, 1927), 52.22—54.21. It is also preserved by the historian Evagrius, *HE* 3.14 (ed. J. Bidez and L. Parmentier, 111–114; trans. M. Whitby, 147–149).

47. Evagrius, *HE* 3.14 (ed. J. Bidez and L. Parmentier, 113; trans. M. Whitby, 149).

48. Zachariah Rhetor, *HE* 6.1 (ed. E.W. Brooks, CSCO 84, 2 (Syriac) and CSCO 88, 1 (Latin); trans. F.J. Hamilton and E.W. Brooks, 133); cf. the letters written to Peter Mongus by the church leaders in Antioch, Constantinople, and Jerusalem (preserved in Zachariah, *HE* 5.10–12; ed. E.W. Brooks, CSCO 83, 233–238 (Syriac) and CSCO 87, 161–164 (Latin); trans. F.J. Hamilton and E.W. Brooks, 126–131).

49. Zachariah Rhetor, *HE* 6.1 (ed. E.W. Brooks, CSCO 84, 2–4 (Syriac) and CSCO 88, 1–2 (Latin); trans. F.J. Hamilton and E.W. Brooks, 133–134).

50. W.H.C. Frend, *The Rise of the Monophysite Movement*, 187.

51. Zacharias Rhetor, *HE* 5.7 (ed. E.W. Brooks, CSCO 83, 226 (Syriac) and CSCO 87, 156 (Latin); trans. F.J. Hamilton and E.W. Brooks, 119).

52. Peter Mongus later also received criticism from Severus of Antioch (ca. 465–538 c.e.) on this matter: see Severus of Antioch, *Epistle to Ammonius, Presbyter of Alexandria* (ed. and trans. E.W. Brooks, *The Sixth Book of the Select Letters of Severus* (London: Williams & Norgate, 1904), 1.2, 286–290 (text) and 2.2, 253–257 (translation).

53. Zachariah Rhetor, *HE* 6.1–2 (ed. E.W. Brooks, CSCO 84, 2–6 (Syriac) and CSCO 88, 1–4 (Latin); trans. F.J. Hamilton and E.W. Brooks, 133–136).

54. The dissemination of Coptic translations of the *Henoticon* along with anti-Chalcedonian commentaries on the text would have contributed to this effort by Peter Mongus and his successors to regain the confidence of such dissident groups: David Johnson, "Pope Peter III Mongus: Conflicts within Egypt," Paper presented at the Seventh International Congress of Coptic Studies, Leiden, Holland (August 2000).

55. Evagrius, *HE* 3.17; ed. J. Bidez and L. Parmentier, 115–116; trans. M. Whitby, 151–153. A further collection of correspondence between Acacius and Peter Mongus has been judged by its editor (and by later commentators) as inauthentic: *Letters of Acacius and Peter Mongus*, ed. E. Amélineau, in *Monuments pour server à l'histoire de l'Egypte Chrétienne aux IVe et Ve siècles* (Mémoires publies par les membres de la Mission archéologique française au Caire 4.1; Paris: Ernest Leroux, 1888), 196–228; cf. M. Cramer and H. Bacht, "Der antichalkedonische Aspekt," in *Das Konzil von Chalkedon*, vol. 2, 324; and Vahan Inglisian, "Chalkedon und die armenische Kirche," in *Das Konzil von Chalkedon*, vol. 2, 369.

56. Zachariah Rhetor, *HE* 6.1 (ed. E.W. Brooks, CSCO 84, 3–4 (Syriac) and CSCO 88, 1–2 (Latin); trans. F.J. Hamilton and E.W. Brooks, 133–134). For a discussion of Zachariah's account of these events in relation to that of Evagrius, see Pauline Allen, *Evagrius Scholasticus the Church Historian* (Leuven: Spicilegium Sacrum Lovaniense, 1981), 133–134.

57. Zachariah Rhetor, *HE* 6.6 (ed. E.W. Brooks, CSCO 84, 11–14 (Syriac) and CSCO 88, 7–9 (Latin); trans. F.J. Hamilton and E.W. Brooks, 142–144, esp. 144). Peter may also have felt free to sharpen his rhetoric because he knew that the church leadership at Constantinople was growing increasingly distracted by a theological rift of its own, a disagreement

with Rome over the validity of the *Henoticon* that came to be known as the Acacian Schism (A.D. 484–519).

58. Evagrius, *HE* 3.17 (ed. J. Bidez and L. Parmentier, 115; trans. M. Whitby, 151).

59. On the subject of heterogeneity in colonial resistance, see Gayatri Spivak, "Subaltern Studies: Deconstructing Historiography," in *In Other Worlds: Essays in Cultural Politics* (London: Routledge, 1987), 204, 211; ibid., "Can the Subaltern Speak?" in *Marxism and the Interpretation of Culture*, ed. C. Nelson and L. Grossberg (London: Macmillan, 1988), 284; Bart Moore-Gilbert, *Postcolonial Theory: Contexts, Practices, Politics* (London and New York: Verso, 1997), 75–76; Nima Naghibi, "Colonial Discourse," in *Encyclopedia of Postcolonial Studies* (London and Westport, CT: Greenwood Press, 2001), 102–107, esp. 103–104. B. Ashcroft, G. Griffiths, and Hellen Tiffin ("General Introduction," *The Post-Colonial Studies Reader*, 4) emphasize ambivalence, complexity, and process in the relationship of colonial societies to empire.

60. On social stratification in colonial cultures, see Ranajit Guha, "On Some Aspects of the Historiography of Colonial India," *Subaltern Studies* 1 (1982), 1–8; Gayatri Spivak, "Subaltern Studies: Deconstructing Historiography," in *In Other Worlds*, 204–206; ibid., "Can the Subaltern Speak?" in *Marxism and the Interpretation of Culture*, 284.

61. Zachariah Rhetor, *HE* 6.2 (ed. E.W. Brooks, CSCO 84, 4–6 (Syriac) and CSCO 88, 2–4 (Latin); trans. F.J. Hamilton and E.W. Brooks, 134–136).

62. The *History of the Patriarchs* (PO 1.4, 1448) reports that John I Hemula was able to secure imperial patronage (gifts of wheat, wine, and oil) for his home monastery, the Monastery of Saint Macarius at Scetis. The editor of the *History* credits this beneficence to Zeno, but this would have been impossible, since Zeno died in 491, five years before John I Hemula became patriarch. If John were the beneficiary of such patronage, it would have been during the reign of Zeno's successor, Anastasius I (491–518).

63. While Severus of Antioch criticizes Athanasius II and John I Hemula (along with Peter Mongus) for not taking a more activist stance in anathematizing Chalcedon, he gives John II Nicaiotes credit for finally demanding that his counterpart in Constantinople condemn Chalcedon as a basis for ongoing agreement over the *Henoticon*: see Severus of Antioch, *Epistle to Ammonius, Presbyter of Alexandria* (ed. and trans. E.W. Brooks, *The Sixth Book of the Select Letters of Severus* (London: Williams & Norgate, 1904), 1.2, 288–289 (text) and 2.2, 255 (translation); cf. E. Schwartz, *Publizistische Sammlungen zum Acacianische Schisma*, 238, note 1; and R. Haacke, "Die kaiserliche Politik in den Auseinandersetzungen um Chalkedon (451–553)," in *Das Konzil von Chalkedon*, vol. 2, 95–177, esp. 128. Zachariah Rhetor (*HE* 6.6; ed. E.W. Brooks, CSCO 84, 14 (Syriac) and CSCO 88, 9–10 (Latin); trans. F.J. Hamilton and E.W. Brooks, 145) gives a different, more favorable, assessment of John I Hemula: according to him, John I was more vocal about his opposition to Chalcedon, even demanding that Flavian, the bishop of Antioch, anathematize the Council. However, several factors might lead us to question the reliability of Zachariah's account at this point. In particular, the structural parallels between this story and Severus' aforementioned account about John II, and the potential for a mix-up in names (Zachariah actually goes on to attribute John I's "namesake and successor" with "believing and acting in like manner") raise the possibility that Zachariah confused the two Johns.

64. Theophanes the Confessor, *Chronicle*, AM 6009; ed. C. de Boor, 162–163; trans. C. Mango and R. Scott, 247.
65. Severus of Antioch, in a *Letter to Dioscorus*, urges him to follow the example of Timothy Aelurus more closely in demanding the anathematization of Leo's *Tome* as a precondition for reconciliation (Severus of Antioch, *Letter to Dioscorus, Archbishop of Alexandria*; ed. and trans. E.W. Brooks, *The Sixth Book of the Select Letters of Severus* (London: Williams & Norgate, 1904), 1.2, 290–293 (text) and 2.2, 257–260 (translation); cf. W.H.C. Frend, *The Rise of the Monophysite Movement*, 229).
66. In a recent paper ("Models for Understanding the Success of Christianity," presented at the Symposium on the Expansion of Christianity in the First Four Centuries, Columbia University, New York, March 30, 2003), Harold Drake argued that the heterogeneity of mass religious movements makes them "inherently prone to fissure."
67. On Anastasius' policies as emperor, see Aikaterina Christophilopoulou, *Byzantine History: Volume I, 324–610*, trans. W.W. Phelps (Amsterdam: Adolf M. Hakkert, 1986), 236–249. On Justin I, see ibid., 261–264.
68. W.H.C. Frend, "Severus of Antioch and the Origins of the Monophysite Hierarchy," in *Orientalia Christiana Analecta* 195 (1973), 271–272. This article is reprinted in W.H.C. Frend, *Religion Popular and Unpopular in the Early Christian Centuries* (London: Variorum Reprints, 1976), XIX, 261–275.
69. On Severus' interpretation of Cyril's "one-nature" Christology as part of his polemics against Chalcedonian theology (which also tried to claim Cyril's writings as support), see A. Grillmeier, *Christ in Christian Tradition*, Volume 2.2, trans. P. Allen and J. Cawte (Louisville, KY: Westminster John Knox Press, 1995), 22–23, 28–46.
70. PO 1.4, 451–455, esp. 452.
71. E. Bolman, ed., *Monastic Visions*, 71, 94, 112, fig. 7.14.
72. For detailed treatments of the theological controversy between Julian and Severus, see René Draguet, *Julien d'Halicarnasse et sa controverse avec Sévère d'Antioche sur l'incorruptibilité du corps du Christ* (Louvain: Imprimerie P. Smeesters, 1924); and A. Grillmeier, *Christ in Christian Tradition*, 2.2, 25–26, 79–111. Zachariah Rhetor (*HE* 9.9–13) and Michael the Syrian (*Chronicle* 9.27; trans. J.-B. Chabot, II, 224–235) both give accounts of this controversy (with a decided bias toward Severus) and preserve portions of the correspondence between the two men. Jean Maspero (*Histoire des patriarches d'Alexandrie depuis la mort l'empereur Anastase jusqu'a la reconciliation des églises jacobites (518–616)* (Paris: Librairie ancienne Édouard Champion, 1923), 94) has correctly pointed out the fact that our knowledge of this controversy is mediated through sources produced "by the Severan party, who ended up triumphing."
73. However, Julian would still argue that the incarnate Word could *freely choose* to endure suffering and death without being corrupted.
74. See, e.g., Severus of Antioch, *Letter to Sergius and Marion*; ed. and trans. E.W. Brooks, *The Sixth Book of the Select Letters of Severus* (London: Williams & Norgate, 1904), 1.2, 404 (text) and 2.2, 358 (translation, with spelling altered slightly); Michael the Syrian (*Chronicle* 9.27; trans. J.-B. Chabot, II, 224) echoes Severus' critique, claiming that Julian believed that the "passion of Christ had been apparent and not real." One of the names given Julian's followers was Aphthartodocetists—i.e., those who believe in an incorruptible, unreal body. For their part, the Julian and his followers called their opponents Phthartolatrae—"worshippers of a cor-

ruptible body" (J.A. Evans, *The Empress Theodora*, 80). On early
Christian Docetism, see Pheme Perkins, "Docetism," in *Encyclopedia of
Early Christianity*, ed. E. Ferguson (New York and London: Garland
Publishing, Inc., 1990), 272–273. Severus also compares Julian to
Eutyches and his followers, who were accused of having dissolved
Christ's humanity in his divinity, thereby denying the reality of the
incarnation (Severus of Antioch, *Critique of the Tomus*; ed. R. Hespel,
CSCO 244, 162 (Syriac text), and CSCO 245, 125–126 (Latin translation);
cf. A. Grillmeier, *Christ in Christian Tradition*, 2.2, 80–81).

75. Julian of Halicarnassus, *Fragments* 13, 71, 72, 147; ed. and trans. R.
      Draguet, *Julien d'Halicarnasse*, 8, 25, 41 (Syriac text); 48, 62, 76 (Greek
      translation) (the page numbers of Draguet's textual edition of the frag-
      ments are asterisked).

76. Liberatus, *Breviarium* 19 (ed. E. Schwartz, ACO 2.5, 134); Ps.-
      Leontius, *De sectis* V.3 (PG 86.1229C); cf. M. Cramer and H. Bacht,
      "Der antichalkedonische Aspekt im historisch-biographischen
      Schrifttum der koptischen Monophysiten (6.–7. Jahrhundert): Ein
      Beitrag zur Geschichte der Entstehung der monophysitischen Kirche
      Ägyptens," in *Das Konzil von Chalkedon*, vol. 2, 315–338, esp. 327.
      Michael the Syrian (*Chronicle* 9.27; trans. J.-B. Chabot, II, 224) and the
      editor of the *History of the Patriarchs* (PO 1.4, 453) both emphasize
      the fact that Severus was forced to move from monastery to monastery to
      escape imperial detection.

77. Ps.-Leontius, *De sectis* V.4 (PG 86.1232). This accounting of events may
      have been based upon the observation that Timothy initially received
      Julian along with Severus.

78. Timothy III of Alexandria, *Fragmenta Dogmatica* (PG 86.268A); cf. A.
      Grillmeier, *Christ in Christian Tradition*, 2.4, 43–44.

79. Zachariah Rhetor, *HE* 9.9 (ed. E.W. Brooks, CSCO 84, 101 (Syriac) and
      CSCO 88, 70 (Latin); trans. F.J. Hamilton and E.W. Brooks, 232);
      Michael the Syrian, *Chronicle* 9.27 (trans. J.-B. Chabot, II, 224); *History
      of the Patriarchs* (PO 1.4, 454).

80. PO 1.4, 454; cf. J. Maspero, *Histoire des Patriarches d'Alexandrie*, 95.
      According to the *History of the Patriarchs*, only seven monks remained
      faithful to Severus. While this is undoubtedly an exaggeration, it is
      noteworthy here that the editor, a patron of Severan theology, is willing
      to admit the widespread gains of Julian's followers under Timothy III
      and Theodosius.

81. The influence of Julian's doctrine was felt not only in Egypt, but in
      other parts of the eastern Mediterranean world as well, even up to the
      ninth century A.D. (Jacques Jarry, *Hérésies et factions dans l'Empire
      byzantin du IVe au VIIe siècle* (Cairo: L'Institut français d'archéologie
      orientale, 1968), 83–88).

82. The dating used for the table in Appendix 3, and for the patriarchs treat-
      ed in chapter four, is adapted from the work of G. Fedalto, *Hierarchia
      Ecclesiastica Orientali. Series episcoporum ecclesiarum christianarum ori-
      entalium II. Patriarchatus alexandrinus, antiochenus, hierosolymitanus*
      (Padua: Messaggero, 1988); and A. Jülicher, "Die Liste der alexandrinis-
      chen Patriarchen im 6. und 7. Jahrhundert," *Festgabe von Fachgenossen
      und Freunden Karl Müller zum siebzigsten Geburtstag dargebracht*
      (Tübingen: J.C.B. Mohr (Paul Siebeck), 1922), 7–23, esp. 23; cf. A.
      Grillmeier, *Christ in Christian Tradition*, 2.4, 88.

83. Ps.-Leontius, *De sectis* V.4 (PG 86.1232A–B); cf. Michael the Syrian,
      Chronicle 9.21 (trans. J.-B. Chabot, II, 193–194).

84. Liberatus, *Breviarium* 20 (ed. E. Schwartz, ACO 2.5, 135); cf. W.H.C. Frend, *The Rise of the Monophysite Movement*, 270.
85. Liberatus, *Breviarium* 20 (ed. E. Schwartz, ACO 2.5, 135); cf. Michael the Syrian, *Chronicle* 9.21 (trans. J.-B. Chabot, II, 193–194).
86. PO 5.1, 34, 36–37, 63; cf. PO 10.5, 447–448, where Gaianite and Julianist (Phantasiast) theology continues to be identified as a threat into the ninth century. At the end of the seventh century, John of Nikiu (*Chronicle* 92.3; trans. R.H. Charles, 145) also gives evidence that the Theodosian-Gaianite strife continued in his time.
87. Theodosius, *Synodical Letter to Severus, Patriarch of Antioch* (ed. and trans. J.-B. Chabot, CSCO 17, 5–11 (Syriac text); 103, 1–5 (Latin translation); Severus of Antioch, *Letter to Theodosius, Archbishop of Alexandria*, CSCO 17, 12–34 (Syriac text); 103, 6–22 (Latin translation); cf. W.H.C. Frend, *The Rise of the Monophysite Movement*, 270.
88. Michael the Syrian (*Chronicle* IX.21; trans. J.-B. Chabot, II, 194); Liberatus, *Breviarium* 20 (ed. E. Schwartz, ACO 2.5, 135).
89. Michael the Syrian, *Chronicle* IX.21 (trans. J.-B. Chabot, II, 194).
90. Liberatus, *Breviarium* 20 (ed. E. Schwartz, ACO 2.5, 134–135).
91. J. Maspero, *Histoire des Patriarches d'Alexandrie*, 124.
92. John W. Barker, "Justinian," in *Late Antiquity: A Guide to the Postclassical World*, edited by G.W. Bowersock, P. Brown, and O. Grabar (Cambridge, MA: The Belnap Press of Harvard University Press, 1999), 531. Among Justinian's attempts to bring Chalcedonians and anti-Chalcedonians into conversation was a synod he convoked at Constantinople in 533, where he advocated Theopaschite doctrine (the belief that one of three persons in the Trinity suffered) as a potential basis for agreement between the two sides. Ultimately, his efforts proved unsuccessful, even though "the conferees' theological beliefs turned out to be surprisingly similar" (W. Treadgold, *A History of the Byzantine State and Society*, 183). For details of what transpired at this synod, see J.A. Evans, *The Empress Theodora*, 75–76. More generally, on Justinian's efforts to forge theological compromise, see John Moorhead, *Justinian* (London and New York: Longman, 1994), 125–134.
93. A. Christophilopoulou, *Byzantine History*, vol. 1, 308–309.
94. Zachariah Rhetor, *HE* 9.19 (ed. E.W. Brooks, CSCO 84, 135–138 (Syriac) and CSCO 88, 93–94 (Latin); trans. F.J. Hamilton and E.W. Brooks, 265–268).
95. On Theodora's lobbying for this Severan "axis" and on the events that led to its break-up, see J.A. Evans, *The Empress Theodora*, 79–84.
96. *History of the Patriarchs*; PO 1.4, 466–467.
97. J. Maspero, *Histoire*, 45, 283. Liberatus (*Breviarium* 23; ACO 2.5, 139.2–4) writes that Paul Tabennesiota "received from the emperor power above the military governor *(dux)* and the tribune *(tribunus)*."
98. Theophanes Confessor, *Chronicle*, AM 6057; ed. C. de Boor, vol. 1 (Lipsius: B.G. Teubner, 1883), 109–110; trans. C. Mango and R. Scott, 354.
99. This view of Apollinaris is given by Chalcedonian and anti-Chalcedonian sources: both Eutychius (*Annales*; PG 111.1069B) and Severus of Ashmunein (*Refutation of Eutychius*; PO 3.2, 202–203) highlight his military pedigree. According to Eutychius (a tenth-century Chalcedonian bishop of Alexandria), Apollinaris used his imperial regiment to massacre a group of anti-Chalcedonians in an Alexandrian basilica (PG 111.1069D). John of Nikiu (*Chronicle* 92.9 and 94.8) gives a more congenial, but contradictory, account of Apollinaris' character and background. Maspero (*Histoire*, 156–165,

esp. 157–158) analyzes these sources in detail and, in the end, judges
John of Nikiu's account less worthy of acceptance.

100. J.A. Evans, *The Empress Theodora*, 84, 87–88. Theodosius gives evidence
of his loyalty to Theodora as his imperial patroness in a sermon he gave
shortly after her death in 548 (ed. J.-B. Chabot, CSCO 17, 40–79 (Syriac
text); CSCO 103, 26–55 (Latin translation); cited by W.H.C. Frend, *The
Rise of the Monophysite Movement*, 288).

101. Theodosius, *Letter to Eastern Orthodox Bishops* (A.D. 563); ed. J.-B.
Chabot, CSCO 103, 68.16–17; and *Synodical Letter to Paul the Patriarch
of Antioch* (A.D. 564): ed. J.-B. Chabot, CSCO 103, 85.24–25; cf. A.
Grillmeier, *Christ in Christian Tradition*, 2.4, 53, 56.

102. Theodosius, *Letter to the Venerable Bishops John, Leonidas, and Joseph* (ed.
J.-B. Chabot, CSCO 103, 95–96); *Letter to the Venerable Bishop Theodore
and those who are in the Thebaid and Arcadia* (ibid., 96); *Letter to the
Alexandrians* (ibid., 96–99); cf. W.H.C. Frend, *The Rise of the Monophysite
Movement*, 292. In these letters, Theodosius authorizes Paul of Antioch to
ordain bishops in Egyptian dioceses that were "destitute" of leadership.

103. Theodosius, *Tome to Empress Theodora*: ed. R. Riedinger, ACO, ser. sec.
1, 326.16–20, 21–25; 327.16–20, 22–25 (Greek fragments); ed. A. Van
Roey and P. Allen, *Monophysite Texts of the Sixth Century* (Leuven:
Uitgeverij Peeters en Departement Oriëntalistiek, 1994), 16–22
(Introduction), 23–41 (Syriac text), 42–56 (Latin translation).

104. On the chronology of this mini-controversy and the theological issues at
stake, see A. Van Roey and P. Allen, *Monophysite Texts of the Sixth
Century*, 3–15; A. Grillmeier, *Christ in Christian Tradition*, 2.2, 362–384.
Primary texts mentioning the *Agnoetai* include Liberatus, *Breviarium* 19
(ACO 2.5, 134); and Ps.-Leontius, *De sectis* V.6 (PG 86.1232).

105. John of Ephesus, *Lives of the Eastern Saints*: ed. E.W. Brooks, PO 18,
690–697; and PO 19, 153–158; cf. W.H.C. Frend, *The Rise of the
Monophysite Movement*, 285–287; also Susan Ashbrook Harvey,
Asceticism and Society in Crisis: John of Ephesus and The Lives of the
Eastern Saints (Berkeley: University of California Press, 1990), 105–106.
Jacob Baradaeus' missionary work laid the foundation for the Jacobite
churches of Lebanon and Syria—the anti-Chalcedonian communion
named after him that survives to the present day: A. Van Roey, "Les
débuts de l'église jacobite," in A. Grillmeier and H. Bacht, eds., *Das
Konzil von Chalkedon*, vol. 2, 339–360.

106. Trinh T. Minh-ha, *When the Moon Waxes Red: Representation, Gender
and Cultural Politics* (New York and London: Routledge, 1991), 16–19.

107. Even as Egypt played an integral, economic role as a producer of grain for
the empire, it had long maintained a tenuous, conflictual relationship with
the imperial court. For over two centuries, no emperor had visited
Egyptian soil (Diocletian had been the last), and Justinian would not
change this trend, opting to administer the territory from a distance (John
Moorhead, *Justinian* (New York and London: Longman, 1994), 122–125).

108. J.A.S. Evans, *The Age of Justinian*, 94. On the nomadic invasions of Scetis,
see D. Chitty, *The Desert a City*, 60–61, 144–145. On the attacks of nomadic
tribes in the Western Desert oases, see Guy Wagner, *Les oasis d'Égypte à
l'époque grecque, romaine et Byzantine d'après les documents grecs* (Cairo:
Institut français d'archéologie orientale du Caire, 1987), 394–400.

109. J.A.S. Evans, *The Age of Justinian*, 250. On Philae as a pilgrimage center
in the cult of Isis (including a discussion of "Philae as Contested Space"
even prior to Justinian's intervention), see Ian Rutherford, "Island of the
Extremity: Space, Language and Power in the Pilgrimage Traditions of

Philae," in D. Frankfurter, ed., *Pilgrimage and Holy Space in Late Antique Egypt*, 229–256. On the adaptation of the Isis temple into a church, see Pierre Nautin, "La conversion du temple de Philae en église chrétienne," *Cahiers Archéologique* 17 (1963), 1–43; on the Christian inscription, see esp., 14–15.

110. Trinh T. Minh-ha (*When the Moon Waxes Red*, 16–17) has noted how territories identified by colonizers as "the margins" become "sites of survival" and "fighting grounds" for the colonized.

111. Annedith M. Schneider, "Center/Periphery," in *Encyclopedia of Postcolonial Studies*, 85–86.

112. Trinh T. Minh-ha, *When the Moon Waxes Red*, 18. In some ways, Theodosius' career bears a striking resemblance to modern colonial representations of the "mimic man"—"a contradictory figure who simultaneously reinforces colonial authority and disturbs it" (Jenny Sharpe, "Figures of Colonial Resistance," *Modern Fiction Studies* 35:1 (1989), 140). Homi Bhabha ("Of Mimicry and Man: The Ambivalence of Colonial Discourse," *October* 28 (Spring 1984), 129) writes that "mimicry . . . in disclosing the ambivalence of colonial discourse also disrupts its authority."

113. On the multiple divisions within the Egyptian church at the end of Justinian's reign, see J. Maspero, *Histoire*, 191–194; and W.H.C. Frend, *The Rise of the Monophysite Movement*, 325–326.

114. The extant historical accounts differ considerably on the subject of this interregnum. The sixth-century writer John of Ephesus (*HE* 4.12; ed. E.W. Brooks, CSCO 106, 146.17–18) reports that ten years lapsed between Theodosius' death and Peter IV's election. By contrast, the eleventh-century editor of the *History of the Patriarchs* (PO 1.4, 470) acknowledges no such delay, probably because such a lapse of leadership would not have been palatable to his Coptic audience.

115. On Dorotheus, see John of Ephesus, *HE* 1.40 (ed. E.W. Brooks, CSCO 106, 34).

116. Michael the Syrian, *Chronicle* 10.6, 19 (trans. J.-B. Chabot, II, 299, 352).

117. Peter IV, *Synodical Letter to Jacob Baradaeus* (ed. J.-B. Chabot, CSCO 103, 161.5–11).

118. John of Ephesus, *HE* 4.12 (ed. E.W. Brooks, CSCO 106, 146).

119. *History of the Patriarchs* (PO 1.4, 470–471).

120. John of Ephesus, *HE* 4.44 (ed. E.W. Brooks, CSCO 106, 171); cf. A. Grillmeier, *Christ in Christian Tradition*, 2.4, 563.

121. On the life and papal leadership of Damian, see C.D.G. Müller, "Damian, Papst und Patriarch von Alexandrien," *Oriens Christianus* 70 (1986), 118–142; and E.R. Hardy, "Damian," in *Coptic Encyclopedia* 3.688–689.

122. Michael the Syrian, *Chronicle* 10.13, 21 (trans. J.-B. Chabot, II, 324, 360–361). This action taken by Peter and James as leaders of the anti-Chalcedonian churches, reiterated the emperor Justin II's earlier action of "erasing his (Paul's) name from the diptychs" (Michael the Syrian, *Chronicle*, 10.2; trans. J.-B. Chabot, II, 289; cf. W.H.C. Frend, *The Rise of the Monophysite Movement*, 321). On the controversy that swirled around Paul of Antioch, see also John of Ephesus, *HE* 4.11 (ed. E.W. Brooks, CSCO 105, 191–194 and 106, 143–145); and E.W. Brooks, "The Patriarch Paul of Antioch and the Alexandrian Schism of 575," *Byzantinische Zeitschrift* 30 (1929–1930), 468–476.

123. C.D.G. Müller ("Damian, Papst und Patriarch von Alexandrien," esp. 126–136) characterizes Damian's "ambition" to have a hand in Syrian affairs as one of the causes for the ensuing rift between Alexandria and Antioch.

124. John of Ephesus, *HE* 4.41 (ed. E.W. Brooks, CSCO 106, 166–168); Michael the Syrian, *Chronicle* 10.17 (trans. J.-B. Chabot, II, 345).
125. John of Ephesus, *HE* 4.45 (ed. E.W. Brooks, CSCO 106, 171); R.Y. Ebied, A. Van Roey, and L.R. Wickham, *Peter of Callinicum: Anti-Tritheist Dossier* (Orientalia Lovaniensia Analecta 10; Leuven: Departement Oriëntalistiek, 1981), 2–3.
126. For a summary of the rise of Tritheism, see R.Y. Ebied, A. Van Roey, and L.R. Wickham, *Peter of Callinicum: Anti-Tritheist Dossier*, 20–25. A Syrian named John Ascoutzanges (or alternatively, John Muqo d-zeqo) is identified as the original proponent of "Tritheist" theology: Elias of Nisibis, *Opus Chronologicum*, Part One, ed. E.W. Brooks, CSCO 62.1, 121 (Syriac text); and CSCO 63.1, 59 (Latin translation); Michael the Syrian, *Chronicle* 9.30, trans. J.-B. Chabot, II, 251; and Barhebraeus, *Chronicle* II.44, ed. J.-B. Abbeloos and T.J. Lamy, volume 3, cols. 223/224. Theodosius' treatise against the Tritheists is edited by J.-B. Chabot, CSCO 17, 40–79 (Syriac text); and CSCO 103, 26–55 (Latin text).
127. On John Philoponos' life and writings, see A. Grillmeier, *Christ in Christian Tradition*, 2.4, 107–146; on his use of Aristotelian categories in his drawing out the philosophical implications of his "one-nature" Christology, see J. Jarry, *Hérésies et factions*, 48–66. Fragments of his Tritheist works, including his treatise *On the Trinity*, have been edited by A. Van Roey, "Les fragments trithéites de Jean Philopon," *Orientalia Lovaniensia Periodica* 11 (1980), 135–163. Ps.-Leontius (*De sectis* VI.6; PG 86.1232D) calls him "the heresiarch of the Tritheists."
128. *Transcript of a Written Statement of Anathema* (ed. J.-B. Chabot, CSCO 103, 111–112).
129. The *History of the Patriarchs* (PO 1.4, 473–475) also attests the presence of other sectarian communities in Egypt during Damian's time in office—specifically, the Melitians and the Acephaloi. The latter are said to have experienced their own internal schism of leadership during this period.
130. According to the *History of the Patriarchs* (PO 1.4, 473), Damian received his ascetic training at the Monastery of John the Little. Recent restoration work at the Monastery of the Syrians in the Wadi al-Natrun has uncovered an eighth-century wall painting that probably represents the patriarch Damian (Fig. 8): see Karel C. Innemée and Lucas Van Rompay, "Deir al-Surian (Egypt): New Discoveries of 2001–2002," *Hugoye: Journal of Syriac Studies* 5.2 (July 2002), 1.3, fig. 3 (on the web at http://syrcom.cua.edu/Hugoye/Vol5No2/HV5N2InnemeeVanRompay.html).
131. W.E. Crum and H.G. Evelyn White, eds., *The Monastery of Epiphanius at Thebes*, Part 2 (New York: Metropolitan Museum of Art, 1926), 148–152, 331–337 (Inscription A), Tafel XV. The full text of the *Synodical Letter* appears in Michael the Syrian, *Chronicle* (trans. J.-B. Chabot, II, 325–334). There is also evidence that the monks at the Monastery of Epiphanius preserved copies of Damian's *Paschal Letters*: two fragmentary examples survive on a pottery shard and on a piece of limestone: W.E. Crum and H.G. Evelyn White, eds., *The Monastery of Epiphanius at Thebes*, Part 2, 12–13, 163 (nos. 53 and 55; Cairo 44674.101 and 44674.116); cited by C.D.G. Müller, "Damian, Papst und Patriarch von Alexandrien," 140. A letter written on a scrap of papyrus that was found in a rubbish hole at the monastery reports about the circuitous route one of Damian's festal letters took on its way to that location. A deacon of the archbishop reportedly brought it to the writer of the papyrus letter (a man named Constantine), who then sent it on to Epiphanius along with

his own greetings. Constantine tells Epiphanius that the deacon had given him the festal letter while traveling northward, because he had originally forgotten to send it to Epiphanius' monastery "when he came southward" (W.E. Crum and H.G. Evelyn White, eds., *The Monastery of Epiphanius at Thebes*, Part 2, 38, 185; no. 131).

132. Michael the Syrian, *Chronicle* (trans. J.-B. Chabot, II, 365); cited by R.Y. Ebied, A. Van Roey, and L.R. Wickham, *Peter of Callinicum: Anti-Tritheist Dossier*, 35. Damian's *Refutation* does not survive in its entirety, although quotations from it are preserved in Peter of Callinicum's later treatise, *Against Damian* (see below for bibliographical information).

133. While Damian's letters to Peter do not survive, some of Peter's writings have been preserved (R.Y. Ebied, A. Van Roey, and L.R. Wickham, *Peter of Callinicum: Anti-Tritheist Dossier*, 9–14). His literary production included an *Anti-Tritheist Dossier* of letters, in which he defended himself against Damian's accusations (*op. cit.*, 44–70, 71–102). The first book of his treatise *Against Damian* is lost, but books two and three survive: their chapter headings have been translated by Ebied, Van Roey and Wickham (*op. cit.*, 104–121). The same scholars have also produced a critical edition of book two with Syriac text and English translation: R.Y. Ebied, A. Van Roey, and L.R. Wickham, *Petri Callinicensis Patriarchae Antiocheni Tractatus contra Damianum*, Volume 1 (CSCO, Series Graeca, 29; Turnhout: Brepols; Leuven: University Press, 1994), 1–367.

134. For detailed accounts of the conflict between Damian and Peter, and the events leading to the breakdown of relations between Alexandria and Antioch, see Michael the Syrian, *Chronicle* 10.22 (trans. J.-B. Chabot, II, 364–271); R.Y. Ebied, A. Van Roey, and L.R. Wickham, *Peter of Callinicum: Anti-Tritheist Dossier*, 34–43; and R.Y. Ebied, A. Van Roey, and L.R. Wickham, *Petri Callinicensis Patriarchae Antiocheni Tractatus contra Damianum*, Volume 1, xiv–xxvi.

135. *History of the Patriarchs* (PO 1.4, 480–483).

136. Michael the Syrian, *Chronicle* 10.26 (trans. J.-B. Chabot, II, 381–393, left column). The text I have quoted from the joint statement of reunion appears on pages 391–392 (trans. R.Y. Ebied, A. Van Roey, and L.R. Wickham, *Petri Callinicensis Patriarchae Antiocheni Tractatus contra Damianum*, Volume 1, xxi). While the authors of the statement are intent on erasing the dispute between Damian and Peter from their common institutional memory, they significantly appeal to earlier anti-Chalcedonian saints—including Severus, Anthimus, Paul, and Julianus from Antioch, Theodosius and Peter IV from Alexandria, and Jacob Baradaeus—to intercede on behalf of their agreement (cf. *History of the Patriarchs*, PO 1.4, 481, where Athanasius of Antioch invokes the "one faith" shared by Severus and Theodosius before his journey to meet Anastasius). Michael the Syrian (*Chronicle* 10.27; trans. J.-B. Chabot, II, 381–394, right column, and 394–399) also preserves three other letters (two by Athanasius, and one by Anastasius) that recount the circumstances of their meeting and announce its results.

137. Michael the Syrian, *Chronicle* 10.26 (trans. J.-B Chabot, II, 391).

138. J. Maspero, *Histoire*, 334–342. Maspero bases his theory of a "Damianite" splinter group on an alternative reading of the original Arabic text of the *History of the Patriarchs*, and on references in the seventh-century writings of Anastasius of Sinai (*Viae dux* 15.16–17; ed. K.-H. Uthemann, Corpus Christianorum Series Graeca 8 (Turnout: Brepols, 1981), 264) to a certain John, who is said to have been "bishop of the Theodosians" in Alexandria for five years.

139. *History of the Patriarchs* (PO 1.4, 479–480).
140. A composite version of the *Life of John the Almsgiver*, adapted from two seventh-century biographies written by (1) Sophronius and John Moschus, and (2) Leontius of Neapolis, has been translated by Elizabeth Dawes and Norman H. Baynes, in *Three Byzantine Saints* (Crestwood, NY: St. Vladimir's Seminary Press, 1977), 199–262. Through such economic patronage, John ingratiated himself to Egyptians regardless of theological affiliation: in fact, his reputation for charity even led the anti-Chalcedonian church to canonize him as a saint (W.H.C. Frend, *The Rise of the Monophysite Church*, 340).
141. *History of the Patriarchs* (PO 1.4, 480). Coordinated with the appointment of John the Almsgiver, the emperor Heraclius and Nicetas, his governor of Alexandria, sponsored "the resettlement of the Roman civil service and the reorganization of the Roman military service" (Alfred J. Butler, *The Arab Conquest of Egypt and the Last Thirty Years of the Roman Dominion*, Second edition, ed. P.M. Fraser (Oxford: Clarendon Press, 1978), 42). It is noteworthy that A.J. Butler compares early seventh-century Byzantine rule in Egypt to "the British administration of India" in the nineteenth century.
142. John of Nikiu, *Chronicle* 97.1–29; trans. R.H. Charles, 157–160.
143. On the Greens and the Blues (as well as the other hippodrome factions), see Alan Cameron, *Circus Factions* (Oxford: Clarendon Press, 1976), *passim*, esp. 45–73; and Charlotte Roueché, "Factions," in *Late Antiquity: A Guide to the Postclassical World*, ed. G.W. Bowersock, P. Brown, and O. Grabar, 442.
144. John of Nikiu, *Chronicle* 97.30–33; trans. R.H. Charles, 160 (slightly modified).
145. John of Nikiu (*Chronicle* 105; trans. R.H. Charles, 166) gives a report of a revolt against local governor named Theophilus that took place in and around the city of Maradâ in Egypt. On Phocas' overthrow of Maurice and his "tyrannical" reign, see A. Christophilopoulou, *Byzantine History*, volume 1, 340–349.
146. John of Nikiu, *Chronicle* 107–110 (trans. R.H. Charles, 167–178); A.J. Butler, *The Arab Conquest of Egypt*, 8–32.
147. Theophylact Simocatta, *History* 8.15; trans. M. Whitby and M. Whitby (Oxford: Clarendon Press, 1986), 234–235.
148. On Chosroes' relationship with Maurice and his motivations for pursuing his war against Phocas and the Byzantine empire, see Mark Whittow, *The Making of Orthodox Byzantium, 600–1025* (Houndmills, Basingstoke, Hampshire, and London: Macmillan Press, 1996), 72–73; and W. Treadgold, *A History of Byzantine State and Society*, 227–236.
149. Jamsheed K. Choksy, "Sassanians," in *Late Antiquity: A Guide to the Postclassical World*, G.W. Bowersock, P. Brown, and O. Grabar, 682–685.
150. Averil Cameron, *The Mediterranean World in Late Antiquity*, A.D. *395–600* (London and New York: Routledge, 1993), 109–113, 186. The Byzantines made their tribute payments to the Persians in gold: 11,000 lbs in 533, 2000 lbs in 545, 2600 lbs in 551, and an annual payment of 30,000 gold *nomismata* promised at the fifty years' peace signed in 561 (with the first ten years paid in advance). For other accounts of Justinian's troubles with the Persians, see J. Moorhead, *Justinian*, 89–98; and J.A.S. Evans, *The Age of Justinian*, 114–119, 154–160.
151. There has long been disagreement over the date of Alexandria's fall to the Persians, a disagreement generated in large part by the lack of consensus

among ancient chronographers. A number of modern scholars have followed Michael the Syrian in assigning a date of 616 or 617 to this event. However, Ruth Altheim-Stiehl, on the basis of another Syrian chronicle along with papyrological and epigraphical sources in Greek and Coptic, has demonstrated that the Persians probably took Alexandria in the year A.D. 619: see especially her articles, "Wurde Alexandreia im Juni 619 n. Chr. Durch die Perser erobert?: Bermerkungen zur zeitlichen Bestimmung der sâsânidischen Besetzung Ägyptens unter Chosrau II. Parwêz," *Tyche* 6 (1991), 3–16; "Persians in Egypt (619–629)," *The Coptic Encyclopedia* 6.1938–1941; and "The Sasanians in Egypt – Some Evidence of Historical Interest," *Bulletin de la Société d'archéologie copte* 31 (1992), 87–96.

152. The late seventh-century writer John of Nikiu (*Chronicle* 109.21; trans. R.H. Charles, 176), for example, quickly passes over this period, offering surprisingly few comments on the Persian invasion.

153. Ruth Altheim-Stiehl, "The Sasanians in Egypt – Some Evidence of Historical Interest," *Bulletin de la Société d'archéologie copte* 31 (1992), 93–94.

154. *History of the Patriarchs* (PO 1.4, 484–486).

155. Arabic *Life of Shenoute*; ed. E. Amélineau, in *Monuments pour server à l'histoire de l'Égypte chrétienne*, volume 1 (Paris: Ernest Leroux, 1888), 340; A.J. Butler, *The Arab Conquest of Egypt*, 87–88.

156. A.J. Butler, *The Arab Conquest of Egypt*, 66–70, 81. While giving credence to the accounts of the Persians' destruction of Egyptian monasteries in the *History of the Patriarchs*, Butler (*op. cit.*, 75–76) expresses doubt concerning the story of the Persians' slaughter of Alexandrian citizens.

157. *Oxyrhynchus Papyri*, vols. 51 and 58, ed. J.R. Rea (London: Egypt Exploration Society, 1984 and 1991), nos. 3637 and 3959–3960); cf. M. Whittow, *The Making of Orthodox Byzantium*, 76.

158. *History of the Patriarchs* (PO 1.4, 484 and 489).

159. *Life of St. John the Almsgiver* 13 and 44B; trans. E. Dawes and N.H. Baynes, *Three Byzantine Saints*, 205–206, 254–255.

160. For a description of this Byzantine recovery led by Heraclius, see M. Whittow, *The Making of Orthodox Byzantium*, 77–82; Averil Cameron, *The Mediterranean World in Late Antiquity*, 186.

161. A. Atiya, *A History of the Eastern Church* (London: Methuen & Co., 1968), 75; cf. A.N. Stratos, *Byzantium in the Seventh Century*, volume 1, (Amsterdam: Adolf M. Hakkert, 1972), 126–127; and J.F. Haldon, *Byzantium in the Seventh Century*, 299. Theophanes the Confessor (AM 6113, A.D. 620/1; ed. C. de Boor, vol. 1, 302–303; trans. C. Mango and R. Scott, 435) is among the early sources that testify to this financial arrangement between the Chalcedonian church and the Byzantine state.

162. J.F. Haldon, *Byzantium in the Seventh Century*, 41ff.

163. ACO², Volume 2.2, ed. R. Riedinger (Berlin: Walter de Gruyter, 1992), 594.17—600.20; Friedhelm Winkelmann, *Der monenergetisch-monotheletische Streit* (Frankfurt am Main: Peter Lang, 2000), 36, 66–67, no. 27. For an explication of the various "one nature" and "two nature" readings of Monothelite doctrine, see Jaroslav Pelikan, *The Spirit of Eastern Christendom (600–1700)* (The Christian Tradition, vol. 2; Chicago and London: The University of Chicago Press, 1974), 62–75.

164. This was perhaps one of the reasons that the emperor Heraclius, already in 638, felt the need to publish a formal *Ekthesis*, in which he demanded adherence to his "one will" Christology throughout all the provinces under Byzantine rule (ACO², Volume 1, ed. R. Riedinger (Berlin: Walter

de Gruyter, 1984), 156.20—162.13; F. Winkelmann, *Der monenergetisch-monotheletische Streit*, 85–86, no. 50).

165. On the Chalcedonian resistance to "Monothelite" doctrine, and the special role played in that resistance by wandering monks, see Judith Herrin, *The Formation of Christendom* (Princeton: Princeton University Press, 1987), 207–211.

166. John of Nikiu, *Chronicle* 116.10; ed. and trans. R.H. Charles, 186.

167. (Ps.-)Benjamin, *Homily on the Wedding at Cana*; ed. and trans. C.D.G. Müller, *Die Homilie über die Hochzeit zu Kana und weitere Schriften des Patriarchen Benjamin I. von Alexandrien* (Heidelberg: Carl Winter; Universitätsverlag, 1968), 84–85, 132–133. The authorship of this homily remains a debated issue: while Müller (*op. cit.*, 9ff.) argues in favor of Benjamin as the author, other scholars have raised doubts about its authenticity: see, e.g., W.E. Crum, "Review of *Ein Mani-Fund in Aegypten*, by Carl Schmidt and H.J. Polotsky," *Journal of Egyptian Archaeology* 19 (1933), 199; H. Brakmann, "Zum Pariser Fragment angeblich des koptischen Patriarchen Agathon: Ein neues Blatt der Vita Benjamin I," *Muséon* 93 (1980), 299–309, esp. 308.

168. The *Life of Samuel of Kalamun* survives in four different versions. Two Coptic versions written in the Sahidic dialect—one complete (Codex A) and one fragmentary (Codex B)—have been edited by Anthony Alcock, *The Life of Samuel of Kalamun by Isaac the Presbyter* (Warminster, England: Aris & Phillips, Ltd., 1983). Alcock also provides an English translation of Codex A, which seems to be the earliest available recension. Codex B represents a later, expanded edition of the work: Alcock's edition of these fragments supersedes the late nineteenth-century edition published by E. Amélineau, *Monuments pour server à l'histoire de l'Égypt chrétienne* (Mémoires de la Mission archéologique français, 4.2; Paris: Ernest Leroux, 1895), 770–789. A third version, again fragmentary, survives in the Bohairic dialect of Coptic: see W.E. Crum, *Catalogue of the Coptic Manuscripts in the British Museum* (London: British Museum, 1905), no. 917. Finally, F.M.E. Pereira, *Vida do Abba Samuel do mosteiro do Kalamon* (Lisbon: Imprensa Nacional, 1894), has edited and translated a complete Ethiopic version of the *Life*. The complete Coptic manuscript (Codex A = Pierpont Morgan Ms. 578, ff. 1–68) has been dated paleographically to the ninth century, but contains elements that suggest contemporaneity with Samuel's life in the first half of the seventh century: see A. Alcock, *op. cit.*, vii; and Robert G. Hoyland, *Seeing Islam as Others Saw It: A Survey and Evaluation of Christian, Jewish and Zoroastrian Writings on Early Islam* (Princeton, NJ: The Darwin Press, Inc., 1997), 286, note 86.

169. *Life of Samuel of Kalamun* 7; ed. and trans. A. Alcock, 6–7 (Coptic text), 79–81 (English translation).

170. *Life of Samuel of Kalamun* 7; ed. and trans. A. Alcock, 7.15–23 (text), 81.11–20 (translation).

171. *Life of Samuel of Kalamun* 8; ed. and trans. A. Alcock, 7–8 (text), 81–83 (translation).

172. *Life of Samuel of Kalamun* 9–11; ed. and trans. A. Alcock, 8–11 (text), 83–85 (translation).

173. F. Winkelmann raises questions about the historicity of martyr accounts associated with this period: see his article "Die Stellung Ägyptens im oströmisch-byzantinischen Reich," in *Graeco–Coptica: Griechen und Kopten im byzantinischen Ägypten*, edited by P. Nagel (Wissenschaftliche Beiträge 48 (I 29); Halle: Martin–Luther–Universität, 1984) 32–34.

174. *Life of Samuel of Kalamun* 18; ed. and trans. A. Alcock, 16.22–24 (text), 92.13–15 (translation).
175. A. Alcock, ed., *Life of Samuel of Kalamun*, x; 122, notes 55 and 61.
176. *History of the Patriarchs*; PO 1.4, 491. Like the *Life of Samuel of Kalamun*, the *History of the Patriarchs* also seems to have been based on earlier source material. F. Winkelmann ("Ägypten und Byzanz vor der arabischen Eroberung," *Byzantinoslavica* 40:2 (1979), 162, note 2, and 172–173) observes that the account of Benjamin's patriarchate (including the martyrdom of his brother) probably derived from an earlier recension dating to the seventh or eighth century: cf. Pierre Nautin, "La conversion du temple de Philae en église chrétienne," *Cahiers Archéologique* 17 (1967), 38ff.
177. The binary oppositions that surface in these martyrologies—the faithful versus the apostate; the victors versus the vanquished, etc.—bear a striking, structural resemblance to the rhetoric of "symmetrical antagonism" promoted by modern "colonialist" discourses. Frantz Fanon (*The Wretched of the Earth* (New York: Grove Press, 1968), 50–51) has described the "symmetrical antagonism" of colonialist discourse as "Manichaean" in character. On this subject, see also Madhava Prasad, "The 'Other' Worldliness of Postcolonial Discourse: A Critique," *Critical Quarterly* 34.3 (1992), 74–89, esp. 74, 79. I want to thank one of my students, Dionis Gauvin, for the idea of applying Fanon's work in this context.
178. *History of the Patriarchs*; PO 1.4, 490.
179. Ibid. The *Homily on the Wedding at Cana*, attributed to Benjamin, indicates that one of his places of refuge was the Monastery of Apa Shenoute (the White Monastery) in Upper Egypt: ed. and trans. C.D.G. Müller, *Die Homilie*, 134–135, 232–233; cf. the Arabic *Life of Shenoute* (ed. and trans. E. Amélineau, in *Monuments pour server à l'histoire de l'Égypte chrétienne*, volume 1 (Paris: Mission archéologique français au Caire, 1888), 340–341.
180. *History of the Patriarchs* (PO 1.4, 489); cf. Michael the Syrian (*Chronicle* 11.8; trans. J.-B. Chabot, II, 432–433) who claims that Cyrus wore "on one of his feet the red shoe of the emperors, and on the other a sandal of a monk, to show that he had imperial and ecclesiastical authority."
181. F. Winkelmann, "Die Stellung Ägyptens," 23–26.
182. F. Winkelmann, "Die Stellung Ägyptens," 26–27. A manuscript of *The Consecration of the Sanctuary of Benjamin* from Luxor (Cod. Luxor., fol. 139b–140b) preserves the tradition that Cyrus (the Muqawqis) was "prefect and patriarch of Egypt": ed. R.G. Coquin (Bibliothèque d'études coptes 13; Cairo: Institut français d'archéologie orientale, 1975), 28–32. A version of the same text from Lower Egypt does not include the reference: *Synaxarium Alexandrinum*, ed. I. Forget (CSCO 47–49, Series Tertia, Tomus XVIII; Rome: Catholicus, 1905–1909), 196–200. The Latin translation of this Arabic text appears in CSCO 78 (1922), 321–326.
183. Frend (*The Rise of the Monophysite Movement*, 349) has read Benjamin's act of leaving the city for the monasteries as the "act of an Egyptian patriarch declaring his non-cooperation with the authorities."
184. In this vein, Aloys Grillmeier (*Christ in Christian Tradition*, 2.4, 82) remarks on the "connection between Egyptian self-consciousness and anti-Chalcedonianism."
185. *Life of Samuel of Kalamun* 7, 9–11 (ed. and trans. A. Alcock, 6–7, 8–11 (text), 79–81, 83–85 (translation)); *History of the Patriarchs* (PO 1.4, 490–493). The term in Coptic is *kauxios* (in Arabic, *muqauqas*).

234 Notes

186. *History of the Patriarchs*; PO 1.4, 498. Under the Arabs, the Monastery of Metras would serve as Benjamin's episcopal residence.
187. Mark Moussa, "The Anti-Chalcedonian Movement in Byzantine Egypt: An Evaluation of Past Scholarship and Current Interpretations," in *Ägypten und Nubien in spätantiker und christlicher Zeit*, Akten des 6. Internationalen Koptologenkongresses, Münster, 20.–26. Juli 1996, Band 1: Materielle Kultur, Kunst und religiöses Leben, ed. S. Emmel, M. Krause, S.G. Richter, and S. Schaten (Sprachen und Kulturen des christlichen Orients 6.1; Wiesbaden: Reichert, 1999), 504–510; cf. A.H.M. Jones, "Were the Ancient Heresies National or Social Movements in Disguise?" *Journal of Theological Studies* 10, new series (1959), 280–298. For a discussion of literary evidence for continued anti-Chalcedonian allegiance to the emperor in the early seventh century, see Friedhelm Winkelmann, "Die Stellung Ägyptens," 11–35, esp. 17–18.
188. *History of the Patriarchs*; PO 1.4, 498. In speaking of a "national culture" here, I borrow the language of Frantz Fanon (*The Wretched of the Earth* (New York: Grove Press, 1968), 206–248, esp. 233), who defines this concept most broadly as "the whole body of efforts made by a people in the sphere of thought to describe, justify, and praise the action through which that people has created itself and keeps itself in existence." On "nation" as a discursively constructed community, see Timothy Brennan, "The National Longing for Form," in *Nation and Narration*, ed. Homi K. Bhabha (London: Routledge, 1990), 46–47; Benedict Anderson, *Imagined Communities: Reflections on the Origin and Spread of Nationalism*, Revised edition (London and New York: Verso, 1991), 5–7; and B. Ashcroft, G. Griffiths, and H. Tiffin, eds., *The Post-Colonial Studies Reader* (London and New York: Routledge, 1995), 151–152. John Moorhead ("The Monophysite Response to the Arab Invasion," *Byzantion* 51 (1981), 579–591) objects to what he calls "the national-religious hypothesis" as an attempt to explain the anti-Chalcedonian "animosity" toward Byzantine rule in the East. However, while I agree in sentiment with his efforts to critique earlier, monolithic political analyses of anti-Chalcedonian discontent, Moorhead's article remains problematic. First, he often reads the historical sources available to him in an uncritical and unbalanced way: for example, he implicitly favors sources friendly to Byzantine interests, labeling them as "orthodox," over against other "Monophysite," writings for which he generally has less sympathy. Second, his analysis falls prey to the same monolithic assumptions as those he wants to critique: specifically, the "national-religious hypothesis" that he constructs as a "foil" proves to be such a one-dimensional construct that it causes him to base his own analysis on simplistic binary assumptions that leave little room for variations or divergences within Chalcedonian and anti-Chalcedonian communal identity.
189. On the function of "minority discourses" in modern post-colonialist contexts, see Madhava Prasad, "The 'Other' Worldliness of Postcolonial Discourse: A Critique," *Critical Quarterly* 34.3 (1992), 75–76.
190. A helpful modern analogy might be drawn here. In Egypt, the Coptic Evangelical (Protestant) churches originally grew out of nineteenth-century American and English missions. However, the membership of those churches today consists exclusively of native Egyptians who claim a multi-generational family lineage in those communities. Despite this fact, the Coptic Orthodox Church views the Evangelical Church as a foreign body. This has most recently been. evidenced in public

addresses by Pope Shenouda III, who (in alleged slips of the tongue) has referred to the Evangelical Church *(al-kinîsa al-ingîlîa)* as the English Church *(al-kinîsa al-inglîzia)*.

191. There were also undoubtedly a complex range of class issues involved that also framed Coptic resistance to Byzantine-Chalcedonian policy: see, e.g., F. Winkelmann, "Ägypten und Byzanz vor der arabischen Eroberung," *Byzantinoslavica* 40 (1979), 175, who raises the question of whether "Benjamin's anti-Byzantine attitude had its root in the separatism of circles of the Egyptian upper class" (my translation).

192. Averil Cameron, *The Mediterranean World in Late Antiquity*, 177, 194–196; G.W. Bowersock, "The Arabs Before Islam," in *The Genius of Arab Civilization: Source of Renaissance*, Third edition, edited by John R. Hayes (New York and London: New York University Press, 1992), 31–32.

193. Walter Kaegi, "Heraclius," in *Late Antiquity: A Guide to the Postclassical World*, edited by G.W. Bowersock, P. Brown, and O. Grabar, 488; cf. A.N. Stratos, *Byzantium in the Seventh Century*, volume 2, 117–118. Sura 30 in the Qur'ân is read by Muslims as prophecy of this Persian defeat at the hand of the Romans: "The Romans have been defeated in the nearer land, and they, after their defeat will be victorious within ten years—Allah's is the command in the former case and in the latter—and in that day believers will rejoice in Allah's help to victory" (*The Qur'ân*, Sura 30.2–4; Arabic text and English translation in *The Meaning of the Glorious Qur'ân*, trans. Muhammad Marmaduke Pickthall (Beirut: Dar al-Kitab Allubnani, 1970), 529–538).

194. Theodore Hall Partrick, *Traditional Egyptian Christianity: A History of the Coptic Orthodox Church* (Greensboro, NC: Fisher Park Press, 1996), 49, 52. J.F. Haldon (*Byzantium in the Seventh Century*, 364) writes that the Arab conquests "dislocated Byzantine society much more fundamentally and dramatically, and at all levels—political, economic, and in terms of beliefs and ideas about the world."

195. Judith Herrin, *The Formation of Christendom*, 134.

196. Ibn 'Abd al-Hakam, *Futûh misr wa-akhbâruhâ* (*The History of the Conquest of Egypt*), ed. C.C. Torrey (New Haven: Yale University Press, 1922), 73; al-Baladhuri, *Kitab futuh al-buldan* (*The Origins of the Islamic State*), trans. P. Hitti (New York: AMS Press, 1968), I.335–351; Eutychius (Saîd ibn Batrîq), *Annales* (PG 111.1105).

197. R. Hoyland, *Seeing Islam as Others Saw It*, 23.

198. *Homily on the Child Saints of Babylon* 36 (ed. and trans. H. de Vis, *Homélies coptes de la Vaticane*, volume 2 (Coptica 5; Hauniae: Gyldendal, 1929); repr. in *Cahiers de la bibliothèque copte* 6 (Louvain and Paris: Peeters, 1990), 100.2–5; trans. R. Hoyland, *Seeing Islam as Others Saw It*, 120–121.

199. John of Nikiu, *Chronicle* 121.2–3 (ed. and trans. R.H. Charles, 200); R. Hoyland, *Seeing Islam as Others Saw It*, 154–155.

200. Michael the Syrian, *Chronicle* 11.8 (trans. J.-B. Chabot, II, 432–433); *Chronicle of 1234* (ed. J.-B. Chabot, CSCO 81, Scriptores Syri 36 (Louvain: L. Durbecq, 1953), I.251–253; Ibn 'Abd al-Hakam, *Futûh Misr wa-akhbâruhâ* (ed. C.C. Torrey (New Haven: Yale University Press, 1922), 58, 73. These sources are cited and discussed by R. Hoyland, *Seeing Islam as Others Saw It*, 132–135.

201. John of Nikiu, *Chronicle* 120.17–28 (ed. and trans. R.H. Charles, 193–194); A.N. Stratos, *Byzantium in the Seventh Century*, volume 2, 110–112, 214–215 (Note XX). The account of Cyrus' alleged suicide in the *History of the Patriarchs* (PO 1.4, 495) is illogical and motivated by bias.

202. John of Nikiu, *Chronicle* 121.1 (ed. and trans. R.H. Charles, 200); *History of the Patriarchs*, (PO 1.4, 495–496).

203. According to the *History of the Patriarchs* (PO 1.4, 495ff.), Sanutius (= Shenoute) functioned as an intermediary between the "exiled" Pope Benjamin and the Muslim commander 'Amr, and later even accompanied the Arabs on their campaign in Pentapolis (Libya). John of Nikiu (*Chronicle* 118.3 and 119.1; trans. R.H. Charles, 187–188, 189) also reports that the leaders of the Green and Blue factions "harassed the Romans during the days of the Moslem," and that some citizens of Lower Egypt "wished to join the Moslem."

204. John of Nikiu, *Chronicle* 115 (trans. R.H. Charles, 183–184).

205. John of Nikiu, *Chronicle* 121.2 (ed. and trans. R.H. Charles, 200); *History of the Patriarchs*, (PO 1.4, 492–493); Ps.-Athanasius, *Apocalypse* 9.1–8 (written before A.D. 744; ed. and trans. F.J. Martinez, *Early Christian Apocalyptic in the Early Muslim Period: Pseudo-Methodius and Pseudo-Athanasius* (Ph.D. thesis, Catholic University of America; Washington, D.C., 1985), 523–529; cited by R. Hoyland, *Seeing Islam as Others Saw It*, 282–285); cf. Michael the Syrian, *Chronicle* 11.3; trans. J.-B. Chabot, II, 412–413.

206. For a more thorough discussion of possible causes, see W. Kaegi, *Byzantium and the Early Islamic Conquests* (Cambridge: Cambridge University Press, 1992), 236–287.

207. R. Hoyland, *Seeing Islam as Others Saw It*, 11–12.

208. R. Hoyland, *Seeing Islam as Others Saw It*, 12–17; A.N. Stratos, *Byzantium in the Seventh Century*, volume 2, 121. For examples of Muslim imitations of Byzantine coins, see W. Kaegi, *Byzantium and the Early Islamic Conquests*, 209, Plate II. Strategies designed to mark "the distinctiveness of Early Islam," such as the use of Arabic in all administrative documents and the minting of aniconic coinage, arise only at the end of the seventh and the beginning of the eighth century (R. Hoyland, *op. cit.*, 16).

209. *History of the Patriarchs*; PO 1.4, 495–497.

210. al-Baladhuri, *Kitab futuh al-buldan (The Origins of the Islamic State)*, trans. P. Hitti (New York: AMS Press, 1968), I.335–351; al-Maqrizi, *El-Mawâ'iz wa'l-i'tibâr fi dhikr el-khitat wa'l-âthâr (Topographical Description of Egypt)* 28, ed. G. Wiet, in *Mémoires publiés par les members de la Mission archéologique française*, volume 30 (Paris: Institut français d'archéologie orientale, 1911), 320–332. On the *jizya* and the concept of *dhimma*, see Claude Cahen, "Dhimma," and "Djizya," *Encyclopedia of Islam*, Second edition (Leiden: E.J. Brill, 1954–), II.227–231, 559–562; and C.E. Bosworth, "The Concept of Dhimma in Early Islam," in *Christians and Jews in the Ottoman Empire: The Functioning of a Plural Society*, Volume 1, edited by B. Braude and B. Lewis (London and New York: Holmes and Meier, 1982), 37–51. For a helpful bibliographical survey of these topics, see R. Stephen Humphreys, *Islamic History: A Framework for Inquiry* (Princeton: Princeton University Press, 1991; repr. Cairo: The American University in Cairo Press, 1992), 255–261.

211. *History of the Patriarchs*; PO 1.4, 495, 498–500 (translation slightly modified). Benjamin's communication with 'Amr and his return to Alexandria appear in PO 1.4, 495–497.

212. Gawdat Gabra, *Coptic Monasteries: Egypt's Monastic Art and Architecture* (Cairo: The American University in Cairo Press, 2002), 56–63, esp. 57–58.

213. For a detailed textual study and edition of the Coptic and Arabic recensions, see René-Georges Coquin, *Livre de la consecration du sanctuaire de*

Benjamin (Bibliothèque d'études copte 13; Cairo: Institut français d'archéologie orientale du Caire, 1975); cf. *History of the Patriarchs* (PO 1.4, 503–518).

214. On factors which support an early provenance for the work, see R.-G. Coquin, *Livre*, 43–49.
215. *Book of the Consecration of the Sanctuary of Benjamin*, fol. 18v.; ed. R.-G. Coquin, *Livre*, 112 (Coptic and Arabic texts) and 113 (French translations).
216. *Book of the Consecration of the Sanctuary of Benjamin*, fol. 26v.; ed. R.-G. Coquin, *Livre*, 138 (Coptic and Arabic texts) and 139 (French translations)
217. W.E. Crum, *The Monasteries of the Wâdi 'n Natrûn*, Part three (New York: The Metropolitan Museum of Art, 1933), 33.
218. Antony, Paul, Pachomius, Macarius, Mark, Peter, Athanasius, and Dioscorus (and perhaps Benjamin as well) all appear in an analogous iconographic program of Egyptian monks and patriarchs in the Monastery of St. Antony at the Red Sea: see E. Bolman, *Monastic Visions: Wall Paintings in the Monastery of St. Antony at the Red Sea* (New Haven and London: Yale University Press and the American Research Center in Egypt, Inc., 2002).
219. Benjamin's solidarity with the martyrs is emphasized in the *History of the Patriarchs* (PO 1.4, 502–503), where at his death he is said to have earned "the crown of exile." In this context, it is significant that the three saints who appear at Benjamin's deathbed and accompany him to heaven are Athanasius, Severus of Antioch, and Theodosius of Alexandria, patriarchs celebrated in Coptic tradition for having suffered exile on account of their faith.
220. Benjamin himself, in his *Sixteenth Festal Letter*, hammers home his opposition to Chalcedonian doctrine by repeatedly invoking the christological precedent of Athanasius, Cyril, and Dioscorus. Out of a total of eighteen explicit patristic citations, these three figures account for eleven. For the Ethiopic text and German translation of Benjamin's *Sixteenth Festal Letter*, see C.D.G. Müller, *Homilie*, 302–351; cf. G. Graf, "Zwei dogmatische Florilegien der Kopten," *Orientalia Christiana Periodica* 3 (1937), 68 (no. 30) and 394 (no. 208).

Epilogue: The Making of the Coptic Papacy

1. Michel Foucault, "On the Archaeology of the Sciences: Response to the Epistemology Circle," in *Aesthetics, Method, and Epistemology*, edited by J.D. Faubion (Essential Works of Foucault, volume 2; New York: The New Press, 1998), 308.
2. In his *Life of Antony*, Athanasius lauds the monk Antony as a "daily martyr to his conscience" (*Life of Antony* 47.1; ed. G.J.M. Bartelink, SC 400, 262). This portrayal of monks as latter-day martyrs may be seen as part of Athanasius' literary patronage of monastic causes.
3. The representation of Saint Mark and (most likely) Saint Athanasius in the northern and southern niches of the same apse reinforces the multiple associations of Peter's image. For a discussion of the iconographic program in Deir al-Malâk (also known as Deir al-Naqlûn), see Wlodzimierz Godlewski, "Naqlun 1993–1996," in *Ägypten und Nubien in spätantiker und christlicher Zeit. Akten des 6. Internationalen Koptologenkongresses, Münster, 20.–26. Juli 1996*, Band 1: Materielle Kultur, Kunst und religiöses Leben, edited by S. Emmel, M. Krause, S.G. Richter, and S. Schaten (Sprachen und Kulturen des christlichen Orients 6.1; Wiesbaden: Reichert, 1999), 160–161; ibid., "Les peintures de l'église

de l'archange Gabriel à Naqlun," *Bulletin de la Société d'archéologie copte* 39 (2000), 89–101; and Gawdat Gabra, *Coptic Monasteries: Egypt's Monastic Art and Architecture*, 69–71, and plates 5.3–7.

4.   To put it in more theoretical terms, the public image of the Egyptian popes was an *intertextual* production, one that was generated through the "interlacing of codes, formulae, and signifiers" (Roland Barthes, "Theory of the Text," in *Untying the Text: A Post-Structuralist Reader*, ed. R. Young (Boston: Routledge & Kegan Paul, 1981), 39. For a helpful introduction to theories of intertextuality, see Graham Allen, *Intertextuality* (London: Routledge, 2000).

Appendix 2: The Election of Alexandrian Patriarchs in the Early Church

1.   Several articles were published on this evidence early in the twentieth century: see (in chronological order) E.W. Brooks, "The Ordination of the Early Bishops of Alexandria," *Journal of Theological Studies* 2 (1901), 612–613; Charles Gore, "On the Ordination of the Early Bishops of Alexandria," *Journal of Theological Studies* 3 (1902), 278–282; W. Telfer, "Episcopal Succession in Egypt," *Journal of Ecclesiastical History* 3 (1952), 1–13; and Eric Waldram Kemp, "Bishops and Presbyters at Alexandria," *Journal of Ecclesiastical History* 6 (1955), 125–142.

2.   Jerome, *Ep.* 146; ed. I. Hilberg, CSEL 56.1 (1996), 310; also PL 22.1194A.

3.   Severus of Antioch, *Letter from Alexandria to a Monophysite Congregation in Emesa*; ed. E.W. Brooks, *The Sixth Book of the Select Letters of Severus* (London: Text and Translation Society Publications, 1902), I.237–238 (Syriac text); II.213 (English translation); trans. C. Gore, "On the Ordination of the Early Bishops of Alexandria," 612.

4.   According to the medieval historian Eutychius (Sa'id Ibn Batriq), the election of the patriarch was in the hands of a council of twelve presbyters until the time of Pope Alexander I, who reigned from 312 to 326 (*Annales*; PG 111.982; excerpt translated by E.W. Kemp, "Bishops and Presbyters at Alexandria," 137–138). In the late fourth century, the writer Ambrosiaster gives evidence that Egyptian presbyters could still play a role in confirming (*consigno*) episcopal candidates if no bishop were present, and alludes to a recent reform regarding such practice: Ambrosiaster, *Commentary on Ephesians* 4.11–12; ed. A. Souter, *A Study of Ambrosiaster* (Texts and Studies 7.4; Cambridge: Cambridge University Press, 1905; repr. Nendeln: Kraus Reprint, 1967), 175–176.

5.   Athanasius, Second *Apology* 6; ed. H.G. Opitz, in *Athanasius: Werke*, vol. 2.1, 91–93. Here, Athanasius defends himself against accusations that he was consecrated secretly by six or seven supporting bishops. Both the Arian accusation and Athanasius' defense take for granted that the patriarchal election required the participation of bishops; the issue was whether Athanasius' election was conducted covertly. Elsewhere, Athanasius weathers criticism from his Arian opponents that he had been consecrated by only two bishops (Philostorgius, HE 2.11; ed. J. Bidez (with revisions by F. Winkelmann), GCS (Berlin: Akademie-Verlag, 1981), 22–24). Again, it is the number of bishops and not their participation that is at issue.

6.   The medieval *History of the Patriarchs* (ed. Evetts, PO 1.2, 149–150) claims that there were other bishops in Egypt as early as Abilius/Avilius, the third patriarch of Alexandria. However, this account is clearly anachronistic (C.W. Griggs, *Early Egyptian Christianity*, 91).

7.   Eutychius (Sa'id Ibn Batriq), *Annales* (PG 111.982; trans. E.W. Kemp, "Bishops and Presbyters at Alexandria," 137–138).

8.   E.W. Kemp, "Bishops and Presbyters at Alexandria," 138; C.W. Griggs, *Early Egyptian Christianity*, 91–92.

9.   On the history of the election of Egyptian popes, see also Mounir Shoucri, "Patriarchal Election," *Coptic Encyclopedia* 6.1911–1912; and Saad Michael Saad and Nardine Miranda Saad, "Electing Coptic Patriarchs: A Diversity of Traditions," *Bulletin of Saint Shenouda the Archimandrite Coptic Society* 6 (2001), 20–32.

Sources of Illustrations

1. Ivory relief depicting Saint Mark with thirty-five successors as Patriarch of Alexandria, early seventh century; Musée du Louvre, Paris, inv. OA3317. Photo: J.G. Berizzi. Photograph reproduced courtesy of Réunion des Musées Nationaux/Art Resource, New York.

   Bibliography: W.F. Volbach, *Elfenbeinarbeiten der Spätantike und des frühen Mittelalters*, 3. Auflage (Mainz: Verlag Philipp von Zabern, 1976), 96–97, no. 144; K. Weitzmann, *Age of Spirituality: Late Antique and Early Christian Art* (New York: Metropolitan Museum of Art, 1979), 544–546, no. 489; C. Haas, *Alexandria in Late Antiquity: Topography and Social Conflict* (Baltimore and London: The Johns Hopkins University Press, 1997), 200–201, figs. 21a–b, and 247.

2. Five ivory reliefs with scenes from the life of Saint Mark, eighth century A.D.; Museo del Castello Sforzesco, Milan. Photographs reproduced courtesy of Civiche Raccolte d'Arte Applicata – Castello Sforzesco – Milano.

   a. Mark preaching in Alexandria
   b. Mark healing Anianus
   c. Mark baptizing Anianus (and others)
   d. Mark laying hands on Anianus (ordination of Anianus as his successor)
   e. Fragmentary scene of Mark walking while carrying a book
   Bibliography: K. Weitzmann, "The Ivories of the So-called Grado Chair," *Dumbarton Oaks Papers* 26 (Washington, D.C.: Dumbarton Oaks, 1972), nos. 7–11. See also W. Volbach, *Elfenbeinarbeiten der Spätantike*, 139–140, nos. 237–241.

3. Wall painting of Saint Athanasius of Alexandria, thirteenth century
   A.D.; Monastery of Saint Antony, Red Sea. Photo Patrick Godeau.
   © 2002 the Antiquities Development Project of the American
   Research Center in Egypt.
   Bibliography: E.S. Bolman, ed., *Monastic Visions: Wall Paintings in the
   Monastery of St. Antony at the Red Sea* (New Haven: Yale University
   and the American Research Center in Egypt, 2002), 94, fig. 6.8.

4. Wall painting of Saint Athanasius of Alexandria, tenth century
   A.D. (A.D. 953); Tebtunis, Fayûm. Photograph reproduced cour-
   tesy of the Egypt Exploration Society.
   Bibliography: C.C. Walters, "Christian Paintings from Tebtunis,"
   Journal of Egyptian Archaeology 75 (1989), pl. XVII.

5. Manuscript illuminations depicting Theophilus of Alexandria,
   early fifth century A.D.; W. Goleniscev Collection, Petersburg
   (three-color plates by Max Jaffé, Vienna). Photographs reproduced
   from Bauer and Strzygowski, pl. VI (recto and verso).
   a. Theophilus, holding a Bible and standing below the mummy of his
   predecessor Timothy (pl. VI, recto).
   b. Theophilus, holding a Bible and standing on top of a pedestal decorated with a bust of the Egyptian god Serapis (pl. VI, verso).
   Bibliography: A. Bauer and J. Strzygowski, *Eine alexandrinische
   Weltchronik: Text und Miniaturen eines griechischen Papyrus des
   Sammlung W. Goleniscev* (Denkschriften der kaiserlichen Akademie der
   Wissenschaften in Wien, Phil.-hist. Klasse, Bd 51, Abh. 2; Wien: Alfred
   Hölder, 1905), pl. VI (recto and verso); C. Haas, *Alexandria in Late
   Antiquity: Topography and Social Conflict* (Baltimore and London: The
   Johns Hopkins University Press, 1997), 180, fig. 17.

6. Wall painting of Dioscorus of Alexandria (depicted wearing a
   monastic hood), thirteenth century A.D.; Monastery of the Syrians,
   Wadi al-Natrun. Photograph reproduced courtesy of Karel Innemée.
   Bibliography: K. Innemée, "The Iconographical Program of Paintings in
   the Church of al-'Adra in Deir al-Sourian: Some Preliminary
   Observations," in M. Krause and S. Schaten, eds., THEMELIA:
   *Spätantike und koptologische Studien Peter Grossmann zum 65.
   Geburtstag* (Wiesbaden: Reichert Verlag, 1998), 153, fig. 6.

7. Wall painting of Dioscorus of Alexandria (on right, with the anti-Chalcedonian patriarch, Severus of Antioch on left), thirteenth century A.D.; Monastery of SaintAntony, Red Sea. Photo Patrick Godeau. © 2002 the Antiquities Development Project of the American Research Center in Egypt.

> Bibliography: E.S. Bolman, ed., *Monastic Visions: Wall Paintings in the Monastery of the St. Antony at the Red Sea* (New Haven: Yale University Press, 2002), 112, fig. 7.14.

8. Wall painting of Pope Damian (?); eighth century A.D.; Church of the Holy Virgin in the Monastery of the Syrians (Deir al-Suriân), Wadi al-Natrun. Photograph reproduced courtesy of Karel Innemée.

> Bibliography: K.C. Innemée and L. Van Rompay, "Deir al-Surian (Egypt): New Discoveries of 2001–2002," *Hugoye: Journal of Syriac Studies* 5.2 (July 2002), 1.3, fig. 3 (on the web at http://syrcom.cua.edu/Hugoye/Vol5No2/HV5N2InnemeeVanRompay.html).

9. Coptic inscription of Pope Damian's Synodical Letter (A.D. 578); late sixth or early seventh century A.D.; Monastery of Epiphanius at Thebes. Photograph reproduced from Crum and Evelyn White, Tafel XV.

> Bibliography: W.E. Crum and H.G. Evelyn White, eds., *The Monastery of Epiphanius at Thebes*, Part 2 (New York: Metropolitan Museum of Art, 1926), 148–152, 331–337 (Inscription A), Tafel XV.

10. Wall painting of Peter I of Alexandria (on right, with Saint Andrew the Apostle on left), in which the image of the archbishop Peter is assimilated to that of Saint Peter the Apostle; A.D. 1025–1030; Monastery of the Archangel Gabriel (Deir al-Malâk), Fayûm. Drawing reproduced courtesy of Wlodzimierz Godlewski.

> Bibliography: W. Godlewski, "Naqlun 1993–1996," in *Ägypten und Nubien in spätantiker und christlicher Zeit*. Akten des 6. Internationalen Koptologenkongresses, Münster, 20.–26. Juli 1996, Band 1: Materielle Kultur, Kunst und religiöses Leben, edited by S. Emmel, M. Krause, S.G. Richter, and S. Schaten (Sprachen und Kulturen des christlichen Orients 6.1; Wiesbaden: Reichert, 1999), 157–162; W. Godlewski, "Les peintures de l'église de l'archange Gabriel à Naqlun," *Bulletin de la Société d'archéologie copte* 39 (2000), 89–101, esp. 92–93 and fig. 2.

Index

This index of names and subjects provides page references to the main text, as well as the appendices. References to the bibliography and notes are not included.